AOL Canada For Dummies

by Marguerite Pigeon and John [...]

MW00965730

Top Emoticons and Abbreviations for Chatting

When you use the AOL Canada chat rooms to communicate with other members, you may want to express yourself in ways that mere words can't accomplish. Use emoticons to convey the facial expressions and body language that accompany spoken conversation but are a little hard to type. Abbreviations enable you to use familiar phrases without typing the entire phrase. (You can find more info about emoticons and abbreviations in Chapter 28.)

:-)	Smile, you're on AOL Canada.
:-D	Big smile. The sun shines brightly on you today.
;-)	Wink, wink. Nudge, nudge. Just kidding.
:-(	Frown. Just got the phone bill, eh?
:-o	Mr. Bill. Oh, no!
AFK	Away from the keyboard
BAK	Back at the keyboard
BTW	By the way
IMHO	In my humble opinion
LOL	Laughing out loud
ROFL	Rolling on the floor laughing

Macintosh and Windows Shortcut Keys

Group	Function	Macintosh	Windows
Editing	Cut	⌘+X	Ctrl+X
	Copy	⌘+C	Ctrl+C
	Paste	⌘+V	Ctrl+V
	Undo	⌘+Z	Ctrl+Z
Mail	Compose new mail	⌘+M	Ctrl+M
	Read new messages	⌘+R	Ctrl+R
People-related	Locate AOL member online	⌘+L	Ctrl+L
	Get info (user profile)	⌘+G	Ctrl+G
	Send an Instant Message	⌘+I	Ctrl+I
Navigation	Go to a keyword	⌘+K	Ctrl+K
	Make current window a Favourite Place	None	Ctrl++ (plus sign)
		Custom Favourites My Shortcuts items ⌘+1 to ⌘+0	Ctrl+1 to Ctrl+0
Documents	Stop incoming text	⌘+. (period)	Esc
	Save a document	⌘+S	Ctrl+S
	Print a document	⌘+P	Ctrl+P

...For Dummies®: Bestselling Book Series for Beginners

AOL Canada For Dummies®

by Marguerite Pigeon and John Kaufeld

Cheat Sheet

Local AOL Canada Access Numbers

Fill in the blanks and use this section as a handy reference guide for your AOL access numbers at home and on the road.

Location	Phone Number	Modem Speed Network
Main local access		
Alternate local #1		
Alternate local #2		

A Few Favourite Places

Record your Favourite Places to go in AOL Canada, along with the keyword that takes you there and a short description of the area. (Refer to Chapter 7 for how to add and organize your Favourite Places, and Chapter 23 for details on how to modify your personal My Hot Keys menu in the Favourites toolbar button.)

Favourite Place	Keyword	Brief Description

Screen Names and Passwords

Use this space to record your AOL Canada screen names and passwords. An AOL Canada account can have as many as seven screen names. (If you fill in the Password area, be sure to keep this card in a safe place!)

Screen Name	Password Name	Screen Password
Primary		

The ...For Dummies logo is a trademark, and ...For Dummies is a registered trademark of IDG Books Worldwide, Inc. The CDG Books Canada logo is a trademark of CDG Books Canada, Inc. All other trademarks are the property of their respective owners.

CDG BOOKS CANADA

...For Dummies®: Bestselling Book Series for Beginners

Welcome to the world of IDG Books Worldwide and CDG Books Canada.

IDG Books Worldwide, Inc., is a subsidiary of International Data Group, Inc., the world's largest publisher of computer-related information and the leading global provider of information services on information technology. IDG was founded more than 30 years ago and now employs more than 9,000 people worldwide. IDG publishes more than 295 computer publications in over 75 countries (see listing below). More than 90 million people read one or more IDG publications each month.

Launched in 1990, IDG Books Worldwide is today the #1 publisher of best-selling computer books in North America. IDG Books Worldwide is proud to be the recipient of eight awards from the Computer Press Association in recognition of editorial excellence and three from *Computer Currents'* First Annual Readers' Choice Awards. Our best-selling *...For Dummies*® series has more than 55 million copies in print with translations in 31 languages. In record time, IDG Books Worldwide has become the first choice for millions of readers around the world who want to learn how to better manage their businesses.

In 1998, IDG Books Worldwide formally partnered with Macmillan Canada, a subsidiary of Canada Publishing Corporation, to create CDG Books Canada, a dynamic new Canadian publishing company. CDG Books Canada is now Canada's fastest growing publisher, bringing valuable information to Canadians from coast to coast through the introduction of Canadian *...For Dummies*® and *CliffsNotes*™ titles.

Every one of our books is designed to bring extra value and skill-building instructions to the reader. Our books are written by experts who understand and care about our readers. The knowledge base of our editorial staff comes from years of experience in publishing, education, and journalism — experience we use to produce books to carry us into the new millennium. In short, we care about books, so we attract the best people. We devote special attention to details such as audience, interior design, use of icons, and illustrations. And because we use an efficient process of authoring, editing, and desktop publishing our books electronically, we can spend more time ensuring superior content and spend less time on the technicalities of making books.

You can count on our commitment to deliver high-quality books at competitive prices on topics you want to read about. At IDG Books Worldwide and CDG Books Canada, we continue in the IDG tradition of delivering quality for more than 30 years. You can learn more about IDG Books Worldwide and CDG Books Canada by visiting www.idgbooks.com, www.dummies.com, and www.cdgbooks.com.

Eighth Annual Computer Press Awards ≥1992

Ninth Annual Computer Press Awards ≥1993

Tenth Annual Computer Press Awards ≥1994

Eleventh Annual Computer Press Awards ≥1995

IDG is the world's leading IT media, research and exposition company. Founded in 1964, IDG had 1997 revenues of $2.05 billion and has more than 9,000 employees worldwide. IDG offers the widest range of media options that reach IT buyers in 75 countries representing 95% of worldwide IT spending. IDG's diverse product and services portfolio spans six key areas including print publishing, online publishing, expositions and conferences, market research, education and training, and global marketing services. More than 90 million people read one or more of IDG's 290 magazines and newspapers, including IDG's leading global brands — Computerworld, PC World, Network World, Macworld and the Channel World family of publications. IDG Books Worldwide is one of the fastest-growing computer book publishers in the world, with more than 700 titles in 36 languages. The "...For Dummies®" series alone has more than 50 million copies in print. IDG offers online users the largest network of technology-specific Web sites around the world through IDG.net (http://www.idg.net), which comprises more than 225 targeted Web sites in 55 countries worldwide. International Data Corporation (IDC) is the world's largest provider of information technology data, analysis and consulting, with research centers in over 41 countries and more than 400 research analysts worldwide. IDG World Expo is a leading producer of more than 168 globally branded conferences and expositions in 35 countries including E3 (Electronic Entertainment Expo), Macworld Expo, ComNet, Windows World Expo, ICE (Internet Commerce Expo), Agenda, DEMO, and Spotlight. IDG's training subsidiary, ExecuTrain, is the world's largest computer training company, with more than 230 locations worldwide and 785 training courses. IDG Marketing Services helps industry-leading IT companies build international brand recognition by developing global integrated marketing programs via IDG's print, online and exposition products worldwide. Further information about the company can be found at www.idg.com.   8/24/99

AOL Canada

FOR

DUMMIES®

by Marguerite Pigeon
and John Kaufeld

CDG BOOKS CANADA™

CDG Books Canada, Inc.

◆ Toronto, ON ◆

AOL Canada For Dummies®

Published by
CDG Books Canada, Inc.
99 Yorkville Avenue
Suite 400
Toronto, ON M5R 3K5
www.cdgbooks.com (CDG Books Canada Web Site)
www.idgbooks.com (IDG Books Worldwide Web Site)
www.dummies.com (Dummies Press Web Site)

Canadian Cataloguing in Publication Data

Pigeon, Marguerite

AOL Canada for dummies

Includes index.
ISBN 1-894413-28-8

1. AOL Canada (Online service). I. Kaufeld, John. II. Title.

QA76.57.A43P53 2001   025.04   C00-933223-5

Printed in Canada

1 2 3 4 5 TRI 05 04 03 02 01

Distributed in Canada by CDG Books Canada, Inc.

For general information on CDG Books, including all IDG Books Worldwide publications, please call our distribution center: HarperCollins Canada at 1-800-387-0117. For reseller information, including discounts and premium sales, please call our Sales department at 1-877-963-8830.

This book is available at special discounts for bulk purchases by your group or organization for resale, premiums, fundraising and seminars. For details, contact CDG Books Canada, Special Sales Department, 99 Yorkville Avenue, Suite 400, Toronto, ON, M5K 3K5; Tel: 416-963-8830; Email: spmarkets@cdgbooks.com.

For press review copies, author interviews, or other publicity information, please contact our Marketing department: 416-963-8830, fax 416-923-4821, or e-mail publicity@cdgbooks.com.

For authorization to photocopy items for corporate, personal, or educational use, please contact Cancopy, The Canadian Copyright Licensing Agency, One Yonge Street, Suite 1900, Toronto, ON, M5E 1E5; Tel: 416-868-1620; Fax: 416-868-1621; www.cancopy.com.

is a trademark under exclusive license to CDG Books Canada, Inc., from International Data Group, Inc.

CDG BOOKS CANADA

About the Authors

Marguerite Pigeon graduated from both journalism and philosophy at Carleton University, in Ottawa, in 1994. She started her career in daily news at CBC Radio, moved on to print reporting and photography at *The Elliot Lake Standard*, and ended up a senior television producer for CTV Television. Since then, she's worked as a freelance producer for a number of news organizations.

She now lives and works in Toronto as a freelance writer, having already published several titles for CDG Books, including *Shopping Online For Canadians For Dummies*, *CliffsNotes Investing in the Stock Market for Canadians*, *CliffsNotes Investing for the First Time for Canadians*, and *CliffsNotes Shopping Online Safely for Canadians*.

She spends the vast majority of her time in Cabbagetown (the best neighbourhood in Toronto), hanging out at the Jet Fuel cafe (the best lattes in the world), boxing at the Cabbagetown Boxing Club, droning on about her hometown, Blind River, and feeling guilty about being behind on e-mails to her massive family.

John Kaufeld got hooked on computers a long time ago. Somewhere along the way, he discovered that he enjoyed helping people understand how computers worked (a trait his computer science friends generally considered a character flaw but that everyone else seemed to appreciate). John finally graduated with a B.S. degree in management information systems from Ball State University and became the first PC support technician for what was then Westinghouse, outside Cincinnati, Ohio. He learned about online services in the Dark Ages of Telecommunication (the 1980s) by guessing, failing, and often doing unmentionable things to his modem.

Since then, John logged more than a decade of experience in working with normal people who, for one reason or another, were stuck using a "friendly" personal computer. Today, he runs Access Systems, Inc (a computer consulting firm) and LinguaPlay (a very fun little division of Access Systems, at www.linguaplay.com). He also conducts seminars for up-and-coming Internet entrepreneurs, and writes game reviews for InQuest Gamer magazine in his copious free moments.

John's other IDG Books titles include *Games Online For Dummies*, *Access 2000 For Dummies*, *Access 97 For Dummies*, and too many other database books to still qualify him as a normal human. He regularly uses America Online (where he's known as JKaufeld) and other online services. He loves to get e-mail and valiantly attempts to answer every message arriving in his mailbox.

John lives with his wife, two children, and (most delightfully) *no* marginally lovable American Eskimo dog, in Indianapolis, Indiana.

ABOUT CDG BOOKS CANADA, INC. AND IDG BOOKS WORLDWIDE, INC.

Welcome to the world of IDG Books Worldwide and CDG Books Canada.

IDG Books Worldwide, Inc., is a subsidiary of International Data Group, Inc., the world's largest publisher of computer-related information and the leading global provider of information services on information technology. IDG was founded more than 30 years ago and now employs more than 9,000 people worldwide. IDG publishes more than 295 computer publications in over 75 countries (see listing below). More than 90 million people read one or more IDG publications each month.

Launched in 1990, IDG Books Worldwide is today the #1 publisher of best-selling computer books in North America. IDG Books Worldwide is proud to be the recipient of eight awards from the Computer Press Association in recognition of editorial excellence and three from *Computer Currents'* First Annual Readers' Choice Awards. Our best-selling *...For Dummies®* series has more than 55 million copies in print with translations in 31 languages. In record time, IDG Books Worldwide has become the first choice for millions of readers around the world who want to learn how to better manage their businesses.

In 1998, IDG Books Worldwide formally partnered with Macmillan Canada, a subsidiary of Canada Publishing Corporation, to create CDG Books Canada, a dynamic new Canadian publishing company. CDG Books Canada is now Canada's fastest growing publisher, bringing valuable information to Canadians from coast to coast through the introduction of Canadian *...For Dummies®* and *CliffsNotes*™ titles.

Every one of our books is designed to bring extra value and skill-building instructions to the reader. Our books are written by experts who understand and care about our readers. The knowledge base of our editorial staff comes from years of experience in publishing, education, and journalism — experience we use to produce books to carry us into the new millennium. In short, we care about books, so we attract the best people. We devote special attention to details such as audience, interior design, use of icons, and illustrations. And because we use an efficient process of authoring, editing, and desktop publishing our books electronically, we can spend more time ensuring superior content and spend less time on the technicalities of making books.

You can count on our commitment to deliver high-quality books at competitive prices on topics you want to read about. At IDG Books Worldwide and CDG Books Canada, we continue in the IDG tradition of delivering quality for more than 30 years. You can learn more about IDG Books Worldwide and CDG Books Canada by visiting www.idgbooks.com, www.dummies.com, and www.cdgbooks.com.

Eighth Annual
Computer Press
Awards 1992

Ninth Annual
Computer Press
Awards 1993

Tenth Annual
Computer Press
Awards 1994

Eleventh Annual
Computer Press
Awards 1995

IDG is the world's leading IT media, research and exposition company. Founded in 1964, IDG had 1997 revenues of $2.05 billion and has more than 9,000 employees worldwide. IDG offers the widest range of media options that reach IT buyers in 75 countries representing 95% of worldwide IT spending. IDG's diverse product and services portfolio spans six key areas including print publishing, online publishing, expositions and conferences, market research, education and training, and global marketing services. More than 90 million people read one or more of IDG's 290 magazines and newspapers, including IDG's leading global brands — Computerworld, PC World, Network World, Macworld and the Channel World family of publications. IDG Books Worldwide is one of the fastest-growing computer book publishers in the world, with more than 700 titles in 36 languages. The "...For Dummies®" series alone has more than 50 million copies in print. IDG offers online users the largest network of technology-specific Web sites around the world through IDG.net (http://www.idg.net), which comprises more than 225 targeted Web sites in 55 countries worldwide. International Data Corporation (IDC) is the world's largest provider of information technology data, analysis and consulting, with research centers in over 41 countries and more than 400 research analysts worldwide. IDG World Expo is a leading producer of more than 168 globally branded conferences and expositions in 35 countries including E3 (Electronic Entertainment Expo), Macworld Expo, ComNet, Windows World Expo, ICE (Internet Commerce Expo), Agenda, DEMO, and Spotlight. IDG's training subsidiary, ExecuTrain, is the world's largest computer training company, with more than 230 locations worldwide and 785 training courses. IDG Marketing Services helps industry-leading IT companies build international brand recognition by developing global integrated marketing programs via IDG's print, online and exposition products worldwide. Further information about the company can be found at www.idg.com.   8/24/99

Dedication

Marguerite dedicates her part of this book to all the average Canadians who aren't afraid to try new things, but need a little help getting started.

John dedicates this book to Jenny, for perpetual help and assistance at precisely the moment it's most needed. Also to J.B. and Pooz, for understanding that sometimes *two* books happen at the same time. And to his friends and compatriots at IDG Books Worldwide, Inc., for the opportunity of a lifetime. Thank you, one and all.

Authors' Acknowledgements

Marguerite thanks everyone at CDG Books, including, above all, Joan Whitman and Melanie Rutledge. Thanks also to everyone involved in the earlier versions of *America Online For Dummies* at IDG Books Worldwide Inc. in the U.S.

She also wants to thank all the people at AOL Canada who made themselves available to answer a million and one silly, obvious, and often redundant questions, most especially Joan Simkins, who deals with everything in a professional and friendly manner to be envied. Thanks also to everyone in the AOL Canada technical department for their detailed technical review of the text.

Many thanks to all involved in the copyediting, layout, and printing of this book.

John wants to thank his project editor, Kyle Looper, without whom this book simply wouldn't be. Thanks for picking up the ball in the middle of the game, and running to the goal in the face of impending deadlines, unforeseen changes, and the peculiar brand of "fun" which surrounds every AOL beta.

Extraordinary thanks also to my technical reviewer, Matt Converse, who made extra-special-sure that the book is actually correct. Without Matt's help, I *never* could have kept the book moving in a sane, orderly fashion. Arrrrgh, matey!

Further up the Editorial Food Chain, thanks to Diane Steele for being one of the best folks to work with on the planet. Way out at the other end of the known world, thanks to Steve Hayes (my acquisitions editor) and Andy Cummings (who runs the Acquisitions Department Asylum).

At America Online, particular thanks go to Kimberly McCreery, who won the PR lottery and got me as a contact. Extra-special "You're the greatest" thanks to Adam Bartlett, Jon Brendsel, Steve Dennett, and Reggie Fairchild, who rank just below Ben & Jerry's Chocolate Chip Cookie Dough Ice Cream in my world.

Another *huge* round of kudos and chocolate goes to the great team of folks in Members Services and Technical Services who took the time to help me make this book all the better: Marc Blackwood, Ben Brown, Kristie Cunningham, Philip Fleet, Keith Jenkins, Charlier Knadler, Martha Lemondes, and Wes Turner. And, of course, a special tip of the hat to Steve Case for the original vision that spawned AOL.

Finally, my sincere appreciation to The Sunday Refugees (another round of Formua De, anyone?), who remind me a little more every day of what *community* really means. Champagne wishes and digital dreams to (in alphabetical order) Art, Barb, Cap, Jen, Lau, Myst, Nick, Ren, Rho, and all the other online friends and acquaintances who helped me maintain a few shreds of sanity while writing this book. Let's JKPARTY, y'all!

Publisher's Acknowledgements

We're proud of this book; please register your comments through our IDG Books Worldwide Online Registration Form located at http://my2cents.dummies.com.

Some of the people who helped bring this book to market include the following:

Acquisitions and Editorial

Editorial Director: Joan Whitman

Associate Editor: Melanie Rutledge

Substantive/Copy Editor: Lisa Berland

Production

Director of Production: Donna Brown

Production Editor: Rebecca Conolly

Layout and Graphics: Kim Monteforte, Heidy Lawrance Associates

Proofreader: Allyson Latta

Indexer: Liba Berry

Special Help

Michael Kelly

General and Administrative

IDG Books Worldwide, Inc.: John Kilcullen, CEO; Bill Barry, President and COO; John Ball, Executive VP, Operations & Administration; John Harris, CFO

CDG Books Canada, Inc.: Ron Besse, Chairman; Tom Best, President; Robert Harris, Vice President and Publisher

IDG Books Technology Publishing Group: Richard Swadley, Senior Vice President and Publisher; Mary Bednarek, Vice President and Publisher, Networking and Certification; Walter R. Bruce III, Vice President and Publisher, General User and Design Professional; Joseph Wikert, Vice President and Publisher, Programming; Mary C. Corder, Editorial Director, Branded Technology Editorial; Andy Cummings, Publishing Director, General User and Design Professional; Barry Pruett, Publishing Director, Visual

IDG Books Manufacturing: Ivor Parker, Vice President, Manufacturing

IDG Books Marketing: John Helmus, Assistant Vice President, Director of Marketing

IDG Books Online Management: Brenda McLaughlin, Executive Vice President, Chief Internet Officer

IDG Books Packaging: Marc J. Mikulich, Vice President, Brand Strategy and Research

IDG Books Production for Branded Press: Debbie Stailey, Production Director

IDG Books Sales: Roland Elgey, Senior Vice President, Sales and Marketing; Michael Violano, Vice President, International Sales and Sub Rights

◆

The publisher would like to give special thanks to Patrick J. McGovern, without whom this book would not have been possible.

◆

Contents at a Glance

Cartoons at a Glance

By Rich Tennant

page 189

page 81

page 299

page 269

page 9

Fax: 978-546-7747

E-mail: richtennant@the5thwave.com

World Wide Web: www.the5thwave.com

Table of Contents

Foreword

● ●

*A*OL Canada is what some people call an Internet Service Provider, or ISP, that you can use to quickly get online from almost anywhere in Canada or around the world. But this is such an underestimation of our services that those of us who work here almost never find ourselves using that term. Instead, since day one, we've always talked about our AOL Canada members belonging to an exclusive online service that's easy to get started, easy to use, and good for everyone from beginners to experts.

We strive to make AOL Canada all of these things and more, from the time you install the free AOL Canada software (most of our new members are up and running with the software in less than 15 minutes), until you become an old hand. We also strive to make your learning curve painless, short, and even fun!

With every new version of AOL Canada, we also add as many new services as possible. Our own AOL Canada team gives you easy access to premiere Canadian content and e-commerce providers and brings you the best of what other AOL services around the world are offering their members. The way we see it, the more convenient we make it the more you'll feel like the world is your oyster as an AOL Canada member.

And speaking of the world, we're especially proud of our fast gateway to the wonderfully diverse world of the Internet and the World Wide Web. Yes, it can seem utterly disorganized and confusing at first, but our easy keyword search guides you to the best content for you and those you care about.

Having said that, we can't catalogue everything there is on the Net. We can barely stay on top of all the content *inside* AOL Canada! That's where this book comes in. The authors have spent time digging deep into the system. Now, they're bringing it to you in this easy-to-read and easy-to-follow guide book. We're confident that it will make your time on AOL Canada more enjoyable, while saving you valuable time.

As I said from the outset, we think of AOL Canada as an exclusive online service for our members. Whatever your interest, whether it be news, research, making new friends, booking your next vacation, or discussing hundreds of different topics with other members, we think you'll find that the more you explore, the more you will think of it that way too. We've built the basics, now it's up to you to make it come alive!

Steven McArthur
President and CEO, AOL Canada Inc.

Introduction

*H*i — welcome to the neighbourhood!

That probably wasn't the first thing you expected to hear when you joined AOL Canada, but it's just the first of many surprises awaiting you. AOL Canada is quite different from those *other* online services. Luckily for you, *AOL Canada For Dummies* is equally unique.

For the first time, just about everything that's interesting, informative, entertaining, and fun about AOL Canada is assembled in one place: right here! This book is your friendly tour guide and road map to an intriguing corner of the digital world. You can find everything you need to get started with (and get the most from) the friendliest and one of the fastest-growing online service in Canada: AOL Canada.

And when we say everything, we do mean *everything*. By now, you've probably noticed the CD-ROM that came with this book. Okay — so maybe you bought the book because you saw the CD-ROM! Either way, that CD is your key to a new world because it holds the AOL Canada software. Once installed — don't worry, the process is painless and we walk you through it in the appendix, "About the CD" — you'll have 540 hours to enjoy AOL Canada for free within your first 30 days (communication charges may apply). After that, you can sign up, stick around, and, like 200,000 of your fellow Canadians, enjoy the ride.

The best part is that you don't need to be some normalcy-challenged computer technoid to make sense of it all. Like the painless software installation, *AOL Canada For Dummies* is simple and easy to navigate. That's because it's written in plain language — the way everyone talked back when *computers* interfaced and *people* had conversations. This book is designed to give you the information you need quickly so that you can get back to the fun stuff at hand.

Don't just take our word for it — jump on in and discover what's here for you. We think that you'll be pleasantly surprised.

Who We Think You Are

To know you is to understand you, and goodness knows, if we can't understand you, we can't help you. With that statement in mind (a challenge in itself), here's what we know about you:

- ✔ You're a Canuck (uh, Canadian), or you just like Canada a lot. (Hey, that's cool too.)
- ✔ You're either interested in AOL Canada or are now using it (and are feeling the effects).
- ✔ You use an IBM-compatible or a Macintosh computer.
- ✔ You have a modem attached to your computer, or connect to the Internet through a cable modem or other high-speed access.
- ✔ You care more about dinner than about modems and computers combined.
- ✔ Terms such as *bps, download,* and *Internet* nip at your heels like a pack of disturbed Chihuahuas.

If these statements sound familiar, this book is for you.

Although the book's instructions are geared primarily toward the Wonderful World of Windows, Macintosh users still benefit from the *AOL Canada For Dummies* Channels Directory, plus all the content information in Parts III, IV, and V. When the 6.0 software for the Macintosh arrives, the instructions from the rest of the book will also be helpful.

It's All English — Except for Parts in "Geek"

Whenever you're working with AOL Canada, it's kind of like being in a two-way conversation: You give commands to the system, and the system displays messages back at you (so be careful what you say!). This book contains stuff about both sides of the conversation, so keep in mind the following ways to help you figure out who's talking to whom:

```
If the text looks like this, AOL Canada is saying something
clever onscreen that you don't want to miss. World Wide Web
sites and other Internet addresses also look like this. It's
the computer book version of the high-tech computer look.
```

If the text looks like this, it's something you have to tell AOL Canada by typing it somewhere onscreen. (Remember to be nice — no yelling.) If you need to choose something from a menu or from one of the funky drop-down menus that pop out from underneath some of the toolbar buttons, the text shows some options separated by an arrow — for example, Mail⇨Write Mail. It means that you should choose the menu or toolbar button marked Mail and then click the Write Mail option. None of the menu items and toolbar buttons shares the same name, so don't fret about clicking the wrong thing.

Because you're using AOL Canada in a Microsoft Windows environment, you also must deal with the mouse. In this book, we assume that you know the following basic mouse manoeuvres:

- ✔ **Click:** Position the mouse pointer and then quickly press and release the mouse button (specifically, the *left* button, if your mouse has two to choose from).

- ✔ **Double-click:** Position the mouse pointer and then click twice — basically, two regular clicks. (Remember that the people who designed this stuff weren't hired to be clever.)

- ✔ **Click and drag:** Position the mouse pointer and then press *and hold* the mouse button as you move the mouse across the screen. As with other mouse actions, use the left button if you have more than one. After the mouse pointer gets to wherever it's going, release the button.

- ✔ **Right-click:** Click the right mouse button. The most popular place to use the right mouse button with AOL Canada is in an e-mail message or Instant Message. Right-click in the area where you write the message to see a pop-up menu of cool options (see Chapter 6 for more about that).

If all this mouse stuff is news to you, we wholeheartedly recommend picking up a copy of *Windows 98 For Dummies* (by Andy Rathbone), or *Macs For Dummies,* 7th Edition, by David Pogue (both from IDG Books Worldwide, Inc.)

Frolicking (Briefly) through the Book

This book is organized into six distinct parts and a special directory. To whet your appetite, here's a peek at what each section contains. Pay special attention to the *AOL Canada For Dummies* Channels Directory. It's your roadmap to the best content on AOL Canada.

Part I: Driver's Ed for the Digital Traveller

This section answers the stirring questions "Just what the heck is AOL Canada, and why do I care?" Part I gives you a broad overview of what the whole service is about. It explains what you generally need to know about online services, walks you through some cool ways to plug AOL Canada into your day (including how to use the CD-ROM that comes with this book), points out the features and highlights of the AOL Canada access software, and gives you some pointers for making the place a little more like home. In short, it's kinda like digital driver's education.

Part II: The Basics of Online Life

As part of their quest to join society, people learn many basic skills — things like walking, talking, ordering in a restaurant, balancing a chequebook, and julienning a potato into french fries (although we somehow skipped that particular session in the school of life).

Likewise, to take your place in the online world, you have to know how to handle the basic tools of this new realm — and that's what Part II is all about. It starts by creating your online persona and then continues with navigating through the digital world, remembering your favourite online hot spots, and expressing yourself through the basic online communication tools (e-mail, Instant Messages, chat rooms, and message boards).

Part II is also where AOL Canada members who've been around for a while should find themselves pleasantly surprised by the new features available in the 6.0 version of the software — yes, the *very same* software that you'll find on the CD-ROM in this book. Those features include more e-mail and Instant Message options, and a cool new toolbar. Get ready to smile.

Part III: Diving into the Fun Stuff

The questions we hear most often from both new and existing AOL Canada members are straightforward: Where's the way-cool online information? Where are the best chats? We're getting hungry — where's the kitchen? The chapters in Part III deliver the goods by focusing on the what's-out-there side of online life. You uncover and explore the lively, topical, and up-to-date AOL Canada content areas; hack, slash, and blast your way through the games; take a trip on the Internet; and fill your computer with new software (courtesy of the voluminous AOL Canada file libraries).

Part IV: Going Your Own Way

This part is especially for you — well, for you, your kids, your neighbours, and various broad strata of the country's entire populace. You see, this part has a chapter for just about everyone. That's the whole point of Part IV: to give you a view of AOL Canada from whatever unique perspective you may have, whether as a parent, a student, an investor, an entrepreneur — or something else. Rather than describe the broad scope of AOL Canada, Part IV turns the telescope around and pinpoints places to go depending on your particular interests.

Part V: Secret Tricks of the AOL Gurus

Shhh. We don't want everyone to hear about this part. Well, at least we don't want *them* to hear about it just yet (you know how spurned technoweenies behave sometimes). Part V contains the collected wisdom of many AOL Canada experts. It's filled with tips and goodies for making your AOL Canada connection truly come alive. Customizing your member profile with new categories and tweaking the toolbar until it's uniquely yours are just two of the cool technotricks documented in this part. Enjoy!

Part VI: The Part of Tens

It just wouldn't be a ...*For Dummies* book without The Part of Tens. In this section, you find tips for getting the most from your AOL Canada experience, code charts that decipher the sometimes peculiar comments in the chat areas, ways to find help when your connection doesn't work, and places to visit when the urge to explore takes hold of your mind. It's a potpourri of things to brighten your digital day.

AOL Canada For Dummies Channels Directory

In yet another attempt to keep you from completely shorting out when faced with all the stuff AOL Canada has to offer, the helpful folks at AOL Canada organize all the content areas into a series of channels. *AOL Canada For Dummies* Channels Directory — a unique book-within-a-book — takes you for a trot through all the channels, introducing you to the goodies within each one. You find out what's available on each channel and in each channel's departments (subsections of a channel, just like departments within a large store). Plus, you uncover tips for making the most of each channel's special features or content.

Icons, Icons Everywhere

To make finding the important stuff in the book a little easier (and to help you steer clear of the technical hogwash), this book has a bunch of icons scattered throughout. Each icon marks something in the text that's particularly vital to your online existence. Here's a brief guide to what these little road signs mean:

If you see a Remember icon, get out your mental highlighter because the text is definitely worth bearing in mind, both now and in the future.

You can benefit from our experience (both good and bad) whenever you spy a Tip icon. Whether it marks a trap to avoid or a trick to make your life easier, you can't go wrong heeding a Tip.

Like it or not, we have to include some truly technical twaddle. To shield you from it as much as possible, we mark the techie stuff with this icon. If you see this turkey, flip — don't lazily turn — to the next page. Really, it's better for everyone this way.

If you need to do something that's just the tiniest bit dangerous (such as strolling through downtown Winnipeg in January in your shorts and sandals), this icon tells you to proceed with caution. Pay close attention to these warnings; they mark the most dire of pitfalls. (Don't worry; they aren't too frequent on AOL Canada.)

This last icon is just a reminder that we place here and there throughout the book, in case you've overlooked the fact that there's a CD-ROM inside the cover containing the AOL Canada 6.0 access software.

Mind Melding: AOL and AOL Canada

As you probably know by now, AOL is a worldwide operation (otherwise, with more than 26 million members, its rosters would account for practically every Canadian man, woman, and child — surely a goal for AOL Canada, but not quite a reality yet. Anyway, what is now global actually began about 15 years ago in the United States. So what does that mean to you? Well, as a Canadian member, you are doubly blessed: you have access to the millions of content windows produced for the entire AOL network (AOL has services in 16 countries and in 8 languages) and you also get thousands of areas devoted solely to Canadians.

Most of the time, the transition between AOL Canada areas and AOL worldwide is seamless. Keywords, for example, which you can learn more about in Part II, often whisk you straight off to an AOL worldwide area. If so, rest assured — the fun, learning, or communing you'll do there is universal enough to be enjoyed by Canadians and non-Canadians alike. Other times, you can *choose* to go beyond the Canadian frontiers (when making new friends through e-mail and chat rooms, for example — hence producing the mind meld in the heading of this section).

It's Time to Get Started!

The beauty of a ...*For Dummies* book — apart from the friendly yellow cover and the cute little Dummies guy — is how it presents information. Unlike many books on the market, you don't have to read *AOL Canada For Dummies* in chapter-by-chapter order. Sure, you can do it that way (after all, it is your book), but the information in here comes out just as easily whether you march sequentially through the chapters or bound and romp from topic to topic. The choice is yours, driven by the needs of your quest for knowledge.

Either way, go on out there and have some fun — and keep this book handy, just in case you need a little help now and then.

Part I
Driver's Ed for the Digital Traveller

The 5th Wave   By Rich Tennant

"It's a free starter disk for AOL."

In this part . . .

Driver's education class is the only thing holding this country together. (Well, besides hockey.) It's a massively shared experience. Everyone, at one time or another, learns how to drive. And we all do it with white knuckles the first time, thinking that 40 kilometres per hour is kinda fast and that maybe we ought to ease it down to a nice, pedestrian 20 kilometres per hour for a while.

The first time you face the vast plains of the online world, that old memory may rise up. Gripping the CD-ROMs with white knuckles, you wonder whether 56,000 bps is just a little fast and perhaps you should just run the modem at 14,400 bps until you get the hang of it.

Hey — it's going to be okay. The truth is that you can surf the Internet, hold an interactive conversation with people all over the country, and receive files from a computer that's 3,000 kilometres away, without knowing (or caring to know) the details of how it all works.

This part gives you an overview of what this wild and wonderful AOL Canada thing is all about and what it can do. It also offers some tips for getting comfortable in your digital habitat and a note or two about working and playing well with others online.

Get ready for the ride of your life. Now, where did those car keys go?

Chapter 1

What You've Gotten Yourself Into (and What You Need to Get Out)

In This Chapter

▶ Discovering what this *online* thing is all about

▶ Scoping out the stuff you need to make it work

▶ Getting online fast with the access numbers

*P*erhaps you just bought a new computer and happened across a stray icon labelled AOL Canada. Or maybe your parent, child, or significant other decided that it was time for you to join the online revolution and endowed you with all the goodies this revolution requires. Or perhaps you don't quite know what to make of all this talk about the information superhighway and worry that you're getting left behind at a rest stop.

For a good understanding of what the term *online* means and where AOL Canada fits into the equation, start here. This chapter explains the introductory stuff, and prepares you for that first trip into the online world. (Don't panic — the journey itself starts in the next chapter.) For now, kick back and get ready to understand what your parent, child, or significant other has been talking about all this time.

What Online Really Means

What is this "*Internet* online service" stuff, anyway? Does it have something to do with the information superhighway? Do you even care? Why or why not? Please write a detailed answer on the inside cover of a matchbook and then set the whole thing on fire, watching with pleasure as it burns to a crisp. Don't you feel better now?

If you do, you're not alone. Many people feel apprehensive about this mysterious electronic world you're entering. Take heart, though. Online services and the Internet used to be much more mysterious than they are today. Don't worry if the whole concept seems more than a little bizarre to you right now. That's okay; the reaction is normal. Those feelings prove mainly that you're not a nerd. Congratulations on passing the test!

Back to the question at hand: What is an online service? Conceptually, it's much like cable TV. With cable TV, you buy a subscription from your local cable company and hook your television into its network with a cable that runs from your television to the wall, then out from your house into the Great Beyond, right?

And, if the technology does what it should, you turn on the TV and choose from among a wide variety of programs, depending on your interests. When it doesn't work, the problem may be in your TV or somewhere between your wall socket and the cable company itself. At the end of the month, you get a bill that you grudgingly pay, all the while wondering whether cable TV is really worth all the time and money you spend on it.

With a few clever substitutions, the cable company example also describes AOL Canada (and those other online services). By hooking a cable into your computer, and running that cable from your computer to a phone jack in your wall, you connect to AOL Canada's network. How? The cable is actually plugged into your computer's modem (an odd little device that acts like a middleman between your computer and AOL Canada's giant and too-boring-to-discuss computers).

If you use a special high-speed connection (like things called DSL or cable modems), you get an even more esoteric device with its own cool cable (more about that in Chapter 24).

As with the cable TV example, if the technology behaves, your computer runs the special AOL Canada software (more on that in a minute) dials a (hopefully) local phone number, and contacts the nerve centre for AOL's worldwide network — its giant computers located in the State of Virginia, in the United States. (Don't worry about long-distance calls to Virginia from Toronto, Montreal, or wherever you happen to live in Canada — you just pay for the local part of the call, while the AOL Canada communications system does the rest.)

After connecting (or, in computer parlance, *going online*), you choose from among a wide variety of services, depending on your interests. When things don't work, the problem may be with your computer, the AOL Canada software, the modem (stupid modems), or somewhere from the phone jack to AOL Canada itself (that Great Beyond we mentioned earlier). At the end of the month, you get a bill you gleefully pay, flush with the happy memory of everything you did online.

By the way, the term *online* means "connected." If you're online with AOL Canada, a link is set up through the phone between your computer and the AOL Canada computers. When you get right down to it, the computers are having this swell digital conversation behind the scenes while you're busy reading the news, sending electronic mail, or doing whatever else you do on AOL Canada.

The entire process looks much like Figure 1-1. Your computer, running the special AOL Canada software, tells the modem to call a particular phone number. The modem dials the number and waits to hear from another modem. The two modems whistle and beep at each other for a while (the technical term for this process is *feature negotiation*, although we always thought of it as some kind of electronic flirting). After the modems settle down, they get to work completing your connection to the AOL Canada computer system.

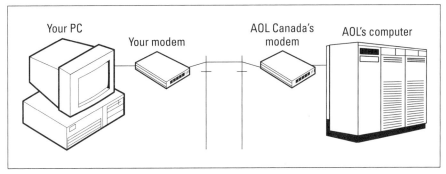

Figure 1-1:
Going online
means
"going on
phone line."

Now for the great part: That's all you need to know about the technology behind AOL Canada. Really — we wouldn't kid you about something like this. All the cool things you can do, all the fun tricks, all the stuff that makes AOL Canada a really wild and woolly place — all these require a great deal of technology, but *it doesn't matter to you.* You don't have to know any of this stuff to use AOL Canada!

All It Takes Is a Bunch of Stuff

Now that you have a conceptual picture of how all this online business happens, you're ready to dig a little deeper and get into some specifics. You need four parts to make the online thing a reality: the AOL Canada software, a computer, a modem, and a phone line. The following sections explore each element just enough to give you a good understanding of what you need without turning you into a computer nerd (ewww — the very thought gives us the shivers).

If you're starting from scratch and need to get everything, we recommend finding a computer guru to give you a hand. Depending on where you find your guru, this help may cost anywhere from a few dozen brownies to a few dozen loonies. If you do seek expert help, make sure that your expert under-stands online services (preferably AOL Canada) and gives sound, unbiased advice. Don't get help from someone you just met whose primary experience in the field comes from working at a computer store or discount electronics place. Check with your friends for the name of a trusted and handy computer guru you can borrow for a while.

First, you need the right software

AOL Canada is a pretty special place, not only because of its content and services but also for the look and feel of its interface (the buttons, menus, and windows that are onscreen). The people who started AOL decided to do things the right way from the start. This decision meant a break with tradition because people would need special software to become a member. Granted, the software was free (and still is today — but more about that in a moment), but the idea itself was pretty risky for the time. Luckily, the risk paid off handsomely in better features, ease of use, and consistency.

Free software? Did somebody say "free"? Yes! As you probably noticed the moment you pulled this book off the store shelf, by purchasing this book you are also getting all the software you need to start using AOL Canada, and you're getting it for *free*! Once you install the software using the shiny new CD-ROM provided, you can try AOL Canada for 540 hours for free (although communication charges may apply), all within your first 30-day period, after which regular charges apply. Read the appendix "About the CD" on installing the free software to do just that.

If some version of the AOL software came preloaded on your computer (both Windows 95 and Windows 98 include it in the Online Services folder on the desktop), make sure that you have the latest, Canadian version. (The first screen you see if you click that icon will ask you to specify which country you live in.) AOL Canada supports all versions back to 3.0; but the most current for the Windows platform is 6.0, and for the Mac it's 4.0. Table 1-1 explains how to politely find out which version you have.

Although knowing your program's version number seems a little nerdy, you have a good reason to find out what it is. This book covers the newest AOL Canada software — that's AOL Canada 6.0, the version included on the free CD-ROM inside the cover of this book. If you're using an older version, you may get confused very quickly (and that's definitely not our goal).

For instructions on how to install the 6.0 access software from the CD-ROM in this book, flip to the appendix, "About the CD." For details on how to connect to AOL Canada, head to the last two sections of this chapter.

Table 1-1		Version, Version, Who's Got Which Version?
Platform	*Version*	*How to Find the Version Number*
Macintosh	4.0	In the Finder, click the AOL Canada icon once and then choose File➪Get Info from the Finder menu or press Ô+I. The version number is in the pop-up information dialog box.
Windows	5.0 and 6.0	With the AOL Canada software running, choose Help➪About AOL Canada from the menu bar. The version number is near the top of the screen (see Figure 1-2).

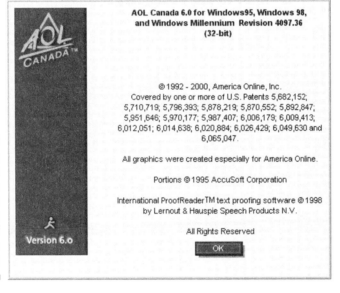

Figure 1-2:
The latest AOL Canada software for Windows shows off its version number.

AOL Canada 6.0 for Windows95, Windows 98, and Windows Millennium Revision 4097.36 (32-bit)

© 1992 - 2000, America Online, Inc.
Covered by one or more of U.S. Patents 5,682,152; 5,710,719; 5,796,393; 5,878,219; 5,870,552; 5,892,847; 5,951,646; 5,970,177; 5,987,407; 6,006,179; 6,009,413; 6,012,051; 6,014,638; 6,020,884; 6,026,429; 6,049,630 and 6,065,047.

All graphics were created especially for America Online.

Portions © 1995 AccuSoft Corporation

International ProofReaderTM text proofing software © 1998 by Lernout & Hauspie Speech Products N.V.

All Rights Reserved

OK

Version 6.0

A computer is a must

You can't get around this one: To use AOL Canada, you must have a computer. Sorry, but that's the way these things go. Having settled that point, the next logical question is "Okay, fancy author-types, what kind of computer?" "Well," we say, "that's up to you."

Because the AOL Canada special access software comes in both Macintosh and Windows versions, you have some leeway in choosing your computer. Choose the type of machine that makes you most comfortable. Don't worry if you use Windows at work but prefer a Macintosh for home (or vice versa). You can still share documents, spreadsheets, and many other files between your computers without any (well, many) problems.

If you buy a new computer for your online adventures, make sure that it has

- ✔ **A fast processor:** A Pentium, Pentium II, or Pentium III for Windows or a PowerPC, iMac, G3, or G4 for the Macintosh crowd

- ✔ **Plenty of random-access memory (RAM):** 32MB to 64MB is a good minimum for either a Macintosh or Windows machine

- ✔ **A high-quality colour monitor:** 15 inches is a good minimum size

- ✔ **Plenty of hard disk space:** 1 gigabyte or more

A modem enters the picture

The next piece of the puzzle is a modem, the device that converts your computer's electronic impulses into whistles, beeps, and various digital moose calls. The modem then yells these noises through the phone line to an equally disturbed modem attached to another computer.

The term *modem* is actually an acronym (and you thought you were safe, didn't you?). It stands for modulator/demodulator, which is a computer nerd's way of saying that it both talks and listens. To find out more than you could possibly want to know about modems, get a copy of *Modems For Dummies*, 3rd Edition, by Tina Rathbone (IDG Books Worldwide, Inc.).

The main things you're looking for in a modem are a well-known manufacturer and blazing speed. Here are our recommendations:

- ✔ **Get a modem made by 3Com/U.S. Robotics or Creative Labs.** Although many other modems are available, these manufacturers stand behind their products better than all the rest.

- ✔ **If you buy a new modem, make sure it's fast.** Modems that run at 56,000 bits per second (bps) are the rage these days. Manufacturers usually call them 56K modems because "K" means roughly 1,000 in the computer world. Condemning yourself to anything slower than 28,800 bits per second just won't do. (We care about your sanity too much for that.) See the following sidebar, "A few words about modem speed," for a little more information about these extraordinarily fleet animals.

- ✔ **Watch those standards when you pick up a new modem.** If you buy a 56K modem, be sure that it supports the V.90 standard. V.90 is the international screeching and whistling specification for 56K modems.

- ✔ **If you have a high-speed access line, you don't use a modem.** Special connections through the cable TV system or with the phone company require some equally special equipment. Chapter 24 guides you through the befuddling maze of high-speed high tech.

A few words about modem speed

A modem's speed is measured in *bits per second (bps)*. The more bits per second, the more information the modem stuffs down the phone line in a given period.

Because AOL Canada doesn't charge extra to use a faster modem, you save a lot of money in the long run by using the fastest modem you can. AOL Canada uses fast 56K modems on most of its local access numbers, although support isn't available everywhere yet. For more about 56K access to AOL Canada, check out keyword **Access.**

Our advice: Pay a little extra and get the fastest, highest-quality modem possible because the money you spend pays you back tomorrow and for many days thereafter. If you own an older 28,800 or 33,600 bps modem, check your modem maker's Web site and find out whether your modem can be upgraded to support higher speeds. Sometimes the upgrade is free — all you need to do is ask.

Many computers include a modem as part of the deal these days. If you aren't sure whether your PC includes one, glance at the back of the machine and look for a place to plug in a phone cord. Congrats — there's your modem!

What about a phone line?

All this other stuff doesn't do you a whit of good if you don't have a phone line to connect it to. The phone is your link with beautiful Dulles, Virginia, USA, which is, as we mentioned earlier, the beating heart of AOL's worldwide network. (See, Toronto isn't the centre of everyone's universe after all!) Luckily, you don't need a special phone line — just about any phone line will work.

The key words in that last sentence are *just about* because not all phone lines are created equal. Many phone lines have been endowed by their subscribers with certain very alien services — such as call waiting — that interfere with a computer's rights and freedoms (and no, computers can't file a Charter case), not to mention its pursuit of a connection with AOL Canada.

(Sorry, we've been studying the repatriation of the Canadian Constitution lately, and got a little carried away. If we had a "We're geeky authors and we're embarrassed" icon, rest assured that we'd insert it here.)

As you probably guessed, high-speed connections don't use a regular phone line at all. If they did, everyone could zip through AOL Canada with lightning speed.

To successfully use a modem, you need an analog phone line. If your home has a single phone line (or two plain, old-fashioned phone lines), you have an analog phone line. Because fax machines need the same kind of phone line, in times of emergency you can unplug the fax and use its phone line to reach AOL Canada.

At work, the story is a little different. Many office telephone systems use digital phone lines. You shouldn't plug a normal modem directly into one of these lines. Please, for the sake of your modem, don't try. At best, the modem won't work this time. At worst, the modem won't ever work again because it's fried. If you're planning to use AOL Canada from the office, contact your telephone folks and tell them that you have a modem and need something to connect it to. Remember to ask nicely, or else they may not give you the answer you're looking for.

Installing Your Free Software Today!

Now that you understand what it means to go online, and you're armed with the knowledge that you really don't have to care about the inner workings of modems, or networks, or any other techno mumbo jumbo in order to enjoy the online experience, it's time to get out there and play.

Proving their commitment to helping you do just that, the people at AOL Canada have made it as simple as possible for you to go online right now! Just pull out the CD-ROM that came inside the cover of this book and follow the easy instructions in the appendix, "About the CD."

If you received this book from a friend (or found it at the library), and the CD-ROM has gone AWOL, don't panic. You can order a FREE AOL Canada Start-Up Kit by calling 1-888-382-6645.

When setting up your AOL Canada account, you'll need a registration number and password. Don't worry. These came with the CD-ROM in this book, or you'll find them with the Start-Up Kit you ordered from 1-888-382-6645.

Access Numbers To Go!

Once you become an AOL Canada member, life will be even sweeter if you understand a thing or two about access numbers. No, we won't bore you with all the details. Just keep the following in mind:

✔ You can connect to your AOL Canada account through access numbers across the country. If you are at the cottage or on the road, you can search for a local connection. However, check with the local telephone company to make sure that you can make a local call to the access number you select. You'll also find it easy to connect while travelling south of the border or across the ocean.

✔ If the access number you are now using is giving you trouble and you don't know why, you can change access numbers (keyword **AccessHelp**). Check with your local telephone company to make sure that the number you select does not result in long distance charges.

✔ If you find yourself in a place where there is no local access number to reach AOL Canada, you can still use a special thing called the *Surcharge Access Number*. It costs more, but depending on your needs, it might be just what you're looking for. To find out more, use keyword **AccessHelp**.

See? That wasn't painful at all. To view a complete list of AOL Canada access numbers, sign on and use keyword **Access**. Figure 1-3 shows just a few of those numbers. The Access window also has simple instructions to follow for changing or adding access numbers so you can get online from just about anywhere.

Figure 1-3:
Here's a portion of the complete list of AOL Canada Access Numbers, which is alphabetical. Hey, Abbotsford! You're online!

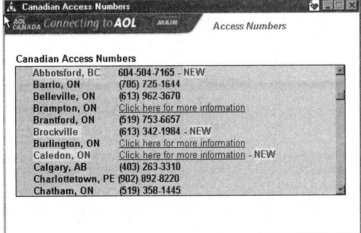

Canadian Access Numbers	
Abbotsford, BC	604-504-7165 - NEW
Barrie, ON	(706) 726-1644
Belleville, ON	(613) 962-3670
Brampton, ON	Click here for more information
Brantford, ON	(519) 753-6657
Brockville	(613) 342-1984 - NEW
Burlington, ON	Click here for more information
Caledon, ON	Click here for more information - NEW
Calgary, AB	(403) 263-3310
Charlottetown, PE	(902) 892-8220
Chatham, ON	(519) 358-1445

For help dealing with stubborn phones, modems, computers, spouses (no, just kidding on that last one) or any other technical concerns, call AOL Canada's technical support line at 1-888-265-4357. If you're not signed on and would like to try answering your own questions, choose Help⇨Offline Help from the menu at the top of your screen. Offline Help is an amazing resource — especially for the 6.0 version of the AOL Canada software.

Chapter 2

I Didn't Know You Could
Do That Online!

. . . .

In This Chapter

▶ Starting your online day

▶ Checking your mail

▶ Reading the rags

▶ Making sense of your loonies and toonies

▶ Grabbing some new software

▶ Surfing the Internet wave

▶ Relaxing with the online games

▶ Shopping — need we say more?

▶ Chatting with the neighbours

▶ And still there's more

. . . .

*B*eep Beep Beep Beep BEEP BEEP! [whack] {yawwwwn} <<strrreeetch>> Ah, good morning! Nice to see that you're up (and, may we add, looking as bright-eyed and bushy-tailed as ever). A full chapter lies ahead, so we're glad that you slept well.

This chapter is a whirlwind tour through the cool stuff AOL Canada offers. Think of this tour as a visual sampler, a platter of digital appetizers, each one delicious in itself but also tempting in the knowledge that still more awaits discovery. Collectively, this chapter gives you a broad idea of what you can do with AOL Canada — and what it can do for you.

For now, kick back and read on. If something piques your interest, take a break and try it online. Each section of the chapter includes the keywords and menu instructions you need.

Before you read on, we need to know this: Have you installed Version 6.0 of the AOL Canada access software? No? Well, grab the CD-ROM that came with this book and get started. You can follow the instructions in the appendix, "About the CD." If you've never used AOL Canada before, prepare to smile. The CD comes with a trial period of 540 free hours in your first month (communication charges may apply), so that you can test drive the latest and best version of AOL Canada yet!

First, You Need to Sign On

Every online experience starts somewhere, and signing on to the service is as good a place as any. Just follow these steps to sign on to AOL Canada:

1. **Turn on your computer, monitor, modem, stereo, food processor, and that cool cordless toothbrush/answering machine in the bathroom. Marvel at what modern technology has accomplished (and how noisy it all is), and then turn off the unimportant stuff.**

   No, you need to leave the computer on for now.

   If you have a Windows machine, your computer should start blissfully and leave you with a ready-to-go desktop screen. If that's you, go on to Step 2.

   If you use an older PC with Windows 3.x, Windows may or may not start automatically. If Windows does fire up on its own, go ahead to the next step. To manually start Windows, type **WIN** at the DOS prompt (C:\>), and then press Enter. In just a moment, the friendly Microsoft advertisement — er, the Windows logo screen — appears.

2. **Find the triangular AOL Canada icon cowering among all your other software icons and double-click it to start the program.**

   In Windows, look on the Start button menu or on the Windows 95 or 98 desktop. After the program finishes loading, it displays the Sign On dialog box.

3. **Choose the screen name you want to use by clicking the down arrow next to the Select Screen Name list box and then clicking the name of your choice.**

   If this is the first time you've picked this particular screen name with the AOL Canada 6.0 software, the program accosts you with another dialog box that demands to know whether you want to store your password. For now, click Cancel and ignore the dialog box. If your curiosity is piqued by this option, flip to Chapter 4 and unpique it with the details awaiting you there.

   Don't panic if the Enter Password text box disappears after you choose a screen name. It means that the password for that name is already stored in the access software.

4. **Press Tab to move down to the Enter Password text box and then type your password.**

   Your password appears as asterisks — not as words. That's a protection feature to keep that guy who's looking over your shoulder from breaking in to your account. What guy? Why, that one right there. (Yipe!)

5. **Click Sign On or press Enter to open the connection to AOL Canada.**

   The software goes through all kinds of cool visual gymnastics while connecting. Granted, it's not a Hollywood masterpiece, but at least it's marginally entertaining.

   If the connection process doesn't work for some reason, make a note of the last thing the software did (initializing the modem, dialing, connecting, or requesting network attention, for example) and then try connecting again. If it still doesn't work, close the AOL Canada software, restart your computer, and give your software one last chance to get things right. (Aren't you glad that your car doesn't work this way?)

   If your software still doesn't connect to AOL Canada, breeze through Chapter 26 for a list of the top 10 problems and how to solve them.

6. **After a moment, the fruits of your sign-on labour pour forth.** The newly designed AOL Canada toolbar at the top of your screen comes to life, the AOL Canada Welcome window appears front and centre on your screen, and the channels menu comes into view on the far left of the screen.

   Congratulations — you're online and ready to get some stuff done.

Although the AOL Canada Welcome window sorta takes over the middle of your screen, the AOL Canada channels are still present and accounted for. You'll find them listed top-to-bottom on a menu that sits on the left side of your screen. If you ever decide you don't want them there, just click the Hide Channels button on the left side of the navigation bar, and they'll disappear. To bring them back, click the same button again — although you'll notice the button is now labelled Show Channels. Clever, eh? Check out the *AOL Canada For Dummies* Channels Directory, your guide to channel mastery — you'll know it by the yellow pages.

Checking the E-Mailbox

Electronic mail (or e-mail) is one of the most popular AOL Canada services. That's why the Read button takes a position of pride and power in two easy-to-access places that you see every time you sign on. It's also presumably why the AOL Canada programmers have improved this service in the new 6.0 software. Here's where to start:

✔ Check for the big mailbox icon at the bottom of the AOL Canada Welcome window. Whenever you've received a message, this button will tell you oh so cheerfully that You've Got Mail, and you'll see AOL Canada's signature yellow envelope sticking out of the mailbox. (On the off chance that you don't have any messages waiting, this button will simply read Mail Centre.)

✔ Look at your AOL toolbar, at the very top left of your screen, for another indication that you have mail. (Don't ever say these people don't give you options!) The Read button mailbox icon will have its flag up and a yellow letter sticking out whenever you have mail waiting (an everyday occurrence in our world, and soon to be a regular feature of yours too). If you don't have any mail waiting, the graphic shows a closed mailbox, like the one shown in the margin at the beginning of this section.

To read your mail, either click the You've Got Mail button or click Read on the toolbar. After the New Mail dialog box pops up, click Read to start through your mail.

✔ If you're paying by the hour and you're writing a mail message instead of reading one, why are you logged on? Sign off from the system and click the Write toolbar button or press Ctrl+M to write your message offline. After you finish, turn to Chapter 8 and read about the myriad ways to send mail.

✔ If you do a lot of e-mailing with AOL Canada and want to save time, we see Automatic AOL sessions in your future. Mark your place here, and flip to Chapter 8 for more about this incredibly useful feature.

As you probably figured out by now, Chapter 8 tells you everything you need to know about addressing, sending, receiving, and generally dealing with e-mail. We had to put the information somewhere, and that seemed as good a place as any.

Say the magic keyword and get there fast

Keywords are the AOL Canada answer to the *Star Trek* transporter. A *keyword* is a single code that immediately takes you to a particular forum, special area, or service on the system. A sidebar in Chapter 7 explains all the details of keywords, but for now, we want to briefly tell you how to use them.

To use a keyword, type the keyword into the big white box on the navigation bar and then press Enter. Was that fast or what?

For the keyboard-centric folks, press Ctrl+K to open the Keyword dialog box. After the box appears, type your keyword and press Enter.

Following the Story

Nothing says "progress" like our ability to wake up to the latest news from Canada and the world — without so much as putting our slippers on to step outside the house. With AOL Canada, you have your choice of not one, not two, but — heck — a slew of newspapers — all at your fingertips. To get there, visit the AOL Canada Newsstand (keyword **Newsstand**). *Calgary Herald*, anyone? What about the *Globe and Mail*? Link to these and other newspapers from across Canada by clicking one of the yellow folders under the heading called Newspapers. Each folder represents one region of the country. Notice that there's an entire folder devoted to International Papers, as shown in Figure 2-1. (That's where you'll find the *Globe and Mail*, by the way).

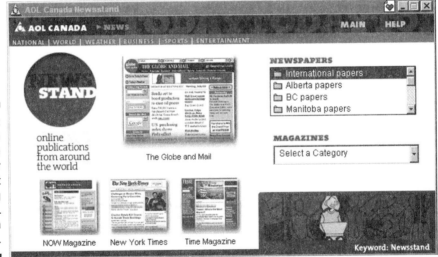

Figure 2-1: Take a trip around the world for the latest news using the AOL Canada Newsstand.

To find out almost everything you could possibly want to know about the channels, check out the *AOL Canada For Dummies* Channels Directory, easily identifiable by its yellow pages.

If magazines are your thing, sample some news and current affairs favourites, including *Maclean's* and *Shift*, or go for the gossip and fun of entertainment magazines like *People* and *Entertainment Weekly*. Use keyword **Newsstand** to bring up the AOL Canada Newsstand window, then choose a folder under the Magazines heading, on the lower right-hand side. Publications are organized into areas of interest like Sports and Business, so it's easy to find what you're looking for.

Still haven't found the magazine you're craving? To curl up with whatever publication suits your fancy, look for a link in your favourite online area, or turn to a likely-looking channel. If you go the channel route, find the Newsstand department (keyword **Newsstand**) and click the button. After you're in the Newsstand department, scroll through the publication list to find the magazine of your desire. The deeper you look, the more you'll find!

Not all the AOL Canada channels have their own newsstands, and not all the newsstands contain specifically Canadian publications. To make your search easier, try the Interests Channel Newsstand (keyword **Interests Newsstand**), and browse the pull-down menu on the left side of the window. This menu is a guide to other channel-specific newsstands.

To have news (and much, much more) screened, attractively formatted, and handily delivered to you by e-mail on a regular basis for free, just subscribe to one of AOL's electronic newsletters. One click of the mouse and you can receive newsletters on topics including business news and computing info. Start at keyword **Newsletters** and dig through the folders until you find one that interests you.

Eyeing the Markets

Managing your stock portfolio has never been easier. The Quotes service (keyword **Quotes**, or click the Quotes button on the toolbar) tracks the stocks closest to your heart and pocketbook.

Columbus, Eriksson, Magellan, and you

New services appear on AOL Canada faster than facial aberrations on a teenager. Something new seems to appear every week. How do you explore it all? Leave it to those clever AOL Canada programmers to think of a couple of great ways: QuickStart and AOL Canada Newsletter.

For all you new members, try the QuickStart new member guide (keyword **QuickStart**). QuickStart includes an overview of what's on AOL Canada, organized by your interests, an introduction to the myriad features of the system, and the requisite syrupy public relations stuff. Don't let that put you off, though, because QuickStart includes some genuinely useful goodies.

Our personal pick in QuickStart is the AOL Canada Features Tutorial, which takes you to

the Best of AOL Canada window. Here, you can learn more about some of the service's coolest stuff, like the Buddy List and Instant Message features. Once you've read about a feature you like, just click the Try It Now link and you're immediately whisked away to that very place.

The AOL Canada Newsletter is another way of staying on top of the newest and most interesting additions to the AOL Canada community. Just click the Subscribe button on the main window at keyword **AOLCanadaNews** and every month you'll get this electronic publication FREE in your e-mailbox. It's just packed with information about (and links to) new areas, seasonal goodies, contest announcements, giveaways, and more.

Figure 2-2:
Be a stock
spy with the
AOL Canada
Quotes
service.

To satisfy a brief curiosity, you can look up a single stock by its symbol. Figure 2-2, for example, tracks well-known Canadian mining company Inco Ltd. stock activity by using the symbol N. If looking at the big picture is more to your liking, the My Portfolios feature (keyword **Portfolios**) follows all the stocks you choose, tracking the current market price and how that translates into a gain or loss for your invested dollars.

- ✔ Don't panic, but the information in Quotes is delayed about 15 to 20 minutes. So, that probably means we can't call it up-to-the-minute information. Hmm — how about up-until-quite-recently information?

- ✔ You can save the portfolio information to a text file by choosing File⇨ Save from the menu bar.

AOL Canada charges no extra fee to use the Quotes and My Portfolios services — it's just part of the package. Flip to Chapter 14 to find out more about the AOL Canada financial news offerings. If you're an investor, try Chapter 21, where you'll find even more personal finance goodies.

Internet On-Ramp, Next Right

At this point in your online life, you've probably heard, read, or otherwise been exposed to *something* about the Internet. If you haven't heard about the Internet yet, don't worry; you're about to.

The *Internet* is the worldwide network of networks that's all the rage these days. You can't get your hair done, shop for tires, or even play cricket without bumping into the Internet somehow. "Oh, is that a new cricket bat?" you ask. "Aye, a player in the `rec.sport.cricket` Internet newsgroup recommended it." See what we're talking about?

The AOL Canada Internet connection (keyword **Internet**) is your portal to the World Wide Web, Gopher, the Internet newsgroups, and much more. The Internet connection makes a great starting point for your jaunts into the digital wilderness.

There's far too much to say about the Internet to do so here, so cruise to Chapter 17 and get ready for the ride of your life.

The Joys of (Nearly) Free Stuff

It seems like everywhere you turn in AOL Canada, you find a software library. You don't have to be anywhere special; just about every service area has something to offer.

Exactly what's available depends entirely on where you are — but the range of stuff out there is utterly amazing. A great place to start is the Daily Download (keyword **Daily Download**), where you'll find, well, a different featured downloadable treat every day. You never know what you'll find there.

In Space Exploration Online (keyword **Space Exploration**), browse through images from the Hubble Space Telescope, photographs of the International Space Station, volumes of news from space programs around the world, and more model rocketry programs than any one person could use. The Food area (keyword **Food**) serves up recipes for every kind of taste and a variety of cookbook programs (both shareware and commercial demonstrations). Try your hand at computer animation in the Animation and Video area's (keyword **A&V**) Windows libraries and resource centre (and pick up trailers from your favourite movies, too).

Thanks to the AOL Canada Internet links, you also have access to the infinite software libraries available through File Transfer Protocol, lovingly known in Net lingo as FTP. Troll the likes of Winsite (`ftp.winsite.com` — widely acknowledged as the world's largest Windows software library), Info-Mac (`ftp://mirror.aol.com/pub/info-mac` — the newly improved version of Stanford's old Sumex library, the home of more Macintosh software than anyone could possibly need), and the Digital River Inc. Archive (`ftp.cdrom.com` — a great spot to find all kinds of programs) with ease. Filling your hard drive has never been so much fun!

Whether it's fonts and clip art, games and playing tips, or something a little more businesslike, in Chapter 16 you can find the details of getting it, unpacking it (watch out for the foam peanuts!), and making it work for you. For FTP info, check out Chapter 17.

Speaking of free stuff, here's a deal: how about a monthly newsletter that keeps you up-to-date on the newest and hottest features on AOL Canada? Look no farther than keyword **AOLCanadaNews**. Just hit the Subscribe button and you will automatically receive the newsletter every month in your e-mailbox. The newsletter includes short, snappy descriptions of contests, promotions, seasonal features, and more (each accompanied by a clickable link so you can jump right there). More on collecting incoming e-mail, including newsletters, in Chapter 8.

Still on the subject of free stuff — and what a subject it is — be sure to drop by AOL Canada's Member Perks area (keyword **Perks**). That's where you'll find out about limited-time deals offered exclusively to AOL Canada members.

Let the Fun and Games Begin!

Because all work and no play makes us really grumpy (and probably does the same thing to you), take a break from the Internet and indulge in some fun. The online world offers games to suit every age, style, and taste.

If you're a shoot-'em-up kinda person, work through your aggression (and sharpen your aim) in Splatterball (keyword **Splatterball**), part of a new breed of interactive online action game. For enthusiasts of more sedate games, AOL Canada offers options like bridge (keyword **Bridge**). For a trip into the imagination of online theatre, check out the Simming area (part of keyword **Games**) or the Games Chat area in the Computing Chat & Messages window (keyword **Computing Chat**).

Some of the games you'll find in AOL Canada's Game Guide (keyword **Game Guide**) will cost you a few extra cents. They're called Premium Games, and you'll generally be charged about 99 cents per hour to play. That's on top of your regular AOL Canada membership charges. AOL Canada will always identify Premium Games before you start playing, so you'll never get caught with a bill you didn't know was coming.

Multiplayer computer games live all over the Internet as well. Visit Yahoo! Games (`games.yahoo.com`) or Excite Canada Games (go to `www.excite.ca`, then click the Games link) for card games like Canasta, Hearts, and Spades; strategy games such as Backgammon and Go; and a cool collection of fantasy sports games. Best of all, the games are free, so play as long as you want (or until your Better Half casually suggests that you stop).

All this fun stuff and more is waiting on the Games channel. For more fun, flip to Chapter 15.

Shopping without the Crowds

Try for a moment to relive the last time you left your Christmas shopping until the last minute. After you regain consciousness, get a drink of water and then come back and keep reading.

Now imagine the same shopping trip with no crowds, no pushy children, and no whining adults. It's a dream, right? No, it's the AOL Canada Shopping channel (keywords **Shop** or **Shopping**, or click on the Shop button in the AOL toolbar). It's your 24-hour shop-till-your-fingers-drop electronic mall.

Take a stroll through the AOL Canada online gift catalogues (keyword **Gift Shop**), where products are just one click away! If books or music are your bag, try the Books and Music category in the AOL Canada shopping channel, where you can shop at Chapters.ca or SamTheRecordMan.com. There are a wide range of categories to browse, including Kids, Toys & Babies; Gifts & Collectibles; Beauty & Wellness; Home, Kitchen & Garden; Pets & Animals; Sports & Outdoors, and Consumer Electronics. Remember, keyword **Shop** takes you there!

Or, if you're ready to dive into a slightly bigger pool, try the AOL Canada Member Classifieds (keyword **Classifieds**), where you'll find millions of listings for buyers and sellers alike. But keep in mind, some of these postings are being made by U.S. residents, so before you dish out any cash, read up on electronic cross-border shopping in Chapter 13. The icon displayed next to the price indicates the currency the price is listed in.

If your credit card is already out, take a break and power-shop through the Shopping Channel in *AOL Canada For Dummies* Channels Directory, the book-within-a-book that sports those eerie yellow pages.

Enjoying a Little Chat

The People Connection (click the Chat icon in the green portion of the toolbar) is the home of the AOL Canada *chat* areas. There, you can interactively talk live with other AOL Canada members. All this chat happens in what the technology jockeys call *real time*, which is a fancy way to say that right after you type a message, the other people in that chat area see the message on their screens, wherever they are.

The chat areas usually hold a maximum of 23 people. AOL Canada does have some larger rooms, known as *conference rooms* or *auditoriums* — you can find out about them in Chapter 9.

When Problems Come Up

Compared to other online services, AOL Canada offers a truly awesome level of support. You can find online chat areas, discussion boards, and even an old-fashioned, pick-up-the-phone-and-call-a-human line. Whew — they really have you covered.

Precisely where you look for answers depends on the problem you're having. Following is a two-step guide to help you find assistance fast:

- ✔ If you *can* sign on but don't know how to do something (for example, send an e-mail or read your Internet newsgroups), look in this book first because that information is probably in here somewhere. If we left it out, you have our apologies (goodness knows, we tried). Now that we're done grovelling, go to the Member Services help centre (keyword **Help**) and click the topic that's causing you grief. Another great resource is the Members Helping Members discussion area (keyword **MHM**). Pose your question there, and fellow AOL members offer their best solutions. Who knows? The answer you're looking for might already be included in the category titled Top AOL Canada Questions. So take a gander!

- ✔ If you can't sign on, call the AOL Technical Guru Department, at 1-888-265-4357. Wade through the menu prompts, cross your fingers, and get ready to work through your problem with one of the helpful (and bilingual) AOL Canada technical-support folks. If you call at one of the system's peak times (like early in the evening), keep some reading material handy because you may be on hold for a while.

For general assistance and live online help, take a look at the AOL Neighbour-hood Watch at keyword **NeighbourhoodWatch**. It covers online conduct, viruses, scams, account security, and more. When you have questions, it's definitely a great place to go. For even more general help with computer-related problems (and who doesn't have these once in a while, eh?), use keyword **PC Help Desk** for a window full of advice and pointers on everything from downloading files to moving icons around.

Handling the Rude, the Crude, and the Socially Maladjusted

Few things spoil a perfectly wonderful online evening quite like an annoying oddball in your favourite chat room, a persistently pestering Instant Message, or an obnoxious e-mail. When problems arise, you need to take action — and this section points you in the right direction.

The following list explains how to handle the various (and unfortunately common) annoyances of online life. If something comes up that's not on the list, check the keywords **Help, NeighbourhoodWatch, Notify AOL,** or **TOSCanada** for suggestions.

- ✔ **Chat room disruptors:** Click the Notify AOL button along the top of the chat window to report the problem and summon some help. Fill out the brief form and then click the Send button.

- ✔ **Instant Message password requests:** Use keyword **Notify AOL** to bring up the Notify AOL window, click on Instant Message Notes, and follow the instructions from there. If you're in a chat room, be sure to warn everyone else that someone is fishing for passwords! If you accidentally did give out your password, go immediately (and we mean right-now-don't-wait-to-think) to keyword **Password** and change your account password.

- ✔ **Annoying instant messages:** Don't close the Instant Message window just yet. Instead, open the Notify AOL window using keyword **Notify AOL** and click Instant Message Notes from the list of options. The instructions here ask you to copy and paste the screen name and the body of the offensive instant message. To do this, go to the instant message window and highlight the screen name by holding down your left mouse button and moving across the words. Then, right-click your mouse and choose Copy from the menu. Return to the Notify AOL window, click into the appropriate text box, right click again, and choose Paste from the menu. The text should appear where your cursor was blinking. Do the same to copy the body of the offensive message. When you've filled everything out, click Send to alert the people at AOL Canada.

- ✔ **Questionable e-mail messages:** To report e-mail problems, click the Forward button in the bothersome e-mail message and send it to screen name `TOSEmail`. If someone you don't know sent you an e-mail message with an attached file, *do not open or download the file!* Instead, forward the message directly to screen name `TOSFiles`. (The odds are very good that the file would mess up your computer or steal your AOL Canada password!)

For help reporting other problems, like raunchy screen names, vulgar member profiles, or tasteless AOL Canada member Web sites, go to keyword **Notify AOL** and click the appropriate button to bring up the correct reporting window.

Wait — There's More!

This chapter doesn't even begin to tell you what's available out in the wilds of AOL Canada. Come to think of it, that's what the rest of this book does:

- ✔ To find out more about a specific channel, look up the area in *AOL Canada For Dummies* Channels Directory, the super-cool, yellow-paged book-within-a-book.
- ✔ To follow your own interests, look in Part IV.
- ✔ If you feel the need to follow other interests, the bathroom is down the hall.

When It's Time to Say Good-Bye

All good things must come to an end, and so it is with AOL Canada. But signing off from the system is quick and painless. Here's a quick list of good-bye (and good-bye–related) options in the AOL Canada 6.0 software:

- ✔ To sign off from the system, choose Sign Off⇨Sign Off from the main menu. This action closes your online connection and leaves you sitting quietly in front of the main AOL Canada software window.
- ✔ To switch to another screen name, choose Sign Off⇨Switch Screen Name from the main menu. In the Switch Screen Name dialog box (shown in Figure 2-3), double-click the name you want to use, and follow the onscreen instructions for typing your new password. In just a moment, AOL Canada signs your other screen name on to the system — and you don't even have to redial the phone! For more about creating new screen names (you get up to seven with each AOL Canada account), see Chapter 6.
- ✔ To shut down the AOL Canada software, choose File⇨Exit. You're done!

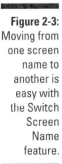

Figure 2-3: Moving from one screen name to another is easy with the Switch Screen Name feature.

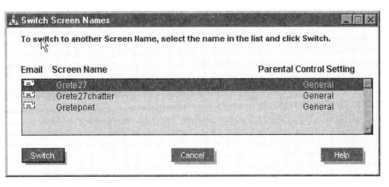

Chapter 3

Surviving the Software

. . . .

In This Chapter

▶ Camping on the new and improved toolbar

▶ Cruising with the slim and sleek navigation bar

▶ Browsing the steadfast menus

. . . .

*U*sing AOL Canada is one thing. But before you can actually use it, you must tangle with [insert scary organ music here] the user interface!

No, it's not something else you need to buy. The term *user interface* is just a fancy way of describing the menus, buttons, and goodies you use to interact with a program. It's like an automobile engineer looking at the layout of a dashboard and thinking, "Golly, that's a clever user interface." (Yes, despite the various specialties, most engineers respond to the simplest stimulus in predictably unintelligible ways — they're just that way.)

This chapter covers the three main parts of the brand-new AOL Canada 6.0 user interface: the toolbar menus, the navigation bar, and the menu bar. It doesn't matter whether you use these tools together or separately, because they make your life a little easier either way (and that's more than you can say for most software on the market.)

If you're reading this book from cover to cover, you might get a bit sick of these reminders, but just in case you've dropped in to this important chapter from the get-go, we want you to know that everything you need to use the latest version of AOL Canada's toolbar (and everything else on the service) is included in the CD-ROM you received with this book. See the appendix, "About the CD," for the basics of the installation process.

Revealing the Toolbar (and Its Way-Cool Menus)

It's always there, right below the menu bar — watching you, daring you, enticing you with coloured buttons. However, the toolbar itself remains a mystery. What do those little pictures mean? Why are there so many of them? Why do some give you a menu and others just do their thing? (By the way, is it time for lunch yet?)

Don't worry if the toolbar looks a little, well, odd at first glance. That's because the AOL Canada 6.0 software features a very different kind of toolbar from those that most programs use today (it's quite avant-garde, for whatever that's worth).

The AOL Canada programmers endowed the 6.0 toolbar with a combination of old-fashioned click-the-button-to-do-something features and newfangled click-the-button-and-watch-the-menu-appear functionality. The new incarnation brings to life a sort of graphical menu filled with possibilities.

All those possibilities start with the five main buttons. Each has a different colour that makes it stand out from the others (and probably to enhance its self-confidence a bit — you know how insecure buttons get sometimes). Each is also divided into a top half (which reveals options within options) and a lower half (revealing at least one icon).

The top half is known as the Menu portion of the button (see Figure 3-1 for an example). It has a name on the left and a small downward-pointing triangle on the right. The triangles aren't anything dramatic, but they are very helpful. They indicate that a whole menu is anxiously waiting to pop into view at the click of a button. (You may have figured that out already, since the word "More" appears beside each triangle whenever you move your cursor over it — as in "Give me *more* options.")

Once you've used the power of the top half of the toolbar to reveal the abounding menus attached to each main button, you'll notice that some of the pull-down options have their own arrows. These look a little different and point not down, but sideways. Follow them to reveal even more options! (Options within options — does this remind you of those little wooden dolls that open up to smaller and smaller dolls?) You can get an idea of how much is in store in the descending menus in Figure 3-1.

The names on the top half of the main toolbar buttons include a *hot key* (the little underlined letter in the name of the button). To use the hot key, just hold down the Alt key and press the underlined letter. Without further ado, that button's menu appears. Talk about speed!

Figure 3-1:
A sample
AOL Canada
toolbar
button.

The bottom half of each button is taken up with buttons *sans* triangle. No menus here, just icons (see Figure 3-1 for an idea of what these look like). Click 'em and they do what they say they do — and what the little pictures hint that they do. These little guys represent some of the most popular areas on AOL Canada. Not only that, but shortly, we'll tell you how you can change some of the icons so that the toolbar truly reflects your individual (and, we presume, refined) tastes.

For now, here's a quick overview of the five main toolbar buttons, starting from the left side of the toolbar (as shown in Figure 3-2):

- ✔ **Mail:** The first group of toolbar buttons governs e-mail. All the e-mail goodies live here, including the customizable mail features — options like adding your very own signature to outgoing mail. For everything you ever wanted to know about e-mail and a little more, check out Chapter 8.

- ✔ **People:** Next sits the People button, which opens the doors to chat rooms, Instant Messages, and discussion areas all over AOL Canada. (Considering all the interaction that happens in the chat areas, it's kinda logical that the icon representing them has all those waving people — but we personally think they should be smiling.) For the scoop on chatting, see Chapter 9.

- ✔ **AOL Services:** The aptly titled Services button covers a bunch of utility functions like the new online calendar, stock quotes, and the People Finder. It's also the gateway to all the cool content available on the worldwide Internet (one click here and you can kiss a few hours farewell as you dive into the amazing bounty of online information). And speaking of bounty, did anyone here want to shop? AOL Services is also your link to an AOL Canada online shopping experience!

- ✔ **Settings:** Do you have kids who are dying to use the Internet? (Uh, are there any kids who *aren't?*) You'll want to check out the Parental Controls and the rest of the wide range of settings that customize your AOL Canada experience. (For more about these settings, see Chapter 4.)

- ✔ **Favourites:** Last, but certainly not least, it's your turn. You get to fill out this area with icons of your choice and links that return you over and over to your favourite places inside AOL Canada and on the World Wide Web. (To find out more about laying claim to an area that's rightfully yours and cramming it full of icons for your favourites-of-favourites, flip to Chapter 23.)

Figure 3-2:
The new
AOL Canada
toolbar.

Now that you know how they're organized, it's time to dig into more of the button details. The following sections rattle off the name and purpose of all the buttons and functions contained in the toolbar.

We've decided to follow the same order as the AOL Canada programmers. That means our explanations appear in the same order as the buttons and menus unfold on the toolbar from left to right — a brilliant preemptive strike on our part to stave off future e-mail from readers beginning, "Dear John and Marguerite, why did Mail Centre come before Favourites?" (not that we don't appreciate your feedback!).

Mail

"Everything about Mail." That's what the helpful little dialog box says if you let your cursor linger over the blue Mail button on the left side of your toolbar, and it pretty much sums up its functions. Clicking the top half of this button takes you into the wonderful world of e-mail quicker than you can say, "Please let there be a new message!" But before we get into the menus, you need to know a bit about the icons on the bottom half of the button.

Read

Clicking this button displays the New Mail section of your e-mail box, just like clicking the You've Got Mail button on the bottom of the AOL Canada Welcome screen (the one that appears when you first sign on). This button works only when you're signed on to AOL Canada.

Write

The toolbar's Write button is a single-purpose button that opens up a blank e-mail window, ready and waiting for your next digital missive. This button does the same thing as pressing Ctrl+M. Write works both online and offline, although you can't send your new mail message until you sign on to AOL Canada. For the details about all things e-mail, check out Chapter 8.

The pull-down menu that emerges from a click of the Mail toolbar button offers one-stop shopping for everything to do with e-mail, from reading new messages to managing your online address book. The following bullets explore the button menu's numerous choices:

✔ **Mail⇨Read Mail:** Here's the first example of a menu option that contains its own set of options. You've got three choices here:

- *Read Mail⇨New Mail*: Read your incoming mail; same as Ctrl+R or clicking the Read toolbar button.

- *Read Mail⇨Old Mail*: Revisit mail you've already read at some point or another. Mail remains here for seven days or fewer, so don't be surprised if something you want to see is gone.

- *Read Mail⇨Sent Mail*: Take another look at the outbound missives (and other types of notes) you sent within the past 30 days or so.

✔ **Mail⇨Write Mail:** Write a new e-mail message; same as Ctrl+M or clicking the Write toolbar button.

✔ **Mail⇨Address Book:** Open up the built-in Address Book and manage your ever-growing collection of online friends. For more on the improved features of the AOL Canada 6.0 Address Book, check out Chapter 8.

✔ **Mail⇨Mail Centre:** Pop in to the Mail Centre, home of all you can know (outside this book, of course) about doing the e-mail thing with AOL Canada.

✔ **Mail⇨Recently Deleted Mail:** Retrieve mail that you deleted (either on purpose or on *whoops!*) within the last 24 hours with the Recently Deleted Mail window.

✔ **Mail⇨Filing Cabinet:** Your filing cabinet is a multipurpose storage unit that keeps all your mail tidily sorted and organized. It's also where you'll find those pretty messages you downloaded while using an Automatic AOL session — meaning you don't have to be signed on to read them.

✔ **Mail⇨Mail Waiting to Be Sent:** Review and send mail you wrote offline (without signing on to AOL Canada). (You'll have to sign on before sending it!)

✔ **Mail⇨Automatic AOL:** Send your AOL Canada software out to carry on an Automatic AOL session (or have the system walk you through the easy setup process).

✔ **Mail⇨Mail Signatures:** Make, modify, or maul your e-mail signatures.

✔ **Mail⇨Mail Controls:** Adjust the e-mail restrictions for your account.

✔ **Mail⇨Mail Preferences:** Display the Mail Preferences window and adjust the details of how AOL Canada handles your incoming and outgoing e-mail.

✔ **Mail⇨Greetings & Mail Extras:** Check out all the cool things you can do with e-mail, like sending electronic cards and such.

People

This friendly-looking toolbar button links you to the wonderful world of the People Connection and AOL Live, home to more great conversation than a convention of talk-show hosts. Just sign on to AOL Canada and click the top half of the People toolbar button to see the entire menu of options, including direct links to chats, presentations all over the system, and other people-related things, like locating members online and searching the member database. "But first," you ask, "what about the bottom half of the People button?" Well, without further ado, here are the icons you'll find there.

I.M.

Hey, this button's even got a cool short-form name. Come on! You've just got to use it to dive in to the world of Instant Messages. Click once and you're on your way. The Send Instant Message window appears, er, instantly.

Chat

Look at all those waving people on the icon. What are they waving about? If they could talk, they'd probably say something like, "Click this button once to meet friends, express yourself, and participate in a 24-hour conversation." This button takes you to the People Connection main window, home of all the system's chat options.

Here's the lowdown on what's available in the pull-down menu under People:

- ✔ **People⇨Send Instant Message:** Drop an Instant Message on a friend's desktop with this menu item; just like pressing Ctrl+I.

- ✔ **People⇨Chat:** Takes you to the People Connection window. From there, just click the Chat Now! option to enter one of the chat lobbies.

- ✔ **People⇨Chat Now:** Another option to take you inside the world of the People Connection.

- ✔ **People⇨Find a Chat:** Seek out a particular chat room by searching for its name.

- ✔ **People⇨Start Your Own Chat:** Click to create a new member chat room.

- ✔ **People⇨Live Events:** Hear celebrities, scientists, singers, and, yes, even authors, as they hold forth on all kinds of fascinating topics; same as keyword **AOL Live**.

- ✔ **People⇨Buddy List:** Display your Buddy List and find out which of your friends are spending a few relaxing hours on the system. For all the details on this innovative tool, see Chapter 12.

- ✔ **People⇨Get Member Profile:** Discover more about the person you just bonked on the head with an Instant Message or bumped into in a chat room; same as pressing Ctrl+G.

- ✔ **People⇨Locate Member Online:** Find out whether a particular screen name is signed on to AOL Canada. If the person is signed on, the system tells you whether that person is in a chat room, a private chat room, or just wandering around the service somewhere; same as pressing Ctrl+L.

- ✔ **People⇨Send Message to Pager:** If someone you know subscribes to the right pager service, send that person a full text-and-numbers page directly from AOL Canada! (Check the information in this area for details about which pagers and services the system covers.)

- ✔ **People⇨Sign On a Friend:** Invite your friends to join the world of AOL Canada.

- ✔ **People⇨AOL Hometown:** Head off to AOL Canada's hopping Web page neighbourhood.

- ✔ **People⇨Groups @AOL:** Are you like us? Do you have family scattered all over the country? If so, you'll want to use this option to create a virtual space where you can meet, talk, laugh, and plan those trips to Grandma's house. An amazing service you can read all about in Chapter 12.

- ✔ **People⇨People Directory:** Discover that special someone by sifting through the millions of profile entries in the AOL Canada People Directory.

- ✔ **People⇨Personals:** Ah! Love is grand, and getting grander all the time now that people are using Love@AOL (same as keyword **Love**). Browse the personals, check out the Advice column, use the Date Planner, and so much more.

- ✔ **People⇨People Finder:** Takes you to the AOL Canada People Finder Web page. Search for long-lost friends and acquaintances by entering a name, city, and province or territory.

- ✔ **People⇨Business Finder:** Like its people-focused neighbour, the Business Finder option helps you to locate businesses across Canada by category (hotel, restaurant, plumber, astrophysicist, and such) or by business name.

AOL Services

Service is a central concept at AOL Canada. As a member, you have access to services big (the Internet, car sales), small (electronic greetings, horoscopes), and novel (the 6.0 version of the software includes the all-new online calendar). Before we get into all that, though, take a look at what the icons on the bottom half of this button can do for you.

Shop

Unless you've been living under a rock for the past couple of years (or maybe raising a horde of kids), you've probably heard something about e-commerce. Well, the beating heart of e-com is online shopping — your ability to find a store, browse merchandise, and pay for just about anything using your computer. The Shop icon takes you to the AOL Canada Shopping channel where you can get a "hands-on-credit cards" education in shopping online. See, learning *is* fun!

Internet

Speaking of living under a rock, we won't discuss how big the boulder would have to be to keep a person from hearing about the Internet these days. Click here for easy access to the World Wide Web, Internet newsgroups, and all the other goodies the international network of networks has to offer.

The AOL Services menu gives you a bit of everything. You'll see what we mean when you read through the following:

- **AOL Services➪Shop:** Shop, shop, shop, shop. (What else is there to add?)

- **AOL Services➪Internet:** Get to the Net using this menu (just follow the right-pointing arrow). You have several options to choose from, including

  - *Go to the Web:* Takes you to the AOL.CA homepage where you can begin a Search, browse the Web Centres and more.

  - *Search the Web:* This option takes you right to the AOL Canada Search page. Use the Canadian categories, or try a keyword search.

  - *Newsgroups:* Go straight to the Usenet Newsgroups window, where a sometimes strange (but always interesting) world of information awaits.

  - *FTP:* Get a head start on filling your hard disk to overflowing with a trip to the Internet's voluminous file libraries, all available directly through the AOL Canada FTP (short for File Transfer Protocol) window.

  - *Internet Connection:* Connect to the Internet through the AOL.CA homepage.

- **AOL Services➪AOL Help:** This option opens the Member Services Help page, where you'll find a list of important contact numbers to reach AOL Canada for customer service and techno-queries.

- **AOL Services➪Calendar:** It's free, it's available wherever you happen to be online, and it's easy to use. It's the online calendar, and you can get there by choosing the Calendar option.

✔ **AOL Services⇨Car Buying:** Powered by Chariots.com, you can use the AOL Canada Auto Centre to buy a new or used car, or just compare the hottest models. You can also use this option to join the AOL Canada AutoClub.

✔ **AOL Services⇨Classifieds:** Buying or selling? This option takes you to millions of postings from people all over Canada and the U.S., thanks to the ClassifiedPlus Web site. (If you decide to buy from a U.S. seller, be sure to check out Chapter 13, where you'll find important information about importing merchandise into Canada.)

✔ **AOL Services⇨Dictionary:** Rely on the reputation of the *Merriam-Webster Dictionary* for all your spelling questions.

✔ **AOL Services⇨E-Greetings:** What could be better than receiving an electronic greeting card? Sending an electronic greeting card for free, of course! That's what you'll find using the E-Greetings option.

✔ **AOL Services⇨Horoscopes:** Hey, baby! What's your sign? Read the stars at the online horoscopes window.

✔ **AOL Services⇨Maps & Directions:** Powered by the well-known Mapquest.com engine, this option lets you search for detailed road maps all over Canada and the U.S. (No more husband–wife disagreements about stopping for directions — we don't need to elaborate, do we?)

✔ **AOL Services⇨Medical References:** You know the saying "At least you've got your health"? Well, truer words were never spoken. Keep up with all the latest health information at AOL Canada Health (same as keyword **Cdn Health**).

✔ **AOL Services⇨Movie Showtimes:** Thanks to *Tribute Magazine Online*, you can find out what's playing in your area tonight.

✔ **AOL Services⇨Personals:** It wouldn't be a real community without the possibility of romance, would it? Explore your options in the AOL Personals.

✔ **AOL Services⇨Recipes:** AOL Canada would not see you stuck at your next dinner party. Look for something new or maybe just a variation on an old favourite at the Food & Recipes window.

✔ **AOL Services⇨Scoreboards:** All the scores, all the time, for all your favourite teams.

✔ **AOL Services⇨Stock Portfolios:** Your direct link to the My Portfolios service, where you can organize and track all your investments. For more on this service, flip to Chapter 14.

✔ **AOL Services⇨Stock Quotes:** Open the AOL Canada stock quoting system to track your market investments (and, depending on the day, to send yourself into blissful ecstasy or hair-tearing waves of angst). This button does the same thing as keyword **Quotes** and works only if you're signed on to AOL Canada.

- ✔ **AOL Services➪Travel Reservations:** The world is shrinking. Get out there and see it all using the AOL Canada Travel channel.

- ✔ **AOL Services➪TV Listings:** 57 channels and nothing on? Don't despair, check out the TV listings to dig up the best of what the tube has to offer.

- ✔ **AOL Services➪People Finder:** One of AOL Canada's most useful services, the People Finder (also known as Find A Person) can help you get in touch with one of your fellow Canucks in a distant part of the country.

- ✔ **AOL Services➪Business Finder:** Millions of business listings await you using the Business Finder Web page.

Settings

Whether you want to browse, add something to your Filing Cabinet, adjust Parental Controls, or set your Preferences, this button takes care of you. In a moment, we'll take you through everything the menu items offer. First, let's look at the single icon you'll find occupying the lower half of the Settings button.

It may be all alone there at the bottom of the Settings button, but the My AOL icon is a powerful little guy. Take a lush tour of the many things you can do to make your corner of the AOL Canada world as cool as can be (same as keyword **My AOL**).

And now, the meat and potatoes of the Settings menu:

- ✔ **Settings➪My AOL:** Begin the process of making AOL home. (Same as clicking the My AOL icon.)

- ✔ **Settings➪Preferences:** Use this option to tweak to your heart's content (same as keyword **Preferences**). Leaf through Chapter 4 for a complete list of all the customizable settings.

- ✔ **Settings➪Parental Controls:** Bring up the Parental Controls window, which explores and explains everything you ever wanted to know about the Parental Controls feature. Check Chapter 4 for the lowdown on the Parental Controls options.

- ✔ **Settings➪My Member Profile:** Create, adjust, or simply blow away your online member profile. (See Chapter 23 for tips about building a very cool profile, complete with custom subject headings.)

- ✔ **Settings➪Screen Names:** Open the screen name management window, where you can create, delete, recover, and generally annoy the screen names on your account (works only if you're signed on with the master screen name — see Chapter 4 for details).

✔ <u>Settings</u>⇨<u>P</u>asswords: Choose this option to change your AOL Canada password, which, of course, you should do every month or two, just for good measure (and to test your memory, too).

✔ <u>Settings</u>⇨<u>B</u>illing Centre: No one can afford to ignore the bottom line. Use this option to learn about the payment options for AOL Canada through the Member Services area.

✔ <u>Settings</u>⇨<u>O</u>nline Clock: If your kitchen clock suddenly poops out, choose this option to see the current time. The online clock also provides a rough estimate of how long you have been online.

✔ <u>Settings</u>⇨Filing <u>C</u>abinet: Open the Filing Cabinet window, your very own digital attic for storing your digital, um, stuff.

✔ <u>Settings</u>⇨Save to Filing Cabinet: If you have an e-mail message, or a newsgroup or message board posting open on your screen, you can use this menu-within-a-menu to store it in one of your Filing Cabinet folders. Here are your default storage options (if you have already created more folders inside your Filing Cabinet, they'll appear just below these ones):

  • *Mail:* If you simply want a copy of a message or posting, use this option to save it to the main Filing Cabinet folder. (All the other folders are held within it.)

  • *Incoming/Saved Mail:* Keeps your message in your general folder for incoming mail.

  • *Mail You've Sent:* Keeps a copy of an important outgoing e-mail.

  • *Create Folder:* Not satisfied with placing a posting or message in the folders we've just explored? Then make a new one using this option.

Favourites

This fifth and final button is both the most flashy (unmistakably purple) and the most personal of all the toolbar buttons. That's because some of the menus and icons are customizable. The menu portion of the button, on the top half, even has a special "More" that comes up when your cursor pauses over the white down-pointing arrow. We'll get to all the "Mores" in a moment, but first, here are your Favourites icons:

One click of the My Favourites icon and the small Favourite Places window magically appears. By default, there are already several folders full of great AOL Canada areas, but you can change them and create more. The idea behind My Favourites is that the longer you use AOL Canada, the more online areas you'll come to enjoy. At some point you need a way to keep track of everything. You use My Favourites to cruise quickly to those areas and for easy navigation anywhere inside or outside AOL Canada. Chapter 7 explains the details of the whole Favourite Places system.

There's nothing like a Perk to, um, perk up your day. (Sorry, bad joke.) But in all seriousness, you'll find plenty to cheer you up every time you click the Perks icon, which whisks you off to the AOL Canada Perks window. Here, you'll find the latest deals, steals, and offers available exclusively to AOL Canada members like you!

This option reveals another sub-menu where those generous AOL Canada programmers have gathered some of the very special deals available to members *only*:

- **AOL Canada Member Perks:** Contests, deals, and exclusive offerings of all kinds can be found in the Member Perks window (same as keyword **Perks**).

- **AOL Gift Reminder Service:** One of our favourites, this free service ensures that you'll never again forget a crucial occasion. How? By delivering a handy reminder right into your e-mail mailbox.

- **Daily Shopping Feature:** Hot deals on quality goods through the AOL Canada Shopping Channel.

- **AOL Canada Gift Shop:** It's one thing to remember an occasion, it's another to celebrate it with just the right gift. This option lends a hand by taking you to the Gift Shop.

If the statement "Time is money" means anything to you, you'll enjoy the Quotes service, accessible by clicking the Quotes icon, or by using keyword **Quotes**. The service lets you keep track of individual stocks as they are traded throughout the day.

If you think you can do better than the Perks and Quotes icons, you're probably right. These two little guys are replaceable (sorry, fellas). All you have to do is follow the simple instructions in Chapter 23, under the heading "Dancing the Toolbar Tango."

Depending on an odd technical detail about your computer, your AOL Canada toolbar may or may not include the last two customizable icons. Even though this seems very odd indeed, one of your computer's screen settings decides the fate of these poor, innocent buttons. You see, your monitor displays information by using a certain number of dots on the screen. Now, *dots* is too simple a term for technology people, so they invented the word *pixel* instead. The number of pixels on the screen tells you the screen's *resolution*. To see the customizable buttons, your screen must have at least an 800 x 600 resolution. Older computers may have a 640 x 480 resolution, which unfortunately cuts the customizable buttons off the screen.

The Favourites menu is as diverse as it is useful. The "More" we discussed before indicates that the menu contains more than meets the eye. Once you begin accumulating Favourites (by following the instructions in Chapter 7), you'll see extra options queuing up at the bottom of the menu — new additions that you create! For now, if you've just signed on for the first time, here are your default Favourites options:

- ✔ **Favourites⇨Favourite Places:** You can use this first option to bring up the Favourite Places window (same as clicking the My Favourites icon).

- ✔ **Favourites⇨Add Top Window to Favourite Places:** Add a Favourite Places item for the cool content area you happen to be in right now.

- ✔ **Favourites⇨Go To Keyword:** Bring up the Keyword dialog box for quick navigation around both AOL Canada and the Internet (same as Ctrl+K).

- ✔ **Favourites⇨My Hot Keys:** This corner of the menu system belongs to you — fill it with up to 10 of your favourite keyword areas. Check out Chapter 24 to find out how.

- ✔ **Favourites⇨AOL's Top Picks:** This sub-menu has 21 options, including everything from a Computer Buyers' Guide to the AOL Canada Women's Channel. Explore them all. You'll be pleasantly surprised.

Sailing around the Navigation Bar

Just below the toolbar is a thin little group of controls, known as the *navigation bar*. Even though the navigation bar is small, it plays a vital role in your time on AOL Canada by acting as both your native guide and skillful scribe.

The navigation bar includes only a few controls, but what they lack in number, these controls make up for in power. Here's a quick breakdown, from left to right, of the cool things awaiting you (for a complete multimedia experience, follow along in Figure 3-3 as you read these bullets out loud — but don't let anybody see you do it, okay?):

- ✔ **Show/Hide Channels button:** Click this button once to bring up the Channels menu that sits on the far left of your screen. It's handy to have around, giving you quick, simple access to AOL Canada's 19 content channels — sort of the backbone of the whole neighbourhood. Click the button again and you can tuck the list away until you need it next.

Figure 3-3: The navigation bar: small, but jam-packed.

Show/Hide Channels Menu Button

Address Window

Keyword Button

Browser Buttons

Search Window

Search Button

⌐ **Browser buttons:** The four buttons on the left side of the navigation bar provide the basic features you need to steer through the Web. (The buttons work with AOL Canada–based information areas, too, although it takes some practice before you get the hang of it.) The right- and left-pointing triangle buttons are Back and Forward. Back takes you to the Web site or information area you last saw, and Forward returns you to the page you were on when you clicked Back. The X-in-a-circle button is Stop, which whacks your AOL Canada software over the head, making it lose its concentration for a moment and stop whatever it's doing. The curly arrow is Reload, which tells your Web browser to reload the current page (it doesn't work with AOL Canada areas).

✔ **Address window:** This handy box saves you time and energy by accepting both AOL Canada keywords and World Wide Web addresses. This always-present box does the same thing as the Keyword dialog box (the one that comes up when you press Ctrl+K in Windows or ⌘+K on the Macintosh). Just type a keyword or Web address in the box and then either press Enter or click Go. AOL Canada immediately whisks you away to the appointed online destination.

If you click the down-pointing arrow on the right side of the Address window, you'll notice a list of places you've recently visited inside and outside AOL Canada. This is called a *history trail,* and you can use it to return to any of the areas listed. You can clear your trail as often as you like by changing your Preferences. Read all about Preferences in Chapter 4.

✔ **Go button:** After you've typed a keyword or Web address in the Address box or chosen an item you already saw from the Address box's pull-down menu, click this button to go there.

✔ **Search window:** Type a few words describing what you're looking for and click Search or Return. Depending on what you typed, you should get back a list of Search Results, including content inside AOL Canada and areas around the World Wide Web. For more on Searching, see Chapter 13.

✔ **Search button:** One click brings up the AOL Canada Search page (same as keyword **Search**).

✔ **Keyword button:** Click to open the Keyword dialog box (same as pressing Ctrl+L).

Running through the Menus

Beauty, as the cyberbard says, is only button deep — and there's more to the AOL Canada interface than mere pretty buttons. How about that menu bar up there? What does it do? Actually, quite a bit. We can't *imagine* trying to figure out AOL Canada without the menu bar.

This section looks at the menu areas one by one, giving you a brief description of both the whole menu area and the individual items that populate it.

File

The File menu governs everything dealing with documents (such as magazine articles, bulletin board postings, and forum announcements), files, and other trivialities such as exiting the AOL Canada access program (but who'd ever want to do that?). Here are the most interesting File menu commands:

- ✔ **File⇨New:** Start the built-in text editor and get ready to create a new plain-text document. We often keep a blank document window open when we're browsing through the system and use it like a notepad for keywords, screen names, and anything else we want to remember. It works really well!

- ✔ **File⇨Open:** Open a document (a plain-text file — not a WordPerfect or Microsoft Word .doc file), graphic, or sound file you downloaded or saved to your computer's disk drive.

- ✔ **File⇨Open Picture Finder:** Display the Open Image Gallery window, which offers a quick way to view, change, and use the graphics files in any folder on your computer. Pick a folder and then click Open Gallery to view a nice thumbnail display of the graphics files there. Click a particular picture to see it full-size.

- ✔ **File⇨Save:** Save the current document (article or discussion board posting, for example) as a plain-text file on your computer's disk drive. If a graphic is in the window (a photo accompanying a news story, for example), then the AOL Canada software automatically offers to save a copy of it, too.

- ✔ **File⇨Save As:** Save the current document under a new filename. If the current document is an article, discussion board posting, or something else in an online area, this command behaves just like File⇨Save.

- ✔ **File⇨Print:** Print the current document. If you choose this option and don't have a printer connected to the computer, your computer may seem to lock up for a minute or two. Be patient — the machine should come back to life, probably complaining that your nonexistent printer is either turned off or out of paper. (Silly computer.)

- ✔ **File⇨Print Setup:** Open the Printer Setup dialog box, where you can change the options for the default printer or temporarily select a different printer.

- ✔ **File⇨Filing Cabinet:** Open your new and improved Filing Cabinet to store e-mail and postings you've sent and received, as well as your downloads.

- ✔ **File➪Save to Filing Cabinet:** Save the current document (article, discussion board entry, or other text item) in a folder within your AOL Canada software's Filing Cabinet. For the whole scoop on the Filing Cabinet, yank open Chapter 8 and check out the section about organizing your e-mail mess(ages), which explains this electronic organizational wonder.

- ✔ **File➪Download Manager:** Fire up the Download Manager, your always-willing accomplice in the task of filling up your hard drive.

- ✔ **File➪Log Manager:** Call forth the Logging dialog box. For more about chat logging, see Chapter 7. Session Log details are in Chapter 14.

- ✔ **File➪Offline Newsgroups:** Open a window with the Incoming/Saved Postings, Postings Waiting to Be Sent, and Postings You've Sent file folders. It works only if you have set up newsgroups to read offline (see keyword **Newsgroups** for more about that — it's kinda advanced).

- ✔ **File➪Exit:** Close the AOL Canada access software.

Edit

Just about every Windows program has an Edit menu. It contains your basic text-editing tools; apart from that, the Edit menu is nothing to write (or rewrite, for that matter) home about. Here are your main choices on this menu:

- ✔ **Edit➪Undo:** Undo the last change you made. We use this command often when writing e-mail messages. Sometimes, we've noticed that fingers can play tricks on the brain by taking charge of the mouse and randomly deleting text. (Don't you just hate that?) For times like those, the brain can take back control by using the Undo command to recover the nearly lost text.

- ✔ **Edit➪Cut:** Remove highlighted text from the screen and put it on the Clipboard.

- ✔ **Edit➪Copy:** Copy the highlighted text from the screen to the Clipboard, leaving the original text in place.

- ✔ **Edit➪Paste:** Insert text from the Clipboard into the current document.

- ✔ **Edit➪Select All:** Highlight all the text in the current document.

- ✔ **Edit➪Capture Picture:** If your computer includes a video camera (like the Connectix QuickCam, for example), this item enables you to shoot pictures on the fly, right from your AOL Canada software. If you don't have a camera, well, it doesn't do a whole lot.

- ✔ **Edit➪Spell Check:** Scour the e-mail message, newsgroup posting, bulletin board entry, or other text document you're creating.

- ✔ **Edit⇨Dictionary:** Open a search screen that scours the online *Merriam-Webster Dictionary* (keyword **Collegiate**) for whatever *correctly* spelled word you enter.

- ✔ **Edit⇨Thesaurus:** Bring up the online version of the *Merriam-Webster Thesaurus* (keyword **Thesaurus**) to help you track down synonyms for your favourite word.

- ✔ **Edit⇨Find in Top Window:** Search the current window for a given piece of text. Open a Web page, an article in the News section, or a discussion board posting, and give this menu choice a try.

If none of these menu items sounds familiar to you, get a copy of *Windows 98 For Dummies*, written by Andy Rathbone and available from IDG Books Worldwide, Inc. You can thank us later.

Print

- ✔ **Print⇨Print:** Click this option to make a paper copy of an online article, graphic, or Web page that tickles your fancy. The Print option sends the contents of the current window (whatever you happen to be looking at right then) over to your printer. It works the same as choosing File⇨Print. Print works both online and offline.

- ✔ **Print⇨Print Setup:** Click this option to tell AOL Canada how or from what printer you want to print your documents; it works the same as choosing File⇨Print Setup.

Window

This menu is a whoa-I-have-too-many-windows-open navigational lifesaver. If you misplace an Instant Message window or lose track of your Web browser, head to the Window menu and find it right away. Best of all, tracking the errant window is merely a two-step process:

1. **Choose Window from the main menu.**

   The Window menu drops down, displaying some marvellously technical options near the top and a numbered list of your open windows at the bottom. On the Macintosh, the windows aren't numbered, but they're still listed at the bottom of the menu.

2. **Click the name of the window you want to display.**

   The until-so-recently-lost window immediately pops to the top of the heap. Is this a great system or what?

Two menu items deserve a quick mention:

- **Window⇨Close All Except Front:** If you're completely fed up with all those open windows (or if it unexpectedly starts raining), close them all with a quick visit to the Window⇨Close All Except Front menu choice. Like it says, choosing this option makes all the open service windows go away, except for the window you're currently looking at. It also helpfully minimizes the Welcome window.

- **Window⇨Add Top Window to Favourite Places:** If you want a way to add things to your Favourite Places without using your mouse, look here. This, as the name implies, adds a link to your Favourite Places for the site in the top window of your screen. You can also use the handy shortcut key Ctrl++ (that's the Ctrl key and the Plus sign key).

As for the other items on the Window menu, don't worry about them. They're for people who care about the difference between tiling and cascading windows — definitely folks with too much time on their hands.

Sign Off

When it's time to hit the trail and mosey off to other matters, the Sign Off menu is the place to go. This menu is not big, but you couldn't get through online life without its two options:

- **Sign Off⇨Switch Screen Name:** Want to change screen names without signing off from the system completely? This menu option does the trick. Choose it, pick your preferred screen name from the pop-up list, type the password, and (thanks to some cool technical magic) sign on with the new moniker.

- **Sign Off⇨Sign Off:** Yes, it's redundant, but it's better than the Windows Start⇨Shut Down combination. Choose this option to close your AOL Canada connection. The software bids a fond farewell to the online world by clipping the link between your computer and the rest of the system.

Help

If you have trouble getting on AOL Canada, check the Help menu for assistance. Help menu options include

- **Help⇨Offline Help:** Displays the AOL Help system's offline help area. This is truly one of the most useful services ever created by the AOL Canada programmers. Without even signing on, you can look through the index for help on everything inside AOL Canada. If the Index isn't working for you, click the Contents or Search tabs for other ways of finding the answers to your questions. Whatever topic you land on, the instructions will appear clearly in the white text area on the right of the window.

For a quick list of help topics related to any of the main items in the offline Help Index, click the option once to highlight it, then click the Display button on the bottom right corner of the window. The full list of related topics instantly appears.

✔ **Help⇨AOL Access Phone Numbers:** Search the world (literally!) for local AOL Canada access phone numbers. Also includes notes about international access and the surcharged 800 numbers (still cheaper than long distance). It's the same as using keyword **Access**.

✔ **Help⇨About AOL Canada:** Show the version information for your AOL Canada software. (Sometimes the AOL Canada technical-support folks may ask you to open up this window — it's a techie thing.)

For help *after* you sign on to the system, check out these Help menu goodies:

✔ **Help⇨AOL Online Help:** Go directly to the free Member Services window (same as using keyword **Help**).

✔ **Help⇨Parental Controls:** Help make your child's online experience safe and fun by setting Parental Controls.

✔ **Help⇨Help with Keywords:** When keywords get you down, try this Help menu for tips and tricks for making the little animals behave.

✔ **Help⇨Accounts and Billing:** View and change your account billing information with this window (same as using keyword **Billing**).

Chapter 4

Making Your Preferences Known

A new AOL Canada account is like a university residence room on the first day of school: completely bare — devoid of anything beyond the institutional necessities of lime-green cinder blocks and grey linoleum. As the new residents move in, they put a distinct face on the nondescript space and make it uniquely their own.

Making yourself at home on AOL Canada means setting things up just the way you want them — and that's what this chapter is all about. It covers the extensive AOL Canada Preferences area, exploring the useful, helpful, and valuable settings, while steering you clear of the odd, esoteric, and nerdy ones.

If you're completely new to AOL Canada, spend some time messing around with the service before digging deeply into this chapter. Several of the preferences (particularly the Mail and Web settings) make a lot more sense after you use AOL Canada for a while. If you want details about creating screen names and online profiles or if you need guidance setting the parental controls, flip to Chapter 6. If you're hungry, go get something to eat. (We don't want you getting faint on us now. This is the good stuff.)

What They Do, Where They Live, and Why You Care

The Preference settings tweak the special AOL Canada software so that it behaves exactly the way you want. (No, you can't install preference settings in your kids.) The options cover every aspect of your time with AOL Canada, from sign-on to sign-off, plus a bunch of stuff in between.

Although AOL Canada remembers your Preferences settings from session to session, you can change them whenever you want. For example, if you're working late and want to keep the sound level down, you hop into the Preferences window (explained in the next section), click the Toolbar and Sound option, and turn off the Enable AOL Sounds option. Later, when you're ready for some noise, you simply turn it back on (and then crank up the speakers).

For members who are not on the unlimited hours billing plan, you'll be happy to know you can also adjust your preferences offline. Finding the Preferences settings takes only a couple of mouse clicks. Dive straight into them by choosing Settings⇨Preferences from the toolbar. The Preferences window (shown in Figure 4-1) immediately hops into action. As always, you can also use handy-dandy keyword **Preferences** to get there.

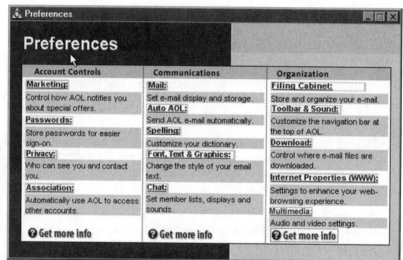

Figure 4-1:
The
Preferences
dialog box,
in its option-
filled glory.

Preferences

Account Controls	Communications	Organization
Marketing:	**Mail:**	**Filing Cabinet:**
Control how AOL notifies you about special offers.	Set e-mail display and storage.	Store and organize your e-mail.
Passwords:	**Auto AOL:**	**Toolbar & Sound:**
Store passwords for easier sign-on.	Send AOL e-mail automatically.	Customize the navigation bar at the top of AOL.
Privacy:	**Spelling:**	**Download:**
Who can see you and contact you.	Customize your dictionary.	Control where e-mail files are downloaded.
Association:	**Font, Text & Graphics:**	**Internet Properties (WWW):**
Automatically use AOL to access other accounts.	Change the style of your email text.	Settings to enhance your web-browsing experience.
	Chat:	**Multimedia:**
	Set member lists, displays and sounds.	Audio and video settings.
❷ Get more info	**❷ Get more info**	**❷ Get more info**

For a quick trip through some of the most popular adjustable preferences, click the **Get More Info** button at the bottom of each column on the main Preferences window. Each button leads to an individual Help screen for Account Controls, Communication, and Organization — complete with a very cool **Set It Up Now** button for each option so you can set your preferences quickly and easily.

Setting Your Preferences

The following sections dive into the preference settings one at a time, offering a quick explanation of the various options available and pointing out the items that truly enhance your online world.

To make the information easier to find, this section lists the Preferences settings in the same order that they appear in the Preferences window, that is, under the three main category headings: Account Controls, Communications, and Organization.

Account Controls

The keyword in the title of this category is *control*. This is where you get to decide how much privacy you want, and how much you want AOL Canada to be your guide to content on the Internet.

Marketing

Neither of us is particularly big on junk mail, pop-up sales windows, and "I'm taking a moment of your time right now" telephone calls. Frankly, we don't like them. This sentiment is most likely born from a combination of personal privacy issues, environmentalism, and the desire to enjoy dinner without the phone ringing off the hook.

If you feel the same way, here's your chance to strike back. By the same token, if you *like* junk mail, telemarketing phone calls, and their various ilk, here's an opportunity to get more of exactly that.

The Marketing Preferences dialog box isn't like the other preference settings. Rather than offering a few distinct options, it brings up a smorgasbord of Preferences settings that cover e-mail, postal mail, online pop-ups, telephone solicitations, and more. Invest a few minutes in browsing the various preference settings — it can only make your life better.

If you're a direct-mail hermit, take special note of the Additional Information button in the Marketing Preferences dialog box. This button leads to some great information about the Canadian Direct Marketing Association's Do Not Mail/Do Not Call service. Briefly, the document explains how to obliterate all traces of your earthly existence (at least as far as the direct-mail merchants are concerned). We highly recommend reading the information and following the instructions therein.

Passwords

Clicking the Passwords button opens a dialog box for storing your screen name passwords. Storing your password offers two distinct (and separate) benefits. First, you can tell the AOL Canada software to automatically enter your password every time you sign on to the system. That makes signing on a quicker process, because your computer never mistypes your password.

The second benefit lets you lock your Filing Cabinet. By storing your AOL Canada account password, you can *password protect* your Filing Cabinet. This feature keeps prying eyes (like those of parents, roommates, and siblings) out of your stored e-mail and newsgroup messages.

As far as we're concerned, the jury is still out on the whole *store your password* feature. It's nice for someone who doesn't really care about passwords (and who might otherwise write the password on a note taped to the monitor). The flip side is that after you store the password, anyone with access to that computer can sign on to AOL Canada with that screen name. Anyone.

Password protecting your Filing Cabinet may be a boon in some cases — particularly when you share a single computer among several people (or simply between one teenage big sister and one 12-year-old little brother).

With all that in mind, here's how to store a password and choose how it's used:

1. **Sign on with the screen name you want to use with the stored password.**

2. **Click the Settings arrow on the toolbar and choose Preferences from the drop-down menu. You can also get there by entering keyword** Preferences.

3. **From the Preferences window, click Passwords.**

4. **Type the password.**

   As you might expect, stars appear in place of the actual password. If you mistype something, press Backspace to delete the whole entry and start again.

5. **To use the password during sign-on, click the Sign-On check box. To use it to protect your Filing Cabinet's contents (that's your FC for all you AOL Canada connoisseurs), click the Filing Cabinet check box. Click OK to save your changes.**

   After you have everything checked (and perhaps double-checked), go on with the next step.

6. **Repeat the process for any other screen names whose passwords you want to store.**

   If you change a password in the future, you must return here and change it as well.

Privacy

Your Buddy List, the cool feature that lets you see when your friends pop online, makes AOL Canada all the more fun. After all, friends make everything better. But sometimes you just want to be alone. Maybe you need to finish some research, update some advertisements in the AOL Canada Classifieds (choose AOL Services➪Classifieds), or spend some quality time with one of the online games. Whatever your reasons, the Privacy Preferences help you hide from the rest of the online world.

The Privacy button opens up the somewhat complex Privacy Preferences window. This is exactly the same window that hops up if you click the Privacy Preferences button in the Buddy List Setup window (keyword **BuddyView**).

Chapter 12, which covers the Buddy List system, explains the Privacy Preferences settings in depth. Flip over there for the short course in online anonymity. (Don't worry — we won't tell anyone where you went.)

Association

This preference makes its first appearance in AOL Canada's Version 6.0 software. The Association preference does only one thing: It tells your computer to use the AOL Canada software any time another program wants to send e-mail, visit a Web site, or perform any other Internet-related task. In geek-speak, this setting associates the AOL Canada software with all Internet tasks, which is how the programmers came up with its odd-sounding name.

If you use AOL Canada as your one and only connection to the online world, click the OK button in this setting's dialog box. If you connect to the Internet through another local or national Internet Service Provider (ISP), leave this preference alone.

Communications

For people to understand one another in the online world, they need to be able to speak the same language and keep track of incoming and outgoing messages in an organized way. That's where the Communications Preferences come in.

Mail

E-mail is one of the most useful features of AOL Canada. But *keeping track* of your e-mail can be one of the most hair-reducing features. Thankfully, help is waiting in the Mail Preferences dialog box, as shown in Figure 4-2.

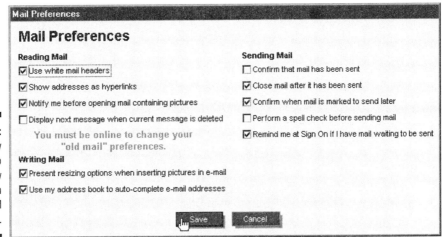

Figure 4-2: Here's how we like to set the new Version 6.0 mail preferences.

The preferences are organized into three easy-to-adjust categories: Reading, Writing, and Sending Mail. Some new features have been added to each category in Version 6.0 of the AOL Canada software, including two that we like very much:

- *Notify Me Before Opening Mail Containing Pictures.* Checkmark this option and you'll always know ahead of time when a downloadable picture is coming your way — something that can come in handy if you suspect the content of the image is objectionable. To learn more about putting your own pictures online, go to keyword **E-mail Help**, where you can read about "Attaching Photos to E-mail," or drop by Chapter 8.

- *Use My Address Book to Auto-Complete E-mail Addresses.* This is genius. Simply genius. Type in the first few letters of an address from your address book and bam! The AOL software automatically suggests the rest of the address.

As you've probably noticed by now, there's a CD-ROM that came with this book, and it contains . . . what else? Yep! The 6.0 Version of the AOL Canada access software. Not only that, but if you've never used the service before, you'll be able to try out AOL Canada for free during a 30-day period for a total of 540 hours. If you're ready to get online, flip to the appendix, "About the CD," and follow the simple instructions to install your new software.

Want to get rid of the Your Mail Has Been Sent dialog box (the one that appears automatically every time you send an e-mail message)? To make that annoying little window go away forever, deselect the check box next to `Confirm that mail has been sent.` Presto — no more mail-confirmation windows!

Auto AOL

Although the AOL Canada software includes a number of tools to make your online life easier, none of them holds a candle to Automatic AOL and Automatic AOL sessions. Automatic AOL sends and receives e-mail, Internet newsgroup postings, and AOL Canada message board postings with incredible ease, saving you both time and effort (and phone time, in case your household includes teenagers).

Automatic AOL helps you manage time by downloading all your e-mail and Internet newsgroup postings to your computer and then signing you off from AOL Canada. From there, you can work offline, reading and responding to your incoming messages and postings. All your replies are saved on your computer. When your replies (and whatever new messages you feel like writing) are ready to go, the Automatic AOL session signs you on to the system and sends them all out in a nice big batch.

Clicking the Auto AOL button in the Preferences window takes you directly to the Automatic AOL setup window. You end up with the same window by choosing Mail⇨Automatic AOL.

For all the details about Automatic AOL sessions and the joys and mysteries of setting these Preferences, flip to Chapter 8.

Spelling

It's official — the AOL Canada software knows its spelling words and grammar rules. To celebrate this achievement, it's only logical that a few new preferences would arrive on the scene. Lo and behold, they have, in the form of the Spelling Preferences settings.

As with several of the other preferences settings in this dialog box, you don't particularly have to adjust anything — the default settings are fine for almost everyone. In fact, the only reason you may want to change some of the settings is if your computer isn't very fast and performs spell-checks with all the speed of a drugged snail. In that case, try turning off some of the grammar checking options under the Advanced button because they demand serious processing power.

Font, Text, & Graphics

Image is everything, right? Well, even if you don't really believe that, you'll want to make sure everything you write inside AOL Canada at least looks presentable (for you serious types), and hopefully pretty (for the more stylish among you). Let's quickly run through your options. You can follow along by checking out Figure 4-3.

Figure 4-3:
Control the look of your AOL Canada compositions using the Font, Text, & Graphics Preferences.

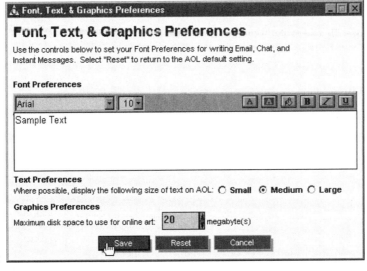

Font

In the past, no matter where you typed on AOL Canada — e-mail, instant messages, or chat rooms, for example — you had a choice of, to paraphrase Henry Ford, any font you wanted, as long as it was Arial. Thankfully, those days are gone. Now, thanks to the Font Preferences, the curtain rises on a brave new world of fontographic choice. Dress up your e-mail, instant message, and chat text with any font installed on your computer!

Use the Font Preferences setting to choose the default typeface (Binner Gothic, Perpetua, or Times New Roman, for example), size, style (bold, italic, or underlined), and colour for your e-mail, instant messages, chat room text, and message boards.

E-mail messages and chat windows include their own font controls, so if you decide on something a little different, changing your settings on the fly is easy. This setting also covers the default font for your signatures in e-mail and discussion boards. Unfortunately, if you already made some signatures, it won't automatically update them to your newly chosen font. (You need to do that yourself.)

Text

The Text option lets you choose how big text appears in many of the areas within AOL Canada. It's a simple concept, but if you like everything to be big, you may want to change the default setting from Medium to Large.

Graphics

Almost every time you wander into a new area within AOL Canada, the system sends all kinds of art files to your computer. They're the artsy buttons, background graphics, and other stuff that make AOL Canada look so cool. However, all that downloaded art hangs out on your hard drive and takes up space. The most important setting in the Graphics Preferences gives you control over how much space the artwork occupies on your hard disk.

The setting in question is labelled `Maximum disk space to use for online art`. The default size is 20MB (or megabytes, short for millions of characters), which is a little small if you use AOL Canada often. If you have plenty of hard drive space available (which most current machines do — after all, it's tough to fill a multigigabyte hard disk), bump this setting up to 40MB or 50MB.

If you can't afford the disk space, nudge the maximum size down to 15MB, but do this *only* as a last resort. The AOL Canada software gets a little irked if you don't give it plenty of space for its graphics — and it doesn't take AOL Canada much time to outgrow that little space.

TIP

Hitting the highlights in one easy step

When you're new to AOL Canada, the options get a bit overwhelming. You have so many things to choose from — where should you begin? What should you change first?

In an effort to reduce your stress and make the settling-in process slightly simpler, AOL Canada collected the most-used goodies together in the cool **My AOL** area.

To get to My AOL, click the My AOL icon on the toolbar (just below the Settings arrow on the toolbar). Click on the Get More Info button at the bottom of each of these screens (there are five: Daily, Interests, Controls, People, and Services) and you'll get to a useful Set It Up Now Help screen for each category. The two most useful settings to look at first are Controls and People. Using these, you can set up and modify settings like your screen name, member profile, and parental controls (see Chapter 6 for details about all of those), as well as Buddy Lists (more about that in Chapter 10), and news and stock portfolios (hiding in Chapter 14).

What happens when the art database grows bigger than the maximum size you set? An electronic version of the old-fashioned spring cleaning, that's what. The AOL Canada software throws out art you haven't used for a while to make room for the new stuff. It happens automatically, although it makes you wait a minute or two while it throws things out. (Maybe it wants you there for moral support.)

You can find out how big your art database is by using Windows Explorer. Check the size of a file named MAIN.IDX in the IDB subdirectory of the AOL Canada software. That file contains the art database, plus a few other digital odds and ends.

Chat

The most interesting settings in the Chat Preferences dialog box are the notification options and the capability to alphabetize the chat group member list.

The notification options tell AOL Canada to let you know when new people join the chat area or when current attendees leave. After hours and hours of personal testing, we loved seeing who just joined the chat room (notify me when members arrive), but seeing when people left (notify me when members leave) got on our nerves. Try turning on one or both notifications for yourself and determine how the results strike you. You can turn on these settings by clicking the appropriate check boxes.

The Alphabetize the Member List option is genuinely handy — we recommend turning it on. If you turn off this setting, the chat area member list transforms into an absolute morass of mixed-up names. Don't let that happen to you. Run — don't walk — to turn on this setting.

As for the Double-Space Incoming Messages setting, we honestly can't think of a reason to turn this on (and take our word for it, we tried). Most chat rooms scroll by pretty quickly on their own, but this setting makes them fly. Unless you feel like practising speed reading, leave this one alone.

Organization

The longer you remain an AOL Canada member, the more you'll realize that taking a few minutes to tweak your storage areas is worth your time. (Trust us, it's gold!) You can stave off a lot of confusion and frustration by reading through the following Organization Preferences and tweaking away!

Filing Cabinet

The Filing Cabinet, that collector of e-mail, postings, Automatic AOL mail, Favourite Places, and all kinds of other stuff, is a useful tool. The options in the Filing Cabinet Preferences dialog box make it even better.

The first preference is set to back up the contents of your Filing Cabinet every four weeks, which also happens to be the least frequent option available. If the contents of your cabinet are vital to you, you can reduce the interval to back it up every three weeks, two weeks, or even once a week.

The backup function for your Filing Cabinet ensures that you'll have a recent saved version of its contents in case something goes wrong. If that happens, choose Settings➪Filing Cabinet and click the Restore button on the bottom of the dialog box. Make your changes and then click the Save button. You can also use this button to manually back up your Filing Cabinet anytime you'd like.

The second preference sets up a warning. It instructs the AOL Canada software to let you know when the Filing Cabinet is trying to single-handedly take over your hard drive. You don't need to change this option — the default should be fine.

On the other side of the scale, you simply *must* turn on the Retain All Mail I Send in My Filing Cabinet option. This one is a winner, particularly if you use AOL Canada with your business. Turn this puppy on and the AOL Canada software automatically drops a copy of all outgoing e-mail into the Mail You've Sent folder (which is available by choosing Mail➪Read Mail➪Sent Mail).

Imagine: No more worrying about whether you replied to someone's message or wondering what you said. Life just doesn't get much better than that, now does it?

The mate to this setting, Retain All Mail I Read in My Filing Cabinet, isn't quite as excellent as its counterpart but still deserves consideration. Like its sibling, this option is great for the times that you need to account for all your correspondence.

For safety's sake, we recommend leaving both the above Confirm check boxes turned on. However, if all the "Are you sure?" messages annoy you too much while cleaning out the Filing Cabinet, feel free to turn them off (at least temporarily).

One word of caution: All this filing uses space on your computer's hard disk, so regularly go through the messages and delete the useless ones. For more about the Filing Cabinet, see Chapter 8.

Toolbar and Sounds

The toolbar looks bolder, brighter, and better than ever these days. Sporting a cool look (and those funky click-to-show-the-menu buttons with icons along the bottom half), the toolbar still has a few tricks up its sleeve. Those tricks live in the Toolbar Preferences dialog box.

Also in Toolbar Preferences is the option to Display the Following in My Toolbar — Text Only. This option lets you pick between the normal toolbar, complete with text and button pictures, and a "lite" toolbar, which contains only the button text. By turning off the pictures, you regain some screen real estate, which means a great deal if your computer has a small monitor.

You can also choose to place your toolbar at the top or bottom of your screen and to clear your History Trail, which may tweak your interest if you share your computer with someone else. Turning on the Clear History Trail allows you to erase all the entries in the drop-down location box on the navigation bar (try saying that three times fast). Basically, it keeps someone else from finding out where you went while you were online. Turn it on and watch your siblings, roommates, or co-workers whine.

The Sounds Preferences can give you peace by allowing you to turn off event sounds, such as Message chimes. This is one you'll probably want to switch from time to time.

And last but not least, our favourite Toolbar & Sounds setting is right in the middle of the window: Auto-Complete. Can't remember the exact spelling of a keyword or Web address? Enable Auto-Complete and the AOL software will suggest the rest of the word or address for you. For those of us possessing an imperfect memory (not mentioning any names, since we forget them), it's a blessing.

Download

These settings govern some trivial (and not so trivial) details about downloading files. The most useful of the bunch are the impressive-sounding Automatically Decompress ZIP Files options, particularly when you choose the When I Download Them option (it should already be set as the default). This setting tells your AOL Canada software to automatically unpack any compressed files (commonly called ZIP files) so that you don't need to do it yourself.

Turn off the Delete ZIP Files after Decompression option until you feel comfortable moving files here and there on your computer's hard drive. That way, if you accidentally delete something, you can pull out a replacement from the original compressed ZIP file.

You may as well leave everything else in the dialog box turned on (with a check mark in the box next to the setting). If you do a lot of downloading, turn off the Confirm Additions to My Download List option, because it may drive you nuts in short order.

Internet Properties (WWW)

Although most of the stuff in the WWW area borders on technoweenie, we want to mention one thing: the Delete Files button.

Although Delete Files isn't really a Preferences setting, you should hit this button every now and then if you enjoy surfing the Web. Every time you view a Web page, the AOL Canada Web browser keeps a local copy of what you see in a *cache*, a temporary storage area for use by the program, within a particular folder on your computer.

Storing information in a cache isn't a nefarious plot to use up your hard disk space — all the popular Web browsers do it. On the plus side, the cache makes your Web browser respond faster when you're bouncing back and forth between a couple of Web pages. The downside, though, is that the cache fills up after a while. Unfortunately, a full cache slows down your Web browser a bit (which is precisely the kind of help the World Wide *Wait* doesn't exactly need).

Luckily, emptying the cache is easy. Just follow these steps:

1. **Click the Internet Properties (WWW) option in the Preferences window, under the Organization heading.**

   The AOL Canada Internet Properties (WWW) dialog box appears, as shown in Figure 4-4.

2. **Click the Delete Files button in the middle of the window.**

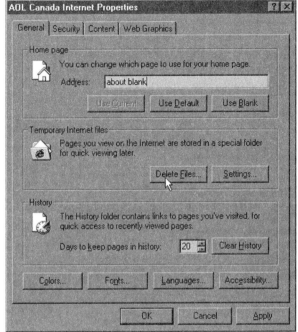

Figure 4-4:
One click
removes
those pesky
temporary
Internet files.

At this point, your hard drive probably sounds like it's going crazy. Believe it or not, that's a good sign. After a few moments (perhaps a minute or more, depending on how long ago you last emptied the cache and how large your hard drive Is), everything quiets down

3. **Click OK to finish the task.**

Multimedia

Your last option under the Organization heading allows you to choose AOL Canada's built-in Media Player so that whenever you want to try out a sound or video file, it will automatically pop up to assist you. We recommend keeping the check mark in the box to the right of this option. It's a simple way to enhance your online experience.

Chapter 5

Dealing with Spams, Scams, Viruses, and Hoaxes

. . . .

In This Chapter

▶ Help — I gave my password to a scammer!

▶ Avoiding password scams

▶ Protecting your mailbox from the junk mail tsunami

▶ Keeping your computer healthy and virus-free

▶ Recognizing an online hoax when you see one

. . . .

*D*ear AOL member, you have seventeen unread AOL Mail messages . . .
*Hello! I'm Bill Gates. I need your help to test my new e-mail tracking
system . . . Walt Disney, Jr., wants to send you $5,000 . . . This really works! Don't
break the chain! Send this to everyone you know and the love you want will
come to you . . . Due to technical difficulties with our membership system, you
must re-verify your account password . . . Hi! We met in the chat room yesterday.
Here are the pix I promised to send you . . . .*

Just when you thought it was safe to visit your e-mailbox, out come the
spams, scams, hoaxes, and other annoyances of online life. Like its snail mail
counterparts, junk e-mail comes in all shapes and sizes, with varying degrees
of official-sounding language and believability. Worse yet, some of the messages
mask outright scams designed to steal your account password, cost you
money, or generally mess up your tidy online world.

Protect yourself from these mailbox perils with the tips and information in
this chapter. The following pages cover the seamy realms of junk e-mail, online
hoaxes, common password scams, and virus infection schemes. Forewarned
is forearmed (as opposed to being four-footed or something), so read these
pages carefully. Do your part to make the online world safe!

AOL Canada *never* sends e-mail or instant messages about password problems. The customer service folks don't know your password now (it's encrypted and stored in one of their computers), they don't want to know your password if you change it, and they certainly don't want your credit card number (well, they may *want* it, but they won't ask).

What If You Just Gave Your Password to Someone?

First, don't panic — these things happen. Change your password to something new and different at keyword **Password**. It only takes a moment.

The best passwords include a combination of letters and numbers, so try things like *blue17hat* or *trainfun47*. Don't make your password obvious (even if it's easy to remember). Never use things like your name, the word *password*, or simple number sequences like *123456* or *000000*.

If Someone Asks for Your Password, Just Say "No"

This ranks as one of the oldest scams in the online world, but it catches people every day. The password scam comes in a variety of flavours, but the bottom line remains the same: The scammer wants your account password and will lie, cheat, and use any trick he or she can to get it.

Regardless of the scam's details, the scammers always ask for your password (some variants ask for your credit card number, but the thought remains the same). If you get an instant message or e-mail asking for either your password or credit card number, do not fall for the trap — *don't give out your information.* The message is a scam.

Defeating instant message scams

Instant message scams are the easiest to recognize and avoid. No company in the world — not AOL Canada, credit card companies like MasterCard or VISA, or phone companies like Sprint Canada or Bell Canada, or anyone else — will send you an instant message asking for account information, credit card numbers, or passwords. They just don't do business that way. Ever. (That kinda simplifies sorting out the real messages from the scams.)

If you get an instant message that asks for your AOL Canada password, credit card number, or any other personal information, immediately open the Notify AOL window using keyword **Notify AOL**. Click the Instant Message Notes option on the left side of the window. Follow the instructions to fill out the date, time, and content of the message you believe to be a scam and click the Send button. Congratulations — you just turned in the scammer!

When a scam appears on your screen while you're in a chat room, take a moment to warn the chat room that a scammer is trying to get passwords. After spreading the warning, use the Notify AOL button (it's at the very top of the chat window) to ruin the scammer's day.

Unmasking e-mail scams

Although some e-mail scams look pretty authentic, they're still just a variation on the *give me your password* theme. If you stick with the basic knowledge that no company in the world will ask you to send them your AOL Canada account password, then you're on pretty safe ground.

Some scammers try the high-tech approach to getting your password by building imposter Web sites using AOL Canada's Web graphics. Because they still have to trick you into coughing up your screen name and password, the scammers most often create a fake page mimicking AOL Canada's AOLMail system (the real one lives at keyword **AOLMail**, which the scammers *can't* fake) or they invent a fictional contest allegedly sponsored by AOL Canada, which requires a screen name and password for entry.

No matter how genuine something looks, remember the basics: AOL Canada won't ask for your password or any other account information. If they do throw a contest, you *never* have to give your account password to submit an entry.

Take a look at Figures 5-1 and 5-2. Take a *close* look, because one of them is a clever fake designed to steal your password.

Here's how to tell the real thing from the *wrong* thing every time:

- ✔ To visit a real AOL Canada-based area, you use a keyword (in the case of these figures, it's keyword **AOLMail**). You can't accidentally go to a fake area by using a keyword, because scammers can't fake a keyword. But anyone can put a fake link in an e-mail message. The moral of the story: If you don't know who sent a message, don't click any links in it.

- ✔ Look carefully at the address displayed in the navigation bar. AOL Canada never uses free Web hosting services like Angelfire (`www.angelfire.com`), Fortune City (`www.fortunecity.com`), Freeservers.com (`www.freeservers.com`), HyperMart (`www.hypermart.com`), Tripod (`www.tripod.com`), or Xoom (`www.xoom.com`) for its information areas.

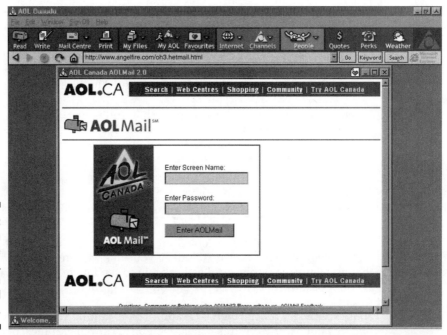

Figure 5-1:
Is this a clever fake of the AOL Canada AOLMail window . . .

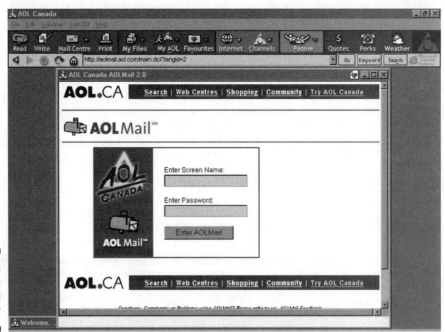

Figure 5-2:
. . . or is this one the real thing?

Instead, it uses the `aol.com` or the `aol.ca` servers. Okay, now the quiz. Which figure is the fake? (Insert appropriate game show theme music here.) And the answer is . . . Figure 5-1. It's pretty sad that the fake looks just as good as the real thing, isn't it?

When you receive an e-mail scam, forward the message to screen name `TOSEmail1` (that's TOSEMAIL with the number 1 attached to the end). The friendly folks at AOL's Notify AOL response team love getting e-mail like that. Find out more about the Notify AOL service by using keyword **Notify AOL**.

For a reminder about what behaviour is acceptable by AOL Canada members, you can always consult the Terms of Service at keyword **CanadaTOS**.

Spam, Spam Everywhere (And None of It to Eat)

When it comes to bulk e-mail, we feel sorry for the Hormel company. Granted, we feel sorry for everyone who deals with junk e-mail, but Hormel gets particular sympathy. Somewhere in the Internet's past, unsolicited commercial e-mail (or *UCE*, as it's officially known these days) earned the nickname *spam*. Thus, Hormel's unstoppable juggernaut of canned cuisine innocently became the household name for e-mail frustration.

How did they find my screen name?

You can run, but you can't hide — no matter how you try, *they* always seem to find your screen name. The next thing you know, the e-mailbox bulges from all the junk. But how did *they* get your address in the first place?

Actually, they went looking for it. Every time you visit a chat room or post your thoughts to an AOL Canada message board or an Internet newsgroup, your screen name gets posted too. (If it didn't, other folks wouldn't know that those clever sayings belonged to you.)

That's where the online *ne'er-do-wells* come in. Using programs written by people with too much free time (and too little life to fill it), these folks harvest screen names from anywhere and everywhere, including chat room lists, message boards — heck, they even pull names from online classified advertisements! With the names in hand, they start the box-filling flow of messages that the rest of us struggle with daily.

No matter what you call it — spam, bulk e-mail, UCE, or digital trash — the stuff pops unbidden into your mailbox. The advertisements run the gamut from questionable penny stock tips to discount long distance phone cards, plus everything you can imagine in between.

The worst thing about bulk e-mail is the simple fact that you can't stop it without blocking your mailbox from most of the digital world. Traditional postal bulk mailers, who pay to send their messages through the postal system, long ago formed groups dedicated to helping people *stop* the junk mail flood. Why? Because postal mail costs money, and the advertising companies don't like throwing their profits away on people who aren't interested.

In the online world, junk mailers don't pay any costs whatsoever (beyond their basic Internet access, that is) to send their messages. Because sending a million e-mail ads costs the same as sending 10,000, the junk e-mailers have no incentive to target their advertising to a particular audience. All a prospective spammer needs to set up shop is a computer, an e-mail account, bulk mailing software, and a fundamental lack of morals (spamming violates the terms of service for every major Internet service provider in the world), so new spammers are joining the fun in a never-ending supply.

In Canada, no federal law specifically prohibits spam. Because it is considered a form of expression (is it just us, or is that a bit of a stretch?), anything the government did come up with to stop spam would have to comply with the Charter of Rights and Freedoms.

So what's the answer? Well, the federal government puts it this way: If the spam amounts to an attempt at fraud or computer-related mischief, then it's illegal and the spammer can be prosecuted. If it's just annoying, then it's up to people in the online industry to put a stop to it through voluntary codes of conduct.

What does that mean to you and your AOL Canada membership? Lots. AOL Canada is a proud member of the Canadian Association of Internet Providers (CAIP), which means they act according to the CAIP's very own code of conduct. You can read it at their Web site at `www.caip.ca`. But they don't stop there. Oh, no. AOL Canada, bent so far backward it hurts, also has its own strict policies about spam, which you can find in the AOL Canada Terms of Service (keyword **CanadaTOS**). What they amount to is that people caught using the AOL Canada neighbourhood to distribute spam can have their account terminated. Gone. Kaput.

And on top of all that heavy information, Canadians have other powers to defend themselves against the rising bulk-mail tide. Here are a few ways to fight back:

✔ If the message includes removal instructions, give them a try. Don't expect success. Spammers are notorious for ignoring removal requests and faking removal e-mail addresses.

✔ Involve yourself in the fight. Visit sites like Safe E-mail Preference Service (www.safeeps.com), Fight Spam (spam.abuse.net), Coalition Against Unsolicited Commercial Email (CAUCE, www.cauce.org), and Junk Email (www.junkemail.org).

✔ If you receive junk e-mail that advertises a pyramid scheme, an illegal product, a lottery, or other such things, use the Notify AOL service (keyword **Notify AOL**) and let their response team track the culprits down.

✔ You can read up about the federal government's position on spam at Industry Canada's Strategis Web site at this not-very-pretty-looking address: http://ecom.ic.gc.ca/english/index.html.

✔ To stay on top of the latest fraud scams being tracked by the RCMP, visit their Web site http://strategis.ic.gc.ca/virtual_hosts/e-com/using/en/spam.html.

On January 1, 2001, a new law (no space odyssey, sorry) will come into effect across this great land to further protect Internet users logged on from Prince George to Cheticamp. Called the Personal Information Protection and Electronic Document Act (for real!), it will impose lots of restrictions and a good number of obligations on how personal e-mail addresses are collected and used. This is bound to nip at least some spam in the bud, since spammers often rely on companies who collect e-mail addresses for their mailing lists. Ah, democracy at work!

Fooling the Bulk Mail Behemoth

Unless you move into the online equivalent of a cave in the hills, you can't completely stop bulk e-mail from dumping into your mailbox. But you can reduce the flow from a torrent to a trickle.

The following sections provide two hands-on ways to protect your mailbox. The first focuses on safeguarding your accounts while chatting away in AOL Canada's People Connection. The other tip centres on the popular Internet newsgroups, where the world swaps ideas, insights, and fanciful conspiracy theories. Since each method protects different parts of your online experience, feel free to apply them both to your AOL Canada screen names.

Make a screen name especially for chatting

Chatting adds community to the often-cold online world. Unfortunately, chatting also leads to a jam-packed e-mail inbox, because spammers spend a lot of time gathering screen names from chat room lists (even though it's against AOL Canada's rules). Protect yourself with a simple technique — make a "chat room" screen name.

Now that AOL Canada gives you seven screen names per account (and 16 characters in each screen name), you have plenty of space for an extra identity or two. Granted, you need to tell your friends about *the new you*, but it's a small price to pay for less junk mail in your mailbox. Here's what to do:

1. **First, pick a new name for your chat identity and create the screen name.**

   If people already know you in the chat rooms, use a variation of your current name with chat, chats, or something like that attached to the end (such as JKaufeldChats or Grete27chatter).

   For help creating a new screen name, flip ahead to Chapter 6.

2. **Set the mail preferences for the new screen name to block all e-mail.**

   This step holds the big key for mailbox protection, because it kills the spammer's main tool. Your chat screen name isn't any good to them, because all the incoming mail bounces off the closed mailbox door. (Don't worry — both your friends and folks you meet in chat rooms can still send you mail. Read on to find the secret!)

   Chapter 6 also offers the lowdown on settings like the mail controls. Look in the Parental Controls area of the chapter for the specifics.

3. **Build a member profile for the chat screen name. In the profile, tell people to send e-mail to your regular screen name.**

   Since the spammer's name-gathering software doesn't intelligently read profiles, your other screen name is protected while you chat the night away.

Protect your e-mail address in Internet newsgroup postings

Use the Newsgroup preferences to add some extra text to the end of your e-mail address, turning it from an innocent address such as jkaufeld@aol.com into jkaufeld@aol.comkillallspam (which is both an incorrect e-mail address and heart-felt personal expression concerning unsolicited commercial e-mail). Putting this protection in place only takes a moment:

1. **Open the Newsgroups window with keyword** Newsgroups.

   If all is well with the online world, the Newsgroups window appears. (If not, then AOL Canada's computers don't feel well right now.)

2. Click the Set Preferences button near the bottom of the window.

This brings up the Global Newsgroup Preferences, a somewhat imposing window with three tabbed pages.

3. Click the Posting tab.

A whole new set of preferences hops onto the screen, including the one you want.

4. Click in the text area next to the Junk Block heading and then type something like nospam **or** nojunk. **After you finish, click the Save button.**

With that setting in place, every time you create an Internet newsgroup message, AOL Canada automatically adds whatever text you typed (the *nospam* or *nojunk* thing) to the end of your e-mail address (because every message includes your address automatically).

Viruses Come in the Darnedest Packages

Despite their best efforts, healthy people sometimes come down with a common cold. They drink the right fluids, eat the best foods, and get plenty of sleep, but the cold still sneaks up and bites them. May we suggest that this could be life's way of saying, It's time to read those new ... *For Dummies* books.

Computer viruses behave the same way, but taking the right precautions dramatically improves the odds of keeping your computer healthy. And what precautions might those be? Glad you asked:

- *Don't download files attached to e-mail from people you don't know.* This is Cardinal Rule #1 of safe computing. Hackers often distribute password-stealing programs in e-mails with a friendly message like "Had fun chatting with you in the room last night. *Here are the pictures I promised!"* It seems innocent on the surface, but it hides a nefarious plot. If you don't readily recognize the screen name sending the file to you, don't download the file.

- *Don't trust file names.* Anyone can name a destructive file "fungame.exe," "screensav.exe," or "coolpic.exe" to camouflage its purpose. (After all, they sure aren't going to name it killdisk.exe.) If you receive a file like that attached to an e-mail message, refer to the previous bullet. Do you know the sender? If not, don't download the file.

- *Watch out for suspicious file extensions.* The file extension is the last part of a filename (the part after the period). Never, never, never download a file with the extension .shs (99 times out of 50 it's a virus). Unless you know what you're doing, don't download files ending in .reg (those files tweak a very important part of Windows known as the Registry). Normal files have extensions like .exe, .com, .zip, .jpg, and .bmp (although program files — the .exe and .com files — often harbour viruses, too). If you get a file that you don't recognize, go back to the first bullet in this section: If you don't know the sender, then it's probably a virus or hacker program.

What if you think the computer already caught a virus? In that case, you need some digital medicine. Visit keyword **Virus info** for virus-killing steps and anti-virus software. If you don't want to tangle with the virus by yourself, coax one of your local computer-savvy friends into helping you (free food makes a great bribe, by the way).

Recognizing Hoaxes: No, Bill Gates Won't Give You $5,000

Free money. Stolen kidneys. Expensive cookie recipes. Modem taxes. Worldwide Internet cleanup day. Free beer. Dying children atop mountains of greeting cards. They all sound soooooo good, but despite a tiny grounding in reality (or simply a plausible concept), they're all classic Internet hoaxes.

When it comes to hoaxes, P.T. Barnum probably said it best: "Get that mule cart off my foot!" (Oh drat — wrong quote.) Mr. Barnum's correct quote has to do with the way that a good story encourages people to suspend their disbelief and join in the fun, which is precisely what happens when an Internet hoax wanders into your mailbox. (Ol' P.T. phrased it a bit differently, but the concept remains the same.)

Rather than getting blindly sucked into a hoax, take a moment to test the information in the message for yourself. Like the various scams discussed earlier in the chapter, Internet hoaxes follow a distinct pattern. After you know the pattern, picking out the hoaxes is easy. Here goes:

✔ **Free money or products thanks to an e-mail tracking system:** This one shows up quite a lot, promising thousands of dollars or free goodies to everyone who forwards the message to their friends. The message guarantees the reward thanks to an "e-mail tracking system," which monitors every move the message makes. *Reality check:* There's no such thing as an e-mail tracking system, and if there were one, the privacy advocates would have collective heart failure over it. Besides, neither Bill Gates nor "A Large International Corporation" really want to give you $5,000.

✔ **Strong statements from vague sources:** Many popular hoaxes rely on official-sounding statements attributed to police ("The Toronto police report that . . .") or highly placed federal government officials. Unfortunately, you can't check on the details of the message because, well, it's not detailed enough. *Reality check:* Look at the Web site of any groups mentioned in the message. Sometimes, the groups in question offer pages of information debunking various hoaxes.

✔ **Send this to all your friends:** Whether hoaxes are spooky or sane, timely or timeless, they all request the same Pavlovian behaviour: Send the message immediately to everyone you know. The message's accuracy isn't the point — quick movement of this "important information" obviously outweighs trivialities like whether the whole thing is correct. *Reality check*: Little if any information really *needs* immediate delivery. Hoaxes count on immediacy because it interferes with research. When hoaxes hit your mailbox, sit on them for a few days before shooting a message back (er, replying to the sender).

For some great virus-stopping resources, including anti-virus Web sites, visit the AOL Canada Virus Information Centre (keyword **Virus Info**). For more general information about Internet hoaxes, visit the RCMP's Web site at `www.rcmp.ca` and take a look through the Latest Scams, the Scams Archive, and the page titled Web Safety (designed especially for parents and children to visit together).

When debunking a hoax, be kind. Reply to both the person who sent the message to you and everyone who received it from your friend. Give a quick explanation that the hoax is, in fact, false, and that they shouldn't bother forwarding it to anyone else. Use the Favourite Places tool to put clickable links into your e-mail message so that people can read the truth for themselves. (For more about adding links to e-mail, see Chapter 8.)

Part II
The Basics of
Online Life

The 5th Wave   By Rich Tennant

"OH YEAH, AND TRY NOT TO ENTER THE WRONG PASSWORD."

In this part . . .

The only thing standing between you and a brain-numbing quantity of mundane details is the AOL Canada access software. You and this program are a team — you'll probably be amazed at what you can accomplish together.

This part shows you how to put the software into action by exploring the fine art of creating screen names, setting the Parental Controls, navigating through AOL Canada, sending e-mail to the world at large, enjoying an online chat, and using the Download Manager to grab programs from the system's online libraries. Part II even includes a section filled with places to find help, if you ever need more than you have right here in your hand. In short, this part covers the basic stuff you need to get your citizenship papers in the Great Online World.

Best of all, we've made sure that it isn't the least bit boring. Really.

Chapter 6

Doing the Screen Name Tango (and the Parental Control Two-Step)

. . . .

In This Chapter

▶ Figuring out the whole screen name thing

▶ Managing screen names

▶ Filling out your profile

▶ Applying some parental controls

. . . .

*O*ne of the best Internet-related cartoons we've seen shows a dog camped happily in front of a computer, talking to another dog that just wandered into the room. (This would be funnier with ocelots, but it probably loses something in foreign translations.) The cartoon caption plays on the anonymous nature of the online world through its pithy caption, "On the Internet, nobody knows you're a dog."

The same idea carries directly into AOL Canada. (The anonymity, that is, not the dog/ocelot thing.) Everybody on AOL Canada knows you by the screen name you create and the information that you put into your profile. That's why choosing the right screen name and filling out your online profile are such big parts of your online experience.

Screen names are more than your online identity. They also play directly into the AOL Canada Parental Controls system, which helps concerned and involved parents take charge of their children's online activities. Without the right screen-name setup, the Parental Controls won't do a bit of good.

This chapter guides you through the ins and outs of the whole *who you are and what you can do online* thing. It starts with screen names, carries on through the member profile, and closes with parental controls. It's a must-see chapter for your online world. (Heck, tell your friends about it too!)

What's in a (Screen) Name?

When you joined an online service in the Days of Online Past, you received an account name mechanically generated by a computer. And this computer was quite proud of itself for calling you 71303,3713. After all, the computer had no problem remembering it — why should you?

AOL Canada was created *by* humans and designed *for* humans. As a direct result, *you* (a human) get to choose the name you use on AOL Canada. You can be yourself if you want: Annie, Jean-Paul, or Svengali. Of course, you can also be a little more daring and become Homeschooler, Elfcognito, or Mungojerrie. Within the bounds of good taste, the choice is up to you (but more about that later).

Every AOL Canada account has space for seven screen names: one primary name plus six others. Your screen name also serves as part of your e-mail address. The *primary name* is the one you choose when you sign on to the service for the first time. This name is special — kind of like your permanent file in school (the mysterious record always spoken of in dark, terrifying phrases such as "You realize, of course, that this incident will go into your *permanent file*"). The primary name is *permanent* — you can't ever change it. However, the other six names can come and go as you please.

AOL Canada only places a couple of limits on screen names. Screen names must be between 3 and 16 characters long and must start with a letter. After the required first letter, you can use letters, numbers, and spaces to create your online identity. Also, the assembled numbers and letters can't cross the line into what Miss Manners might call "poor taste." (For more about that, see the "Now be nice!" sidebar in this chapter.)

Here's a quick overview of the technical rules covering AOL Canada screen names:

- ✔ You can have seven screen names in your account — one primary screen name and six others.

- ✔ The primary screen name is permanent; you can't ever change it. But you can create and delete the other six screen names at your whim.

- ✔ By default, only the primary screen name can make new screen names and adjust Parental Controls. If you want to give that ability to other screen names in your account, you can do so by making the new name a master screen name. See the section "Creating a new screen name" later in this chapter to find out how to create a master screen name.

- ✔ Choose your primary name carefully; it's yours forever.

Now, be nice!

A creative screen name is your tool for carving out a unique identity in the world of AOL Canada. You're *supposed* to be creative — that's the whole point. However, a subtle line separates *creative and obnoxious*.

Here's a simple guideline for creating a good screen name: Make it as creative as you want, but if you blush at the idea of explaining it to your children, parents, spouse, or significant other, your screen name is probably beyond the bounds of good taste.

One final thought about choosing a screen name: Make it appropriate. A screen name for official business e-mail is quite different from one for chatting online about a multi-player game like Battle Tech. If you want to be BoogerDigger, that's your choice, but your new e-mail address (boogerdigger@aol.com) may look a little funny on a business card.

✔ Screen names are 3 to 16 characters long, start with a letter, and contain any combination of letters, numbers, and spaces your imagination can dream up (within the bounds of good taste).

Dealing with Screen Names

Managing the screen names in your account isn't just a job — it's a creative adventure. The following sections go through everything you need to know to keep your screen names in order.

These instructions don't apply to your account's primary name. Short of quitting AOL Canada and signing up again, you can't change that. Ever. So there.

Creating a new screen name

We think the people who started AOL Canada read too much Shakespeare, because the whole screen name system is outlined in *Romeo and Juliet*. In the play, Romeo can't decide on a screen name. Juliet tries to calm him with the observation "What's in a name? That which we call a rose by any other name would smell as sweet." His confidence thus buoyed by this botanic observation, he sets off to create a new screen name.

Kids — don't try this at home alone. Romeo and Juliet did, and look what happened to them. (If you don't know what happened to Romeo and Juliet, you can find out on the Internet. For a stroll through the classics, turn ahead to the section about the OCF Online Library in Chapter 27.)

Making a new screen name only takes a few moments. Just follow these steps:

1. **Sign on to AOL Canada under your account's primary name or any master screen name.**

   The primary name can create new screen names, as can any other screen name that has master screen name status (more about that later in this chapter).

2. **After safely connecting to the service, choose Settings⇨Screen Names from the toolbar (or use keyword Screen Names).**

   The AOL Screen Names dialog box opens. If you haven't read the screen names sidebar "Now be nice!" earlier in this chapter, now is an excellent time to do so.

3. **Click the Create a Screen Name option in the dialog box (it's on the right, under the heading Screen Name Options). After the Create Screen Name information box appears, click the Create Screen name button.**

   A dialog box appears with the very long title AOL Screen Names Step 1 of 4: Choose a Screen Name. Once you've managed to read that title, this is where the fun starts.

   If AOL Canada protests that `your account already has the maximum of 7 screen names,` you must delete an existing name before creating a new one. For more about that, see the section "Deleting an old screen name," later in this chapter.

4. **Type your proposed new screen name in the text box and then click the Continue button.**

   If the screen name you typed is available, AOL Canada creates it and a new dialog box (aptly titled AOL Screen Names Step 2 of 4: Choose a Password) appears. Yes, you do have to make up a clever password. If this is the message you get, skip ahead to Step 6. If someone else thought of the screen name before you, the system suggests that you choose something else, as shown in Figure 6-1.

Figure 6-1:
Drat! You
have to
choose
something
else.

AOL ⊠

ⓘ The name you requested is already in use. Please try another name.

OK

5. **If AOL Canada tells you that the screen name you want is not available, click OK to make the information dialog box leave you alone, go back to Step 3 and try again.**

The big computers at AOL Canada sometimes feel creative and attempt to help you create a valid screen name. The outcome is much like having your three-year-old "help" you make a cake from scratch. Figure 6-2 shows the computer's suggestion for an attempt to set up Bird as a screen name (an anglo variation of Marguerite's francophone last name). If you reach this point, heed the advice "You may be a Pigeon, but you're no numbered bird!"

After you and AOL Canada agree on a screen name (which may take several tries), the Choose a Password dialog box appears, asking you to set a password for the new screen name.

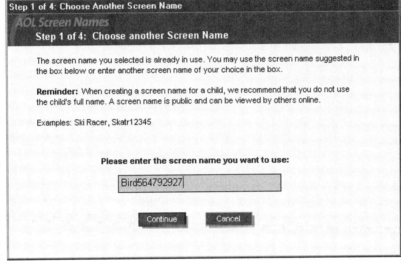

Figure 6-2:
Don't let the
computer
"help" you
make screen
names.
Baaaad
idea.

6. **Type the password twice and then click the Continue button.**

AOL Canada passwords have to be between six and eight characters long. As you type a password, little stars (asterisks) appear onscreen. Yes, it's *supposed* to happen that way — it's a security thing.

Because you can't see what you're typing, AOL Canada makes you enter the password twice so that you're sure you didn't make a typing mistake. Type the password in the box on the left and again in the box on the right. If the two entries don't agree, the software warns you and makes you try again.

After the password is accepted, the Parental Controls dialog box appears. Hey, guess what the title is? Yep! AOL Screen Names Step 3 of 4: Select a Parental Controls Category. See the sidebar "Psst — what's the password?" later in this chapter for some important thoughts and warnings about passwords.

7. **Select an access level for your new screen name by clicking the appropriate radio button in the Parental Controls dialog box. Click OK to finish creating the screen name.**

   If you choose the 18+ setting, AOL Canada then asks you whether this screen name should be a master screen name. For more about that, continue with the next step. For all other types of screen names, skip ahead to Step 9.

   Although the Parental Controls dialog box offers some guidelines for picking the right access level, the actual decision is up to you as a parent. AOL Canada doesn't require kids to have a particular access level — it's not their job. You, the parent, have the full and final say in the matter.

   You can always change the access level for a screen name if you find that it's too restrictive or too loose. For more information about the other parental controls, see the section "Parental Controls: Taking Away the Online Car Keys," later in this chapter.

8. **To designate the new screen name as a master screen name, click Yes. Otherwise, click No.**

   Master screen names can create and delete screen names in your account, change parental controls, and generally do anything the primary screen name can. You may make your significant other's screen name a master screen name, but you don't want to give that ability to the kids.

   After choosing the master screen name setting, AOL Canada takes you to the last, aptly titled dialog box, AOL Screen Names Step 4 of 4: Confirm Your Settings. It also outlines what the screen name can do with the access you selected back in Step 7, and gives you the opportunity to make some last-moment tweaks to the screen name's Parental Controls settings. Click Accept Settings if everything looks just fine.

9. **To use the new screen name, sign off from AOL Canada by choosing** Sign Off➪Sign Off **and clicking** Sign Off **in the dialog box that appears.**

   The sign-on screen clears, and the Goodbye dialog box bids you a fond farewell.

10. **Click the down arrow next to the Screen Name list box and choose your new screen name from the list.**

11. **Press Tab to move to the Password box and type the new password you created.**

    A dialog box appears giving you the option of storing your password. If you decide to store it, type the new password in the text box provided, then a second time, and click OK. If you'd rather not store it, just click Cancel. For more on the pros and cons of storing your password, flip to Chapter 14.

12. **Click Sign On.**

    Poof — it's the new you!

AOL Canada automatically sends a "welcome aboard" e-mail message to the new screen name, describing the powers conferred on a screen name, offering some thoughts about good online citizenship, and mentioning other topics. The system also sends a reminder e-mail to your primary screen name saying that a new screen name just joined your account.

If you ever find one of those "Thanks for making a new screen name" messages in your mailbox when you haven't made a new screen name, immediately call the AOL Canada Screen Name or Password Problems help line, at 1-888-265-4357. Although it may be nothing more than a computer glitch, calling AOL Canada to find out what's going on is a good precaution.

Deleting an old screen name

Even screen names reach the end of their usefulness. When that time comes for the screen names in your account, delete them and go on about your business. Just follow these steps to delete a screen name:

1. **Sign on to AOL Canada with your primary screen name or a master screen name.**

   If you aren't familiar with master screen names, see the brief description in Step 8 of the preceding section.

2. **After connecting, choose Settings⇨Screen Names from the toolbar (or use keyword Screen Names).**

   The AOL Screen Names dialog box appears.

3. **Click the Delete a Screen Name option under the heading Screen Name Options, in the dialog box.**

4. **When AOL Canada displays the aptly named Are You Sure? dialog box, take a deep breath and click Continue.**

   The Delete a Screen Name dialog box appears, looking just the tiniest bit somber in its fateful duties.

5. **Click the screen name you want to delete and then click Delete.**

   Be *darn sure* that you want to delete this screen name before clicking the Delete button. Although theoretically you can restore deleted screen names, it's an inexact science. Translated into English, restoring a deleted screen name is up to the impish whims of the AOL Canada computers. Maybe they'll let you restore the name, and then again, maybe they won't. Who knows how these machines think?

6. **After doing the dirty deed, AOL Canada issues the brief, generic obituary shown in Figure 6-3.**

Figure 6-3:
The bird's
history (so
to speak).

You can't delete the primary screen name. Also, any master screen name on your account can delete other screen names.

Changing a screen name

What if you have a screen name and decide that you want to change it a little? Well, you're out of luck. To paraphrase the wisdom of Yoda, the Jedi master from *Star Wars*, "There is no *change,* only *delete.*"

Your only option is to delete the existing screen name and create a new one from scratch. Sorry to break the news to you like this, but that's just life in the online service world.

Restoring a deleted screen name

Having second thoughts about deleting your favourite screen name, eh? Who could blame you? (After all, that really *was* a great screen name!) Thank goodness, AOL Canada offers the Restore a Screen Name option. If all goes well, after a couple of quick clicks, your old screen name (complete with its online profile) will be back, as good as new.

Psst — what's the password?

Just like music and cooking, making a good password is an art. Here, in two sentences, is our collective knowledge on the subject.

The best passwords string together two common but unrelated words (such as GRAINFUN) or add a number to the end of a word (TRAIN577, for example). Your password should not be your name, birth date, spouse's name, dog's breed, shoe size, or anything else that someone can find out about you.

By the way, if you're setting up a screen name for a child or a password-phobic adult, you can configure the AOL Canada software to automatically enter that screen name's password.

Notice that we specified "if all goes well." As you may suspect, things *can* go wrong with the restoration process — like the simple problem of the AOL Canada computers saying, "No, you can't have that name back." Precisely why they do this, we don't understand. It probably has something to do with zebra migrations, cat hairballs, and the number of lawyers worldwide telling the truth at any given moment.

Now that you've had fair warning that the process may not work, here are the steps to restoring a deleted screen name:

1. **Sign on to AOL Canada with your primary screen name.**

2. **After you connect, choose Settings⇨Screen Names (or use keyword** Screen Names**).**

   The AOL Screen Names dialog box appears.

3. **Click the Restore Screen Name option, under the heading Screen Name Options in the dialog box.**

   The Restore Previous Screen Name dialog box pops up, as shown in Figure 6-4.

4. **Look through the listed screen names, click the one you want to restore, and then click Restore.**

   Assuming that the AOL Canada computers feel cooperative, the system restores your screen name and gleefully pats you on the back to celebrate.

Figure 6-4:
The bird is
back — if
you want it!

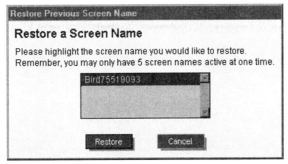

If the name you want isn't on the list or if the AOL Canada computers decide that you can't recover it, you have our condolences (we've lost a few screen names this way too). See the section "Creating a new screen name," earlier in this chapter, because that's your next stop.

Turn a Bit and Let Us See Your Profile

When you see people on the street or in the office, the first thing you notice about them is how they look. Beyond that, they're mysteries until you meet them, talk with them, and invest some time getting to know them.

In the world of AOL Canada, your screen name determines how you "look" to the outside world. But AOL Canada has something else, too — something really neat that we wish existed in real life: the member profile.

A *member profile* is a collection of tidbits and trivia about the owner of a particular screen name. For example, Marguerite's member profile appears in Figure 6-5. Despite what you may think, she's an average, small-town Canadian girl, writer, and piano-learner. (She also writes books, but you already knew that.) If she's chatting with someone online and the other person wants to know a little more about her, all that person has to do is choose People⇒Get Member's Profile from the toolbar (or press Ctrl+G), type Marguerite's screen name in the Get a Member's Profile dialog box, and click OK. Presto! Her member profile appears onscreen.

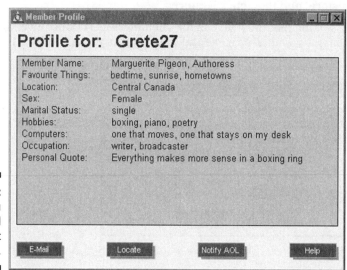

Figure 6-5:
Now you
know all
about
Marguerite.

Profile for: Grete27

Member Name:	Marguerite Pigeon, Authoress
Favourite Things:	bedtime, sunrise, hometowns
Location:	Central Canada
Sex:	Female
Marital Status:	single
Hobbies:	boxing, piano, poetry
Computers:	one that moves, one that stays on my desk
Occupation:	writer, broadcaster
Personal Quote:	Everything makes more sense in a boxing ring

E-Mail   Locate   Notify AOL   Help

So where does all this profile information come from? From you — that's where. (Marguerite's came from a small town in Northern Ontario, but that's another story.) It's up to *you* to create a member profile for your screen name. If you don't create a profile, other members can't find out about your likes, interests, and hobbies. In short, you'll barely exist on Planet AOL.

✔ Please, oh please, fill out your member profile. Leaving it blank is like moving into a new neighbourhood because you heard that it had lots of fun people, and then acting like a hermit.

✔ There's another reason to fill out your member profile: so that people who share your hobbies and interests can find you by searching the People Directory. Chapter 13 explains the details.

✔ Although this falls under the heading of plain old common sense, we want to drive home a point. Do not put your phone number, address, or other truly personal information in your profile. On a scale of good to bad, this is reeeeaaaaaally bad. Parents, check your kids' profiles every now and then just to make sure that they didn't put anything too personal or (too) weird in there.

✔ If you use more than one screen name, you need to fill out a member profile for each one. Every screen name has its own member profile.

✔ Some parts of the service (such as the online simulation and role-playing games at keyword **Games**) rely on information in your member profile as part of the game. For more about these cool entertainment options, see Chapter 15.

To create (or update) your member profile, follow these steps:

1. **Make sure that you signed on to AOL Canada with the correct screen name.**

   Because every screen name has its own member profile, pairing the right name and profile is important.

2. **Choose Settings⇨My Profile from the toolbar.**

   The Edit Your Online Profile dialog box appears. If you're *creating* a member profile, the dialog box is blank. If you're *changing* the member profile, your current information appears in the spaces (just like Marguerite's, as shown in Figure 6-6).

   Her profile window looks like a mess because she customized it — added new categories and things like that. It's dangerously close to nerd territory, but if having a profile that's truly your own sounds intriguing, check out Chapter 22 for the scoop.

3. **Fill out the Member Profile form. After you finish, click Update.**

   Don't worry if you seem to type past the end of the boxes for Hobbies, Occupation, and Personal Quote. You have plenty of room to type — the text scrolls through the box until you can't enter any more text. At that point, the box is full. Use your directional arrow, Backspace, and Delete keys to correct any typing or editorial errors.

   After you click the Update button, AOL Canada replies with a little dialog box telling you that your profile is being updated. Although the update process usually happens immediately, it occasionally takes a little while (usually 10 minutes or so, but more if the system is busy).

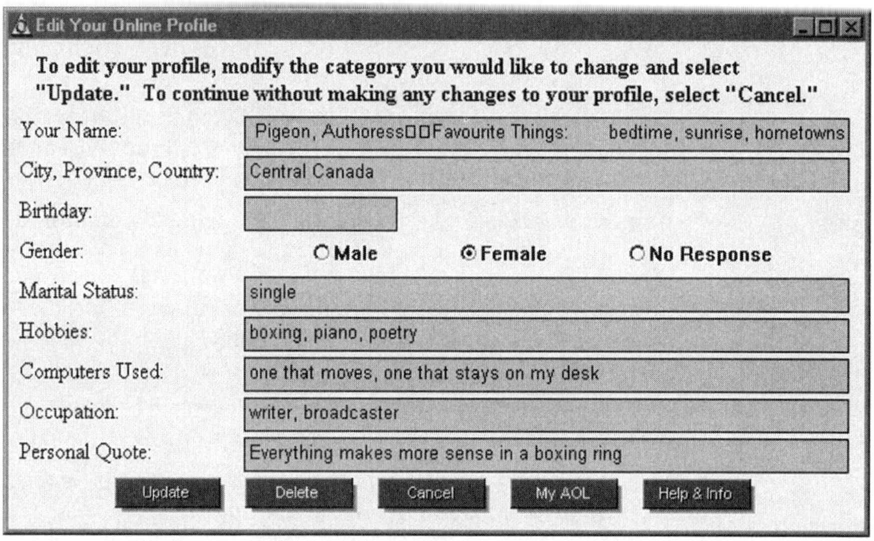

Figure 6-6: Here's Marguerite's member profile "under construction." The strange boxes are part of the secret of creating a custom profile (see Chapter 22).

The dialog box shows:

Edit Your Online Profile

To edit your profile, modify the category you would like to change and select "Update." To continue without making any changes to your profile, select "Cancel."

Your Name:	Pigeon, Authoress□□Favourite Things: bedtime, sunrise, hometowns
City, Province, Country:	Central Canada
Birthday:	
Gender:	○ Male ⊙ Female ○ No Response
Marital Status:	single
Hobbies:	boxing, piano, poetry
Computers Used:	one that moves, one that stays on my desk
Occupation:	writer, broadcaster
Personal Quote:	Everything makes more sense in a boxing ring

Update   Delete   Cancel   My AOL   Help & Info

Parental Controls: Taking Away the Online Car Keys

Like any major city or tourist destination, AOL Canada has much to see and do. Unfortunately, the similarities don't end there. Every big city also has a section that the tourist guide suggests avoiding, as well as a small, eerie population of less-than-moral people. If we said that AOL Canada was immune to this concept, we'd be very foolish (no editorial comments from readers who know either of us personally, please).

Whether you like the thought or not, the online world contains some places (and some people) that your kids really don't need to visit. That's what the Parental Controls are all about. They offer you, the parents, control over what your kids can and can't do with AOL Canada.

Before going into the details, here are a few thoughts to set the stage:

- ✔ Different people have different views about what kids should and shouldn't do (just look around your neighbourhood for proof). Please understand that we're not hopping onto a moral high horse and proclaiming what's right and wrong for your kids and that we're not passing judgment about what's available out there (although the thought *is* tempting sometimes). We're just explaining the tools available and giving some very general advice for parents whose kids know the Internet better than they do.

✔ To make the Parental Controls really work, only you, the parent, should know the password to the master screen names (the screen name you created when you first signed up for AOL Canada, plus any screen name you created with master screen name privileges).

✔ Create a screen name specifically for your child to use. Remember that each AOL Canada account can have up to seven screen names at no extra charge — one primary name plus six others. To give each child in the family a different level of access to AOL Canada and the Internet, create separate screen names for everybody.

✔ If you're curious why we're making such a big cloak-and-dagger deal out of who's using which screen name, here's the reason: Master screen names are special. *Only* a master screen name can set parental controls and create new screen names on your account. If your child uses a master screen name for online access, she can simply turn off whatever parental controls you turn on. (Whoops!) Instead, create a screen name especially for her, place the controls on it, and keep the master screen name for yourself.

Starting the Controls (And Backing Safely Down Your Digital Driveway)

Open the Parental Controls screen by either choosing Settings⇨Parental Controls from the toolbar or using keyword **Parental Controls**. Either way, the Parental Controls information screen appears. It offers general thoughts about the whole parental control thing, plus tosses out some cool tips and suggestions concerning online safety and the AOL Canada premium services (the ones that cost extra to use). When you're ready, click the Set Parental Controls button at the bottom of the screen.

AOL Canada provides two levels of parental control, depending on how much you want to tweak the digital knobs and levers. The basic level offers four general options (Kids Only, Young Teen, Mature Teen, and 18+). When you choose one of these, AOL Canada sets a bunch of default restrictions governing what that screen name can access both within AOL Canada and outside on the Internet (when accessing the Internet with the AOL Canada built-in Web browser and other Internet tools).

The more advanced level is *Custom Controls*. This à la carte approach to the Parental Controls helps you pick and choose specific limitations for chats, instant messages, downloads, Web use, e-mail, and Internet newsgroups. Although using these settings takes a bit more knowledge of AOL Canada, you create an online experience tuned exactly to your child's needs.

How do you choose the right controls for your kid? It depends. Consider the age and maturity of your child. Granted, our kids are all above average in intelligence and everything else, but for this one moment try to be especially objective. How responsible is your child? How naive? How trustworthy? Yes, these are tough questions, but this decision is very important. Here are a few general guidelines:

- ✔ For children 12 or younger, we recommend using the Kids Only default option. That lets them get into Kids Only, the area within AOL Canada that's specifically designed for that age group, plus kid-friendly Web and Internet sites. You can feel comfortable that your little one won't run across anything incredibly weird (except, of course, other kids).

- ✔ The teen years are more challenging. (Stating the obvious is one of our strengths.) If you use any controls at all, start with the appropriate teen-access setting. If your online child finds that setting too restrictive, try relaxing things by using some specific Custom Controls options (discussed in the following section). If you use the Custom Controls feature, we recommend blocking member rooms in the Chat control, FTP in the Download control, and any Internet newsgroup containing the magic words *sex* or *erotic* in the Newsgroup control. That combination maximizes the widely acceptable stuff while blocking off the Internet's most (ahem) *colourful* content.

- ✔ If you feel comfortable giving your kids free run of the world, that's cool. In that case, use the 18+ option, which gives them full access to both AOL Canada and the Internet. Nothing says that you *must* use the controls — they're just available tools.

You can change the settings at any time, so don't worry about ruining your children forever by making the wrong choice. Pick the settings, talk to your children, and see how everything works. If you need to make adjustments, do so. Most of all, work with your children and let them know that you're interested in their online world. That makes a bigger impact than any control ever can.

Tailoring Online Life with the Custom Controls

Sometimes (well, *okay,* more often than not) the one-size-fits-all solutions just don't fit. If your child needs more access here and less access there than the Kids Only or teen access controls allow, try customizing the Parental Controls. From the main Parental Controls window (keyword **Parental Controls**), click the Set Parental Controls option near the bottom of the window. This leads you to the do-it-yourself side of the parental controls (as shown in Figure 6-7), where you, the parent, take complete control over what your kids can and can't do online.

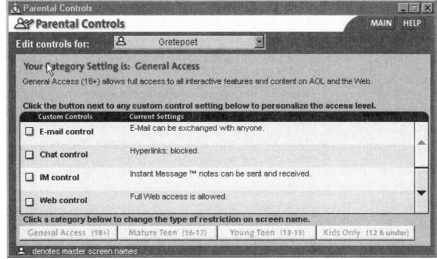

Figure 6-7:
The custom
controls
give you
incredible
flexibility to
tailor your
child's online
access.

The options in this window govern the most important interactive parts of AOL Canada. Each option is described in its own section later in this chapter.

None of these controls protects a child who has access to a master screen name on your AOL Canada account (master screen names always have permission to change the Parental Controls for any screen name in your account). To take advantage of the Parental Controls, you must create a separate, non–master screen name for your child.

E-mail control

E-mail is a powerful communications tool, although it can also be powerfully annoying. With the new AOL Canada Mail controls, however, you can take command of your e-mailbox and, more importantly, protect your kids from mail they shouldn't get.

The Mail controls fall into two distinct groups: general limitations on all mail and specific restrictions based on a set of e-mail addresses. Here's a look at your options by group:

- ✔ **General limitation controls:** These options establish simple, wide-ranging limits on all mail sent to a particular screen name. The three options are

    - **Allow All E-Mail:** Anyone on AOL or the Internet can send e-mail to this screen name.

    - **Allow E-Mail only from AOL members:** This option blocks all Internet-based e-mail.

- **Block all E-Mail:** So much for the e-mail thing — it was nice while it lasted.

✔ **Specific address-based controls:** Unlike the blanket controls, the address-based controls filter mail based on a list of e-mail addresses that you, the parent, enter into the system. The options on this side of the fence are

  - **Allow E-Mail from AOL Members and only from the Listed Internet Domains and Addresses:** Any AOL member can write to the screen name, but only listed Internet addresses can do so.

  - **Allow E-Mail Only from the Listed AOL Members, Internet Domains and Addresses:** You can receive mail from any AOL or Internet e-mail address, as long as you put the address on the list in the dialog box.

  - **Block E-Mail from the Listed AOL Members, Internet Domains and Addresses:** This option allows all mail except items from the listed addresses.

These six controls have a great deal of flexibility — hopefully, enough for everyone. Our favourites on the list are Allow E-Mail Only from AOL Members (great for easily blocking Internet junk mail), and Allow E-Mail from All AOL Members and Only from the Listed Internet Domains and Addresses (because it's a slightly looser version of the preceding option). Although at certain moments the hermit-like Block All Mail option is interesting, we think defining who is acceptable is more powerful than blocking those who aren't.

To put up some e-mail controls, follow these steps:

1. **Sign on with your master screen name and then choose Settings⇨ Parental Controls.**

   The general Parental Controls window opens.

2. **To fire up the screen you need, click the Set Parental Controls option, near the bottom of the window.**

   The detailed Parental Controls settings window appears.

3. **In the Edit Controls For box at the top of the screen, click the down-arrow to see a list of your account's screen names. Click your child's screen name in the list.**

   The window resets itself to display the current Parental Control settings for the selected screen name.

4. **Click the button next to the E-Mail Control entry in the Custom Controls area in the middle of the dialog box.**

   The Mail Controls window appears, ready to help protect your kids.

5. **Click the radio button for the proper level of mail control. If necessary, enter any AOL Canada screen names or Internet e-mail addresses in the Type Mail Address Here box and then click the Add button.**

   Because these are radio buttons, you can choose only one mail control setting at a time (even if you really want a combination of two).

6. **After you're done, click Save and then close the Parental Controls window.**

   Your mail controls are now in place and running.

Chat controls

The People Connection chat rooms are a popular attraction on AOL Canada. Unfortunately, the word *popular* often translates into *time-consuming*, because it's so easy to completely lose track of time while chatting the night away.

To keep your kids (or even yourself) out of the chat rooms, follow these instructions:

1. **Sign on with a master screen name and choose Settings⇨Parental Controls.**

   The general Parental Controls information window appears.

2. **Click the Set Parental Controls item near the bottom of the window.**

   The detailed Parental Controls setting window hops energetically to the screen.

3. **In the Edit Controls For box at the top of the screen, click the down-arrow to see a list of the screen names on your account. Click the child's screen name in the list.**

   The window resets itself, displaying the current Parental Control settings for the screen name you chose.

4. **Click the button next to the Chat Control entry in the Custom Controls area in the middle of the dialog box.**

   The Chat Controls window appears, filled to the brim with detailed information about the chat controls (as shown in Figure 6-8).

5. **Click in the check boxes next to your child's screen name for each chat control you want to turn on.**

   Table 6-1 explains each of the four options, including a Severity option that offers an opinion of how draconian that particular setting is.

6. **After you're done, click Save.**

   AOL Canada responds with a brief note that your changes are saved.

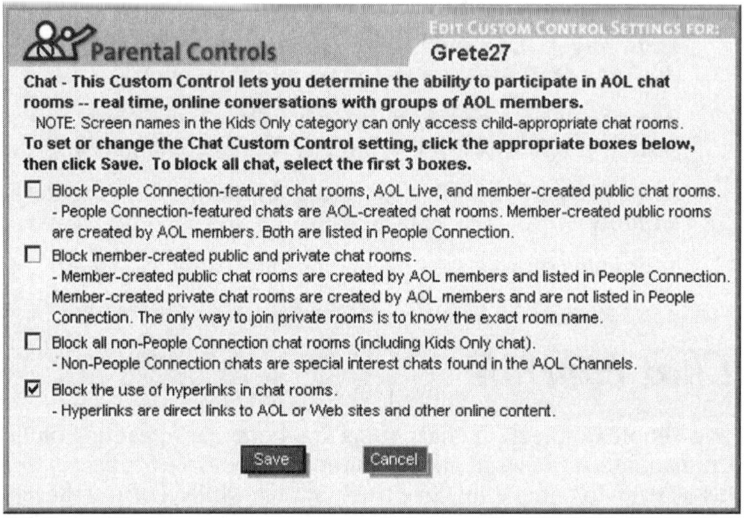

Parental Controls

EDIT CUSTOM CONTROL SETTINGS FOR:
Grete27

Chat - This Custom Control lets you determine the ability to participate in AOL chat rooms -- real time, online conversations with groups of AOL members.
   NOTE: Screen names in the Kids Only category can only access child-appropriate chat rooms.
To set or change the Chat Custom Control setting, click the appropriate boxes below, then click Save. To block all chat, select the first 3 boxes.

☐ Block People Connection-featured chat rooms, AOL Live, and member-created public chat rooms.
   - People Connection-featured chats are AOL-created chat rooms. Member-created public rooms are created by AOL members. Both are listed in People Connection.
☐ Block member-created public and private chat rooms.
   - Member-created public chat rooms are created by AOL members and listed in People Connection. Member-created private chat rooms are created by AOL members and are not listed in People Connection. The only way to join private rooms is to know the exact room name.
☐ Block all non-People Connection chat rooms (including Kids Only chat).
   - Non-People Connection chats are special interest chats found in the AOL Channels.
☑ Block the use of hyperlinks in chat rooms.
   - Hyperlinks are direct links to AOL or Web sites and other online content.

Save   Cancel

Figure 6-8:
Keep younger kids out of chat rooms with a couple of well-chosen controls.

7. Click OK and then close all the Parental Controls windows.

Another one's done!

Turning off the chat options is as easy as turning them on. Just repeat the preceding steps and click in each check box again, removing the mark for it.

Table 6-1	Parental Control Options	
Control	*Severity*	*Description*
Block People Connection– featured chat rooms	10	Blocks all general AOL chat areas, including AOL Live and the People Connection, but still gives access to conference rooms.
Block Member-created public and private chat areas	2	Prevents access to member-created and public and private chat areas, but allows the use of the regular People Connection areas.
Block all non-People Connection chat rooms	9	Blocks conference rooms throughout AOL including the Kids Only chat areas.
Block the use of hyperlinks in chat rooms	4	Prevents the screen name user from clicking a hyperlink that someone types in a chat room.

Instant message controls

Instant messages are the immediate communication windows that appear out of nowhere (sometimes scaring the living daylights out of you, depending on the hour of the day and how hard you were concentrating at that moment). Instant messages let you carry on a private, one-on-one chat with someone else on AOL Canada or on the Internet (through the AOL Canada Instant Messenger software — see keyword **Instant Messenger** to find out the scoop about that, or flip to Chapter 10).

Depending on the age and maturity of your child, you may or may not want her using instant messages. (John turned the whole instant-message thing off on his kids' accounts, but his kids are in the under-10 bracket.) To limit your child's access to the instant message system, follow these steps:

1. **Sign on to AOL Canada with your master screen name and choose Settings⇨Parental Controls and click Set Parental Controls Now.**

   The Parental Controls settings window appears, eager to help.

2. **In the Edit Controls For box near the top of the window, click the down-arrow to see a list of screen names in your account. Select the child's screen name.**

   The window displays the current Parental Controls settings for the screen name you selected.

3. **Click the button next to the IM Control entry in the Custom Controls area in the middle of the dialog box.**

   The Instant Messages control window hops to the screen, just like the one shown in Figure 6-9.

Figure 6-9:
Keep instant messages off your child's screen with the Block Instant Message Notes option.

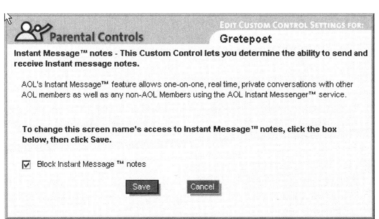

Parental Controls   EDIT CUSTOM CONTROL SETTINGS FOR: **Gretepoet**

Instant Message™ notes - This Custom Control lets you determine the ability to send and receive Instant message notes.

AOL's Instant Message™ feature allows one-on-one, real time, private conversations with other AOL members as well as any non-AOL Members using the AOL Instant Messenger™ service.

To change this screen name's access to Instant Message™ notes, click the box below, then click Save.

☑ Block Instant Message ™ notes

Save   Cancel

4. Select the Block Instant Message Notes check box for this screen name if you want to disallow instant messages to your youngster.

The choice is clear: Let them use instant messages or not. This isn't a shades-of-grey kind of decision.

5. After you're satisfied with the control settings, click Save to save them. Close the Custom Controls window (click the X button in the upper-right corner of the window) when you're done.

The instant message controls are in place (and you can breathe a little easier).

Web controls

Few things in the world change faster than the World Wide Web (although the flux-filled policy statements of many career politicians do come close). Although the Web is filled with thousands of clever and informative sites, it's also the home of many pages best left unseen by little eyes. To keep curious youngsters pointed toward the truly educational things rather than the *woo-hoo-hubba-hubba* educational ones, try applying some Web controls.

These controls limit the sites the AOL Canada built-in Web browser can connect to. The decisions about which sites are in and which are out come from the Learning Company, which rates the sites by the type of content they contain. The Web controls include Kids Only (a limited list of sites for ages 6 to 12), Young Teen (another limited list for ages 13 to 15), and the Mature Teen block list (which allows full Web access but blocks specific inappropriate sites). The system's other option grants full access to the Web.

For younger kids, stick with the Kids Only approved site listing. After your child blossoms into the terrible teens, give her either the appropriate teen setting or full access (as long as she can handle the responsibility). Because so much of AOL Canada's content is Web-based, we can't recommend completely shutting down Web access for any account.

To apply the Web controls, follow these steps:

1. Sign on to AOL Canada with a master screen name and then choose Settings⇨Parental Controls. Click the Set Parental Controls button to continue.

The detailed Parental Controls window soundlessly enters the room.

2. In the Edit Controls For box at the top of the window, click the down-arrow to see a list of screen names in your account. Click on the child's screen name.

The window updates itself and displays the current Parental Controls settings for the screen name you chose.

3. **Click the button next to the Web control entry in the Custom Controls area in the middle of the dialog box.**

   The Web Controls window pops onto the screen.

4. **Click the radio button next to the level of Web control you want.**

   Because the settings are radio buttons, you can pick only one setting per screen name.

5. **Click Save to store the settings; then close the Parental Controls window.**

   The Web controls are ready to serve and protect.

Additional master (screen name)

In the world of screen names, only a few are masters — the rest, simply subordinates. That's a good way to keep things as a parent with online kids. By default, only your primary screen name (the one you created when you first signed on to AOL Canada) is a master screen name. If adding another master screen name would simplify your life, open the Screen Names parental control and get to work.

The Screen Names window accomplishes only one thing: It turns normal screen names into master screen names. It doesn't *create* screen names (for that, choose Settings⇨Screen Names from the toolbar), change screen names, or even smirk at screen names. This is one seriously focused window.

Do *not* give your child a master screen name! That's the digital equivalent of loaning your beloved teenager the keys to your 1966 Corvette, signing over the vehicle's title, handing her your gold credit card, and casually mentioning that you're on the way out the door for a two-year-long world cruise. In short, it's free rein for the child to do whatever she wants in the online world. Because master screen names can set parental controls, only parents should use the master screen names.

With that warning ringing in your ears, here's a run through the process of changing the master screen name settings:

1. **Sign on with the master screen name and then choose Settings⇨ Parental Controls from the toolbar. After the general Parental Controls window appears, click Set Parental Controls.**

   The Parental Controls settings window finally appears, ready to work.

2. **In the Edit Controls For box at the top of the window, click the down-arrow to see a list of screen names in your account. Click on the child's screen name.**

   The window updates itself and displays the current parental control settings for the screen name you chose.

3. **Using the down-arrows on the side of the Custom Controls area, scroll down to the additional master setting and click the button next to setting's entry.**

   After that little romp, you land in the Additional Master Screen Names window.

4. **Click the check box at the bottom of the window to bestow master-screen-name status on this lowly screen name.**

   Only three of your seven screen names can be master screen names. Your primary screen name automatically has master status, so you can assign as many as two more masters on your account.

5. **After you finish setting the Master check box, click OK.**

   AOL Canada stores your preferences and updates the online records for your screen names. As a security precaution, AOL Canada automatically sends to the primary screen name a notification e-mail that gives the time and date that each screen name received master status.

If you open your e-mailbox one day and find a letter saying that one of your screen names recently received master status but *you* didn't do it, immediately call the AOL Canada Screen names and Passwords help line at 1-888-265-4357 and enlist its help to find out what's happening with your account.

Download controls

Of all the parental controls, the Download controls are probably the least important. Granted, there are some things in the world that we don't want our kids downloading from AOL Canada or the Internet, but that's hardly the biggest concern about online life.

If it's a bigger worry in your life than in ours, follow these steps to limit your child's access to downloadable files:

1. **Sign on to AOL Canada with your master screen name and then choose Settings⇨Parental Controls. After the window appears, click the Set Parental Controls option at the bottom of the window.**

   If everything works just right, the Parental Controls settings window appears.

2. **In the Edit Controls For box at the top of the window, click the down-arrow to see a list of the screen names for your account. Click the screen name for your child.**

   The window updates itself and displays the current parental control settings for the screen name you chose.

3. **Using the arrows on the side of the Custom Controls area, scroll until the Download control item appears and then click the button next to its entry.**

   The vaguely impressive Downloading Control dialog box leaps into view.

4. **To turn on the download controls, click one or both of the check boxes in the window. After you're done, click Save.**

   An energetic dialog box pops up, letting you know that your changes are saved.

   We wouldn't bother with Block AOL Software Library Downloads, but turning on the Block FTP Software Downloads option is a good idea. FTP (File Transfer Protocol) copies files through the Internet, and there's no telling what your inquisitive kiddo may find out there.

5. **Click OK and then close the Parental Controls windows.**

   Download controls are now in place!

As you may have guessed by now, to undo the download controls, you simply repeat the steps to create them. The big difference is that this time you click the check boxes *off* rather than turn them on.

Newsgroup controls

Of all the custom parental controls, Newsgroup is the most valuable. Internet newsgroups are an incredible resource, filled with discussions about almost every topic imaginable. However, not all the conversations out there are designed for the eyes of those under age 18.

To block out the most (we're being kind here) *exotic* material the newsgroups offer, follow these steps:

1. **Sign on with the master screen name and then choose Settings⇨Parental Controls. Finish your trip by clicking the Set Parental Controls button.**

   The Parental Controls settings window appears.

2. **In the Edit Controls For box at the top of the screen, click the down-arrow to see a list of your account's screen names. Find your child's screen name in the list, then click it.**

   The window resets itself so you can see the current parental control settings for the selected screen name.

3. **Using the arrows on the right side of the window, find the Newsgroups controls entry. Click the button next to the Newsgroups option.**

   The Newsgroups control window pops into view.

4. For most kids, we recommend setting the controls as shown in Figure 6-10. When you finish the settings, click Save.

The example setting blocks your child from any Internet newsgroup with, shall we say, *stimulating* words in its name. This one setting quickly blocks off most of the content that many parents are concerned about.

This setting does *nothing* to keep your kids out of the more explicit areas of the World Wide Web — it just takes care of the newsgroups (which really need taking care of, by the way). For that, see the section "Web controls," earlier in this chapter.

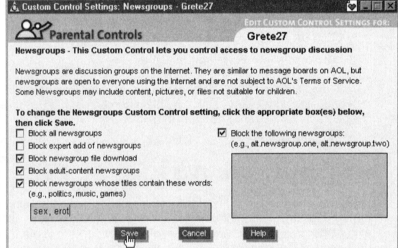

Figure 6-10: These two little words keep your kids out of so much trouble that it's amazing.

5. Close all the various open windows and continue with your regularly scheduled day.

Your child is now mostly safe from the Internet newsgroups.

To undo these restrictions, work back through the preceding steps. In Step 4, delete the entries in the Block Newsgroups text area. Remember to click OK after you're done!

Premium services

Your monthly AOL Canada fee covers an awful lot of ground. It provides e-mail access, Internet access, plus chat rooms, message boards, and lots of other goodies that AOL Canada offers. Even so, some areas of the service (notably, some of the cool multi-player games) bring an extra hourly fee. If your kids enjoy computer games as much as John's do, then keeping junior (or juniorette) out of the for-pay games could spell the difference between fiscal responsibility and financial disaster.

There must be some parents at AOL Canada, because all of the generic age restriction settings (Kids Only, Young Teen, and Mature Teen) automatically block access to premium service areas.

If you *want* to give your children access to the pay-by-the-hour games and other premium fee areas, follow these steps:

1. **Sign on with the master screen name, then choose My AOL⇨Parental Controls from the toolbar. Complete the journey by clicking the Set Parental Controls item at the bottom of the screen.**

   The Parental Controls settings window appears onscreen.

2. **In the Edit Controls For box at the top of the screen, click the down-arrow for a list of your account's screen names. Click on your child's screen name in the list.**

   The window resets itself so you can see the current parental control settings for screen name you clicked.

3. **Using the arrows on the right side of the window, find the Premium Services entry. Click the button next to the item.**

   The Premium Services window hops into view.

4. **Click the Block Premium Services check box to pick your premium services settings.**

   To block your child's access to premium service areas, select the check box. To allow your child into the pay-by-the-hour areas, de-select the check box (click in the box until the check mark disappears).

5. **With your setting in place, click Save to, well, save your settings. Close the various Parental Controls windows, then carry on with your regularly scheduled online time.**

   That's it — the settings are good to go!

Chapter 7

Navigating the System and Marking Your Favourite Destinations

In This Chapter

▶ Looking through the digital windows

▶ Setting My Places (actually, your places) in the sun

▶ Staying organized with Favourite Places

*Y*ou don't need to travel much before you start collecting a mental list of places you enjoy, locales you dislike, and restaurants you never quite found, despite splendid directions from the hotel concierge. It's human nature — we know what we like, and, when in doubt, we usually choose the known rather than the unknown (particularly because we can go there without getting lost).

Human nature being what it is, by now you have probably wandered the online highways and byways, got lost among the windows a few times, and discovered several (perhaps many) likable haunts on both AOL Canada and the Internet. But remembering your favourite spots and finding your way back to them is a problem sometimes — after all, computer monitors have only so much physical space for little sticky notes before you can't see the screen anymore.

That's where this chapter fits into your life. It looks at the main windows of your online world, explores the gentle art of navigating the system, and then explains how to rid your monitor of sticky notes, thanks to the built-in My Favourites option. If you're tired of stumbling across something cool and then losing the note that got you there (or if you're just tired of getting lost), kick back, put your feet up, and flip through this chapter. It's here to help.

Your Windows on the World

Everywhere you go on AOL Canada, you find windows. Welcome windows, channel windows, information area windows — *sheesh*, spring cleaning around here must be a *total* nightmare.

Although the windows are a little confusing at first, they make AOL Canada the special place that it is. Unlike other online services, AOL Canada was designed with the Macintosh and Microsoft Windows graphical way of life in mind. And it shows.

This section introduces and explains the basic AOL Canada navigation windows. The details of the content areas (the stuff *in* the windows) come later in this book. For everything you ever wanted to know about the channels, turn to *AOL Canada For Dummies Channels Directory*, in the yellow pages in this book. For now, though, sit back, grab a bottle of spray cleaner, and head for the windows of your digital world.

AOL Canada Welcome Window: Road map, cheerleader, and department store greeter rolled into one

If you're looking for the right place to start your online expedition, try the AOL Canada Welcome window, as shown in Figure 7-1. From here, your news, e-mail, calendar, and more are a quick jump away. Life just doesn't get better than this.

Figure 7-1: How's this for a warm welcome and a taste of what's to come?

Every time you sign on to AOL Canada, you're greeted by an explosion of activity. The main toolbar lights up. At the same time, two windows appear. One is the Channels menu, on the far left side of your screen. (If you find it useful, leave it there. If you don't like having it around all the time, click the Hide Channels button on the far left of the navigation bar.)

The other window that opens is — *ta-dah!* AOL Canada Welcome, offering a great big "Hi there — welcome to the system!" This window is like an electronic version of a department store door greeter, only better. This greeter doesn't just wish you well; it says hi, tells you the top news headlines, keeps tabs on your e-mailbox, and never hits you with a shopping cart. Not even Torontonians have it this good.

Figure 7-1 shows the AOL Canada Welcome window the way it would appear on an average day. It's a straightforward affair, organized into several specific information areas: utility buttons (mail, calendar, and such), Today on AOL goodies, and service areas.

The *utility button*s sit along the bottom of the AOL Canada Welcome window. These handy fellows tell you if e-mail awaits your attention. The utility buttons also provide quick access to an online calendar and the very popular People Connection Chat rooms (keyword **Chat**). Just click the button and you're off!

Next on the agenda is the Today on AOL Canada area. This serves up brief descriptions of a few highlighted areas on AOL Canada, along with links that take you to each one. These entries change all the time, so don't worry if your screen doesn't show exactly the same items as Figure 7-1. In general, though, a Top Story holds a place at the left of the window, keeping you informed about Canada and the world. Next to it is the Today in Entertainment area, where you can often find links to AOL Live's regular celebrity chats. Moving toward the right, keep an eye out for Daily Deals offered through the Shopping channel.

Last but not least, you'll find links to a bunch of popular service areas along the right side of the AOL Canada Welcome window. These include AOL Canada Search, Top News stories from the AOL Canada News channel, weather conditions, and My Places (a new feature you can read all about later in this chapter).

There are even more service links at the bottom right of the AOL Canada Today window. Use them to bring up the AOL.CA homepage (your link to the Internet), set Parental Controls, or request help.

The keyword for the AOL Canada Welcome window is pretty self-explanatory: it's simply **Welcome**. Still, if you'd like explanations about other less-obvious keywords, see the sidebar "Psst — what's the keyword?" later in this chapter. As you flip through the AOL Canada channels, you'll always find a reference somewhere on the channel menu to its keyword. Be sure to check the title bar (along the top of the window). If you can't find it there, try the window's bottom right corner.

While we have your attention, here's some more stuff you should know about handling the channels:

✔ Getting back the Channels window is never hard. Just click the Show Channels button on the far left side of the navigation bar and it reappears. To get to a specific channel, just click its name once and you're there.

✔ To pick up more information about what each channel contains, flip to the *AOL Canada For Dummies Channels Directory* — a special section on yellow paper near the middle of the book.

Individual content windows: The heart of AOL Canada

The digital foot soldiers of AOL Canada are the individual content areas. Hundreds, if not thousands, of content areas are out there, and each has its own unique interface window. Some of the windows have lots of artwork and feature buttons (like Figure 7-2). Others are plain to the point of being utilitarian (see Figure 7-3 for a to-the-point example). Both kinds of interfaces do basically the same things, except that the fancy ones do it with more panache.

Figure 7-2:
A truly fancy service window.

A fancy service window always contains some *feature and function* buttons. These graphical buttons lead you to special parts of the service, help you search the service's archives, or otherwise do something truly fun for you. Read the button descriptions carefully — don't rely too much on the picture to tell you what the button does.

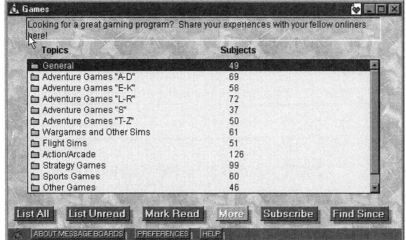

Figure 7-3: The essence of simply presented content.

Somewhere in the window is the service's keyword. It usually sits in the lower-right corner, but not always — it migrates all over the place, depending on the service. If you're not familiar with keywords, you should be. Look in the sidebar titled "Psst — what's the keyword?" for more information.

Last on the tour is the list of *service areas* — see Table 7-1. Most of the time, both kinds of content windows contain this list, but not always (fancy content areas sometimes replace the list with a series of buttons). The list is in whatever order the service feels like using (in other words, don't bank on things coming up in alphabetical order). To get into an area on the list, double-click its entry.

Table 7-1	Service Areas
Icon Name	*Meaning*
File Folder	Leads to an individual service window, which in turn contains more icons
Chat	Takes you into a conference chat room within a content area

(continued)

Table 7-1 *(continued)*

Icon Name	Meaning
Document	Shows a document explaining something about the service
Open Book	Displays a searchable database (found mostly in the various Research sections)
Disks	Opens a library of downloadable software
Globe	Usually points to an item on the World Wide Web
Bulletin Board	Opens a window of discussion boards
Special	Often a Web page but may be just about anything

Psst — what's the keyword?

Almost every service in AOL Canada has a *key-word*. It's like a magic carpet that whisks you wherever you want to go. Using keywords saves you time, and makes the system all the easier to use, too.

To use a keyword, click the icon button marked Keyword in the top right corner of the AOL Canada toolbar, or in the big white text area on the navigation bar along the top of the screen. (Keyboard lovers in the audience should press Ctrl+K to bring up the Keyword dialog box.) Type the keyword and press Enter. If everything works as it should, you immediately jump to that keyword's window.

Jot down the keywords for your favourite services on the Cheat Sheet in the front of this book and use that list as a memory jogger or to plan your online sessions.

For some keyword ideas, click the Keyword button located to the far right of the navigation bar. Click Keyword List and you'll find Keywords of the Day and AOL Canada's Top Ten Recommended Keywords.

Keywords are added all the time, so you sorta have to feel your way around to get to know some of the new ones. Also, keep in mind that there are plenty of AOL keywords that aren't specific to Canada. Yep, another nod to the more than 26 million AOL members around the world. That means there are hundreds more keywords that you can (and should) check out. So where do you go to find them? That's the sticky part. A master list of AOL keywords that includes Canadian keywords is still under construction by the programmers at AOL . . . cold comfort, we know. But when it's done, you'll find it, strangely enough, at keyword **Keyword**.

For now, you'll have to use a roundabout method to access the mostly non-Canadian keywords. First, open the Computing and Games channel (keyword **Computing**). Click Search and Explore at the bottom left of the window, then Ultimate Keyword List from the list of options. This brings you to a window where you can browse thousands of keywords by popularity, alphabetic order, or channel. Very cool!

Don't expect every service to look just like every other service. Some are very plain; others are quite fancy. Just relax and go with the flow — you're doing fine.

Adding Your Picks to My Places

As part of their ongoing effort to help you find the coolest online places (and to herd everyone in roughly the same direction — toward the ads), the AOL Canada folks added a new tool to your navigational arsenal: the quasi-customizable My Places links (as shown in Figure 7-4). They camp on the right side of the AOL Canada Welcome window, ready to send you wherever — well, *mostly* wherever — you want to go.

Figure 7-4: Customize your AOL Canada Welcome window with My Places.

"Wait a minute," we hear you cry in navigational confusion. "What do you mean *quasi-customizable*? And what's with the *mostly wherever* crack?"

Unfortunately, we mean just what we said. The My Places area, unlike the whatever-you-want-to-put-there Favourite Places system and the My Hot Keys do-it-yourself menu, is *quasi-customizable*. Yes, you choose where the buttons take you, but you can only pick from a preset list of links that AOL Canada provides. If you love the online game shows, the AOL Canada customizable news page, or the Business Finder, then My Places completes your life. If your tastes run toward more unique things (like Web graphics or home schooling forums), you're out of luck with My Places. Instead, use either the Favourite Places or My Hot Keys for quick access to those areas.

The AOL Canada programmers (secreted away somewhere very mysterious) assure us that they included the "most popular" online areas in the My Places options. Still, it would have been nice to include an "Other" entry to add your favourite keyword or Web site. But alas, there isn't one. (At least, not yet.)

The first time you sign on with the AOL Canada 6.0 software, the AOL Canada Welcome window displays an uncustomized My Places area, emblazoned with the suggestion that you should nip right over and pick some places of your own. The setup process only takes a moment:

1. **With your computer signed on to AOL Canada, click the Set Your Places button on the right side of the AOL Canada Welcome window.**

   The somewhat simple Change My Places window pops onto the screen.

   The settings for My Places are unique to each screen name, so you need to repeat the setup process for each name in your stable. (See Chapter 6 for more about screen names.)

2. **Pick a slot for the new My Places link, then click the Choose New Place button next to it.**

   A drop-down menu slides into view.

3. **Run your mouse through the drop-down menu until you find an interesting topic. When you find the right topic area, click it once.**

   The topic takes its position in the chosen slot.

4. **Repeat Steps 2 and 3 until you fill the five possible My Places slots.**

5. **Click Save My Changes after you finish.**

   AOL Canada saves the My Places for this screen name (not for all screen names in your account).

Check the New Place menus every now and then to see if AOL Canada wised up and either added more places or gave us an "Other Location or Web site" option. (But for now, all we can do is hope. That, or send in your opinion on the matter to the AOL Canada Suggestions Box, keyword **Suggestions**).

Organizing the Places of Your Heart

There's a new button in town — and it's appearing on a toolbar near you. Say hello to My Favourites and its sidekick, the Favourite Places window — both of them working hard to organize the online areas you know and love.

The Favourite Places system doesn't bring any law into your digital life (hopefully, Parliament won't either), but it promises a *lot* of order. Rather than limit yourself to just 10 favourite places socked away on the My Hot Keys menu (see Chapter 23 for the details about that), you can store as many favourites as you want! Is that just too cool or what?

Figure 7-5 shows a hardworking Favourite Places window in action. The heart entries link to services within AOL Canada or to Web pages and gophers on the Internet. For example, the item highlighted in Figure 7-5 is the AOL Women's Channel Beauty & Fashion forum. Folders (such as Member Exclusives and AOL's Top Picks) apply some order to the impending chaos.

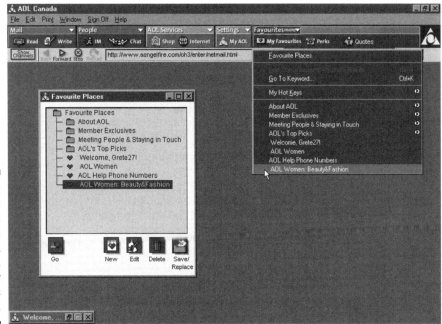

Figure 7-5:
The famous
Favourites
Places
dialog box
and its twin,
the My
Favourites
toolbar icon.

Figure 7-5 also shows another cool feature of the AOL Canada software: The Favourite Places *menu item list* that automatically appears beneath the Favourites button on the toolbar. When you add an online area to your Favourite Places, it automatically appears in both the Favourite Places window and on the menu list under the Favourites toolbar button. (Life's getting better all the time, isn't it?) Items in both places work the same way, so you can end up in the AOL Canada Shopping Channel whether you double-click its heart entry in the Favourite Places window or just choose it from the Favourites drop-down menu.

Here are some other random musings about the Favourite Places system:

> ✔ Even though all the items in your Favourite Places window are also displayed on the Favourites drop-down menu, you can make changes to the entries only in the Favourite Places window. The Favourites drop-down menu notices the changes on its own, so don't worry about that.

> ✔ You're not limited to the folders shown in Figure 7-5. You have the freedom — yes, even the right and responsibility — to create equally peculiar folders for yourself.

Using folders in the Favourite Places window

We almost forgot to mention this but, luckily, two brain cells, firing somewhere between John's overused cerebrum and Marguerite's grey matter, reminded us that double-clicking is the key to using the Favourite Places window:

> ✔ To open a folder, double-click it.

> ✔ To close the folder after you're done with it, double-click the folder again.

> ✔ To take off for a favourite place, double-click it.

Flip back into single-clicking mode when you're using the drop-down menu under the Favourites button. Because it's a menu and not a list of items in a window, you click once to choose destinations there.

Adding a favourite place

Including a new favourite place is a cinch. You can do so in two ways: the Easy Way and the Other Way. This section tells you how to handle them both.

The Easy Way is for areas inside AOL Canada or Internet-based Web pages and gophers you've browsed your way into:

1. **Display an area you're fond of, either inside AOL Canada or on the Internet.**

2. **Click the heart-on-a-document icon in the window's upper-right corner.**

   A little dialog box appears (see Figure 7-6), demanding to know what you intend to do with the link to this online area.

   Not every window in AOL Canada has one of those cute little heart document icons. It's unfortunate but true. If the window you're looking at doesn't have one, you can't add it to the Favourite Places list.

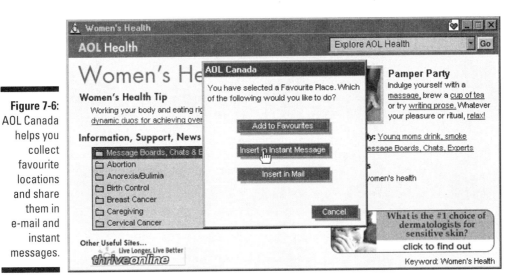

Figure 7-6:
AOL Canada
helps you
collect
favourite
locations
and share
them in
e-mail and
instant
messages.

3. **In the little You Have Selected a Favourite Place dialog box, click the Add to Favourites button to include an entry for this online area on your Favourite Places list.**

   Your new entry takes up residence at either the top or bottom of both the Favourite Places window and the drop-down menu under the Favourites button on the toolbar, just as Figure 7-7 shows. (Which end of the list it lands on seems to depend entirely on how your AOL Canada software feels at the moment. Strange, isn't it?)

Figure 7-7:
The new
entry lands
at the
bottom of
the list.

If you click the Insert in Instant Message button, a new Instant Message window appears, complete with a ready-to-use link to this favourite place. Clicking Insert in Mail does much the same thing, except that a blank e-mail message pops up, with the link in the body and a friendly Check Out (Name of Content Area or Web page here) notice on the Subject line, and a handy hyperlink at the top of the text box so that whoever received your message can, er, check it out with just one click.

Use the Other Way when someone dashes up and says, "I just found the neatest Web page — you've *gotta* check it out!" The Other Way assumes that you have the address of a Web page and want to include it manually in your list of favourite places:

1. **Click the My Favourites icon on the toolbar.**

    The Favourite Places window appears.

2. **Click the folder in which you want to store the new item.**

    If you don't know where to put the item, click the Favourite Places folder at the top of the window. That's as good a place as any — and you can always move the entry somewhere else later.

3. **Click New at the bottom of the Favourite Places window.**

    The Add New Folder/Favourite Place dialog box (designed by the Use No Articles Programming Team) appears.

4. **Type a name for this entry in the Enter the Place's Description box, press Tab, and then type the entry's address in the Enter the Internet Address box.**

    Figure 7-8 displays a finished entry, ready to be saved for posterity.

5. **Click OK to add the entry to your Favourite Places window.**

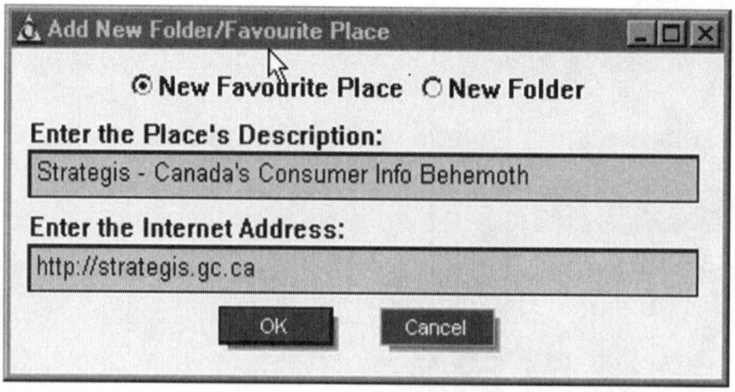

Figure 7-8:
The useful
Strategis
Consumer
Information
Web site is
ready to
join your
Favourite
Places.

Add New Folder/Favourite Place

⊙ **New Favourite Place** ○ **New Folder**

Enter the Place's Description:

Strategis - Canada's Consumer Info Behemoth

Enter the Internet Address:

http://strategis.gc.ca

OK   Cancel

Adding a folder

Adding all kinds of favourite places to your system is great, but you need some organization to keep everything in order. That's why those clever AOL Canada programmers included folders.

Folders can live in the Favourite Places area or inside other folders (see Figure 7-9). Either way, creating a folder is easy. Here's how (assuming that you already have the Favourite Places window open):

1. **Click the Favourite Places button on the toolbar.**

   The Favourite Places window pops to attention.

2. **Click the Favourite Places folder at the top of the window.**

   The Favourite Places folder is highlighted (this is a good sign).

3. **Click New.**

   The Add New Folder/Favourite Place dialog box appears on your screen (another good sign).

4. **Select the New Folder radio button.**

   The dialog box suddenly shrinks to half its previous size, shedding those unwanted pounds and inches in no time at all.

5. **Click in the text box under** Enter the New Folder's Name **and then type the name of your new folder. Click OK after you're done (see Figure 7-10).**

   Your new folder appears at the bottom of the Favourite Places list.

6. **Move the folder wherever you want it on the list.**

   If you're not sure how to move the folder, look in the next section.

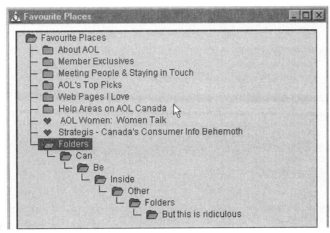

Figure 7-9:
An example
of folder
creation run
amok.

Figure 7-10:
Now there's
a safe place
to keep
those
otherwise
forgotten
Web sites.

Moving folders and favourite places

Creating folders and favourite places is one thing, but organizing them is another. The little guys tend to land wherever the AOL Canada software feels like putting them. But moving them around is easy after you get the hang of it.

The technique is the same for both folders and favourite places. After you open the Favourite Places window, follow these steps:

1. **Decide which item you want to move and where it's headed.**

2. **Put the mouse pointer on the chosen item and press and hold the mouse button.**

   The technical term for this manoeuvre is *click and drag,* but there's no reason to mention it, so we won't. (Oops, as Britney Spears might say, we did it again!)

Figure 7-11:
The Web
Pages I
Love folder
before . . .

Figure 7-12:
The Web
Pages I
Love folder
after . . .
adding a
cool site!
Fuller!
Better!

3. **While holding down the mouse button, move the item to its destination and then release the mouse button.**

   The item settles down, safe and sound in its new home (see Figures 7-11 and 7-12 for a before and after of the moving process).

Modifying folders and favourite places

A point comes in every life when it's time to make some changes. When that time in the life of your Favourite Places window arrives, have no fear. Although change is never fun, at least it's easy in the Favourite Places window. Open the Favourite Places window and then follow these steps:

1. **Click the folder or favourite place and then click Edit.**

   For a folder, the cursor appears at the end of the highlighted folder name. For a favourite place, the description and Internet address dialog box appear.

2. **Make your changes (usually to the name of the item) and then click OK.**

   If you change your mind and don't want to make any changes, double-click in the upper-left corner of the box.

Deleting folders and favourite places

Favourite Places entries, like other impetuous flashes in the dark sky of fading youth, have a limited life span. When it's time to delete an entry, just do the deed and go on as best you can. Solemnly open the Favourite Places window, and then morosely proceed through the following steps:

1. **Click the item you want to delete.**

2. **Click Delete and then Yes in the pop-up dialog box.**

The entry is no more. Remember; ask not for whom the Delete button clicks — it clicks for thy once-favourite place.

Chapter 8

E-Mailing the World, One Mailbox at a Time

*Y*ou'll pardon our abandon when we state wholeheartedly that e-mail is the communications medium of the millennium. It seems like everybody has an e-mail account at the office, at home, or both. Messages travel quickly, arrive safely, and rarely get delayed by any of the obscure national holidays that shut down the post office so frequently.

Through AOL Canada, you can send e-mail to virtually anyone on the planet. (No kidding — we're not even exaggerating.) One way or another, your e-mail message flies on the wings of technology from your online mailbox to its destination, whether the message is headed to another AOL Canada e-mailbox or to an Internet e-mail address.

This section tells you how to join in the fun, from sending Internet mail, to attaching multiple documents to an outgoing message in a jiffy, to organizing your messages by date, subject, type, or e-mail address using the new 6.0 version's sorting capabilities. No matter what you want to know about e-mail and AOL Canada, this chapter is the place to look.

Sending E-Mail to an AOL Canada Member

You're surrounded by other AOL Canada members (not to mention members worldwide) every time you sign on. So, the odds are good that you'll send at least a few messages to one of these people. That's what the e-mail system was designed for in the first place, so trading messages with other members is pretty easy. The mail system also has some special features, like *unsend*, that work only when you're writing to another AOL Canada member. (If unsending a message sounds interesting, check out the "Stupid mail tricks" sidebar later in this chapter.)

Before sending e-mail to someone, you must know the person's screen name. Upper- and lowercase don't matter, but spelling *does*. For example, you could enter John's screen name as **JKaufeld** or **jkaufeld** and the mail would still go through. But if you try **JKaufield**, don't expect a reply — at least not from *this* John Kaufeld — because the name is misspelled.

Before sending your first few messages, take a second to look through these tips and suggestions for making your e-mail stand head and shoulders above the crowd:

- ✔ Writing e-mail messages is a little different from any other kind of communication. Good e-mail takes a bit of care, the right words, and a willingness to type until the message is clear. If you're new to e-mail, don't panic — we were new once, too (and look what happened to us!).

- ✔ Please don't type your messages in one huge paragraph. That makes them really hard to read. Press Enter (or Return) a couple of times every now and then to break the behemoth into smaller, more digestible chunks.

- ✔ According to the AOL Canada official Rules of the Road (also known as the Terms of Service agreement by lawyers and other people who create official-sounding language because they enjoy it; keyword **CanadaTOS**), you can't send unsolicited advertisements through the e-mail system. If someone specifically asks to receive information from you, that's perfectly okay, but blanketing everyone in a chat room with e-mail about your company's new Web site falls on the Not Okay side of the chart.

Enough of this talk — it's time to hit the keyboard and start e-mailing! To send an e-mail message, follow these steps:

1. **If you *aren't* using the Unlimited Hours pricing plan and you signed on to AOL Canada to compose an e-mail message, sign off now.**

   Unless you're an excellent typist, need to send a very short message, or just don't care how high your AOL Canada bill goes this month, don't compose messages online if you pay for access by the minute. Instead, write your message offline (unconnected from AOL Canada) by continuing with Step 2 below. (Your credit card bill will thank us next month.)

2. **Create a new mail message by clicking the Write icon on the toolbar or pressing Ctrl+M.**

   A blank e-mail window mystically appears onscreen.

3. **Type the recipient's AOL Canada screen name in the Send To box.**

   To send the same message to more than one screen name, keep typing screen names in the To box and separate them with commas.

   If the screen name is in your address book, click the Address Book button, highlight the screen name and then click the Send To option. The screen name pops into your Write window's Send To box. Click the X at the top right corner of the address book to make it go away.

   Even easier, if the name is already in your address book, all you have to do is start typing it into the To box, and the screen name or e-mail address will automatically appear. Magic!

   You can freely mix AOL Canada screen names and Internet e-mail addresses when sending a message. Just separate each entry with a comma, and the AOL Canada e-mail system makes sure that the message goes to the right place. When you include a group of recipients from the Address Book window, the AOL Canada software automatically adds commas for you. Isn't that helpful?

4. **Press the Tab key to move the blinking cursor into the CC box. Enter the screen names of people who should get a copy of the message but should not be listed as a main recipient**

   Odds are, you won't ever use the CC, or *carbon copy* feature, but we had to mention it anyway, just for the sake of being thorough — authors do this!

   Don't bother putting your own screen name in the CC area. You automatically get a copy of every message you send. Choose Mail⇨Read⇨Sent Mail to see them. Copies only stick around for about 30 days, so if the message is *really* important, print it and keep the paper.

   To save your messages *and* a few trees, try storing vital messages in your Filing Cabinet. Just open a sent message, click the Save To Filing Cabinet button along the bottom of the window, and choose a folder. Congratulations! Your message has been preserved for posterity!

5. **Press Tab again to put the cursor in the Subject box. Type a brief (50 characters or fewer) description of the message.**

   Write your message subject so that the other person can tell right away what it's about. If the message is *really* important, write something like *URGENT* at the beginning of the subject and be sure to include some details after that. Because your reader may have 35 other messages to look at, making the subject descriptive helps her figure out which message to check first.

6. Press Tab once more to get into the message area at the bottom of the screen. Type your message text there.

Enter the text as though you're using a word processor; for example, don't press the Enter (or Return) key at the end of every line. Press Enter (or Return) a couple of times every now and then to break the message into easy-to-read paragraphs (see Figure 8-1).

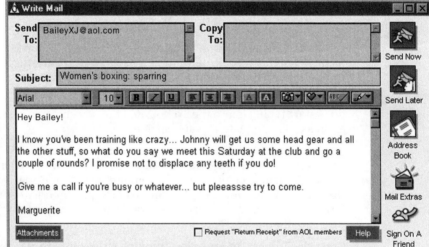

Figure 8-1:
Leave some white space in messages to make them easy to read.

To jazz up your messages, add some cool formatting or live links to your favourite Web sites. For all the details, flip ahead to the section "E-Mailing with Panache," later in this chapter.

7. If you're sending a file, click Attachments. In the Attachments dialog box, click Attach one more time. Finally, in the Attach dialog box, find the file you want to send and double-click it (or highlight it and click the Open button — don't worry the file won't actually open, but it will be attached).

After you pick the file (whichever way you do it), the Attach dialog box vanishes, leaving you in the Attachments dialog box. The name of the attached file appears in the middle of the window. Click OK to make the Attachments dialog box go away and leave you alone.

To attach several files to the same message, hold down Ctrl while you click the name of each file once. It's as easy as pointing and clicking. In fact, you can attach as many files as you want, and the AOL Canada software automatically compresses them into a ZIP file for you. Isn't technology wonderful (at least, when it works)?

If you change your mind about attaching the file, click the Detach button (it's right next to Attach in the Attachments window — what a strange coincidence).

What if you want to see just a list of the files you attached to the message? Just click the Attachments button again. After perusing the list, click Cancel to make the little window go away.

8. **If you're signed on to AOL Canada, click Send to mail the message. If you aren't signed on right now (which is important if you pay by the hour!), minimize the mail window and then sign on. After you're on, use the Window function on your topmost menu to toggle to the message and then click Send.**

AOL Canada automatically reassures you with a little message, Your mail has been sent, but that reassurance gets old if you send a great deal of mail. To stop the annoying little dialog box from popping up, turn off the Confirm Mail After It Has Been Sent option in the Mail Preferences window. (See Chapter 4 for everything you never — er, ever — wanted to know about preference settings.)

The section "Doing E-Mail the Automatic AOL Way," later in this chapter, explains the Send Later button and why it's the coolest thing since, um, well, they started tracking cool stuff.

AOL Canada automatically keeps copies of all your outgoing mail for about 30 days. To review these old messages, choose Mail⇨Read Mail⇨Sent Mail. If you're truly attached to your correspondence, tell your AOL Canada software to squirrel away copies of all outbound messages in your Filing Cabinet. Then find them by choosing Settings⇨Filing Cabinet and opening the Mail You've Sent folder with one click of your mouse. To find out more about this setting, along with the many other fascinating and tweakable items that control your AOL Canada experience, flip to Chapter 4 and look in the "Mail" section.

Writing to the @'s: Sending Internet E-Mail

Using AOL Canada as your e-mail link to the Internet is easy. In fact, you can pretend that you're just sending mail to another AOL Canada user, except that the person has a very weird screen name.

To send mail through the Internet, you go through exactly the same steps as you do to send e-mail to another AOL Canada user. The only difference with Internet e-mail is in how you address the message.

Stupid mail tricks

As though it weren't enough that you can send e-mail to anyone on AOL Canada, those zany programmers threw in some extra features designed to make your mind do loops. Look for these options along the bottom of the Online Mailbox window (get there by clicking the Read icon on the left side of your toolbar) or on the right-click pop-up menu (right-click a mail message's entry in the Online Mailbox to see the menu).

✔ **Read (button):** Opens a highlighted message for viewing.

✔ **Save to Filing Cabinet (button):** AOL Canada's e-mail system took a major leap forward by adding this useful function that lets you save a highlighted message to the folder of your choice in the Filing Cabinet. Just click the button with the friendly triangle once and an equally friendly drop-down menu appears displaying all your current Mail folders. Click a folder once and your message is saved there.

If none of the folders in the menu seems like an appropriate place for your new message, you can create a new folder by choosing the Create Folder option at the bottom of the menu. A nifty little dialog box appears asking you to name your folder. Type the name, click OK, and bam! You've got a new folder ready to welcome new messages. Next time you visit your Filing Cabinet (by choosing Settings⇨Filing Cabinet), you'll find your message safely stored away in whichever folder you selected. If you've created a new folder, you'll also see it among the other Mail folders.

If you're house-cleaning and find yourself with dozens of messages in the Online Mailbox (story of our lives), you can save several messages at the same time to your filing cabinet. Just hold down the Ctrl button and click each message once, then click Save To Filing Cabinet and choose a folder from the menu. The AOL software goes to work saving all the messages you've high-lighted. (You'll know things are going well when you see a Status box appear under the navigation bar.)

✔ **Keep as New (button):** Click Keep as New and you remove the red check mark that usually adds itself to all the messages that you've opened. This works on an individual highlighted message or on a group of messages — hold down Ctrl and click each message once to create a group. The goal of the Keep as New button is to tell the AOL Canada software to act as though you had a new unopened message in your Online Mailbox, even after you've opened it. That way, the little red flag goes back up and the You Have Mail title reappears on the Welcome toolbar. This is sort of like a string around your finger to remind yourself to get back to a certain message . . . instead of having it shifted into the Old Mail area, where it could be forgotten, or worse, purged!

✔ **Delete (button):** Get that message out of your Online Mailbox!

✔ **Status (button):** Want to see whether your buddy hasn't read the mail lately or is just ignoring you? Click the mail message you sent and click Status. AOL Canada returns a dialog box with the screen name of the person who read the letter and the time and date it was read. If it's still in unread limbo, the time and date are replaced with not yet read. The Status option only works for mail you've addressed to an AOL screen name.

✔ **Unsend (button):** If you send a message that you quickly regret, AOL Canada lets you reach through the system and pretend that the message never happened — as long as the message is sent to another AOL member and the person hasn't read it yet. To unsend a message, open your mailbox and click the Sent Mail tab. Find the message you're embarrassed about, click it, and then click Unsend. If the message hasn't been read yet, AOL Canada yanks it from the other person's e-mail basket and throws the message away. If the person has read the message, it's truly too late — Unsend won't work now.

Unsend doesn't work for mail sent to Internet addresses.

✔ **Ignore (pop-up menu):** When junk mail (or any other mail you don't want to see) fills up your box, this option makes a great antidote. As its name implies, the Ignore option disregards the current message, automatically consigning it to the Old Mail page of the Online Mailbox without actually opening it. If you get a great deal of junk e-mail, the Ignore option promises to warm your heart. To ignore a message, right-click the message's entry in the Online Mailbox and choose Ignore from the pop-up menu.

The key to sending Internet e-mail is getting the address right. Most Internet mail addresses look a little bizarre to uninitiated eyes, but that's not an issue — in a moment, you'll be initiated. Rather than simple, straightforward things like JKaufeld, or the not-so-straightforward but very creative Grete27, Internet mail addresses look like this: imrappaport@stagetheatre.com. The part to the left of the @ is the person's ID (the Internet term for screen name). The other half is the address of the computer the person uses for e-mail (in this case, it's one of those other online services). Put the whole thing together and you get an Internet e-mail address.

These addresses get complicated sometimes (the one for a friend of John's in France contains about 50 letters, numbers, and various punctuation symbols). An easy way to get the address exactly right is by asking your friend to send you a message first. When it arrives, add it to your address book with the Add Address button (on the right side of the mail window, as you read the friend's message). Now you don't have to worry about the gory, technical address stuff anymore — just pick the entry from your address book and you're done. (We get in to all the details of the address book later in this chapter.)

Because you're on AOL Canada, you have an Internet e-mail address too; it's your screen name with @aol.com glued to the end. If your screen name is Mungojerrie, your Internet e-mail address is mungojerrie@aol.com. The Internet address doesn't use the space or the capital letters in the screen name — it just ignores them.

By the way, remember to use the person's *screen name* or *Internet address* rather than her *real name* when you're sending an e-mail message. Although both AOL Canada and the Internet use advanced technology, the computers still don't know people by their given names (and we sort of hope that they never get to that point!).

E-Mailing with Panache

In these image-conscious times, looking good is almost as important as sounding good. Thanks to advances in the AOL Canada software, e-mail messages are more powerful and flexible than ever. HTML capabilities — don't worry, the acronym isn't as confusing as it is imposing — let you send and receive Internet-based information. Formatting buttons put you in charge of the text size, style, alignment, and even colour while you're creating e-mail. The possibilities for including Web-based information, choosing font size, colour, and alignment are endless (for your message's sake, we hope that your design skills are better than ours).

Most of the formatting options (including HTML) work with Instant Messages too. Don't let your e-mail have *all* the fun — add some formatting and dress up your instant messages.

The buttons just above the message area control the formatting magic. They're grouped into sets by what they do. Here's a quick rundown of the sets, from left to right:

- ✔ **Font and text size:** Pick any of your installed fonts and select the size that meets your purpose. If the person receiving the message has that same font installed and uses the AOL Canada 4.0 software or higher, she sees your message in the font you chose.

- ✔ **Text formatting:** These are the Bold, Italic, and Underline buttons, as their labels demonstrate.

- ✔ **Text alignment:** Like any good word processor, the AOL Canada e-mail system understands left, centre, and right justification.

- ✔ **Text colour:** Change the colour of the text with the first button. Use the second button to change the background colour of the entire message (not just a small portion of it). Remember that blue text on a blue background doesn't show up very well!

- ✔ **Insert picture:** The camera button inserts a graphical image into your e-mail, so you can tell Aunt Sarah about the holiday party *and* show off the digital pictures. To insert a graphic, click the camera button, select an image file, and — *poof!* — the graphic appears in your message.

✔ **Favourite Places:** You loved them as a Toolbar button, and now they're back in the e-mail window. The Heart button opens your Favourite Places window, making it easy to drag-and-drop Favourite Places links into your e-mail messages (see the next section for more about that).

✔ **Spell check:** Clicking the ABC button checks your spelling (yes!) to prevent embarrassing speeling misteaks.

✔ **Insert Signature File:** The last button on the list made its first appearance in AOL Canada Version 5.0, and continues to take a proud place on the far right of the formatting options in Version 6.0. The pencil button stands for *Signatures* (don't ask how you start with "pencil" and end up with "signature" — we don't make 'em up, we just report 'em). In e-mail terms, a *signature* is a little bit of text, usually no more than four lines, that you can make your e-mail software add to the end of your e-mail messages. It can include just about anything you want — but usually people like to add their name, other contact information, and some pithy quote or brief advertising message. Click the Pencil button to build a new signature, set your default signature, or use an existing signature in your current message. Don't be afraid to get creative. It's one of those features that's sure to impress your friends and family!

The font, formatting, colour, and alignment buttons all work the same way. To use them with new text, click the buttons for your choices and start typing. The software applies the fonts, formatting, and whatever else you choose, to the text as you type. To format text that's already in the message, click and drag across the text you want to change and then click the various formatting buttons. Presto — the old text looks new! To remove some formatting, highlight the text in question and click *off* the format options you don't want.

For some really fun goodies, click the Greetings button (along the lower-right side of a Write Mail window). This little bonus area offers some great freebies to spice up your e-mail. The freebies include a smiley reference guide, simple drawings to drop into messages, a stock of generic e-mail–brightening photos, plus a neat digital stationery maker. The Online Greeting Cards are a lot of fun to create and send (and hopefully receive). Beware, though — once you try them, online greeting cards get *really* addictive!

Linking with Ease

Almost every time we wander AOL Canada or surf the Web for a while, we run across something that's really neat and worth sharing with our friends. In the past, this required laboriously copying the Internet address or AOL Canada keyword into a mail message — and sometimes messing it up in the process. Today, though, we never miss an address because we let the AOL Canada software insert the link for us.

Before trying this trick, you have to understand how the Favourite Places area works and what it does for you. If you're not familiar with Favourite Places, flip to Chapter 7 and find out more about it before attempting this link thing.

When you want to include a link to either an AOL Canada keyword or an Internet site in an e-mail message, follow these steps:

1. **Go to the keyword area or Internet site so that it's in a window on your screen.**

   If the keyword area doesn't have a Favourite Places icon in its window, you can't send a link to it using this method. Sorry — it's just how life goes sometimes.

2. **Click the Favourite Places heart in the upper-right corner of the window.**

   A small dialog box appears and wants to know what it should do with your Favourite Places link.

3. **Click the Insert in Mail button.**

   After a few moments of thinking, the AOL Canada software displays a fresh e-mail window with your link ready and waiting in the message body.

4. **Address the message, type a subject and body, and then send the message just as you normally would.**

   The AOL Canada software makes this mail-the-link thing easy, doesn't it?

If there's a Web address you'd like to include in an outgoing e-mail that doesn't have a Favourite Places heart icon, don't despair. You can still get the job done using the Insert Hyperlink option. A hyperlink is just that: a link that takes you to an Internet page with a single click (as in "What a *hyper*-fast way to get to where you want to go!") Just click into the text area of your outgoing message, right-click your mouse, and choose Insert a Hyperlink from the menu options. A dialog box appears asking you to type in a brief description and the *exact* Internet address. (We stress *exact* because unless you type in the address just the way it shows up in the navigation window, your recipient will not be able to use the hyperlink.) Double-check your work, click OK, and watch as the link appears in your message in the bright blue that has become the trademark of hyperlinks everywhere. As long as your recipient has a recent enough version of the software to support hyperlinks, that little link will take him or her straight to the Web page.

HTML and e-mail, together at last

Among the improvements made to the AOL Canada 6.0 software — have we mentioned enough times yet that the software is on the CD-ROM that you got when you bought this book? Yes? Well, we just don't want you to miss it, that's all! . . . Anyway, as we were saying, one of the best things about 6.0 is your ability to include HTML-formatted text in your outgoing messages (and to receive these kinds of messages from other people).

HTML (HyperText Markup Language) is kind of boring, but it's what makes Web sites look so good compared to regular ol' text. Up to now, if you tried to copy some of that good-looking stuff into an outgoing e-mail message, it would

be magically transformed into boring stuff by the software (not good, eh?) Now, with 6.0, you can copy it in and the good-looking stuff remains intact.

Confused? Give it a try. Go to a Web page you like. Try highlighting part of the text and some of the pretty formatting — like fancy borders. Right-click your mouse and choose Copy. Now, click into the text area of a brand-new e-mail message, right-click again, and choose Paste. There you go! That's what you call a little hands-on scientific proof.

By the way, this technique also works for instant messages. So go online and get creative!

Incoming Missive, Sir!

Sending mail is only half the fun. After you send something, you get a reply! If you think that a mailbox full of junk mail is a lift, just wait until you sign on to AOL Canada and find a message or two in your e-mailbox. Someone out there cares!

To check your online mailbox, click the Read button on the Toolbar or the You've Got Mail button on the bottom left of your AOL Canada Today window. Either way, AOL Canada whisks you away to the New Mail window.

To read a message, either double-click the message in the New Mail window or click it once and then click Read (on the bottom left of your Online Mailbox). Your message hops up into its own window.

To reply only to the person who sent the message, click Reply. To share your comments with the sender *and* everyone else who received the message, click Reply All. To send a copy of the message to someone else (even out to the Internet, but not to a fax or postal mail address), click Forward. After you're done with the message, click Send Now (or Send Later if you are not signed on to your AOL Canada account). Once you send your e-mail, a dialog box appears to tell you "Your mail has been sent." Click OK to close the window.

Sniffing out an e-mail buddy who's online

Have you noticed something strange about your Buddy List (the little window on the right of your screen) when you open e-mail? Yes? Excellent! Two points for being so observant. Thanks to changes in the 6.0 version of AOL Canada, your Buddy List automatically rearranges itself to include a group called Mail Contacts whenever you open an e-mail message. So why do you care? Hey! Two more points for highly developed curiosity. Here's the deal: If the owner of that address is still online, you'll see his or her screen name or Internet e-mail address at the very top of your Buddy List. Now you know for sure whether friends, family, and co-workers are available to receive more e-mails, or better yet, instant messages. For all the details on Buddy Lists, see Chapter 12. For more on instant messages, drop by Chapter 10.

✔ To keep a message in your inbox after you read it, click the message in the New Mail window once and then click Keep As New. Unread messages live in your AOL Canada inbox for 30 days after arriving. After that, they turn into very small pumpkins and are shipped to your local grocery store, never to be seen or heard from again.

✔ To save an important message, either print it or save it in the Filing Cabinet (the AOL Canada software's built-in storage spot). To print, choose Print⇨Print from the menu at the very top of your screen. To store the message in the Filing Cabinet, click the Save to Filing Cabinet button on the bottom left of the Online Mailbox and choose a folder where you'd like the message stored. For more about the Filing Cabinet, see the next section in this chapter, "Organizing Your E-Mail Mess(ages)." For the option of sorting your messages, read the section called "Sorting as You Please," later in this chapter.

✔ After you first read a message, it hangs out in the Old Mail area for anywhere from a few days to a couple of weeks. (In the Mail Preferences setting, you can tell the AOL Canada computers to store incoming e-mail for at least seven days — see Chapter 4 for more about that). To reread an old message, choose Mail⇨Read Mail⇨Old Mail. Doing so brings up the Old Mail dialog box. Double-click the message you want to read.

Organizing Your E-Mail Mess(ages)

Both of us absolutely *live* on e-mail. Maybe it's this job or the peculiar people we work with (or perhaps it's that nasty nerdy side showing again — we hate it when that happens), but we spend a great deal of time each day fielding incoming messages and unleashing an outbound correspondence flood. Thankfully, our faithful digital assistant, the Filing Cabinet, keeps all that e-stuff organized.

The Filing Cabinet tracks incoming and outgoing e-mail, discussion board postings, and e-mail and newsgroup messages retrieved with Automatic AOL sessions. It even covers file downloads. Best of all, it's built right into the AOL Canada software, so you have nothing to download and nothing to buy.

To open the Filing Cabinet, choose Settings⇨Filing Cabinet. The window hops on the screen, looking much like Figure 8-2. The file folders along the left side of the window represent different storage areas. The buttons along the bottom control the Filing Cabinet.

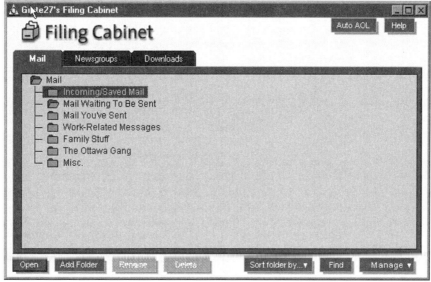

Figure 8-2:
The Filing
Cabinet
stores your
digital
information
in electronic
manila
folders.

You have much to work with here, and this area is easiest to understand when you play with it. Before turning you loose, here are some basic ideas about how the Filing Cabinet works:

✔ In AOL Canada Version 6.0, the Filing Cabinet is divided into three areas: Mail, Newsgroups, and Downloads. Use the tabs to move between the areas. (You'll store your e-mail in the Mail area.)

✔ To open a folder, double-click it. To close it, double-click it again. When you open a folder, the software displays all the items the folder contains (which can be a lengthy list). Don't be surprised if you have to scroll up and down to see everything in a folder.

✔ To view a piece of e-mail, a newsgroup posting, or something else inside a folder, double-click the item. Double-clicking an entry in the Download Manager area displays the description for that file, but only if you're signed on to the system.

- To create a new folder, click the top folder of the area (like Mail, for example) and then click Add Folder (along the bottom of the Filing Cabinet window). Type a name for the new folder and then click OK. The new folder appears underneath the top folder. Isn't automated organization amazing?

- Folders can be inside other folders, just like in the real world.

- Moving things from one folder to another is easy. Just move your cursor over the item you want to move, click and hold down the mouse button, and drag the item to its new home. When the mouse arrow is pointing to the item's destination, release the mouse button. The Filing Cabinet gently puts the item in place.

- If you misplace an e-mail message, click Find to have the Filing Cabinet ferret it out. You can search for the item's title or the full text of messages. Spiffy, eh?

- Speaking of misplacing (or better yet, of attempts to avoid misplacing) e-mail messages, there's a new option along the bottom of the Mail area window in the Filing Cabinet. It's called Sort Folder By and it gives you the option of displaying the messages in any folder according to date, subject heading, type, or sender/recipient. (For details, check out the next section in this chapter, called "Sorting as You Please.")

- In the Mail Preferences (choose Settings⇨Preferences, then choose the Mail option from the Preferences Guide), you can tell AOL Canada to automatically store copies of all your mail (both sent and received) in the Mail folder of the Filing Cabinet. The idea is cool, but it eats up disk space pretty quickly. Try turning this feature on and see whether you like it (but regularly delete the old messages that you really don't need to keep).

Sorting As You Please

There's a new option in town and it's going to add dimensions to your e-mail world (okay, *dimensions* is a bit over-the-top, but we like hyperbole almost as much as we like hypertext and hyperlinks). It's called Sorting and it's ready for you to become addicted to in the AOL Canada Version 6.0 software that you'll find on the CD-ROM included *free* inside the cover of this book. (Did we mention that it's FREE?)

Sorting is a simple principle, but until now, those AOL Canada programmers just hadn't got around to applying it. It means you can choose to display your e-mail messages according to several priorities (like when the message arrived, what it's about, what kind of message it is, or who sent it to you). This applies to mail in your Online Mailbox and all the messages you've saved into your Filing Cabinet's Mail folders.

The best thing about Sorting is that you're never committed to one sorting method. (Really, even you commitment-phobes can breathe a sigh of relief.) Resorting by a different method is as quick as a single click of your mouse button. If you try out a new method but find it isn't for you, just click the option you usually sort by and move on.

Sorting Messages in Your Online Mailbox

Sorting in your Online Mailbox is a temporary feature. By default, the AOL Canada software sorts your mail by date. If you close your mailbox and re-open it later, you'll have to take a moment and click one of the other sorting options to re-sort.

Here's how to use the Sorting function in your Online Mailbox.

1. **Click the Read icon on the far left of your toolbar.**

   Your Online Mailbox appears, organized into three areas: New Mail, Old Mail, and Sent Mail. You can move among the areas by clicking the labelled tabs.

2. **Click one of the Sorting options. You'll find them above the window where your messages are listed. A white arrow will appear next to the option you click, indicating that you are now sorting using that method.**

From left to right, here are your sorting options:

- ✔ **Type:** This option lets you sort your messages according to what kinds of messages are sitting in your mailbox. For example, the software understands that messages with attachments are different from regular text messages. Sorting by Type will group together mail in the following order (with oldest messages appearing at the top, newest messages last):
    - Mail with attachments and embedded images
    - Mail with attachments only
    - Mail with embedded images only
    - Regular text messages

- ✔ **Date:** Sorting by date makes a lot of sense. So much so that the AOL Canada software defaults to this sorting method throughout your Online Mailbox.

   When you sort messages by date in the New Mail area of your Online Mailbox, you'll notice that the little white arrow beside the word "Date" points down. This indicates that you'll see oldest unread messages first, followed by newer and newer messages. The opposite is true in the Old Mail and Sent Mail areas. Sorting by date in those areas places the latest messages at the top of the list (as indicated by the cute up-pointing white arrow).

✔ **E-mail Address:** Are you facing the prospect of digging up all the correspondence from a very full mailbox? No problem. Click the E-mail Address sorting option, and messages are immediately regrouped according to who sent the message to you (or who received messages you sent, if you're sorting Sent Mail) in descending alphabetical order.

✔ **Subject:** Your last option lets you sort mail by subject. This is especially handy if you're trying to retrace a thread — a series of e-mails you sent and received on a particular subject.

Sorting Messages in Your Filing Cabinet

Sorting has a more lasting effect in your Filing Cabinet. Switch the sorting method in a particular folder, and it will stay that way until you decide to change it back. Now that's custom organization!

Here's how to sort all the mail you've stored in your Filing Cabinet:

1. **Choose** **S**ettings⇨**F**iling Cabinet **from the toolbar.**

 Your own personal AOL Canada storage space comes cheerfully into view.

2. **Choose the Mail tab to view saved e-mail messages (you should probably be there already, since the software defaults to this tab rather than Downloads or Newsgroups).**

 The Mail window appears with its folders within folders. (If you want to review the process of saving messages and creating new folders in Filing Cabinet, go back to the preceding section in this chapter, called "Organizing Your E-Mail Mess(ages)."

3. **Choose the folder you would like to re-sort by highlighting it with one click of your mouse.**

 If you want to see the messages before and after re-sorting, click the folder again to reveal its contents before moving on to Step 4.

4. **Click the Sort Folder By button on the bottom of the Mail window and choose one of the sorting options from the menu.**

 Your sorting choices are almost the same as those described in the previous section, "Sorting Messages in Your Online Mailbox," except that instead of the Date option, you can choose to display messages starting either with the Oldest or the Newest. The first puts your oldest messages at the top of the list in your folder. The second puts your newest messages at the top.

Sorting in your Filing Cabinet applies to individual folders. If you want to apply a new sorting method to another folder, you'll have to repeat the steps above.

Catching People with Your Address Book

You start meeting people right away in AOL Canada. Join a discussion, drop in for a chat, or attend a live presentation, and suddenly you have online friends. You also have a problem: How do you keep track of the members of your newfound social club?

It's time to invoke the familiar refrain "Luckily, the AOL Canada programmers thought of that." Yup, those clever folks did it again. Step right this way, and meet the new and improved AOL Canada Address Book.

Thanks to improvements made in the 6.0 version of the AOL Canada software (that just so happens to be on the CD-ROM attached to the cover of this book), your Address Book is now accessible to you wherever you happen to be online. That's right, you can use it when signed on to AOL Canada as a guest from another AOL member's computer.

The reason you can use your Address Book from anywhere with the 6.0 software is that the information in it is actually stored on AOL Canada's computers, something the techno-geeks call a *host-based* service. Take it from us, you don't want to know all the details. Suffice it to say, when you sign on, you'll notice a status bar while AOL *synchs up* the data in your address book (a chit-chat between your computer and the AOL computers that brings both up-to-date on any offline changes).

Address Book entries are specific to each screen name. If you sign on with one of your extra screen names for the first time, you might think your entries have disappeared. Don't panic! They haven't. You'll just have to switch back to your original screen name to use them. (Choose Sign Off⇨Switch Screen Names to effortlessly slip from one screen name to another without hanging up.)

As address books go, AOL Canada's is simple. It handles entries for single screen names or big, honking mailing lists (assuming that you're into large, noisy name collections).

> ✔ For an individual, the Address Book holds just about everything you'd ever want to know about a person, including his or her real name, screen name, work title and company, Internet e-mail addresses, home and work mailing addresses, phone/fax numbers, home page URL, birthday and anniversary dates, spouse and family names, and any other notes you can dig up if you happen to be part of CSIS (the Canadian secret service). Phew! That's a lot of information — don't worry, you don't have to fill it all out if you don't feel like it.

✔ For a mailing group, the entry consists of a descriptive title and a list of the assembled crowd's e-mail addresses (you can add people from your existing Contacts List and new addresses). You can also choose whether to keep the group list private or share it. If you choose to share the group, you are automatically whisked off to the setup page for Groups@AOL. This service is simple, wonderful, and just a bit time-consuming to set up, so we'll save the details for Chapter 12.

Your address book's contact list contains both individual entries and groups in one master alphabetized list.

Adding Address Book entries

Before you can use the Address Book to send messages, you have to put some addresses in it. With that marginally deep thought in mind, here's the fastest way to add a new address or screen name to your address book (a not-so-fast way will follow):

1. **Open an e-mail message that you've received from someone you'd like to add to your Address Book.**

   If you don't already have a message open, click the Read icon on your toolbar and look for a message from that person in your Online Mailbox.

   If you're not signed on to AOL Canada, look for a message from that person in the Mail area of your Filing Cabinet by choosing Settings⇨ Filing Cabinet.

2. **Click the Add Address button on the lower right side of the message window.**

   The address is automatically placed in a Contact Details window. Just start typing your contact's name into the First Name text box and continue filling out any other information you want to add to your new entry.

3. **Click Save.**

   That's it! You've just added an entry to your Address Book contact list. (Whoever came up with "No pain, no gain" was dead wrong.)

To see your new entry, choose Mail⇨Address Book to open your Address Book and scroll through the contact list on the left of the window. Click your new contact's name once, and all of the information you've entered about her or him is displayed on the right side of the Address Book window.

You can add multiple entries to your contact list by following Step 1 and highlighting several addresses or screen names from an e-mail message while holding down the Ctrl button. Click the Add Address button, and the new entries will be added to your Address Book.

These days, you can't go to a party or a business meeting without someone handing you an e-mail address on a crumpled piece of paper. Here's how to start a new entry for your Address Book from scratch (remember, you don't have to be signed on to AOL Canada to carry out these steps):

1. **Open the address book by choosing Mail⇨Address Book or clicking the Address Book button in a blank Send Mail window.**

   The Address Book window pops up, all bright and cheery.

2. **To add an entry for a person, click New Contact. To build a group entry, click New Group.**

   A blank New Person or New Group dialog box appears.

3. **Fill in the appropriate spaces in the dialog box and then check your work carefully, especially the e-mail address entry (or addresses, as the case may be).**

   When you're creating an individual contact entry, the process starts with the Contact window. You can then click the tabs labelled Home, Work, Phone, and Details, to add even more information about the individual.

   Making a group entry is a little different. The Manage Group window, shown in Figure 8-3, is broken down into five easy steps that walk you through the process of naming the group, adding addresses from your

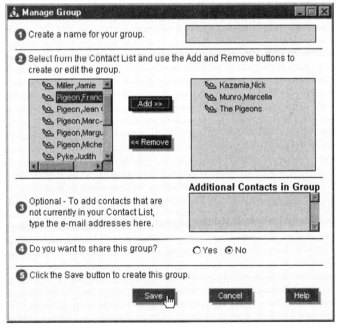

Figure 8-3:
A group
takes shape
in the
Address
Book.

existing contact list, adding brand-new addresses (separate these by a comma), and specifying whether to keep the group to yourself or share it. (Choosing to share will bring you to the Groups@AOL setup page, which you can read all about in Chapter 12.)

Although capitalization doesn't count here, spelling definitely does! For example, you can enter John's screen name any way you want (JKaufeld, Jkaufeld, jkaufeld, or jKaUfElD all count), and AOL Canada figures out that you mean *this* John Kaufeld. If you put in **jkaufield** (with an *i*), however, the system gets all confused and doesn't send the mail to him.

4. **After you finish, click Save.**

   The new entry pops into the Address Book window in alphabetical order.

Repeat the process until your address book overflows with friends, acquaintances, business associates, and other online contacts.

You can view all the information you've saved about a contact by clicking the entry once. It comes into view in the right window of the Address Book. If you can't see the right window, you've probably got your Address Book condensed (shrunk)! To expand it, click the Show Details button.

Sending an e-mail using the Address Book

Now that you know everything there is to know about creating and expanding your Address Book's contacts list, it's time to use it. Just follow these easy steps:

1. **Open a new e-mail message window by clicking the Write icon on the toolbar.**

   Hey! There's a brand-new message window waiting to be addressed. The anticipation is killing us.

2. **Open your contacts list by clicking the Address Book button on the right side of the window.**

   Your contacts are listed alphabetically in the window on the left side of the Address Book window.

3. **Click an entry in your contacts list, then click the Send To button once. Close the Address Book by clicking the X on the top right corner.**

   The screen name or Internet e-mail address is now firmly in place in the Send To area of your new message.

   To send a message to multiple recipients, hold down the Ctrl button and double-click several entries in your contacts list in Step 3.

To add a CC to your new message (a carbon copy of your message that you send to someone for their edification), use the same steps as above but in Step 3 click the Copy To button along the left side of your Address Book window instead of the Send To button. For a blind copy (or BCC, a copy you send to one recipient without the other recipients knowing it), click the Blind Copy button.

If the person you're sending the message to is already in your Address Book, you can just start typing his or her screen name or Internet e-mail address in either the To or CC box. The screen name or e-mail address will automatically appear. Easy!

Deleting Address Book entries

So now you may have an Address Book full of stuff, and it's getting unwieldy — plus you can't remember who half these people are. No problem — that's what the Delete button is for. Deleting is a quick and painless process. Here's how to do it:

1. **Open the address book (if you haven't already) by choosing Mail⇨ Address Book.**

   Of course, you can also click the Address Book button in the e-mail message window if that's where you happen to be when the inspiration hits.

2. **Scroll through the Address Book contacts list (on the left side) until you find the entry you want to dispose of.**

3. **Click the description once to highlight it and then click Delete.**

4. **When the software wrings its little hands and asks whether you're serious about this deletion business, click Yes.**

   If you just want to see what the Delete button does and how the program will react when you use it, click No. Apologize to your software for even *thinking* of tricking it like that. Shame on you.

Changing Address Book entries

Because things change at a ridiculous pace, particularly in the online world, keeping your Address Book up-to-date is a never-ending task. That's why your Address Book has an Edit button.

Here's the scoop on changing an existing Address Book entry:

1. **Open the address book (if it's still closed) by choosing Mail⇨Address Book or by clicking the Address Book button in a brand-new mail message.**

2. **Click once on the entry you need to change.**

   This step highlights the entry.

3. **Click Edit.**

   The Contact Details window comes back. It's the same window you used to create the entry.

4. **Make your changes as necessary.**

   Everything is open for change, so make whatever modifications you must. If you're working with a list, you can freely add and delete screen names.

   All the standard Windows text-editing tricks work here: highlight, delete, insert, click and drag, and the rest. Edit (and play) as much as you want.

5. **After you're done with the changes and are pleased as punch with them, click Save to save your work.**

   Click Cancel if you want to abandon your carefully wrought editing and keep the record the way it was.

   Whichever button you click, the Address Group dialog box vanishes, and you're back to the Address Book screen.

Two more functions in the AOL Canada Address Book should round out this section nicely.

   ✔ The *Look Up* function makes it easier to dig up an address if you have a lot of contacts. Just start typing the person's last name (or group name) in the Look Up window and the Address Book will look for a match, displaying contact information in the right window.

   ✔ To save time, use the *auto-complete* function to address a new message. Just open a blank message by clicking the Write icon on the toolbar and start typing the address in the Send To area. As long as you've previously saved that address into your Address Book, the 6.0 version of the AOL Canada software will attempt to guess the rest of the address and fill it in for you.

Doing E-Mail the Automatic AOL Way

Do you want to save money? Do you want to save time? Well, then, step right up, folks, step right up and see the working person's miracle, a technological time-saver: Automatic AOL. This little beauty lets you type your e-mail offline, that's right, *offline*, folks, not signed on at all — step back, son, you bother us. Save yourself some money right then and there. But it doesn't stop with that, no siree. It doesn't want to save you a *little* money, folks; it wants to save you a lot. That's why it au-to-matically gets your new mail when it's sending the old stuff off. Read your messages, write your replies, and then tell the little fellow to go do it all again. Every time you use it, you can't *help* but save money. Like money in the bank, folks, that's Automatic AOL for you.

Okay, so AOL Canada probably didn't use old-time carnival barkers to announce Automatic AOL, but they sure could have. This technology is incredibly useful, and it's built right into your AOL Canada Version 6.0 access software. You have nothing else to buy; no salesperson will call. Even if you belong to the all-you-can-use unlimited online time plan, Automatic AOL still simplifies life by managing all your online communications with one easy tool. And if you pay by the hour, Automatic AOL is your key to low monthly AOL Canada bills!

To work with Automatic AOL, choose Mail↪Automatic AOL. The Automatic AOL dialog box pops up in the middle of your screen. For all its power and usefulness, Automatic AOL is easy to set up and use.

You don't have to be signed on to the system to configure Automatic AOL — in fact, it's probably a good idea if you aren't.

Here's what Automatic AOL does for you (be sure to sit down before reading the list — it's pretty amazing):

- ✔ Sign on with one, a few, or all your screen names, and gather new mail for offline review.

- ✔ Send outgoing mail that you wrote offline and saved with the Send Later button.

- ✔ Automatically download files attached to mail messages (or not, depending on your preference).

- ✔ Retrieve postings from Internet newsgroups you marked for offline reading.

- ✔ Retrieve items from your favourite AOL Canada discussion boards (the ones listed in the Read My Message Boards window at keyword **Myboards**).

- ✔ Post your responses to Internet newsgroups and discussion boards.

- ✔ Bring down files you marked with the Download Later button in either e-mail messages or AOL Canada file libraries. For tips on finding the downloads you want on AOL Canada, flip to the section called "Finding Cool Programs and Nifty Files" in Chapter 13.

- ✔ Perform all these actions at regular intervals (every half-hour, hour, or two hours, for example) or whenever you tell the program to do so.

Automatic AOL is flexible, so you can do whatever you want. For example, your Automatic AOL session can retrieve new mail, leave attached files online, send outgoing mail, and not mess with the Download Manager. And you can change the settings at your whim.

You can choose from two ways to set up Automatic AOL: Either click the Walk Me Through button, which asks you questions and does the settings based on your answers, or use the options that appear on the setup page for what we like to call an Expert Setup, and follow these steps to gear up your Automatic AOL by yourself (do whichever is more comfortable for you; heck — do them both if you want):

1. **If you haven't already done so, sign off from AOL Canada.**

   Feel free to get a glass of your favourite beverage (Marguerite likes tea) and a handful of snacks before continuing. Food makes software configuration less painful.

2. **Choose Mail⇨Automatic AOL.**

   The Automatic AOL dialog box appears, as shown in Figure 8-4.

   If you want the AOL Canada software to take you step-by-step through the whole configuration process (which isn't necessarily a bad idea), click the Walk Me Through button. Otherwise, stay where you are and follow the next steps.

Figure 8-4:
You can have AOL Canada help you with the setup process for Automatic AOL by clicking the Walk Me Through button.

3. **Click the Select Names button.**

   The Select Screen Names dialog box appears.

4. **Select the check box next to each screen name you want to use with Automatic AOL. Enter the password for each screen name you select. Click OK after you're done.**

Type the passwords carefully. If a password is misspelled, Automatic AOL doesn't work correctly (and you don't want *that* to happen, do you?).

5. Tell the software which actions Automatic AOL should take.

Table 8-1 has a brief breakdown of the settings, what they do, and how we suggest that you set them.

6. After all your settings are completed, close the window by double-clicking in the upper-left corner.

Congratulations — Automatic AOL is ready to go.

Table 8-1	Automatic AOL Activities	
Setting	*Recommendation*	*Description*
Send mail	Turn it on	Sends any mail messages you write offline and save with the Send Later button. Another must-have feature of Automatic AOL. Use it.
Get unread mail	Turn it on	Copies new mail messages from AOL Canada to your computer so that you can read them offline. Definitely use this option — it's a time- and money-saver.
Download files attached to unread mail	Turn it off	Automatically downloads files attached to mail messages, which can be good and bad. If you get a number of files by e-mail, this feature is useful. In that case, go ahead and turn it on.
Send postings	For advanced use	Posts replies to your read-offline list of Internet newsgroups.
Get unread postings	For advanced use	Retrieves new messages from your read-offline list of Internet newsgroups and AOL Canada message boards.
Download files marked for later	Turn it on	Invokes the Download Manager and gets any files you have marked. If you download lots of shareware, this feature shines.

You may have noticed that we ignore the Schedule Automatic AOL button (on the top left of your setup window). Although we think that this feature is interesting, we don't want our computers deciding on their own that it's time to call AOL Canada and check for mail. If automating the process sounds like a hot fudge sundae to you (it sounded like cold asparagus soup to John, like liver to Marguerite), click the Help button on the bottom right of the setup window for help in setting the scheduling options.

We leave out two other settings, namely the ones relating to Internet newsgroups. Using Automatic AOL with newsgroups is a slightly complex process (much like assembling a child's tricycle on Christmas Eve — if you're a parent, we know that you can relate). If you *really* want to do newsgroups with Automatic AOL, sign on to the system, go to keyword **Newsgroups**, and get the details by clicking Read Offline and then clicking the Help button.

Using Automatic AOL is even easier than setting it up (be thankful for small favours, eh?). To start Automatic AOL, choose Mail⇨Automatic AOL from the toolbar and click the Run Automatic AOL Now button. The Run Automatic AOL Now dialog box appears. If you're happy with the settings you made earlier, click Begin. If you want to briefly review things, click Set Session instead. An information window pops up to give you the blow-by-blow commentary on the Automatic AOL session in progress. After the session is done, close the Automatic AOL Status dialog box.

To read incoming mail, select the appropriate screen name from the main AOL Canada window and then choose Mail⇨Filing Cabinet from the toolbar. You can read, reply, and do whatever else you want with the messages. After all your replies are done, set off another Automatic AOL session to send them on their way. Remember, almost all of this is done while you are signed off — something that saves you both time and money.

If your teenagers have their own screen names, they probably won't want to be part of your time- and money-saving Automatic AOL. Why? Well, it's a privacy thing — and you remember how important privacy was when you were young. Because you don't need to type a password to read mail that came in through an Automatic AOL session, anyone in the family could read the teen-mail by selecting the screen name and choosing the Filing Cabinet option. (You can protect your Filing Cabinet with a password. Flip to Chapter 4 to find out how.)

Chapter 9

Chatting the Day (and Night) Away

*I*nteracting with your fellow members is at the very heart of AOL Canada. There's never been an online service that's as into the idea of community as AOL Canada — and darn it, people in a community should talk to each other. The People Connection exists so that you can chat informally with others, make friends from all over the world, and redeem yourself in the eyes of your mother, who still thinks that you shouldn't spend so much time alone with your computer.

This chapter introduces the People Connection chat rooms and goes into detail about how the whole chat thing works. It also explains the AOL Live auditorium, home to some of the finest online presentations ever shown, um, online. Turn off the TV, let the newspapers stack up by the door, and get ready to boldly go where a whole lot of people eagerly await your arrival.

Ambling into a Chat Room

Getting into a People Connection chat room is easy. In fact, you've probably fallen into one more than once by just wandering around the system and clicking a few random links.

To formally set sail for the Wonderful World of Chatting, use keyword **Chat** or click the Chat icon on the toolbar (on the bottom half of the green People button). Welcome to the People Connection window. Just click the Chat Now! option, and after a moment of intense thought, the AOL Canada software launches you into a randomly selected chat room. To find a particular destination, click Find a Chat and then double-click one of the hundreds (or on some nights, thousands) of chat rooms. After you saunter in, look around, and generally get comfy, your screen should resemble Figure 9-1.

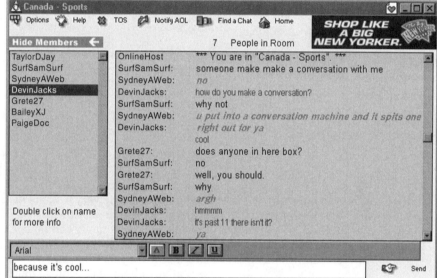

Figure 9-1:
Welcome to
the chat
room —
dive in and
enjoy!

Because the People Connection rooms are, after all, for chatting, the *chat text area* fills most of the window. Opposite the chat text is the *people list,* a roster of the members sharing the chat room with you. Along the bottom of the window is the *message box,* where you compose your witty comments before pressing Enter (Return) or clicking Send to share them with the room.

At the very top of the Chat window are the *control buttons,* which work like a transporter beam to various chats:

✔ **Options:** Leads to a roster of Chat options including

• **Parental Controls:** Guide your kids toward the best that chatting has to offer by adjusting the options in the Parental Controls window. Find out more about the process in Chapter 6.

- **Chat Preferences:** Opens a dialog box containing the various chat settings (just like choosing <u>S</u>ettings⇨<u>P</u>references from the toolbar and clicking Chat in the Communications Preferences).

- **Edit My Profile:** You want to look good out there in cyberchat-space, don't you? Well, what people have to go on is your Member Profile. Use this link to get to the Edit Your Online Profile window, where you can tweak to your heart's content. See the next sidebar for more good reasons to make your profile zing.

- **Search AOL Member Directory:** Find people with similar interests by scanning other member profiles for keywords (same as keyword **Member Directory**).

- **Locate AOL Member Online:** Find out if another AOL member you know is online at the same time you are. Just enter her or his screen name in the dialog box and click OK. You'll get your answer instantly (same as choosing <u>P</u>eople⇨<u>L</u>ocate Member Online from the toolbar).

- **Chat Schedule:** Find out what special chats are coming up on AOL, or read about regularly scheduled chats like Canada's own Back Bacon Caf-eh.

- **Private Rooms**: Leads you to the quiet world of invitation-only chat rooms.

- **AOL Live:** This is the good stuff. AOL Live is where you get to talk in real-time to the famous and the informed. Find out who's talking today, and who's scheduled to drop by the neighbourhood at a later date.

✔ **Help:** Takes you to the Member Services Help window, with a host of answers to your questions about chatting online, including etiquette and where to find the chat you're looking for.

✔ **TOS:** Know your responsibilities and those of other members toward you within the AOL community by reading through the AOL Canada Terms of Service. There's a lot in here that can arm you against inappropriate behaviour within the chat rooms.

✔ **Notify AOL:** Speaking of inappropriate behaviour, if you believe someone is breaching the Terms of Service by trying to steal people's passwords, endangering other people's safety, or some other equally offensive behaviour, report him or her! For more about how to do it using the Notify AOL service, read the section in Chapter 2 called "Handling the Rude, the Crude, and the Socially Maladjusted."

✔ **Find a Chat:** Lists both regular and member-created public chat rooms.

✔ **Home:** Takes you and your screen name out of said chat room and back to the main People Connection window . . . where, we suppose, you could choose another place to go make new friends.

Why you simply must fill out your profile

Before getting too far into the fun and frolic of the People Connection, you need to know about member profiles. Your member profile is a little online dossier you write. It contains whatever you want other AOL Canada members to know about you, such as your real name, your birthday, and the computer you use. You don't have to fill out every line — leaving some parts blank is perfectly okay.

Why fill out your profile? Well, if someone meets you in a chat room or reads a message you

posted and wants to find out more about you, she checks your member profile. People often search the member profiles, looking for other AOL Canada members with the same interests. John's wife scored an interview in a national magazine because the writer read her profile and liked what she found there.

Making a profile isn't hard. Flip to Chapter 6 for all the details. To make a truly amazing profile, check out Chapter 22 for tricks of the profile masters.

A standard chat room holds 23 people at a time. If you try to get into a room that's full, AOL Canada either offers to send you to another chat room (particularly if you're heading for a Lobby or other popular public chat area) or digitally shrugs you off, saying that the room is full (which it usually does if you try to enter an overflowing member-created chat room). If AOL Canada shrugs, all you can do is wait a few moments and try again.

If your kids use AOL Canada, you definitely need to know about the Parental Controls for chat rooms. Check out Chapter 6 for the details.

Finding Conversations among the Keystrokes

It's only fair, both to you and to non-computer portions of your life, to say this right up front: Chatting in the People Connection is almost too much fun for words. If you like people, thrive on conversation, and enjoy typing, you may as well put a pillow and blanket next to the computer, because you've found a new home.

The People Connection chat rooms are the AOL Canada answer to clubhouses, meeting halls, corner pubs, and your living room (except that chat rooms are a little tidier under the chairs). Put simply, chat rooms are digital gathering spots where you and 22 other folks type about life, the universe, and what's for dinner.

When you first arrive in a room, the chat text area is blank except for a brief note from a computer named OnlineHost that announces which room you're in. After a few moments, the chat text area comes alive with messages. (Don't try to talk with the OnlineHost — it never listens.)

The key to a successful chat room conversation is knowing how to read your screen. Flip back to Figure 9-1. The chat text area is a mess, isn't it. That's because whenever anyone types a message in a chat room, everyone can read it. It's like a conference call where everyone talks at the same time *all* the time.

To follow the flow of a chat room, you have to skip around. The chat text in Figure 9-1 shows just how fast conversations move and shift online. Here's a breakdown of the action.

First, notice that Marguerite has entered a chat room called Canada Sports, using her screen name Grete27, and that six other screen names are on the members list on the left side of the screen, indicating who is participating in the chat.

Starting at the top, we "hear" SurfSamSurf ask everyone to get the ball rolling. SydneyAWeb dismisses the request. (Yuck!) But luckily, DevinJacks picks up the ball and asks SurfSamSurf how to start. That inspires SydneyAWeb to get into the spirit and make a joke. DevinJacks finishes this thread with a simple comment. Now, Marguerite intercedes with — what else? — a boxing-related question. This is, after all, a sports chat room. Unfortunately, the rest of the exchange is a bit drab. No one there was interested in pugilism, it seems.

Stop chat room junk mail in its tracks

Although chatting makes the online world come alive with friends (both old and new), it also makes your mailbox strain at the sides with junk mail. Unfortunately, junk e-mailers scan the screen name lists in chat rooms and send out hundreds, if not thousands, of useless and often downright lurid advertising messages. Left undefended, your mailbox may get 30 to 100 junk e-mails or more during a single chatting session!

So what can a dedicated chatter do to stem the tide? Create a dedicated chatting screen name, that's what! It's your simplest yet most powerful weapon against junk e-mail.

The idea is simple — and, thanks to the fact that all AOL Canada accounts get up to seven screen names — easy to use. Create a new screen name for your chatting experience and then use the Mail Controls (keyword **Mail Controls**) to block all e-mail to the account. In the member profile for your chatting name, include a note directing people to your e-mailable screen name. That way, the chat room bulk e-mailers won't bother you, but your friends can still drop you a line.

For more about screen names and member profiles, see Chapter 6. To find out more about junk e-mail (and how to fight it), flip back to Chapter 5.

Now take a look at the text box at the bottom of the chat window. See how Marguerite was getting ready to send off another part of the conversation? Well, she'd better get in there fast because those last five replies came in within seconds!

Tossing your own thoughts into the chat room maelstrom is easy. Basically, start typing. Whatever you type appears in that long, thin box along the bottom of the chat room window. After you're done typing, press Enter (or Return) or click Send. In a moment or two, your words of wisdom appear in the chat text area for all to see. A single chat room comment holds only 92 characters, so choose your letters, numbers, and punctuation marks carefully (or split your thought into two lines — that works, too).

If you type a comment but your text *doesn't* appear in the box at the bottom of the chat room window, click the mouse anywhere in the box. When you see the blinking toothpick cursor way over on the left side of the box, go ahead and start typing again.

There's much to tell about chat rooms, but little of it follows any kind of organization. With that bit of rationalizing out of the way, here are some randomly assembled thoughts and tips about the wild world of chatting:

✔ To get someone's attention in a chat room, start your comment with their screen name. If the person doesn't respond in a minute or two, try it again. If all else fails, send the person an instant message asking whether they saw what you typed.

✔ To quickly read a fellow chatter's member profile or send the person an instant message, scroll through the People list until you find the person's screen name and double-click it. A little dialog box pops up. At the bottom of the box are two buttons destined to make your life easier: The Send Message button sends an instant message to the selected person and the Get Profile button displays her member profile. To get back to the chat room, close the little dialog box. Before making another comment in the chat room, click the mouse anywhere in the long box at the bottom of the window and then start typing (otherwise, what you type doesn't appear onscreen).

✔ If a person is getting out of hand or you just don't like listening to him, find the person's screen name in the People in Room list, double-click it, and click Ignore. From then on, nothing he types appears on your screen. (Isn't technology wonderful?)

✔ If you wander into a game chat, someone may ask you to "roll dice" in the room. For wonderful yet mysterious reasons, all AOL Canada chat rooms understand the special command //roll. This command tells the AOL Canada computer to pretend to roll some dice and print the results in the chat room. By default, it "rolls" two six-sided dice (just like you do in Monopoly and other board games). You can also specify the number of sides and number of rolls by typing `//roll-dice xx-sides yy` (replace *xx* with the number of dice and *yy* with the number of sides on each die). So, to roll four eight-sided dice, type `//roll-dice 4-sides 8`.

✔ If you see people writing comments like `afk`, `bak`, `LOL`, and `ROFL!`, don't worry — they're not making fun of you. That's standard chat room shorthand for things like "away from the keyboard," "laughing out loud," and other ever-necessary comments. For a quick primer in chat room-ese, use keyword **Shorthand** or check out Chapter 28.

Beware the Password Scammers

We both wish that we didn't have to include this section, but we must. Password scamming is alive and well in the chat rooms. The good news is that AOL Canada actively fights the jerks who do it; the bad news is that more jerks are *always* available to replace the ones who get caught.

Don't *ever* give your password to anyone — *anyone* — who asks for it, whether it happens online or some other way.

Nobody from AOL will ever ask for your password. Period. Never. It won't happen. No matter what the person says, who the person claims to be, or what she threatens to do, ignore and report anyone who asks for your password.

Figure 9-2 shows actual samples of password scammers we bumped into on AOL. We want to emphasize that: *We did not make these figures up — they are real.*

If you get an instant message that looks like the ones in these figures, don't bother to reply or say anything catty (leave that to people like us); just get ready to ruin the scammer's day. Here's how to report a password scammer to AOL Canada:

1. **If you're in a chat room when a password-scamming message appears, type a note in the room explaining that someone is fishing for passwords.**

   Be sure to give the screen name of the person who sent you the instant message. It never hurts to remind everyone to *never* give out their passwords — think of it as your good deed for the day.

2. **Click the Notify AOL button (one of the buttons along the top of the chat window) to bring up the Notify AOL window.**

   Under the heading Type of Violation, click the Chat button. To file your report, first select the Room Category from the drop-down list and type the chat room name where the violation took place. The name of chat

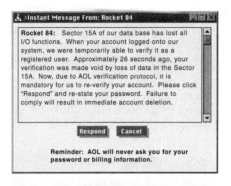

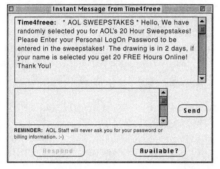

Figure 9-2: They promise anything to get your password.

rooms is always centred along the top of the text area in a chat window. Now, fill in all the required information, including date and time, the offender's screen name, and the content of the message you're complaining about. For this last one, you'll have to go back to the offending Instant Message and highlight the text, right-clicking and choosing Copy from the menu options. Return to the Notify AOL window, click into the text box, right-click again and choose Paste. Finally, hit Send to fire off your complaint.

3. **If you want to add any comments with your report, type them in the text area at the bottom of the Notify AOL dialog box.**

4. **After everything is filled out to your satisfaction, click Send Report.**

5. **Close the scammer's Instant Message window and proceed with your regularly scheduled evening.**

If you gave out your password before realizing that the person requesting it was a scammer, all is not lost. *Immediately* (like, *right now*) go to keyword **Password** and change your account password. After that, go through the preceding steps and report the scammer.

Enjoying a Little Private (Room) Time

Whether you're talking business or catching up with a friend, the People Connection's private room feature gives you all the benefits of a chat room without the inconvenience of filling it with strange people. Private rooms are great for reunions, parties, brainstorming sessions, and regional meetings.

Private rooms are just that — private. Nobody can get in without knowing the name of the room (a name *you* make up, by the way). AOL Canada doesn't keep a master list of active private rooms. People outside the room can't monitor the discussion in a private room.

Private chat rooms still have *some* limitations, though. For example, a private room holds only 23 people (so you can't have a really *whopping* party). And you get unexpected guests every now and then. Someone thinks up the same name *you* used and *poof!* —that person appears in your private room. Don't worry, though — that doesn't happen very often. Also, private chat rooms, unlike their public counterparts, don't include a Notify AOL button in the chat window. To report a problem, use keyword **Notify AOL**.

To create or join the discussion in a private chat room, follow these steps:

1. **Choose People⇨Start Your Own Chat from the toolbar.**

   The Start Your Own Chat dialog box appears.

2. **Click the Private Chat button.**

   The Enter a Private Chat dialog box hops nimbly to the screen

3. **Carefully type the name of the private room you want to either join or create and click Go Chat.**

   The chat room window reappears, with the name of the private room emblazoned across the top.

If you're creating a new private chat room, just make up any name for it you want. If you're joining someone else's room, type the name exactly as she gave it to you (assuming that she sent you the room name when she invited you in).

If you were heading into a private chat with some friends but find yourself alone in an empty private room instead, make sure that you typed the name right (capitalization doesn't count, but spelling does). If you unexpectedly waltz into someone else's private room, blush profusely, type a brief apology, close the window, and start over at Step 1.

If you spend a great deal of time chatting with folks on your Buddy List, the Buddy Chat feature promises to make your life a little easier. Flip to Chapter 10 for the details.

Attending AOL Canada Live Chats (and Enjoying Them)

Chat rooms cater to small, informal groups of people. For something a little larger (such as, oh, about 500 people), AOL Canada offers AOL Canada Live, where you can interact with popular media figures, captains of industry, authors, and lots of other fascinating folks. AOL Live is a more controlled environment than the chat rooms, but it's still loads of fun.

To get into AOL Canada Live, use keyword **Live** (or choose People⟹Live from the toolbar). The AOL Canada Live window appears, looking much like Figure 9-3. All the AOL Live auditoriums look alike and work in basically the same way.

Figure 9-3: Appearing now in AOL Canada Live!

When you enter one of the AOL Live theatres, you're randomly assigned to a row in the virtual auditorium with as many as 16 other people (just like sitting in a theatre). To find out who else is in your row, click the Who's in My Row button. A dialog box that lists your row-mates appears. To say something in your row, type your thoughts in the text box along the bottom of the window and click Send (just as in the regular chat rooms). What you type appears in the chat text area, with your row number in parentheses before the comment. In-row comments are visible only to people in the row with you, so you can say just about anything you want.

To ask a question of the person onstage, click the Participate in Event button, type your question in the dialog box, and then click Ask a Question. If the presenter answers your question and asks for more details from you, click the Participate in Event button, type your comments, and click Send a Comment.

Sometimes the audience votes or bids on things. (No, we don't know exactly *what* you vote or bid on, but we have it from the best authorities that the process is very important.) To take part in it, click the Participate in Event button, type your vote or bid (whatever it is), and click either Vote or Bid.

As with chat rooms, you need to know many other things about theatres to make your enjoyment complete:

- ✔ To focus on the event and stop annoying chat from people in your row, click Who's in My Row and then click Turn Chat Off.

- ✔ To change rows (if you're allergic to someone you're sitting with), click the Who's in My Row button, then click Other Rows and double-click Row. Remember that each row holds only 16 people. If the row you choose is full, AOL Canada Live sends you to a nearby row.

- ✔ Take your newly developed chatting skills for a test drive at John's America Online For Dummies monthly chat. Currently, it's the third Monday of each month at 9 p.m. ET in AOL Live (keyword **Live**). For 45 minutes, he answers questions and keeps everyone filled in on the latest AOL content and Internet game news. It's a hoot! Even though John specializes in the AOL (U.S.) interface, as a Canadian you're sure to get something out of his witty banter and insightful ways, if we do say so ourselves.

- ✔ Did you miss a theatre presentation you wanted to attend? No problem — just look for a transcript. Use keyword **AOL Live** and click Event Transcripts. Because all transcripts are plain text files, you can read them with any word processor.

- ✔ For a list of upcoming AOL Live events, use keyword **Live Guide**, or click the Coming Soon button in the Today on AOL Live window. Events in this folder are organized by date. Scroll through the list and double-click whatever event looks interesting to get the details.

Can(ada) We Talk, Eh?

Once you've honed your chatting skills, you'll want to take advantage of some Canada-specific chat areas. Besides the open-to-all "Canada Lobby-1," where you usually find yourself if you choose the Chat Now! option from the People Connection, there are several regularly scheduled chats with a little more direction available on AOL Canada. Three in particular deserve mention right now:

✔ **The Country Cabin** (keyword **Country Cabin**): What could be more Canadian — and more cozy — than a log cabin? The Country Cabin is the virtual equivalent. Pull up a chair and get ready for some relaxed conversation. You'll find some regulars and a lot of nice folks here when the cabin opens nightly at 10 p.m. Eastern time.

✔ **National Town Hall** (keyword **TownHall**): News junkies unite! In a country this big, there's always something in the news worth discussing by the end of the week. That's why the National Town Hall chat room opens the floodgates every Sunday evening between 9 p.m. and 11 p.m. EST. (On your way in, be sure to read up on the Hot Topics in the news by following the links on the right side of the Town Hall window. They'll take you to recent articles filed in the AOL Canada News channel.)

✔ **Back Bacon Caf-eh** (keyword **BackBacon**): Had a long day at work? Feel like a little light banter? Then stroll into AOL Canada's nightly pub, affectionately known as the Back Bacon Caf-eh.

Recording Your Conversations

For whatever reason (whether it's simple paranoia or something more complex), you may want a record of what went on during a chat. Perhaps you're attending a forum conference centre presentation and need to review the chat for ideas. Or maybe you're just feeling a little cloak-and-dagger today and want to spy on your chat room friends. Whatever the reason, keeping a copy of your chats is easy.

To record the chat room you're in, choose File⇨Log Manager from the menu bar. This selection opens the Logging dialog box with the name of your chat room in the Room box. Click the Open button in the Chat Log area (near the top of the screen). In the Open Log dialog box, the chat room name automatically appears as your log name (you can change it if you want, by typing a new name for the file). Either click Save or press Enter to open the Log file. From that point on, any new chat text appears onscreen and gets saved on your disk drive. Text that was already onscreen before you started the log isn't in the file.

Chapter 10

Dropping a Quick "Hello" with Instant Messages

*Y*ears ago, when the world was young and we thought brick-size desktop calculators and LED watches were still pretty neat, saying "Hi" to your friends meant either calling them on the phone or sending them a quick note through the (gasp!) postal mail. As time went by, immediate gratification won out over genteel manners; thus phone calls became the norm.

The online world took immediate gratification to a whole new level by delivering messages anywhere in the world within moments. It also introduced new problems because the friends who used to live next door now live in the next time zone (or, worse, the second continent on the left just past that ocean over there). E-mail still flies through the wires with the greatest of speed, but it's not interactive — you can't enjoy the back-and-forth exchange of ideas that a good, old-fashioned phone call provides.

Because programmers abhor missing features, the clever developers at AOL Canada came up with the Instant Message system. *Instant messages* blend the immediacy of e-mail with the interactivity of a phone call by letting you type back and forth with someone else on the system. It all happens right now — or, as the computer people say, in *real time* (as opposed to fake time . . . well, you know what we're getting at) — like a private, one-on-one chat room.

This chapter explores the Instant Message system and details how to send and receive instant messages (or IMs, for short), how to encourage people who aren't (yet) using AOL Canada to get into the act, plus how to shut the little charmers off when you want to concentrate for a while.

Online Telepathy with Instant Messages

Sometimes, you just want to drop a quick "Hi!" to someone you happen to bump into online. That's what the AOL Canada Instant Message feature is for. It's an easy way to have a quick conversation with someone regardless of whatever else either of you is doing at the time (see Figure 10-1). Instant messages are private, too — only you and your correspondent see what passes between you.

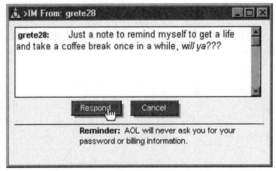

Figure 10-1:
An instant message appears.

The title bar of the box tells you the screen name of the person who just "dinged" you. Just below that is the message area itself, where your online conversation takes place. Along the bottom of the Instant Message window sit two action buttons:

- **Respond** ships a message right back to the original sender.
- **Cancel** makes the message go away, never to be seen or heard from again.

If you do decide to respond, a new box will add itself under the original incoming message. Use the big white text area to write your message, then choose one of the two action buttons along the bottom of the text area, as shown in Figure 10-2:

- **Send** ships a message to the original sender.
- **Cancel** makes the message go away, never to be seen or heard from again. (That's in case you write something but like it better in your imagination than on someone's screen.)

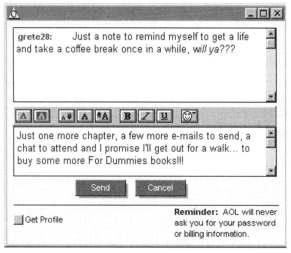

One more option is presented on the bottom left corner of the window:

✔ **Get Profile** allows you to retrieve the IM sender's Member Profile (if
they were so kind as to fill one out like a good citizen. (Enough with the
preaching, eh? Okay. No more . . . for now!)

Starting your own Instant Message is easy — here's how they work:

1. **Click the IM icon below the People button on the toolbar and select
Instant Messages.**

   A brand-new, never-before-used Instant Message window appears, ready
   to be fired.

2. **To see whether someone is online, you've got three options: type the
screen name into the text box along the top of the Instant Message
window and click the Available? button along the bottom, check your
Buddy List, or use the Locate command (Ctrl+L).**

   The Buddy List system is a great tool for tracking your friends online. To
   find out more about it, see Chapter 12.

   You can send instant messages only to someone who's signed on *and*
   has the Instant Messaging option turned on in the AOL Canada Parental
   Controls area (keyword **Parental Controls**). You can also send to someone
   who's signed on to AIM (AOL Instant Messenger). Find out how AIM
   works later in this chapter, under the title "Bringing Others into the IM
   World Using AIM."

2. **If you found your target with the Locate command, click the Send IM button in the Locate dialog box. If you used the Buddy List, click the person's name and then click IM.**

   Either way, the Send Instant Message dialog box pops up.

3. **If it's not there already, type the person's screen name in the To box and press Tab to move the blinking cursor into the text area. Then type your message.**

   Keep instant messages short — 10 to 12 words is great. If you have something long to say, use e-mail.

4. **After you finish typing the message, click Send.**

   If the message's recipient is signed on and accepting instant messages, the Instant Message window briefly disappears from your screen and then reappears in the upper-left corner.

   If something goes wrong along the way (like the person isn't online right now or has blocked instant messages), the AOL Canada software displays a message to keep you informed.

When your friend gets the message, he can reply by clicking the Respond button. His message then appears on your screen, and you can start a running dialog. (That's assuming, of course, that your buddy wants to talk to you today. Never quite a sure thing.)

Turning Off Instant Messages Because Sometimes You Just Want to Be Alone

Life on AOL Canada sometimes resembles a huge commune. The moment you sign on, one (or sometimes several) of your friends immediately sends you an instant message and wants to chat. For hours.

If you want to check your e-mail in peace and quiet or perhaps do a little online research, you can easily hang out the Do Not Disturb sign by turning off incoming instant messages. The setting is temporary, so the next time you sign on to the system, instant messages are automatically turned *on* again.

To temporarily turn off the Instant Messaging feature, follow these steps:

1. **After signing on to AOL Canada, your Buddy List should appear on the right side of your screen. If the Buddy List window does not appear on your screen, select Buddy List from the People menu.**

2. **Click the Setup button in your Buddy List window. A Buddy List Setup window hops onto the screen.**

3. **Click on the Preferences button, and then click on the Privacy tab.**

4. **Choose the privacy preference that best suits you. You can block all Instant Messages, list the people that you want to block, or list the people from whom you will accept Instant Messages.**

5. **Select the "Buddy List and Instant Message" radio button and click Save.**

To turn the Instant Messaging feature back on without signing off from AOL, just repeat this process and select the Allow ALL Users to See and Contact Me option.

Bringing Others into the World of IMs using AIM

Whether or not it's smart, there are still a lot of Canadians who are not members of AOL Canada. It's true. Some of them may even be your friends or (gasp!) your relatives. Oh boy. How are you going to enjoy an Instant Message dialog with *them*? Easy: with AIM.

AIM (AOL Instant Messenger) is a little software program that anyone can download and use *for free*. Use keyword **AIM** to find out more, or visit the AOL.CA homepage, your starting-point for Internet jaunts of all kinds (keyword **AOL.CA**) or tell your friends who aren't using AOL Canada but have access to the Internet to visit www.aol.ca/aim. There, you'll find all the steps necessary to download the program. The whole process should only take a couple of minutes. Check out Figure 10-3 for an idea of what the software looks like once you're signed on.

To use AIM requires setting up a screen name (like your AOL Canada screen name but without all the extra privileges and content that come with an AOL Canada membership) and a password. Once people are signed on to AIM, you can send them an Instant Message using their new screen names, and they can send Instant Messages back. The dialog is on!

Some extra features to consider when recommending AIM to a friend include access to a continuous news ticker that parades the latest AOL Canada News channel headlines across your screen, as well as a stock ticker that keeps track of the ups and downs of a favourite company's performance on the stock market. AIM has a lot of impressive features and they're worth reading about. You can do that by clicking the AIM link under the Free Products heading at the AOL.CA homepage. We particularly like the FAQs you'll find there.

Figure 10-3:
AIM, or
AOL Instant
Messenger,
vastly
increases
the number
of people
who can
share the
Instant
Message
experience
with you.

Catching Password Scammers

Whenever you collect 26 million people in one place (even if it's a virtual place), somewhere in the mix you're bound to find a few undesirable characters. At home, it's the telemarketers. At work, it's the slightly unhinged co-worker who lines his cubicle with aluminum foil to block CSIS thought-control transmissions. In the online world, it's the password scammers.

These bottom-feeders want only one thing: your account password. Nobody — *nooo-body* — from AOL Canada or any other company will ever ask for your password. It won't happen! No matter *what* the person says in his or her message, no matter who he or she claims to be, he or she is *lying.* Pay no attention to this kind of drivel. Instead, get ready to report the person to AOL Canada.

If someone sends you an Instant Message or an e-mail asking for your password, credit card number, or anything else like that, report the person *immediately* with the Notify AOL service (for details, flip back a few pages to Chapter 9). Whether the person claims to be from the AOL Canada billing department, a credit card company, or Mars (which is where she *should* be), it's all a lie. You can find out more about this subject in Chapter 5, including a couple of sample scams, plus detailed instructions for nailing — er, reporting — these lowlifes.

Chapter 11

Cogitating, Consternating, and Conflagrating on the Message Boards

In This Chapter

▶ Frolicking in the folders

▶ Peeking at the messages (and adding some of your own)

▶ Touring the Canadian boards

You can't turn around on AOL Canada without running into a discussion. Whether you want to talk about music, mayhem, or something in between (like Cape Breton fiddling music — Hey! It's become very popular!), AOL Canada has a place for you somewhere.

After finding your online home, it's time to join the fray by diving into an online discussion. Of course, you need to know a few things to make sense of the whole thing. This chapter looks at these parts of the discussion world, guiding you along the sometimes obscure path toward joining a discussion group and posting your opinions in the message boards for all to see.

Wending Your Way through the Message Folders

Before joining a discussion, you have to find one. To do that, cruise around in your favourite online areas and look for an item labelled something like *Chat and Messages, Message Boards, Discussion Boards*, or perhaps just *Boards*. Any of these is a strong clue that you found a discussion area with message boards awaiting your thoughts.

Because details always make more sense if you know the terminology involved, here's a quick romp through the top message-board terms. Ready? Here goes:

- ✔ Message boards contain a bunch of individual *topics*, each of which is like a miniature bulletin board.
- ✔ *Topics*, in turn, list the member-created discussion subjects.
- ✔ *Subjects* contain one or more member-written *postings*.
- ✔ *Postings* hold your thoughts, carefully arranged and presented for maximum effect among your fellow discuss-ees.

With all that firmly in mind, press onward for a more detailed explanation of the whole menagerie.

After finding a likely-looking message board, you encounter a window like the one shown in Figure 11-1. This window gives you an overview of every *topic* and *folder* in a particular discussion area. The board shown in Figure 11-1 lists a bunch of topics — individual mini-bulletin boards focused on different discussions. Other message boards may include folders in this window's list. A single folder can hold a number of topics and may even contain other folders. Because the online staffers in charge of each discussion area organize the boards however they see fit, the organizational details of each area vary wildly among online forums.

Figure 11-1:
This
message
board
contains
several
topics and
one folder
(which leads
to more
topics).

⚠ Vegetarian & Vegan	❤ _ □ ✕
AOL Food: Vegetarian and Vegan recipes here. Please review the message board guidelines.	

Topics	Subjects
🗂 Vegetarian Appetizers & Snac	0
🗂 Vegetarian Beverages	0
🗂 Vegetarian Desserts	0
🗂 Vegetarian Entrees	0
🗂 Vegetarian Favorites	1
📁 Vegetarian Issues	6
🗂 Vegetarian Main Courses	0
🗂 Vegetarian Pasta	0
🗂 Vegetarian Sandwiches	1
🗂 Vegetarian Sauces and Condiments	0
🗂 Vegetarian Side Dishes	0
🗂 Vegetarian Snacks	0

List All	List Unread	Mark Read	More	Subscribe	Find Since

ABOUT MESSAGE BOARDS	PREFERENCES	HELP

Below the topic descriptions sit the *feature buttons*. You usually see six buttons there. Table 11-1 lists the buttons, along with brief descriptions of what each one does. These buttons are your tools for filtering the postings on a particular message board. Use them well (particularly the Find Since button) to make short work of keeping up with your favourite boards.

Table 11-1	Pressing the Message Board Buttons
Button Title	**Action**
List All	Opens the highlighted bulletin board topic and lists all the messages in it, whether or not you previously read them.
List Unread	Opens the current topic and displays only the messages you haven't read.
Mark Read	Marks all the messages in the current topic as though you have read them.
More	Lists the rest of the topics on the bulletin in the window (available only if a particular message board has numerous topics on it).
Subscribe	Adds the selected topic to the list of message boards you can read offline through Automatic AOL sessions. The list is kept at keyword **Read my boards**.
Find Since	Helps you search the message board for specific message posting dates or time periods. Choose either the New radio button, to see messages since you last visited, or the In Last (?) Days option, to specify a time period. Or you can click into the bottom row of text boxes to create a time period between two dates.

Here are a couple of tips and tricks to keep in mind with the message boards:

✔ Don't fret if you double-click a message item and AOL Canada replies with a terse message saying This message is no longer available. It just means that the message was posted so long ago that it was erased to make room for new ones. *Remember:* Old messages never die — they just scroll off the system.

✔ Use the Signature option in the Message Board Preferences window (it's one of the buttons on the very bottom) to automatically add a few words about yourself to the bottom of each posting. Remember that it's automatic — don't accidentally embarrass yourself.

✔ After your first visit to a topic area, save time by using the Find Since button to filter out old messages. That way, if you subscribe to an hourly price plan, you don't have to wade through everything you've already read while the online clock is ticking.

Reading, Replying To, and Generally Browsing the Messages

When you find an interesting topic, double-click its entry to display a window like the one shown in Figure 11-2. These topics are discussion subjects themselves — the real meat of a message board.

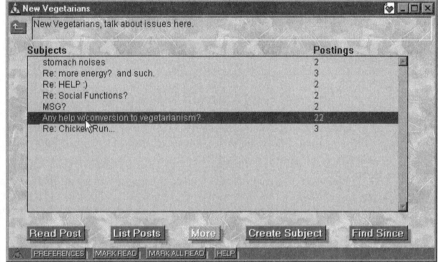

Figure 11-2:
The discussion is off and running in the subject window.

In the middle of the screen is the Subjects list, which displays the first 40 or so subjects that are open for debate. The Subjects list shows the title of the subjects and the current number of responses. To see a message within the subject, double-click the subject entry in this list, or click it once and then click Read Post.

The feature buttons along the bottom of the window let you do all sorts of fascinating things:

  ✔ Read Post does the same thing as double-clicking the subject name: It puts you in the discussion message window and displays the first posting for the selected subject.

   When you double-click a subject (or highlight one and click the Read Post button), the message appears in a window like the one shown in Figure 11-3. After all that effort, this window is surprisingly easy to use.

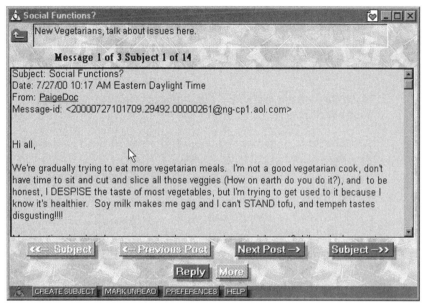

Figure 11-3:
Finally — a
message.

✔ List Posts generates a list of all posts within a particular topic, including who wrote the posting, how long it is, and the date and time it was written.

✔ The More button, like its counterpart in the topics window, comes into play only when you have so many messages that AOL Canada can't display them all on the first try. In that case, click More to tell the system that you want to occ more messages.

✔ Create Subject is your ticket to making a new discussion subject dedicated to whatever you jolly well want (is that ultimate power or what?).

✔ Find Since works just like it does in the topics window — it displays matching messages for each subject within the current topic.

✔ Cowering along the bottom of the window is the Preferences button (containing your bulletin board signature settings plus other preferences regarding which posts are displayed, how they're displayed, and how many are downloaded).

✔ Mark Read and Mark All Read are down there as well to let you ignore whatever messages you want.

✔ Help is AOL Canada's version of this checklist — you get an online explanation of all the buttons, similar to our descriptions here. (Although, surely, ours are more refined, given our literary skills and independence of spirit. Sorry, we couldn't resist.)

The message text dominates the windows (as it should — after all, that's why you came). Every AOL Canada message begins with a brief header giving the message's vital statistics: subject, posting date, author, and a grim-looking message ID that makes you wonder whether it's harbouring some secret code. The message follows.

Along the bottom is a whole raft of feature buttons that do just about anything your heart desires:

✔ The forward arrow and backward arrow Subject buttons move you to the next subject for this discussion.

✔ The Previous Post and Next Post display other thoughts on the current subject.

✔ Use Reply to add your thoughts to this group (*or thread*) of messages within the subject.

✔ Use More to, uh, see *more* postings.

Canadian Message Boards

Now that you've got the basics of message boards down pat, you'll want to know what other Canadians are interested in, right? The Canadian Message Boards (keyword **Cdn Boards**) are the place to start. Here, you can browse the entire collection of Canadian-based boards by clicking Main Collection, or scroll through the list on the right-hand side of the window under the heading Message Boards.

If you're trying to publicize a not-for-profit or charitable event in your area, you'll definitely want to check out the Community Bulletin Boards link in the Canadian Message Boards window. The people at AOL Canada designed this area specifically for postings about community-based events and information. Just click the area of the country you'd like to explore, and see what's going on in your neighbourhood.

Chapter 12

Where's Your Buddy?
Where's Your Pal?

● ●

In This Chapter

▶ Creating, deleting, and changing your Buddy List

▶ Maintaining your privacy

▶ Making your preferences clear

▶ Gathering in Groups@AOL

● ●

*G*athering your buddies for a chat meeting is always fun. After all — what would your life have been like these past few years without your best friend (or your cadre of best friends)? When you meet a new friend on AOL Canada, you can keep track of her screen name with the AOL Buddy List and avoid the frustrating experience of meeting a new best friend one day and losing her forever the next — all because you forgot her name!

This chapter explores the world of digital friend tracking, including creating, adding to, and deleting from your AOL Canada Buddy List. In case you find yourself in a talkative mood, you also find out how to send instant messages to your buddies and gather them for a cozy private chat, and how to use your Buddy List to tell if an e-mail recipient is online and ready for an Instant Message. Then we'll take you through the process of setting up your own private place on the Web to gather for chats, exchanging postings, scheduling events, and even posting pictures with friends and family using a new feature called Groups@AOL.

Who's Your Buddy?

At a glance, the Buddy List tells you which of your friends is online. It even organizes your buddies into groups, making the task of discerning the office crowd from the gang at last week's online Jell-O diving competition an easy one. (After all, the difference may be important, even if a few names overlap between the two.)

Your Buddy List jumps into action by default every time you sign on to AOL Canada, hanging out in the upper-right corner of the screen. (If you don't want the list to always come up, you can adjust the Buddy List's behaviour with the Buddy List preferences, covered later in this chapter.) As your buddies sign on and off the system, the list updates itself automatically.

The following sections cover all the important stuff you need to know about building, using, and changing your Buddy List on AOL Canada. For information about privacy preferences and Buddy List preferences, see the sections "Privacy Preferences: Please, I Vahnt to Be Alone" and "Setting Your Buddy List Preferences," later in this chapter.

What if some of your friends don't use AOL Canada? Are they lost forever? Goodness, no! Tell your other Internet-based friends about the cool AOL Instant Messenger feature (better known as *AIM*), which lets them send and receive instant messages, create a Buddy List, and do many other nifty tricks. Find out more about AIM in Chapter 10. For all the details, go to keyword **AIM** or www.aol.ca/aim (for your *Net.friends*).

Adding someone to a Buddy List

Including people on the Buddy List is a snap. Here's how to do it:

1. **In the Buddy List window, click the Setup button.**

   The Buddy List Setup window appears, just like the one shown in Figure 12-1.

   If your Buddy List window isn't already onscreen, use keyword **BuddyView** to open it.

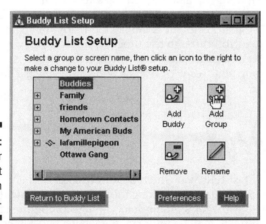

Figure 12-1: Tweak your Buddy List groups from this window.

2. **Highlight the name of the Buddy List group you want to bulk up with new members, by clicking it once with your mouse.**

   You can also right-click a group name to begin editing. This opens a menu that matches the options in the Buddy List setup window, except that you'll find one more option called Share Group. For details on how this option works, skip ahead to the section in this chapter about Groups@AOL.

   To create a new Buddy List group, see the following section, "Creating a new Buddy List group."

3. **Click the Add Buddy button in the setup window, or choose the Add Buddy option from the right-click menu.**

4. **In the Add New Buddy box, type the screen name of your buddy and then click Save.**

   Your buddy's screen name takes its place among the other members of that group.

5. **Repeat Steps 3 and 4 until all your buddies are in there.**

Creating a new Buddy List group

You've met a whole slew of new people in a particular chat room, on a message board, or through an e-mail mailing list. Keep track of them by creating a unique Buddy List group just for them:

1. **In the Buddy List window, click the Setup button.**

   The Buddy List Setup window appears, eagerly awaiting your new creation.

2. **Click the Add Group button to make a new Buddy List group and add people to it, or choose the Add Group option from the right-click menu.**

   The Add New Group window hops onto the screen, ready to accept a name for your new group.

3. **Type a name (up to 48 characters long) for the new group and then click Save.**

   The Buddy List now includes your new group, as shown in Figure 12-2.

4. **Follow the steps in the previous section, "Adding Someone to a Buddy List," to store all your buddies' screen names in your new group.**

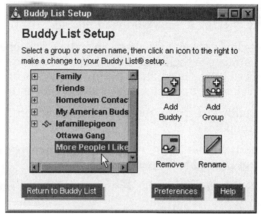

Deleting someone from a Buddy List group

Sad to say, sometimes buddies become ex-buddies. Your interests change, their interests change, and suddenly you no longer correspond. Or maybe your friend simply changed screen names, which means that you need to add her new screen name and delete the old one. Whether deleting a buddy from a Buddy List group is traumatic or transitional, AOL has provided a way to get the job done:

1. **In the Buddy List window, click the Setup button. The Buddy List Setup window appears.**

   If your Buddy List window isn't onscreen, keyword **Buddy** brings the Buddy List setup window to attention.

2. **Click the plus sign (+) to the left of the Buddy List group that contains the passé screen name or absent friend.**

   The Buddy group opens up, revealing the buddies you've previously added.

3. **Highlight your buddy's screen name in the group list and click the Remove button, or choose Remove from the right-click menu.**

   A small dialog box appears, asking you whether you're *sure* you want to delete this buddy.

5. **Click Yes to make the dialog box go away.**

   The Buddy List setup window shows its face again. This time, you see one fewer buddy in the Buddy List group you just edited. You can click the minus sign (–) to close up that particular group if you like neatness, but you don't have to — the job's already done.

Deleting a whole Buddy List

Once a year or so, you get the urge to clean house. Take a look at your Buddy List groups and see whether the urge also applies there. If you've been hanging on to Buddy List groups that contain no members, groups that track outdated interests, or lists of e-mail business addresses for the job you left 18 months ago, a little window cleaning may be in order:

1. **Click the Setup button on your Buddy List window to open the Buddy List Setup window.**

   If your Buddy List window isn't handily onscreen, use keyword **Buddy** to bring the Buddy List Setup window immediately into view.

2. **Click once on the Buddy List group you want to get rid of forever, to highlight it, and hit the Remove button, or select the Remove option from the right-click menu.**

   A small dialog box worriedly rushes to your screen, asking whether you truly want to delete the entire Buddy group.

3. **After you click Yes, the Buddy List setup window adjusts to the change, displaying one fewer Buddy List group in its collection.**

   Be very sure that you want to delete a Buddy List group before you click OK to delete the list. If you mistakenly delete the wrong list, you have to re-create that Buddy List group from scratch. This has already happened to you? Bummer. See the section "Creating a new Buddy List group," earlier in this chapter. It's not so bad.

Renaming a Buddy List group

You woke up this morning and realized that you'd found the perfect name for one of your existing Buddy List groups. Never fear — changing that Buddy List name is a snap:

1. **Click the Setup button in the Buddy List window to bring up the Buddy List Setup window.**

   If your Buddy List window is hiding from you, keyword **Buddy** calls the Buddy List setup window to your screen.

2. **Highlight the Buddy List group you want to rename and click the Rename button, or choose Rename from among the right-click menu options.**

   The Rename window jumps to attention.

   If you've used the right-click option, your cursor simply pops into the existing name — just start typing to begin renaming. This shortcut lets you skip the last step in this list.

Watch carefully — it even does tricks!

Now that you have these cool new Buddy List groups, what do you do with them? Well, plenty!

Want to know where your friend is hanging out online? Find her fast by highlighting her screen name and clicking the Locate button. (This also works by right-clicking a screen name and choosing Locate from the menu.)

Quickly send your friend an instant message by highlighting her screen name and clicking the IM button. (This option is also available in the right-click menu for individual screen names.) An Instant Message window opens onscreen with your friend's screen name already filled in.

If you had a more face-to-face discussion in mind, use the Chat feature to invite your buddy to a private chat room with the two of you (and whomever else you want to invite). See the "Buddy Chat" section, later in this chapter, for all the details.

The Buddy List gives you other helpful indications to let you know who is ready and able to "buddy around" right now — sort of the techno-equivalent of being able to keep an eye on the door for people who are arriving at or leaving a very cool party:

✔ You can always tell which of your buddies has most recently signed on because you'll see an asterisk beside her or his screen name in your Buddy List.

✔ Likewise, you'll see parentheses around the screen name of the buddy who has most recently signed off.

✔ Also, check out the numbers listed on the right of a Buddy group name. They should look something like (3/7) or (0/7). This tells you how many of your buddies in that particular group are signed on (three of seven in the first case, none in the second — hey! where are those guys?)

✔ Planning to step away from your computer? (How dare you, when so many buddies require your attention?) The least you can do is let them know you've got other responsibilities (like eating and bathing) by using the Away Message option that you'll find on the bottom left of your Buddy List window. Choose one of the default messages or edit your own, and while you've stepped away the system automatically responds to instant messages with something like "Auto response from Grete 27: I have stepped out to lunch."

---

3. **Type the new name for your Buddy List group.**

   Choose a name that's representative of the whole group or one that helps you remember why you've placed these screen names together.

4. **Click Save to make your changes a reality.**

   After the dialog box disappears, you see an updated Buddy List setup window that proudly displays your new Buddy List group name.

Privacy Preferences: Please, I Vahnt to Be Alone

You don't have to be a movie star to want a little privacy every now and then. Sometimes, you just want to get away from it all and enjoy some peace and quiet. That's why the Buddy List system includes a whole collection of privacy preferences.

If you don't want people to track your screen name with a Buddy List, that's easy to set up. Here's what to do:

1. **In the Buddy List window, click Setup.**

   If your Buddy List window isn't visible, use keyword **BuddyView** to make it magically appear. Then click the Setup button.

   The Buddy List setup window appears onscreen.

2. **Click the Preferences button in the Buddy List setup window and click the Privacy tab (it's the last on the right, near the top of the window).**

   You see the Privacy Preferences window, very similar to the one shown in Figure 12-3, jump to the screen.

   Although it looks rather daunting, this window is easy to configure. The left side of the window shows two sections — *Choose Your Privacy Preferences* and *Apply Preferences to the Following Features*. Each section contains two or more radio buttons; clicking one to select it deactivates all the others.

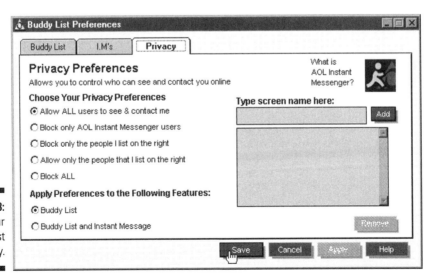

Figure 12-3: Regain your Buddy List privacy.

3. **Select the radio button to activate whichever privacy level you prefer.**

   • **To allow everyone who uses instant messages to see and contact you (including AOL Instant Messenger users on the Internet):** Select the Allow ALL Users to See and Contact Me option.

   • **To narrow down the people who can contact you to AOL members only:** Select the Block Only AOL Instant Messenger Users radio button.

   • **To either allow or prevent a few users from tracking you on their Buddy Lists:** Select either the "Block only the people that I list on the right," or the "Allow only the people I list on the right" radio button. Then type the specific screen name you want to block or allow in the Type Screen Name Here box and click Add. Add as many screen names as you want to block (or allow).

   • **To completely block yourself from Buddy Lists all over AOL worldwide (including AOL Instant Messenger users on the Internet):** Select the Block All radio button.

4. **Decide whether to apply these preferences for your Buddy List only or for both your Buddy List and Instant Messages.**

   We recommend using the Buddy List setting rather than the Buddy Lists and Instant Messages option. The latter option is best if you want to strictly limit who can see you with a Buddy List or send you instant messages.

5. **After you finish setting your privacy preferences, click Save.**

6. **Click the upper-left corner of the Buddy List setup window to close it.**

   Continue with your regularly scheduled online experience, free from unwanted interruptions.

Setting Your Buddy List Preferences

Some days, you want sound in your world; other days, the mere thought of extra noise makes your head pound. Set your general Buddy List preferences to match your mood. Opt for or against sounds when your buddies come and go, and tell the system whether you want to see your Buddy List every time you sign on.

To set your Buddy List preferences:

1. **Click the Setup button in the Buddy List window to bring the Buddy List setup window to attention.**

   If your Buddy List window is nowhere to be seen, keyword **Buddy** wakes the Buddy List setup window, and it jumps smartly to attention.

2. **Click the Buddy List Preferences button to open the Buddy List Preferences dialog box.**

   If it's not already front-and-centre, click the Buddy List tab to bring the Buddy List Preferences window to the fore.

3. **To see your Buddy List every time you sign on, select the check box that says** Show Me My Buddy List At Sign On.

   The default setting is to display your Buddy List when you sign on. If waiting that few extra seconds for the Buddy List window to load every time you sign on really annoys you, de-select it and use keyword **BuddyView** to see your Buddy List whenever you want to.

4. **Make sound decisions (sorry — you couldn't expect us to resist a pun like that one).**

   The two remaining options deal with sound. To hear a sound when your buddies arrive, select the Play Sound When Buddies Sign On check box. To hear sound when your friends leave, select the Play Sound When Buddies Sign Off check box.

   Click only one if you want to be notified by sound only when friends sign on or off; click both to hear when they come and go. If your Buddy List groups are large and their members active, the constant noises may grate on your nerves after a while. If that happens, use the Buddy List Preferences dialog box to de-select the sound options.

   To hear Buddy List sounds, you need to download the Buddy Sound Installer file. The default sound for your Buddy List is an opening and closing door; if you select the sound options and don't hear the door when the next buddy comes or goes, click the Go to Sound Library button in the Buddy List Preferences window to open the Buddy List Sounds information. Then click the Download Buddy Sound Installer Door Theme button to open the download window for the sound installer. Click Download Now to begin the download.

   If you want to see other available Buddy List sounds, click the Buddy List Sound Library button in the Buddy List Sounds window. Download any of the sounds in the list that tweak your fancy.

7. **After you finish setting your Buddy List preferences, click Save.**

   You now find yourself back at the friendly Buddy List setup window.

8. **If you're happy with the Buddy List preferences and don't want to change anything else, click the upper-left corner of the Buddy List setup window.**

   It merrily retires to windowland to await your next summons.

Building an Online Treehouse with Buddy Chat

Instant message conversations have their place, but for extended chatter, using the AOL chat rooms is better. Chat rooms offer a larger text area for scrolling messages and the ability to talk to more than one person at a time. (Flip to Chapter 9 for more on chatting.) With the AOL Canada Buddy Chat feature, the system quickly creates a private chat room and invites the screen names you specify.

Here's how you create a Buddy Chat of your own:

1. **Select the name of a buddy you want to chat with and then click the Chat button in the Buddy List window.**

   The Buddy Chat window appears with the screen name of your buddy already in the Screen Names to Invite window.

   To invite a whole bunch of buddies, click a Buddy group entry (like Family or Friends, for example) rather than clicking a single buddy's screen name.

   AOL fills in the screen names of your selected buddy or buddies, as the case may be. Their names appear in the Screen Names to Invite box. You can now add more names (separated by a comma), or remove names you'd prefer not to invite this time.

2. **Alter the buddies in your list as you like by erasing names and filling in others.**

   Invite only one person or as many as you can reasonably fit into a chat room (23 people total, including you) and still have a good time.

3. **In the Message to Send box, type a reason for getting together.**

   AOL helpfully starts your message with `You are invited to`; either complete it or replace it with a phrase of your own.

   Some invitations, like "You are invited to a public beheading," tend to turn people off. Spend a couple of seconds to make it sound inviting if you want your friends to attend your chat.

4. **In the Name of Private Chat Room window, type a superior-sounding name for your chat room.**

5. **Change any (or all) of the chat room names to make them more friendly.**

   AOL Canada also provides help here, giving you a chat room name made up of your screen name and some other stuff (numbers, usually). Either leave it as is and click Send to whisk the invitation off to your buddies, or click into the text box and get inventive!

AOL chooses these chat room names to minimize the chance of having someone you don't know drop in to your private chat room. If you change the chat room name to something more generic, such as I love dogs or Jane, you may receive a surprise visitor every now and then as someone else coincidentally thinks up your chat room name. If this happens, simply tell them that you're sorry, but their chat room name is already taken. Most of the time, they leave as quickly as they came.

6. **After you add, alter, and amend your invitation to your heart's content, click Send.**

   Your Buddy Chat invitation wings its way to your friends.

   To ensure that you're not forgotten, an invitation appears on your screen too. Figure 12-4 shows you a sample.

   The invitation also features an IM button. You may receive an instant message from a buddy in a teasing mood or from someone who had a momentary brain lapse on your screen name's identity.

Figure 12-4: Anyone for a private Buddy Chat?

7. **Click Go to enter the chat room.**

   You arrive in the chat room you created and await your buddies. After you're in the room, you find that it works just like a normal private chat — mostly because it is a private chat room. (For a quick refresher on private chat rooms, flip to Chapter 9.)

8. **Greet your buddies as they drop in to the room, and have a great conversation!**

Finding a Web-Based Home Using Groups@AOL

So you've learned to like gathering people together using things like the group contacts in your Address Book (more on these in Chapter 8), private chat rooms (described at length in Chapter 9), message boards (all about these places in Chapter 9), and now Instant Messages (Chapter 10) and the Buddy List (this very chapter). Phew! You've learned a lot, haven't you?

But if you still hunger for more gathering options, you're in luck. With AOL Canada Version 6.0 software, you have another very powerful tool to bring family, friends, classes, or any other group of people you can think of, together in a private spot on the Web: Groups@AOL. You set it up, you control it, you choose who can see it, and, if need be, you dismantle it. It's truly a place to call your own, and it gives you, the person who sets up the group, a ton of free benefits, including

- ✔ A private Web page that only you and the people you invite can see.
- ✔ An online meeting place where you can post messages, schedule events, list favourite places, and even build a picture gallery.
- ✔ A customizable spot that can be tweaked to suit family, friends, classrooms, or clubs.
- ✔ The ability to tell when members of your group are visiting your group's Web page using your Buddy List, and a group entry in your Address Book so you can send e-mail to all your group members at the same time.
- ✔ The power to invite non–AOL Canada members to join, attend scheduled events, or assist in maintaining things like a photo gallery.

The setup process for Groups@AOL is a bit involved, consisting of lots of steps — although none is very difficult. You just need a bit of patience. Trust us, the results are worth the effort. Begin by choosing People⇨Groups@AOL from the toolbar. Take some time to read through the guidelines and help areas before you begin.

Remember, everything you need to begin your journey into the world of AOL Canada is on the CD-ROM inside the cover of this book. It holds Version 6.0 of the access software — the latest and best yet!

1. **To get to Groups@AOL, choose People⇨Groups@AOL or use keyword** Groups.

2. **Type your group name in the dialog box.**

You'll also be asked to type a brief description that will let invited group members know what the group is all about, and you'll also be asked to select a time zone (after all, this is a very big country). Then click Submit.

As the person creating the group, you are known as the *Founder*, and you will also have to review and agree to AOL's guidelines and Terms of Use before going on to the next step. Only AOL Members can be group founders. However, anyone can be invited to join a group.

3. Choose a title and theme.

The title will be displayed at the top of your group's main page. Select a theme that will organize the page according to the type of group you want to create: family, friends, or an activity group.

Choosing the Family Theme displays any posted pictures at the very top of the page, the Friends Theme gives priority to postings by members, while the Activity Groups Theme brings events to the fore.

4. Choose one of the available styles.

Hey, looks count. You want people to feel at home, right? Decorate your group's page with one of the styles available. They include several fun combinations of colour and symbol options.

5. Create your member profile.

The founder and group members can each create a member profile that includes the person's name and birth date. You can also choose an image or icon to represent yourself. And you can specify who can see your member profile — only AOL members, or anyone invited to a group (which includes non-AOL members).

Entering your birth date is fun, because once you've saved it as part of your member profile, it is automatically added to your group's list of upcoming events — no more excuses for other members missing such a crucial occasion.

Congratulations! You've just founded a group. You can visit your new group using the hyperlink displayed on the Congratulations page, review the settings you've chosen for your group, or, better yet, start inviting members to your group. After all, what's a founder without members to enjoy what is founded?

To begin the process of inviting right away, just click the link provided. You'll immediately arrive at the Invite page, where you can type in screen names or Internet e-mail addresses as you please.

Soon after you complete the process of creating a Group@AOL, you'll get an e-mail from the good people at AOL Canada explaining the privileges and weighty responsibilities that come with this accomplishment. Follow the links imbedded in the message to learn more about groups, and enjoy! The more you use your Groups, the more they'll start to feel like home.

There's more than one way to join a group, You don't always have to be a founder. Other founders can set up a group and invite you to join as a member. Later, you can even participate in the management of the group by becoming an *owner* (a member who helps the founder maintain the group's main page and membership list).

Parents who have set up restricted-access screen names for their children using the Kids Only or Young Teen categories will receive a copy of any invitations their kids receive to join a group. As a parent, you then have to give permission to your kids to join. Remember, Groups@AOL are private and aren't monitored for content by AOL Canada. We strongly encourage you to read the Note to Parents in the Groups@AOL user guide for a more complete set of warnings that will arm you and your children against inappropriate content or behaviour in the groups.

Part III

Diving into the
Fun Stuff

The 5th Wave   By Rich Tennant

"HONEY! OUR WEB BROWSER GOT OUT LAST NIGHT
AND DUMPED THE TRASH ALL OVER MR. BELCHER'S
HOME PAGE!"

In this part . . .

Okay, so you're not easily impressed — e-mail doesn't do much for you, discussion boards warm your fires only a little, and chats leave you utterly cold. You tend to repeat the question time and again: "So what can you really *do* with AOL Canada?" Yet you know that the online world truly is the Next Big thing and you want to join in the fun.

Welcome to Part III — your field guide for the Digital Age, offering tips for finding the who, what, and where of digital life; techniques for researching the topics that tweak your curiosity; and suggestions for picking out the *perfect* game to play while frittering away the hours. To make this part complete, we also include an Internet chapter, with the lowdown on everything from gophers to the Web.

Chapter 13

Finding People, Places, Things, and Information

In This Chapter

▶ Uncovering the Search button

▶ Finding people and businesses

▶ Discovering great online places and resources

▶ Digging up deals

▶ Finding disk-filling files and programs

· ·

*I*f we could get a nickel for every time someone asks us how to find things in the online world, we'd ask for a loonie instead. (A nickel doesn't buy anything these days.) Whatever the payment, we would be up to our eyeballs in money. That's because tracking stuff down on AOL Canada and the Internet is (ahem) challenging — or at least it was challenging before those clever programmer types invented the supercool search systems.

Whether you want something specific or feel like browsing aimlessly for a while, start your hunt here, with the various search systems available throughout AOL Canada. This chapter reveals the search oracle's mystic secrets, starting with the Search button and continuing with a romp through all your search-related tools. Whether you seek an online area, Web page, favourite quotation, obscure fact, e-mail address, or business phone number, the AOL Canada search tools make quick work of the job.

Finding People: Sniffing Out Friends, Acquaintances, and Other Novel Folks

Even though the world of AOL Canada is packed with information covering every topic under the sun, it's the people that make life fun — people who populate the chat rooms, fill the message boards, and pack the audiences at live online events. No matter what brought you to AOL Canada, the community is what keeps you there.

Find it all with AOL Canada Search

It's time for a quick experiment.

With no special equipment and nothing up our sleeve (at least nothing that household remedies can't treat), we shall now attempt to link two ideas within the recesses of your mind. Ready to begin? First, think of the word *look*. Got it? Good. Now, use keyword **Search** or click the Search button on the right end of your navigation bar to open the very slick AOL Canada Search window. Softly repeat the word *look* as

you gaze at the AOL Canada Search window. Whenever you want to *look* for something but you don't know where to start, think of AOL Canada Search, the single best AOL Canada starting point for the whole search experience.

From this one window, reaching all the system's search services is a snap. Whether you seek people to meet, places to visit, or things to do, AOL Canada Search has the tools you need.

Locating folks to see who's around

The AOL Canada Locate command gives you a quick way of finding your friends. If you know your pal's screen name, the Locate command tells you whether your compatriot is signed on at the moment and also reports whether she is in a chat room. If your friend is chatting the light fantastic in a public chat room, auditorium, or conference room, the Locate system automatically offers to take you right to that chat. (Ahh . . . this is definitely one of those "Isn't technology wonderful?" moments.)

Speaking of technology, AOL Canada also includes a way for you to prevent people from finding you with instant messages and in your Buddy List. To find out more about the built-in privacy options, stealthily slink on to Chapter 12.

To quickly find someone online with Locate, follow these steps:

1. **Either press Ctrl+L or choose People➪Locate AOL Member Online.**

   The Locate Member Online dialog box appears onscreen, ready and willing to do its thing.

2. **Type the screen name in the dialog box and either press Enter or click OK.**

   The system searches hither, thither, and even yon to see whether the person you seek is signed on to AOL Canada or anywhere on the AOL worldwide network.

If the person is signed on right now (and if he didn't block you through the Buddy List system's privacy preferences), AOL Canada displays the Locate dialog box, as shown in Figure 13-1. The system giddily announces that it found him and tells you whether he is in a public chat room or private chat room or just skulking around the system waiting for you. If your pal is in a public chat room, the dialog box also gives you the room name and offers a Go button so that you can join him there. The dialog box also offers a button to send the person an Instant Message.

If the person you seek is not online at the moment, a vaguely sad dialog box tells you so. In that case, be sure to check your spelling because AOL Canada doesn't say, "Whoops, you misspelled the screen name" — instead, it looks for a person with the screen name you typed, whether or not it's a valid AOL Canada screen name.

Figure 13-1:
Hey —
Marguerite's
signed on
with that
weird
screen
name of
hers!

grete27 is in chat room "Lobby" in public category "Canada."

Go   Send IM   Cancel

Searching the Member Directory

It doesn't matter whether you like to dress up like the late, great Maurice "Rocket" Richard (even outside hockey season), or meditate in front of the TV while considering Zen and its effects on game show hosts. With more than 26 million members of AOL around the world, you're very likely to find people just like (or significantly similar to) you somewhere on the system. The trick is finding them — and being found yourself.

To ensure that you are found, fill out your online profile. If you haven't done your profile yet, there's no time like the present. Mark your place in this book, sign on to AOL Canada, choose Settings⊅My Member Profile from the toolbar, and fill out the profile dialog box. After you finish, click Update to save your profile information and then come back to the book (yes, we'll wait for you). Now that your profile is done, you're part of the Member Directory. Congratulations.

If you want an incredibly fancy profile that's sure to make people stop and say, "Hey, that's an incredibly fancy profile," flip to Chapter 22.

Now that your information is in the system, try searching the Member Directory for friends-to-be. To do that, follow these steps:

1. **Use keyword** Member Directory **to bring up the Member Directory dialog box.**

   The Member Directory Search dialog box appears.

2. **Type something that describes the people you want to find: a hobby you enjoy, the city you're from, your occupation, or whatever else you can think of.**

   Short descriptions work best. Check your spelling — you don't want a typo standing between you and your friends-to-be!

3. **Click Search to see whom you can see (like the bear going over the mountain — remember that tune from childhood?).**

   If AOL Canada reports that it can't find anyone, check your spelling again (it never hurts) or search for some other unique characteristic. If everything works, the dialog box overflows with possible new friends. (Okay — it doesn't really overflow, but that's poetic licence for "There are so many entries that a scroll bar appears next to the list.")

4. **Double-click anyone who looks interesting. Jot down the screen name (or add it to your Address Book), write a "Hi, how ya doing?" e-mail message, and see where it goes from there.**

When you reach this last step, remember that you get only one chance to make a good first impression. Make your introductory e-mail message witty, genteel, interesting, and, most of all, polite. If the person in question never writes back to you, don't take it personally — just search the Member Directory again and look for someone else to correspond with instead.

Finding friends with the AOL Canada People Finder

AOL has more than 26 million members worldwide, but that number pales against the countless millions who inhabit the Internet worldwide. Even though nothing exactly like the AOL Member Directory exists for the Internet, the AOL Canada People Finder makes a good start.

The AOL Canada People Finder is just what it sounds like — a white-pages–style listing of names, addresses, phone numbers, and e-mail addresses for Canadian residents. Because the information in the People Finder is drawn from publicly available sources (such as the paper-based white pages), the odds are good that both you and your friends are already listed. Even though you're in the system, there's no guarantee that the information about you is accurate. (Ah, the joys of information in the electronic age, eh?)

In addition to address and e-mail information for individuals, the system also includes a whole section devoted to business information. The Business Finder works in much the same way as does the version for individuals, so just pay attention to the prompts as you work through the dialog boxes; your business searches should go as successfully as your other explorations.

Searching the system involves only a few steps. Here's what to do:

1. **Either use keyword** People Finder **or choose** People⇨People Finder **from the toolbar to open the AOL Canada People Finder.**

   The Web browser pops up, filled to the brim with the People Finder Web page. You'll see the Find a Person heading front and centre.

   If you want to look for business listings, scroll around this page until you find a link to the Business Finder. Click the link to start your business search. Looking for someone outside Canada? Scroll down until you see the International Directory link.

2. **Fill in whatever information you have about the person (such as the name, city, and province), and then click Find People.**

   The People Finder engine chews on your information for a while and then displays its search results.

3. **If the system found your person (or a group of people, if you did a more general search), it lists the name and address it came up with from the Finder's database.**

   If you see more than one name, scroll through the list until you find the specific person you want.

   On the other hand, if the system doesn't find your person, try leaving off the first name or shortening the name to just the first few letters. Searching for Dave, for example, won't find your person if he's listed as David. Try using Dav for the search because that matches both variations.

Finding Places: Tracking Interests and Meeting Informational Needs

Do you ever sit in front of your computer, staring at the AOL Canada screen, knowing that what you want to know just *has* to be in there somewhere? If only you knew where to look . . . [insert wistful sigh here].

The next time that feeling strikes, fire up one of the AOL Canada topical search systems. These routines search not only the content areas within AOL Canada but also the wealth of stuff on the World Wide Web to match you with precisely the place you want.

When you're looking for a particular topic, start with AOL Canada Search first (keyword **Search**), then use one of the other Web search engines discussed later in this chapter (read the section called "AOL.CA"), as a backup.

You can also try typing a few words into the small text box on the right end of the navigation bar and clicking the Search button.

Find it on AOL Canada

To track down an online community for your favourite topic, try the handy AOL Canada Search system. AOL Canada Search takes any word you type (like *homework, finances,* or *photography*) and looks for that subject in the database of interesting Internet sites. The system lists everything it finds relating to your subject.

The search begins

To start searching, sign on to AOL Canada and follow these steps:

1. **In the text box on the right side of the navigation bar, type the word or words you're looking for and click Search.**

   After a moment, the AOL Canada Search page pops up, displaying the results of your search, just like in Figure 13-2. The system splits your results into sections: Recommended Sites (features Web sites and AOL Canada areas), Matching Categories (lists of related sites), and Matching Sites (other individual Web sites and AOL Canada areas that match your search terms).

   If the system displays a window apologizing that it couldn't find any matches for the topic you entered, don't worry — you didn't do anything wrong. Instead, close the gee-I'm-sorry-I-failed-you window and search with a different word. If you run out of terms, take your search out to the World Wide Web through AOL.CA Search, discussed later in this chapter.

   You can also begin your search by using keyword **Search**. This brings you straight to the AOL Canada Search window. Now, type the word or words you're looking for into the search box and click Search.

2. **Browse through the search results to see what AOL Canada found for you. To view something on the list, click its entry. To see more matching sites, click one of the Next links.**

Figure 13-2:
Whether
your topic is
general or
a little
esoteric, the
odds are
good that it's
somewhere
on AOL or
the Internet.

When you click an item in the Results list, the information hops into view, either in the Web browser window (where the search information was just a moment ago) or in an entirely new window (if the area lives inside AOL Canada itself). Pretty cool, eh?

3. **After you're done with that particular area, go back to the Search Results window to look for other items of interest.**

   If the stuff you looked at replaced the Search Results window, use the Back button on the navigation bar to flip back to the search information. (Or, if all else fails, just start your search over again.)

4. **To start another search, close the various windows and start over at Step 1.**

   If you don't feel like looking for anything else right now, feel free to close all the search-related windows. (There's no penalty for tidiness.)

The plot thickens

Once you get cozy with the basics of an AOL Canada Search, dare to go the next step: Explore the Search Options. How? Here we go:

1. **Use keyword** Search **to open the AOL Canada Search window.**

2. **Click the yellow Search Options link (to the left of the Help link under the Search box).**

   The not-so-flashy but very handy Search Options window appears and asks you to follow three simple steps before clicking that tempting Search button.

3. **Type one or more words into the Must Contain text box, then choose a radio button to specify whether you want to look for all the words at the same time, or any one of them.**

   This step gives AOL Canada Search some *parameters* (good word, eh? it means guiding principles) in order to focus its efforts. If you're interested in dogs, for example, you might try typing `dogs training tricks` into the Must Contain box, then choose the All of These Words radio button to look for all the terms at once.

   The more specific you are in your choice of search words, the better your chances of finding what you want. If you only enter one word (`dog`, for example), your search might yield too many results that won't interest you. . . . Then again, maybe you're just one of those people that *cannot* get enough of canines. Hey, it's a free country!

4. **Type one or more words into the Must Not Contain text box, then choose a radio button to specify whether you want your search to ignore all the words at the same time, or any one of them.**

AOL's American and Canadian versions face off in search of information

Now, there's a title that's worthy of a diplomatic row! As we discussed in the introduction to this book, some of AOL's keywords and channels link you to not-specifically-Canadian content areas. These areas are generally a product of the U.S. version of AOL. Most of the time, though, the information you'll find in those areas is universal enough to suit people everywhere.

Well, what's true for keywords and channels is also true for searches. Depending on how you conduct your search, you'll either end up in the AOL Canada Search window, or the AOL Search window. "Which is better," you ask, "the Canadian or the U.S. search system?" That probably depends on what kind of passport you hold! Okay. Joking aside, the searches are essentially the same.

Likewise, if you use keyword **Search** (as we describe under the heading "Find It on AOL Canada" earlier in this chapter), you will also be whisked away to the AOL Canada Search window. Using keyword **Search** is also good because the AOL Canada Search window has Canadian categories for you to browse. (For more on this, see the section titled "AOL.CA Search.")

This step is optional, but it's designed, once again, to give AOL Canada Search even tighter parameters (there's that great word again). Using our dogs example, then, you might try typing `breeding exotic` into the Must Not Contain box, then choose the Any of These Words radio button to reject results that would steer your search away from dog training.

5. **Choose where you want AOL Canada Search to look for results, by selecting one of the radio buttons.**

   You have three options: AOL Canada and the Web, AOL Canada only, or the Web only. Obviously, the first option will give you the biggest pool to search through.

6. **Click Search to begin your search.**

   After a moment, your results are displayed in descending order, starting with the sites that most closely fall within the, um, parameters (sorry) you set up. Hey! Look what we found! A site that sells the "Amazing Dog Trick Training Video." Hey, Fido, come here, boy!

Surfing — er, searching — the channels

When the folks at AOL Canada redesigned the channel lineup, they moved things around, pushed the content areas into different cubbyholes, and generally gave the whole place a clean, freshly painted look. They also added a cool tool to your arsenal of goodies: a vastly improved channel search system. (To find out more about the channels, visit the yellow *AOL Canada For Dummies Channels Directory* in this book.)

Although every channel needs a search option, not every channel has one. As we write this, several of the Canadian channels don't have their own search. For example, the Health channel includes search systems focused on finding particular health problems, but nothing that scours the whole Health channel.

The search system includes cool features, such as content limits that control where you want to find information and a filter to adjust how narrowly or broadly you want to search. All in all, the channel search system is a big improvement over the old way of searching the channels. You do, however, need to invest a few minutes in figuring out how to make the channel search system work.

To simplify that task, we present you with the following steps. They guide you through the channel search process in an utterly painless way. (If your personal pain quotient is low today, feel free to slam your head into the wall between steps.) Here's what to do:

1. **Go to a channel you want to search.**

   If the channel window is nowhere to be seen on your screen, click Show Channels on the far left side of your navigation bar, then click the channel name that interests you.

2. **Click the search item for that channel.**

   After a moment of deep thought, the channel's Search window pops up.

   The Search window occasionally hides in the channel windows (it's a little shy — you know how software sometimes gets), but if you look carefully, you can find it.

3. **Browse through the list of available topics on the item list.**

   When you find a description that looks interesting, click its *hyperlink* (the colourful underlined text) to visit the area.

Digging a little deeper

The Search system has more than one button and a cool window. In fact, you'll find lots of searching resources all over AOL Canada. The trick, as usual, is knowing where to look. (*Yes,* it's frustrating when you can't find the sites to help you look for things, but at least *now* you know where they are!)

The following bullets point out the other search-thingies lurking on the AOL Canada toolbar menus and skulking around the system:

✔ **Find Public and Member Chats (choose People⬦Find a Chat from the toolbar):** Click the Search All People Connection Chats to bring up the Search Featured Chats window, where you can browse through the featured chat or member chat room lists or search through the chats by room name to find *precisely* the one you want.

✔ **General AOL Canada Help (keyword Help):** Cruise through the Member Services area for tips and information about life in the online world.

✔ **Canada Message Boards (keyword Cdn boards):** Find other Canadians who've spoken up and pinned up electronic messages to one of the Canadian electronic bulletin boards. Subject areas range from Sports to Canadian News.

✔ **AOL Canada Newsletter (keyword AOLCanadaNews):** There's nothing sweeter than free insider tips. Get lots of those and lots more by subscribing to the *AOL Canada Newsletter.* It's delivered once a month to your mailbox and will keep you on top of new additions to the AOL Canada community . . . and did we mention it's free?

✔ **AOL Canada Chat Schedule (click the Chat icon on the toolbar):** Click the AOL Chat Schedule option to bring up the Canada Chat window, where all the regularly scheduled Canadian chats are listed, including chat groups created by AOL members themselves.

AOL.CA Search

It seems like almost everybody (including the local plumber) offers information through the World Wide Web these days. That diversity makes the Web an incredible repository of information — like a library filled with the collected knowledge, opinions, and ramblings of a measurable percentage of the world's populace. Sounds almost too good to be true, doesn't it?

Well, you're right — there *is* a catch. Although the Web world is filled to the brim with cool stuff, organizationally speaking it's a mess. Imagine a library organized by a tornado, with assistance provided by every kindergartner in your hometown. Not a pretty picture, is it?

Shortly after the Web came to be, many clever people built indexes and search systems to tame this wild digital frontier. Some of these tools catalogue sites and then help you search the list by a keyword you entered. Others take a slightly different approach by building a topic index you browse by clicking onscreen menus. Both systems have their advantages, depending on what you want to find and how you feel like looking for it.

The AOL Canada foray into the world of Web searching is AOL.CA Search. Just click the Internet icon on the toolbar and the AOL.CA home page jumps to attention. Now, type the word or words you're looking for into the Search the Web text box and click Search. AOL.CA goes poking all over the Web to dig up likely matches.

AOL.CA gives you the best of both worlds, by offering both a searchable database and a browsable subject index:

✔ **Go topic hopping through AOL.CA:** Just click one of the Web Centres, Shortcuts, or Shopping links at the bottom of the window. Each leads to more detailed lists. Keep clicking until you dig your way down to a particular site that meets your needs. If you click your way to the bottom of the barrel without finding a good match, try a keyword search instead.

✔ **Use AOL.CA Search's fill-in-the-blank search option:** Type a word or two describing your topic into the text box in the middle of the AOL.CA window. (It's hard to miss because it's set against a bright red banner.) Then click the ever-exuberant Search! button. After chewing on your request for a few moments, AOL.CA Search returns with a list of matching sites. To view any of the matches, just click the site's entry. Sometimes, AOL.CA uncovers so many possible matches that they don't fit on one screen. In that case, AOL.CA presents a Next button at the bottom of the window. Click that button to view the next page of matching entries.

If AOL.CA Search can't come up with anything that matches your topic, it quietly tells you of its failure and often implies that the problem is somehow your fault. Don't believe it — it lies. If this happens during your search, take your topic to another of the Web's search engines, listed in Table 13-1. Some engines provide automatic links to other popular search systems when they display your search results (just in case you want to try your luck elsewhere).

Table 13-1	**Search Engines for Scouring the World Wide Web**
Search Engine	*Web Address*
AltaVista Canada	www.altavistacanada.com
Canada.com	www.canada.com
DejaNews	www.dejanews.com
Dogpile	www.dogpile.com
Excite Canada	www.excite.ca
Google	www.google.com
Infoseek	www.infoseek.com
Lycos	www.lycos.com
Yahoo! Canada	www.yahoo.ca

Search engines like Dogpile (what a name!) conduct *meta*searches, a fancy way of saying they search other search engines — a major time-saver if you're planning to do a lot of research online.

Browsing through some great resources

Sometimes nailing down precisely what you want to find isn't easy. Instead of being a simple, cut-and-dried topic, your goal is more vague — sort of an I'll-know-it-when-I-see-it feeling. Even so, you still need some places to start looking. The general areas listed in the preceding section may meet your needs, but sometimes a more narrowly focused source sparks your imagination in a way that a more general one can't.

The following is a selection of searchable resources from all corners of AOL Canada. Some areas offer news, and others come bearing general introductory notes. All these resources are free, which makes them your friends by default:

✔ The king of all general references has to be the Research & Learn area's More Subjects window (keyword **More References**). Here you'll find several major categories of subjects — each packed with subcategories. In Arts, for example, you'll find subjects ranging from dance to opera. No matter what kind of information you seek, the More References list makes a great starting point.

✔ Every schoolchild knows that it's hard to stump the encyclopedias (keyword **Encyclopedias**). Putting these general reference guides online makes browsing and searching their content even easier.

✔ In addition to the encyclopedias, AOL Canada offers many other classic references, such as a dictionary (keyword **Dictionary**) and a thesaurus (keyword **Thesaurus**). AOL goes a step farther by offering specialized word references too, such as Word Histories (keyword **Word Histories**), Other Dictionaries (keyword **Dictionaries**), and the beginning connoisseur's friend, the *Wine Dictionary* (keyword **Dictionaries**, and then double-click Wine Dictionary on the list).

✔ Writers require strong research areas to find facts for their stories, but sometimes they also need information that's a little off the beaten path. For days when you either want a good laugh or feel like adding to your storehouse of the odd and mystifying, check out Straight Dope (one of our favourite areas, at `www.straightdope.com`).

✔ What report, theme, or presentation couldn't use a good quotation to spice it up? Choose the best sound bites from several volumes of quotations in the Research and Learn channel's Quotations folder (keyword **More References**, and then double-click Quotations in the References area).

✔ When your research sends you looking for ethnic information, try areas such as Ethnicity (keyword **Ethnicity**), Jewish Community Online Canada (keyword **Jewish**), or NetNoir (keyword **NetNoir**). Each one includes resources, discussions, and chats that may lead you to still other resources in the Great Out There.

✔ Digging into the world of business? For a veritable plethora of business resources, try Canadian Finance Company Research (keyword **Company Research**) where you can search through business news articles or link to major finance-related Web sites like Canada Newswire (with its searchable database of corporate news releases); and the news by company ticker system (keyword **Company News**) for the latest news wire tidbits about your favourite firms.

✔ Looking for some culture in your life? Give Infoculture a go. It's part of the CBC's massive online presence, and you'll find it at keyword **Music**, then by choosing the Infoculture option from the drop-down list of resources at the bottom left of the window.

✔ It's a frightening thought, but the federal government is one of the largest publishers in Canada. It also generates more statistics than should be allowed by law. To dip into the wellspring of numbers bought with your tax dollars, check out the Statistics Canada Web site, at `www.statscan.ca`. The site's even got a page where you can get the latest and most media-friendly statistics every day. It's called *The Daily* and you can find it at `www.statcan.ca/cgi-bin/DAILY/mdaily.cgi`.

✔ There's an amazing selection of helpful finders in the AOL Services menu. Just click the top half of the Services button and try these out for size:

- Find an appointment using My Calendar (keyword **Calendar**).

- Find a new or used car at the AOL Canada Auto Centre (choose <u>A</u>OL Services⇨Car <u>B</u>uying).

- Find deals or buyers with the AOL Canada Classifieds (keyword **Classifieds**).

- Find out a little something about your future by reading your horoscope (keyword **Horoscopes**).

- Find directions and shortcuts (keyword **Maps**).

- Find out what's playing at a movie theatre near you (keyword **Movie Finder**).

- Find someone to call your own at Love@AOL (keyword **Personals**).

If you need to collect information about a topic on an ongoing basis, check out the News Profiles system, at keyword **News Profiles**. You define what kind of stories you want to see, and the News Profiles system scours the news wires, automatically forwarding any matching stories directly to your mailbox. Setting up a profile takes only a moment, but it keeps going and going, just like an electronic news version of that annoying pink bunny.

Finding Things: AOL Canada's Shopping Channel

One of the most practical things the Internet can offer the average person is the option of shopping from the comfort (and, in Canada, the relative warmth) of your own home. Just think of the possibilities! With downloadable images, you can browse through the merchandise at the click of a button. With encrypted — meaning safe from cyber thieves — online payment systems, you can check out right then and there. Finally, with easy delivery, you can get your new purchase home ASAP!

AOL Canada is on top of this online shopping revolution, bringing you an entire channel devoted to finding the object of your desire from Canadian merchants who are online and have brand-name recognition. It's called the AOL Canada Shopping channel (keyword **Shopping** or click the Shop icon on the toolbar).

Start by browsing the 16 categories — including everything from Apparel to Books, Music & Videos, to Consumer Electronics to Toys, Kids & Babies, to Pets & Animals, and more! In most categories, you'll find quality Canadian merchants like Chapters.ca, SamtheRecordman.com, TheShoppingChannel.com, CompuSmart, Hickory Farms, and Uniquely Canada. If you can't find what you are looking for in one of these categories featuring Canadian merchants, click the U.S. channels area, then select shopping and — *poof!* — the virtual door opens to cross-border shopping! (Before you go, read the sidebar later in this chapter, "A word or two on cross-border shopping in cyberspace.")

While you're in the Shopping channel, be sure to check out the free AOL Canada Gift Reminder Service, and follow these easy steps to ensure you never again forget that important birthday, graduation day, or anniversary:

1. **Use keyword** Reminder **to open the Gift Reminder window.**

   The Reminder Service pops onscreen with its fashionable, easy-to-use commands.

2. **Click Create Your Reminder.**

   Your personalized Reminder List appears, ready for new additions. If you've created Reminders before, you'll be able to see each of them in this window, including the name of the recipient, the type of occasion, and the date.

3. **Click Add Personal Reminder.**

   Guess what? The Add a Reminder window opens up smack in the middle of your screen, asking you for all the vitals: name of the recipient, type of occasion, date, and whether it's an annual event. In the bottom portion of the screen, you can also tell the Reminder Team a little about the recipient, such as gender and age, to help the Reminder Team in providing you with appropriate gift suggestions.

4. **Fill out all the required information and click Save to store your Reminder.**

   The Add Personal Reminder window disappears, and your personalized Reminder List magically re-appears, sporting the new occasion you've just created. From here on in, it's smooth sailing. You'll get an e-mail from the AOL Canada Reminder Team 14 days before that birthday, anniversary, or whatever type of occasion you just specified. If you ever decide you don't need reminding anymore, just highlight that Reminder and click Remove.

If you're more worried about upcoming holidays than birthdays, use the Holiday Reminder button. Just click the radio button beside whichever holiday is prone to slipping your mind, and yes, an e-mail will come your way two weeks before the fact. Want a reminder of when holidays are this year? Click on the Important Dates You Shouldn't Forget area and you will see a list of all holidays for that year. Isn't it grand?

A word or two on cross-border shopping in cyberspace

Let's face it. Online shopping was a more-or-less U.S. invention. We Canadians are getting there, with new cyber stores opening up all the time, but the selection of merchants operating south of the border is hard to resist. If you do decide to buy from a U.S. vendor, there are a few extra costs to keep in mind:

✔ **Exchange:** Most American merchants list prices in U.S. dollars. You'll have to figure out the exchange rate to get the real price. AOL Canada gives you a hand by providing a Cash Converter (keyword **FX**) whenever you're shopping in non-Canadian areas. It's simple to use and instantly gives you the rate of exchange for just about any currency you'd like.

✔ **Duty:** Depending on what you buy, you may be responsible for duty — the fee collected by Customs Canada for bringing goods across the border. The North American Free Trade Agreement (NAFTA) got rid of duty on some merchandise, but otherwise, you still have to pay up. To find out more about duty and GST costs, visit the Canada Customs Web site for individuals at www.ccra-adrc.gc.ca/customs/individuals/menu-e.html

and read the downloadable pamphlet called *I Declare* (available at www.ccra-adrc.gc.ca/E/pub/cp/rc4044em/README.html).

✔ **Tax:** And now for the bad news. Almost everything you bring in to Canada is subject to provincial sales tax (PST) or the harmonized sales tax (HST), depending on where you live. Yeah. It does suck.

✔ **Shipping:** No matter what you buy online, you're going to have to get it home. That means shipping. Many big merchants have a system in place that makes shipping as easy as typing in your address. Many will also waive the shipping fee to attract business. Keep in mind, though, that many U.S. merchants still do not ship to Canada through their Web sites (such as Gap and Old Navy). But if you buy from an individual (say, through online auction houses such as eBay), you will probably have to make your own arrangements with either the postal service or a courier company. See Chapter 25 for the Web sites of some popular shipping companies.

Still wondering how this AOL Canada service works? Click the area labelled How Does This AOL Service Work and you will see a list of FAQs (frequently asked questions), as well as additional useful information about this free service.

Finding Cool Programs and Nifty Files

After working through the initial euphoria (and the first credit card bill) of owning your computer, the next thought that usually goes through your mind is something like, "I wish that the computer could do X," where X is some incredibly important task that none of your current software and hardware setup comes even *close* to performing. Worse, if you're like most people (ourselves included), X is quickly followed by Y, Z, and a whole horde of functions that start with peculiar math symbols you barely remember from school.

It sounds like you need software — and lots of it at that! Purchasing commercial programs to accomplish everything is a great idea, but your credit card is still on life support from getting the computer. Copying your buddy's program is out of the question (the software makers frown on that in a big, ugly, nasty way). What's a computer owner to do? Search the file libraries of AOL Canada, that's what!

The hundreds of file libraries on AOL Canada contain programs that process words, mangle (sorry, *manage*) data, implode unfriendly aliens — the list goes on. And these programs keep your budget happy because they're either freeware (free programs donated to the world by proud developers) or shareware (try-before-you-buy programs that require only a small payment to the author). You may even find demonstration versions of commercial applications.

To help you find the software needle in the online haystack, AOL created the Software Search system. This system quickly puts the software you need right into your hands — or, more precisely, right on your hard drive, which is an infinitely better place for a program (software stains wickedly if you get it on your clothes).

Get into the FileSearch system by using keyword **Filesearch**. A little dialog box happily pops up with a three-step system to help you find what you're looking for. Check out Figure 13-3 to get an idea of what to expect, then follow the commands.

1. **Choose a time frame.**

   Since new downloadable software (programs, screen savers) is being added to the software libraries all the time, you might want to specify a search through the recent additions. Otherwise, choose the All Dates option.

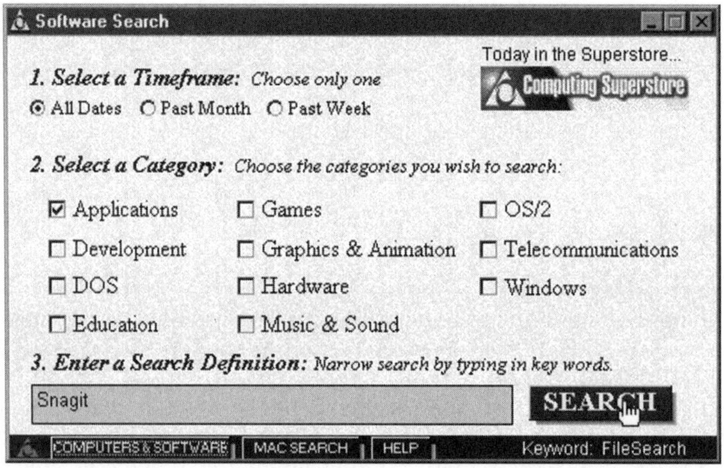

Software Search

Today in the Superstore...

Computing Superstore

1. Select a Timeframe: *Choose only one*
⦿ All Dates   ○ Past Month   ○ Past Week

2. Select a Category: *Choose the categories you wish to search:*

☑ Applications   ☐ Games   ☐ OS/2
☐ Development   ☐ Graphics & Animation   ☐ Telecommunications
☐ DOS   ☐ Hardware   ☐ Windows
☐ Education   ☐ Music & Sound

3. Enter a Search Definition: *Narrow search by typing in key words.*

Snagit   **SEARCH**

COMPUTERS & SOFTWARE | MAC SEARCH | HELP   Keyword: FileSearch

Figure 13-3:
FileSearch
guides you
to the
software
you crave.

2. Choose a category.

What are you looking for? Games? Music? Tell FileSearch and it will narrow down your search results accordingly.

3. Specify a definition.

If you know the name of the program you're looking for, type the name in this text box. The search engine will hopefully root it out among AOL Canada's various catalogues. Otherwise, type in a few words describing the type of program you're looking for.

4. Click Search.

If your search was successful, in a moment you'll see a dialog box with a list of results matching your search criteria. So, what are you waiting for? Download away! To learn exactly how to do that, flip to Chapter 15.

By default, the Windows search system appears, but Macintosh software isn't far away. To switch to the Mac search system, click the Mac Search button at the bottom of the Software Search window.

In the unlikely event that you can't find what you want in the voluminous AOL Canada digital catacombs, point your Web browser to either Download.com (www.download.com) or Shareware.com (www.shareware.com). These two sites (both part of the huge CNET Web presence) carry software for almost any use and occasion, including business applications, utilities, games, and more. There's no cost to use the areas (and no salesperson will call).

Did we mention that AOL has tons of software worth downloading? You can dig through the Canadian Viewz Software libraries (start at the Computing and Games channel, click Search and Explore, and scroll down to the Download Software area, then click the Viewz Software Libraries link.) There's too much to say about it here, so visit Chapter 15 for the whole story on downloading until your computer's heart's content.

Don't forget to check out some of the fun and free Canadian downloads available through keyword **Cdn Boards**. Just click the Software Libraries link on the left side of the window and browse the categories, including Shareware and even a gallery of thoroughly Canadian images.

Chapter 14

Tracking News, Weather, Markets, and More

. . . .

In This Chapter

▶ Browsing through the news

▶ Collecting stories with a session log

▶ Checking on the weather

▶ Examining the business side of news

▶ Keeping In Toon with editorial art

. . . .

*N*ews plays a big role in our lives. It's our link to the community, the country, and the world. (Can't you almost hear the national anthem playing?) AOL Canada must think that news is very important because it offers so many kinds of news — headlines, international, business, technology, features. The list goes on — and costs you nothing extra because it's part of normal AOL Canada service. Is this a deal or what?

Thankfully, AOL Canada gives you lots of tools for dealing with the influx of news, weather, sports scores, and stock prices. This chapter looks at your options for picking up news, ranging from a casual romp through the channel to a detailed analysis of the markets.

Look back at this chapter two or three times over the coming months. Your information needs change over time, and a quick peek here may help you open up precisely the news source you need.

Getting the News

Most of the online news lives (no surprises here) on the newly redesigned AOL Canada News channel, as shown in Figure 14-1. It displays top headlines from business, politics, entertainment, and the world in general. The News channel

Figure 14-1:
The AOL
Canada
News
channel
hosts top
stories and
links to
specialized
online news
areas.

also provides links to in-depth coverage in the various news departments. Each department, in turn, narrows the focus, giving you an ever-more-carefully-winnowed collection of stories.

Analysis on the go

Some of the most interesting news areas sit deep inside the News channel. For example, reading a relatively short news wire story about a development on the federal political scene is one thing, but reviewing an in-depth analysis of that same development by one of Canada's most respected journalists is quite another.

That's exactly what you'll get from AOL Canada's Print Weasels (keyword **Print Weasels**). AOL has gathered some of this country's finest to ponder and pontificate about everything from politics to everyday life, including Mike Duffy (he could take care of that political development we mentioned), John Daly (business news guru), and Gary Dunford (columnist with intelligence and wit).

To view a Print Weasel column, just click the title link on the main window. If you like what you read (or better yet, if you dislike it intensely), fire off an e-mail using the icon provided. You can also post a message to one of the Weasel's message boards.

He may not be in one of the AOL Canada Print Weasels, but if you want analysis from a highly, er, recognizable source, look no farther than Don Cherry. Yes, the king of Canadian hockey commentary is on AOL Canada at keyword **Don Cherry**. Explore the Coach's Corner at your own risk.

Filling your mailbox with news you want

A little-known feature of the AOL Canada news system could save a *bunch* of time if you like to watch for stories about particular topics or companies. Considering all the resources on the News channel, you often don't have time to sift through tons of stories to find that all-important informational nugget. The AOL Canada News Profiles service (keyword **News Profiles**) solves this problem for you by delivering directly to your mailbox the latest stories about the topics you choose.

To build a news profile, go to keyword **News Profiles** and follow the instructions in the How to Create a Profile section. Start with something simple, like a single topic (we tried *espionage*) or a company name. Let the profile do its thing for a couple of days so that you can judge how many new e-mail messages it adds to your box. Adjust the items in your profile or the story-limit setting to manage the incoming story flow.

This service comes at no extra charge with your AOL Canada account, so it's definitely worth a look. One word of caution: If you track a popular topic (like *Microsoft*), your mailbox fills up in no time! Also, keep in mind that News Profiles draws its news mostly from U.S. news services.

For those whose appetite for punditry and analysis of all kinds is insatiable, you'd better hit the AOL Canada Newsstand (keyword **Newsstand**). From here, you can link to newspapers across the country, where op-ed pages abound, or try one of the magazines, such as *Maclean's*.

There are also specific news-related keywords worth checking out. Go deep into the world's financial realm with keyword **EIU** to reach the *Economist Intelligence Unit*, or try the respected U.S. publication the *Financial Times* (keyword **FT**), or *Time* (keyword **Time**).

Searching the News channel

In this day and age, it's not where you get the news that matters, it's where you get the news *you want*. With so many news sources producing stories "24/7" (the new lingo for 24 hours a day, 7 days a week), a Search function is essential for any online news provider. Of course, you'll find just that in the AOL Canada News channel.

Click the Search News button to begin your search for topics that interest you. Here are a few tips for searching the News channel:

✔ If the system can't find any stories that match your search, try searching for something more general (*music* rather than *new rock groups*, for example).

✔ Likewise, if you're suddenly the proud owner of hundreds of matches, narrow your search terms (*small business* rather than *business*) to cull the reports you really want. Also, try limiting your options with the special search commands (see Table 14-1 for more details).

✔ To conduct a more detailed search, try using the tools AND, OR, and NOT. The table shows you how.

Table 14-1		Special News Search Commands
Command	*Example*	*Description*
AND	government *and* waste	Links two words or phrases; finds only articles that contain *both* examples
NOT	software *not* buggy	Finds only articles that contain the first word or phrase and do not contain the second; prevents unwanted matches (and occasionally provides moments of humour)
OR	Windows *or* Macintosh	Finds articles that contain either example *or* both of them

Rolling Your Articles into a Log

With so many easily accessible news areas, you can spend all day doing nothing but wandering from place to place, browsing through the stories. Obviously, that can affect your regularly scheduled day. Luckily, a tool built right into your AOL Canada software captures all the stories you see onscreen and packages them into a single file, which you can put on your laptop, print on paper, or even download to your personal digital assistant.

The tool is the *session log* (part of the Log Manager that's built into your software), the AOL Canada answer to a very fast-writing scribe. The session log automatically copies into a plain text file on your computer any articles you display. What's an *article?* It's a news story, picture caption, bulletin board posting, or other text that appears in a window onscreen. Menu items and things like that don't count — it's only paragraphs of text that land in the log files.

Follow these steps to create a session log of your reading activities:

1. Choose File⇨Log Manager from the menu that sits at the top left corner of your screen.

The Logging window, small though it is, hops on the screen.

2. **Click the Open Log button in the Session Log portion of the dialog box.**

   The Open Log window, shown in Figure 14-2, appears.

3. **AOL Canada automatically offers to name the file SESSION.LOG, which is fine for most purposes. Click Save.**

   If you want to save the session log files for posterity, you may change the name to today's date instead. If you reuse the same name each day (always naming the file SESSION.LOG, for example) when you click Save, Windows asks whether you want to overwrite the old file with a new one. Click Yes when it asks.

4. **Browse through the news stories just as you always do.**

   From this point on, your session log file is active and working behind the scenes to capture all the stories you display onscreen. Do what you normally do: Find a story that looks interesting and then click it to bring it up in a window. You don't need to actually scroll through the story yourself; just making it appear in the window is good enough for the session log.

5. **After you finish looking through the stories, choose My File⇨Log Manager from the menu to open the Log Manager, and click Close to save the log file.**

   Your file is safely tucked away on your computer. At this point, you can do anything you want with it, including opening it in a word processor, printing it, or copying it to another computer or a personal digital assistant.

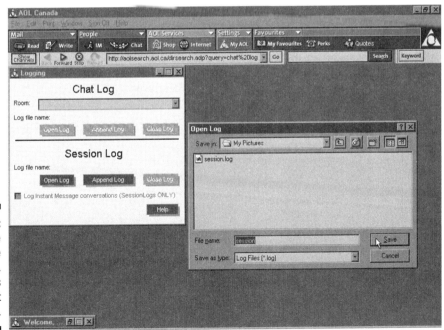

Figure 14-2:
Using the default name SESSION. LOG works well for most everyone.

> TIP
>
> If you copy the log file into a personal digital assistant (such as a Palm Pilot or Franklin REX), remember to erase it when you finish indulging your desire for news. Otherwise, the stories take up the very valuable (and limited) memory space in your little device.

The Weather Outside — Is It Frightful?

How much you care about the weather seems to depend directly on where you live (does anyone in Barbados, for example, *really* check the forecasts, except during storm season?) and which generation you belong to. If you come from the generation of mothers and fathers who "walked through three feet of snow to get to school, uphill both ways, with inadequate boots," a little rain might not seem like such a big deal. You know who you are! If, on the other hand, you're from the generation of spoiled North Americans who take umbrellas to work, or worse, if you ride your bike to the office (Marguerite's got her hand up for that one), you'll want to know what to expect.

To avoid problems, check out the AOL Canada Weather channel, at keyword **Weather**. It's one-stop shopping for every kind of weather information imaginable (plus some you just don't *want* to imagine). Among other things, the Weather area (shown in Figure 14-3) offers a quick forecast for anywhere in Canada, plus detailed forecasts for both Canada and the U.S. Get familiar with weather terms using the Learn function, read through recent weather-related articles with the News link, or even send your weather questions to The Weatherman (thanks to a partnership with The Weather Network). It's all waiting for you at AOL Canada's Weather channel.

Figure 14-3: No matter what kind of weather info you want, it's available in the Weather window.

If you're a serious weather buff, or if you're planning a trip across the border, make sure to check out the USA link at the top left of the main AOL Canada weather window. There, you'll find maps, satellite images, and specific forecasts for golfers and skiers, among other weather resources. To visit The Weather Network, type its URL (`www.theweathernetwork.com`) into the long white text box on the navigation bar and click Go.

Watching the Markets

Considering the amount of work and worry some people put into fretting over their stock market investments, stuffing all your cash into a mattress suddenly looks like a marginally attractive idea. At least you don't spend all your time wondering whether your funds are safe, because what kind of thief is going to walk off with a big . . . um . . . Hey! Where did the bed go? Hmm — perhaps there is something to be said for putting your money in the markets, after all.

If you've parked some money in stock investments, you probably want to see how your investments are performing. AOL Canada offers two unique tools for tracking these investments. The first is the Quotes system, which pulls up the current (delayed by 15 to 20 minutes) price for whatever stock or mutual fund you want. The other system is Portfolios, which makes short work of watching a whole group of investments. The following sections look at each of these tools individually.

 If you're going to be using the Quotes and Portfolios services, you've probably already achieved "small individual investor" status in the eyes of friends, loved ones, and, of course, your smiling broker! If so, you'll want to keep up with all the latest investment news by subscribing to the *Canadian Investor* newsletter (keyword **Cdn Investor**). Just click the Subscribe button and you'll automatically receive this monthly missive for free via e-mail. It includes highlights culled from the month's biggest business and market news stories. This way, you can save your energy for the work involved in upgrading to "big-time individual investor" status. For more investor resources, flip to Chapter 21.

 Remember to visit keyword **Newsletters** for a list of all the free and informative newsletters available for subscription at the click of a mouse.

Quotes (keyword Quotes)

The only way that checking stock prices could be easier than the AOL Canada Quotes system is if the system could read your mind — but if it did that, who knows *what* it would discover? Perhaps the world is a better place if we just keep the Quotes system the way it is and don't let computers peer into our thought processes.

Getting a stock quote takes only a moment. Here's what to do:

1. **Open the Quotes window by using keyword** Quotes **or clicking the Quotes icon on the toolbar.**

   Whichever way you choose, the Quotes window hops into action.

2. **Type the company's stock ticker symbol in the Symbol box and click Get Quote.** Make sure that the symbol button is chosen and that you have selected the exchange that your stock is traded on.

   After a moment or two, the stock's information appears in the large window on the left side (see Figure 14-4). What's more, if any recent news stories have been written about that company, you'll also find a list of clickable headlines in the News box along the bottom of the window. Now you can be sure to stay on top of the latest.

   If the window mechanically mutters no quote information available, double-check the spelling of the ticker symbol you entered. If worse comes to worst, click the Lookup button to find the symbol you need.

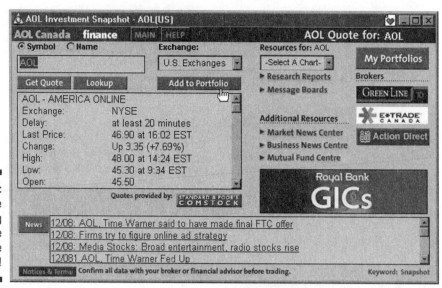

Figure 14-4: Things are looking good for the stock of the day!

When you're looking up a quote for a Canadian stock traded on a Canadian exchange, the price you're quoted is in Canadian dollars (of course). But when you're quoted a stock price for a U.S. stock on one of the U.S. exchanges, the price is, yes, in U.S. dollars (a tad different, eh?).

Repeat the process for however many stocks you want to see. To track a number of investments, it's easier to use the Portfolios system, as discussed in the next section. That system gives you some extra perks, by offering more information about your particular investments.

In addition to the stock price search system, the Quotes window offers a host of newsy goodies of interest to both serious investors and part-time plunkers. Here's a quick rundown of what's waiting there:

- Research Reports (keyword **Company Research**) offers an expert perspective on the markets. Find useful research tools in the list box that will provide you with analyst reports, financial statements, earnings reports, and more!

- Message Boards is a great place to find out how other AOL Canada investors are faring.

- The Market News Centre (keyword **MNC**) offers quick graphs for everything from the Dow Jones Industrials to the Japanese Nikkei 225, plus selected news headlines.

- AOL Canada Business News (keyword **Business News**) delivers the latest in wire stories of business deals and the companies that make them. Check out the section called "Business News," later in this chapter, for more details.

- Mutual Fund Centre (keyword **Mutual Fund**) brings up the AOL Canada Mutual Fund Centre. RRSP season is never far off, and the smart investor will want to explore the dozens of leading mutual fund companies available through AOL Canada, or track your fund's performance in the Top Ten Overall Mutual Funds list, updated daily. For all the details on the AOL Canada Mutual Fund Centre, check out the section called "AOL Canada Brokerage and Mutual Fund Centres," later in this chapter.

- Broker Buttons give you the option of going directly to three prominent Canadian online trading sites, E*TRADE Canada, Action Direct, and TD Mutual Funds.

Invest carefully, and don't believe everything you hear on the Personal Finance discussion boards. To repeat this warning, and to hear several others like it, flip to *AOL Canada For Dummies* Channels Directory, the mini-book in this book (you can tell that you're there by the yellow pages), and check out the Personal Finance channel.

If you are interested (or invested) in U.S. stocks, you should also try the Historical Quotes service (keyword **Historical Quotes**). It thumbs through previous years of pricing to clearly show how U.S. stocks have performed in the past. (Remember, as the gurus say, previous performance is no guarantee that we won't all lose our socks on this sucker the next time around.)

Economies of Scale: U.S. versus Canadian financial information

Okay, so they're bigger than us. We'll admit it. And when it comes to the financial news and information on AOL, sometimes the content gives a nod to the in-larger-numbers-than-us U.S. investors. For example, the Investment Research service (described in the preceeding checklist), offers excellent stock reports prepared by an American research company. But we also found an excellent stock report on Canadian mining giant Inco Ltd., so don't be afraid to look around. When using the Portfolios services, you'll run into the same kind of thing. While AOL Canada has enhanced the service to allow you to include Canadian stocks and mutual funds in your portfolio, some Canadian securities still cannot be tracked this way. Expect even more Canadian content from all the financial services on AOL in the future.

AOL Canada also offers a complete suite of tools that will help you make investment decisions that are tailored to meet your individual needs.

- Registered Retirement Savings Plans (keyword **RRSP**) can present themselves in a confusing manner. To understand the basics of investing in an RRSP and to stay on top of the latest investing trends, check out this informative area.

- You can find the full picture of a mutual fund's performance, holdings, investment strategy, fund management, and commission structure, at AOL Canada's exclusive Fundata Canada area (keyword **Fundata**).

  This area also allows you to monitor interest and mortgage rates.

Portfolios (keyword Portfolios)

The other side of the AOL Canada built-in stock-tracking tools is the Portfolios system, at keyword **Portfolios**. Unlike its little sister the Quotes window, Portfolios easily handles a whole, well, portfolio of stock investments. Your portfolio shows, at a glance, your positions for all stocks, including the number of shares, the stock's current price, the price you paid for it, and your total gain (or, horrors, loss).

All the tools you need for creating and managing a portfolio live in the Portfolios window. Your first portfolio, cleverly named Portfolio #1, is automatically created when you tell AOL Canada that you want to add a stock to your portfolio. Open your portfolio by either double-clicking it or clicking once to highlight it and then clicking Display.

With your portfolio open onscreen, you can do any of the following:

- ✔ **Add another stock or mutual fund to the portfolio:** Use the Add Item button. You need to know the stock or mutual fund ticker symbol, the number of shares you own, and the price you paid for the stock or mutual fund.

- ✔ **Remove a stock or mutual fund:** Click the stock or mutual fund you want to get rid of and then click Remove. When AOL Canada asks whether you're sure, click OK.

- ✔ **Transfer a stock or mutual fund to a different portfolio:** Click the stock or mutual fund and then click Transfer. AOL Canada displays a nice dialog box asking to which portfolio you want to move the investment. (Of course, you need at least two portfolios before trying this little trick. For more about making a new portfolio, see the text after this list.)

- ✔ **Edit an entry:** Click the entry you want to change and then click Edit. You can adjust the number of shares and the purchase price, but you can't change the ticker symbol. To do that, you need to delete the entry entirely and then create a new one.

- ✔ **Check the details:** Click the stock or mutual fund entry you want detailed information about and then click Details. After a moment or two of serious consideration, the system displays a window filled to the brim with expanded price information, links to recent news stories, and buttons to create historical charts. All very cool stuff when you've got money invested in a company!

- ✔ **Refresh the display:** Click Refresh to get the latest prices for all the investments in your portfolio.

You can create and manage multiple portfolios through the system as well. Click Display All to return to the main Portfolios window (or use keyword **Portfolios**), and then pick your task from these items:

- ✔ **Create a new portfolio:** Click Create Portfolio. When asked, type a name for the portfolio, and click OK. The new portfolio appears in the Portfolios window.

- ✔ **Delete a portfolio:** Click the portfolio you don't want any more and then wave solemnly at it while clicking Delete Portfolio. When the system asks whether you really, really want to delete the portfolio, click OK.

- ✔ **Rename a portfolio:** Click the portfolio with the weird name and then click Rename. When AOL Canada asks you for a new name, type it, and click OK.

Be careful when you're deleting a portfolio. Make doubly sure that you clicked the correct portfolio because after you click that fateful OK button, that portfolio is gone forever. There's no Oops key, so don't let mistakes happen to you.

Use the Customize Columns button at the top right of any open portfolio to choose exactly what kind of indices you want displayed for each stock in that portfolio (with a maximum of seven columns).

Business News

AOL Canada is a great source of business news for both the ardent investor and the casual follower of the world of finance. Use keyword **Business News** to open the main Business News window, and try out these great features:

- Read the latest articles in seven categories including Canadian Business, International, Resources (that's natural resources — the stuff this country was built on!), Markets, U.S. Business, Technology, Consumer Briefs, and Currency.

- Skim the very best and the very hottest business news from the Canadian Press (CP) Business Summary, updated daily. You'll find it open and ready to be scrolled through on the right side of the main Business News window.

- Search for the news that matters to your investments by clicking Search on the bottom of the window. (This search works exactly like the general news search that we described earlier in this chapter.)

- Sit back and enjoy the daily audio- and video-enhanced Fund News Network Daily Market Update, presented by TD Mutual Funds. This is what being online is all about. It's fun. It's free. It's also a launch pad to check out mutual fund prices or set up an online trading account with TD. You can also get there by typing www.tdbank.ca/mutualfund/ into the long white navigation bar box and clicking Go.

AOL Canada Brokerage and Mutual Fund Centres

For moments when you want another opinion or want to buy something now, the AOL Canada Brokerage Centre (keyword **Brokerage**) and the AOL Canada Mutual Fund Centre (keyword **Mutual Fund**) supply everything you need, from financial analysis information to links for online brokers.

At the Brokerage Centre, use the links to set up an online account with some of Canada's most reputable securities houses, or check out the always-up-to-date summary of Canadian and U.S. stock exchange action.

At the Mutual Fund Centre, you get another always-up-to-date summary. This time, it's the daily Top Ten Overall mutual funds. Using the Mutual Fund Resources drop-down menu, you can link to dozens of prominent mutual fund companies. In the middle of the main window, you'll also find a link to Fundata Canada (keyword **Fundata**), an amazing resource for the mutual fund investor. Find out which funds were winners and losers after a day of trading, use the Dictionary to look up investment terms, or check out the *valuation dates* for your fund — useful information, especially if you want to track the fund's performance in your AOL Canada portfolio. (Look up the fund in the alphabetical list and you'll find the date in the upper-right corner of the fund's window.)

In Toon with the Times

Even the most serious-minded news junkie (and Marguerite confesses she's got it bad) needs something lighthearted — or at least satirical — once in a while! Thus, the editorial cartoon was born.

In its bid to bring you all the news that's fit to print, AOL Canada also brings you a daily selection of editorial cartoons at keyword **In Toon**. (Catchy name, eh?) The art is Canadian, while the topics range from federal politics to just about anything that catches the artists' attention.

Chapter 15

Frolicking in the Games

● ●

In This Chapter

▶ Sorting out the free games from the premium ones

▶ Playing the coolest games on the system

● ●

Games, games, games — they're a great pastime, a relaxing way to spend an evening, and a challenging contest aimed at sharpening your mental blades. They're also one of the top reasons people buy a computer in the first place (whether or not they admit it).

Being part of the AOL Canada community brings a whole new dimension to games. Rather than playing a game *against* the computer, how about playing the game *through* the computer with a live opponent hundreds of miles away? Whether you want to challenge others or swap tales of gaming in the good old days, the games and game forums on AOL Canada are definitely the places to do it.

This chapter looks at the free and premium (as in *not free*) games available through AOL Canada and offers some tips about online games to try and love.

If There's No Free Lunch, Are There at Least Free Games?

Yes, Virginia, there *are* free games on AOL Canada. And the system also has pay-per-play games that charge an hourly fee. No, the fee doesn't apply to all games on the system. Yes, it does cover some. Yes, you get plenty of warning before entering a pay-by-the-hour gaming area, so you can't accidentally wander into one. That would be like "accidentally" driving your car through a shopping mall and then claiming that the pedestrians didn't get out of the way fast enough.

Most of the for-pay (or *premium*) games live in two areas of the Games channel: the Game Parlour (keyword **Game Parlour**) and Xtreme Games (keyword **Xtreme Games**). The individual games are provided and supported by two big-league online game companies — GameStorm (keyword **GameStorm**) and WorldPlay (keyword **WorldPlay**).

As their names imply, each game area focuses on a different kind of game. The Game Parlour contains classic parlour games, like backgammon, cribbage, hearts, and spades. Just to keep things interesting (and, we think, because they couldn't figure out where else to put them), it also includes some non-parlour games, like Splatterball (keyword **Splatterball**) and Virtual Pool.

The Xtreme Gaming side of the world offers action-oriented titles like Air Warrior III, Harpoon Online, Magestorm, Multiplayer Battletech, and Warcraft II. (Just for fun, see whether you can read that last sentence in one breath. Why should you? Well, why not?)

As you play the premium games, your AOL Canada account is charged per hour, which is the smallest amount of billable time the AOL Canada computers understand. As we write this book, Game Parlour titles cost 99 cents per hour, and Xtreme Gaming titles are also 99 cents per hour, but the prices change periodically so check the details in each game. The billing is automatic and begins after you pass through the This Costs Money curtain (okay, it's really a window), shown in Figure 15-1, which reminds you, in no uncertain terms, that it costs money to step beyond this point.

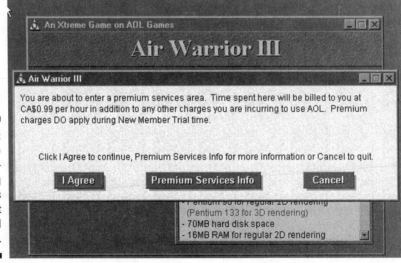

Figure 15-1:
Make no
mistake —
the billing
clock starts
the moment
you click I
Agree.

Opening the door to premium games

By default, only the master screen name (the first screen name you created on AOL Canada) can play the way-cool premium games. All the other screen names on your account start out blocked from the games. If someone signs on with one of those other screen names and tries to play a premium game, a message pops up saying, basically, that AOL Canada would just *love* to let them play, but some heathen scoundrel (namely, the keeper of the master screen name) won't let them. After riling the would-be player into a frenzy, the window then suggests that she take up the issue with the account holder.

If you *want* to allow your other screen names to play premium games, you have to tell AOL Canada. To do that, sign on to the system using your master screen name (that is, the one that you created when you registered for AOL Canada) and then use keyword **Parental Controls**. When the window appears, click the Set Parental Controls button. When the Set Parental Controls window appears, select the appropriate screen name, then scroll down to Premium Services and click on the green box. When the new window pops up, clear the Block Premium Services check box by clicking on it.

To prevent a screen name from playing the premium games (thus protecting your credit card bill from accidental inflation), make sure that the Premium Services Current Setting reads "Access to Premium Services is not allowed."

For the latest information about premium games, including hourly fees, special offers, and other details of online gaming, go to the AOL Games Premium Services Guide, at keyword **Premium**.

Can't find the game you're looking for? First, try the A–Z list of games available in the How To Play Games on AOL Canada window (keyword **How To Play**). Each listing provides a game description (including its status as premium or non-premium) as well as a link so you can start playing ASAP! If you still can't find the game of your dreams, don't worry. There's a much bigger list of games at keyword **Games Help**.

The free games live in Game Shows Online (keyword **Game Shows**), shown in Figure 15-2, and the Gamers Forum (get there using keyword **Game Guide**, then click the folder called Gamers Forum). These games lean more toward the thinking side of life than their premium game counterparts, but it doesn't mean that they aren't just as exciting. Games such as Strike-a-Match (keyword **Strike a Match**), Slingo (keyword **Slingo**), and Out of Order (keyword **Out of Order**) definitely raise your blood pressure — believe us — and the Simming and Role Playing areas in the Gamers Forum stretch your imagination to new heights. Other free games include a huge variety of trivia titles, online role-playing games, and word puzzles.

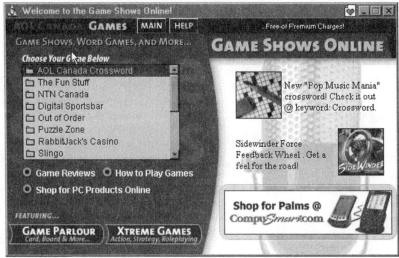

Hopping into the Best Free Games

In our fast-paced society, time is a scarce thing at work and at home. That makes the time you devote to online gaming even more rare! In the hopes of helping you spend most of that precious time actually playing games instead of fruitlessly wandering around looking for them, we've put together the following list of popular (and mostly free) games available on AOL Canada.

Each section includes the name of the game, the keyword for getting there (when there is one), and a quick description of what the game (or game area) is like. If you have to pay a fee for playing, there's a note about that as well.

So, with no further delay, explanation, or meandering text, here are the AOL Canada games and game areas you don't want to miss:

✔ If you love trivia games, the AOL Canada games of trivia anxiously await you. Keyword **NTN** leads to trivia games in the NTN Studio. Zealot science fiction trivia can be found at keyword **Z**. For a real challenge, check out the International Trivia area (keyword **Trivia**; then double-click the International Trivia item). For a patriotic turn, put away that Canadian encyclopedia and try to remember what John A. MacDonald meant to this country, in the Canadian Trivia area (keyword **Trivia**; then double-click the Canadiana Trivia item).

✔ To satisfy the word puzzle addict in you (or at your house), turn to the Puzzlezone (keyword **Puzzle**), as shown in Figure 15-3. Thanks to a partnership with Boxerjam.com, AOL Canada gives you access to free daily puzzles, including Crossword Plus, anagram challenges from Elvis-

Figure 15-3:
The
Boxerjam
Puzzlezone
offers word
puzzles for
every skill
and
patience
level.

Lives, and Clink, a stream-of-consciousness game that defies rational explanation (makes you immediately want to find out how it works, doesn't it?).

✔ Vying for the dual titles of "visually darkest online area" and "most likely to keep you coming back" is Antagonist, Incorporated. Antagonist is a combination game review and online gaming site, with lively discussion and late-breaking stories in the world of both computer and console games (the Nintendos and Segas of the world). Not content to merely talk about the games, the Antagonist also offers Antagonist Trivia, which you can find at keyword **AT**.

✔ VGA Planets (keyword **Games**; click Strategy/Wargames and then VGA Planets) was one of the first turn-based, multiplayer space strategy games on the market. Its success spawned other similar games, like Stars (keyword **Games**; click Strategy/Wargames and then Stars). These games enjoy some of the largest and friendliest game communities on the Net. Check them out for yourself, and join in the fun!

✔ Fantasy role-playing games are an extraordinarily popular pastime in the gaming chat rooms of AOL Canada. The Gamers Forum includes several of these creativity-laden entertainment areas, including the Simming forum, the Role Playing forum, the Red Dragon Inn, and the Stars End Spaceport. These games are a riot to play, as long as you're up to the challenge. Check the forums for more information about their various games and venues.

✔ The folks at BoxerJam Productions (keyword **Boxerjam**) supply some of the most delightful game shows in the whole of AOL Canada. Strike-a-Match (keyword **Strike A Match**), Take 5, and Out of Order are fast-playing and challenging, with a high replay factor. Don't blame us if you get hopelessly hooked on them!

✔ Finally, we'd be seriously remiss if we failed to mention the Collectible Cards forum (keyword **Gaming**, and click Collectible Cards). Collectible card games are the hottest new game trend in years. Led by games like the Star Wars Customizable Card Game, Star Trek: The Next Generation, and Magic: The Gathering, collectible card games continue to entrance new players every day with their combination of game play, collectibility, and old-fashioned horse swapping, as anxious players trade cards in hopes of collecting a full set. Find out all about the collectible card game world here, and join the fun for chats and live, online tournaments.

✔ There's much more to do in the world of online games than the things on AOL Canada. To dive in to the depths of live, multiplayer action, pick up a copy of *Games Online For Dummies*, written by our very own John Kaufeld (IDG Books Worldwide, Inc.). It covers more of the AOL games and opens the door to the games of the Internet.

Keep an eye on the Game Shows Online (keyword **Game Shows**) and Gamers Forum (keyword **GameGuide**, then click the folder called Games Forum) areas to watch for new games joining the system. Lots of cool stuff is coming — don't miss it!

AOL Canada For Dummies Channels Directory

The 5th Wave

By Rich Tennant

"From now on, let's confine our exploration of ancient Egypt to a site on AOL."

In this directory . . .

Cable TV is a fixture of modern life. These days, people expect to sink into their favourite couch, chair, or yoga position (ouch!) and flip aimlessly among 763 different channels of equally mindless programming. Thank goodness society sets its sights so high.

The 19 Canadian content channels are AOL Canada's version of cable TV (and a mighty nice substitute it is, too). The channels sit at the heart of AOL Canada, creating a structure for all of the other information areas on the system.

In keeping with their central position, this directory devotes page after page to the channels, describing what the channels offer, covering the primary information areas inside each channel, and, whenever possible, listing keywords for quick access to everything. It's truly the informational surfing experience. (Now where did that remote control go. . . .)

AOL Canada For Dummies Channels Directory

Some days, nothing feels as good as camping in your favourite chair, sucking down a cold pop, and channel-surfing the moments away. After all, with dozens of specialty channels available on TV, you're bound to find something that tickles your fancy (even if it's just the relaxing sight of the different channels flipping by).

Even though the channels themselves provide some small amount of entertainment value, their main purpose in life is to organize the TV programs so that consistently finding reruns of *The Beachcombers* or *The King of Kensington* doesn't completely whack our brains. (Okay, maybe these aren't the shows you're looking for, but you get the idea!) Combined with a good printed reference, the various TV channels make viewing less of a chore and more of a time-consuming obsession.

The 19 channels on AOL Canada do the same thing — organize information, that is, not turn our online time into an obsession. (If you're like us, you're quite capable of doing the online obsession thing on your own, thank you very much.) The channels give you a ready-to-use, subject-oriented guide to all the content on AOL Canada. Just pick the channel that sounds like it matches your interests, and start browsing. You never know what you may find!

AOL Canada Welcome Screen

The AOL Canada Welcome screen (keyword **Welcome**) ranks right up there as one of the world's best inventions since the concept of evenly apportioned bakery goods (sorry — make that sliced bread). The AOL Canada Welcome screen rolls a little bit of everything into one place and offers links to some of AOL Canada's most popular areas.

Top Story

Keyword **News**

All day, every day, news pours in from across Canada and around the world. The Top Story area displays the current top headline and links you straight to the AOL Canada News Channel (covered later in this section) for everything from the news of the world to the tidbits of your neighbourhood.

Mail Centre

Keyword **Mailbox**

You've Got Mail! If the mailbox's flag is up and letters peek out, then new messages await your attention. If you haven't been lucky enough to have received e-mail, this icon will read Mail Centre. (Don't worry, you can always check back later to see if your luck has changed!)

Keyword

Keyword **Keyword**

If there's one little trick that makes using AOL Canada fun and easy, it's keywords. These things will get you around the system faster than you can say, "Take me *there*!" And since the people at AOL Canada know this better than anyone, they made it really easy to use keywords by adding a nice big Keyword icon to the AOL Canada Welcome Screen. One click of those gold keys and the Keyword window springs into action! Now, you can either enter a keyword in the text box and click Go, or, if you aren't sure exactly what you're after, check out the Keywords of the Day or the weekly Top 10 Recommended Keywords. If you're still having trouble getting the hang of things, you can click the link beside the title "New To Keywords?" for easy-to-follow instructions, or try the new AOL Canada Help Search system. It's another easy way to find the content you're looking for.

Hot Tip: Although the Keyword icon on the AOL Canada Welcome screen is the flashiest way to bring up the Keyword window, you can still get there the old-fashioned way by pressing Ctl+K on your keyboard, or by using the small but equally cute Keyword button on the far right of your navigation bar. For more about how to use keywords, visit Chapter 7.

My Calendar

Keyword **Calendar**

Thanks to the My Calendar button, your life is about to become more organized! Using this free AOL Canada service, you can schedule appointments months in advance, mark upcoming events like birthdays and anniversaries, or even the next big game, movie premiere, or CD release date. AOL Canada even provides a comprehensive Event Directory to help you choose what not to forget, no matter where you live in Canada.

Chat

Keyword **People Connection**

Want to pass the time with some new (or old) online friends? Click the Chat button and join the fun. This button takes you directly to the main People Connection window, where a world of people talk in a universe of chat rooms.

Search

Keyword **Search**

AOL Canada and the Internet both offer amazing amounts of cool information. The AOL Canada Search system makes finding the good stuff quicker and easier than ever. Find both Web sites and AOL Canada content areas with one-stop searching.

Headlines

Keyword **News**

Click the blue link here to bring up a breaking story from the AOL Canada News channel.

My Weather

Keyword **Weather**

Although looking out the window gives you a snapshot view of the day, sometimes your plans require a bigger weather vision. For moments like that, click My Weather, which takes you straight to the Current Conditions window of the AOL Canada Weather channel.

My Places

Keyword **My Places**

Sure, it's already full of great online places to visit, but the AOL Canada Welcome screen still needs a personal touch before it's truly your digital home away from home. My Places, a new

arrival with the AOL Canada 6.0 software, lets you add five links from a pre-selected list of My Places to the AOL Canada Welcome screen. By putting some of your favourite AOL Canada areas within clicking distance, My Places makes your online life easier. (For more about the *other* customizable areas of the AOL Canada software, flip ahead to Chapter 23.)

Go to Web

Keyword **Internet**

You can learn more about the Internet in Chapter 17, but we also recommend letting curiosity be your guide to the wonderful world of the Net. Click this button to begin your journey at the AOL.CA homepage.

Parental Controls

Keyword **Parental Controls**

Even though AOL Canada gives a neigh-bourhood feeling to the online world, the kids still shouldn't wander around unsupervised. Focus your child's online time (and keep their fingers out of the digital cookie jar) by setting the Parental Controls for their screen names. Chapter 6 explains the controls in detail, so head there for more information.

AOL Help

Keyword **Help**

Despite what the computer company ads say, your computer doesn't *always* do things right the first time — sometimes it fails on the second, third, seventeenth, and eighty-sixth times, too. When you feel overwhelmed, frustrated, or want to drop-kick your modem over the balcony, check the topics in the Member Services AOL Canada Help area for tips and tidbits to make your online life better.

Computing & Games Channel

When computers made their first appearance in the 1940s, they were an incomprehensible morass of wires, tubes, huge boxes, and cooling fans. Thanks to the wonders of modern technology, the computer of the year 2001 bears little resemblance to its long-antiquated counterpart. Computers are now an incomprehensible morass of boards, chips, little boxes, and cooling fans. Fills you with hope for the future, doesn't it?

Given this confusing state of affairs, the AOL Canada neighbourhood would not be complete without a substantial area devoted to discussing the things that can go wrong (breakdowns, upsets, crashes, and plain ol' obsolescence), and all the wonderful things that can go right (games, games, and more games) with your home computer. Well, ladies and gentlemen, may we introduce the AOL Canada Computing & Games Channel (keyword **Computing** or keyword **Games**).

The channel window has three main sections. On the left, from top to bottom, are a series of options you can select by clicking the orange and black bullets. Each option links to a different computer or game-related service, including computer shopping, a free computing newsletter, and a handy feedback area. In the middle of the window is the features and departments area (shaped into a raised oblong of buttons). These buttons lead to all the games areas and a lot more. On the upper right side of the window are the Spotlight areas. Sometimes fun, sometimes educational, but *always*

useful, these buttons change frequently, highlighting all kinds of timely content on the Computing & Games channel. What follows is a more complete list of the options you'll find in the main channel window.

Shop for PC Products Online

Thanks to a partnership with CompuSmart, a leading Canadian computer superstore, you can buy pretty much any computer product your heart desires through the PC Products link. Browse the Departments, including Top Sellers (turns out 3-D games are very popular these days), PC desktops (not as exciting, but everyone wants 'em), modems (yawn), digital cameras, and much more. Or, better yet, use the Find function to dig up more deals. CompuSmart guarantees all its products, so be sure to read through the return policies using the Our Deal With You link on the right side of the window.

Computing & Games Newsletter

Nothing is static inside AOL Canada. Combine that with the ever-changing world of computers and you have a recipe for missing out if you happen to blink! What's a techno junkie to do? Stay on top of changes to the Computing & Games channel, including new reviews, downloads and games demos with the Computing & Games Newsletter. Just click the Subscribe button, and every Wednesday, AOL Canada and *Viewz* (a Canadian online PC computing magazine) drop a free summary of all the latest into your online mailbox.

IBM Community Centre

Keyword **IBM Community Centre**

Is there any company more synonymous with quality and innovation in computing than IBM? Take a tour through all the solutions this granddaddy of the PC biz has to offer both individuals and small businesses at the IBM Community Centre. There's a complete product index in the pull-down menu under the heading Information. If you find something you like, you can shop from home at the IBM online store. Select How to Buy from the Shopper's Guide menu to find out more.

Feedback

Do you like the look and feel and functions of the Computing & Games channel? No? Well, by all means, let AOL Canada know about your problems or concerns. Just type in your comments and click Send to keep those computing experts on their toes.

Search and Explore

Keyword **Search Computing**

This helpful area lays it all out: It's a virtual tour of everything the Computing & Games channel has to offer. Read through the brief explanations listed on the left of the window. If something grabs you, click the blue link to be transported away. (Hey, that must be where the "explore" comes from in the Search & Explore title.) On the right of the window, you'll find some cool general interest links, including Great Places on AOL, an enormous master list of keywords (some less useful than others), the Research & Learn area, and the Random function.

Chat and Messages

Keyword **Computing**

If your life is (horrors!) devoid of computer or gaming people, or if you just want to swap tips with whoever wanders by, check out the various chat and discussion areas in the Chat & Messages department. They are great places to find solid technical help because you never know *whom* you may run into there. Stuck on Level 1 of your new favourite game? Post a message on one of the games boards and let another gamer come to your rescue. For the more technically inclined, you'll also find dozens of postings on serious technical topics like computer upgrades, maintaining a Web page, and even digital photography. Chat and Messages is also your entry point to the live *Viewz* chat rooms, where you can exchange tips on PC computing in real time. By the way, *Viewz* (keyword **Viewz**) is one of AOL Canada's partners-in-content, not to mention a cool online PC Computing magazine in its own right.

Play Games

Keyword **Play Games**

Okay, now for the really good stuff: Play Games is split into three distinct areas. Starting on the left are the games themselves, including the Game Parlour (keyword **Game Parlour**), Game Shows (keyword **Game Shows**), and Xtreme Games (keyword **Xtreme Games**). We discuss each of these below.

Along the bottom of the window lurk the Computing & Games departments. That's where the fun really starts, as you link up with other gamers, swap tips, download programs, and generally wreak havoc with your computer. Taking up the right half of your window are the current featured areas. These are usually devoted to various premium games, although the game shows, contests, and general information areas pop up from time to time.

Remember: All the games in the Game Parlour and Xtreme Games belong in the *premium* category, meaning that each game costs to play. By default, only the original master screen name (the first one you made when you signed up for AOL Canada) can play the premium games. To allow your other screen names into the area, go to keyword **Parental Controls** and change the Premium Services setting. For more about premium games, flip to Chapter 15.

The Game Parlour

Keyword **Game Parlour**

Even though the rough-and-tumble super–3-D action games garner most of the headlines, the truth is that more people play online card games than those explosion-laden digital destruction fests. On AOL Canada, that means visiting the Game Parlour, the home of card, board, and other games of a quiet persuasion. Your playing options in the parlour include classic card games, like gin, hearts, spades, and poker, plus arcade-style multiplayer games such as Splatterball and Virtual Pool.

Game Shows Online

Keyword **Game Shows**

Few things in life beat the fun and value of the Game Shows Online department, including the AOL Canada Computing & Games channel. What's so great about online game shows? They're challenging and engaging, of course, and (hang on to your hat) they're *free!* That's right — free. What a deal! Enjoy the multiplayer challenges of games like Strike-A-Match (keyword **Strike A Match**), Slingo (keyword **Slingo**), and the Puzzlezone

(keyword **Puzzlezone**), or settle down in front of the computer for a quiet round of crossword (keyword **Crossword**). While you're there, be sure to try the Canadian NTN trivia challenge (keyword **NTN**) — there's even a Canadiana category for all you proud Canucks. All that and more awaits you in Game Shows Online.

Xtreme Games

Keyword **Xtreme Games**

If a game explodes, roars, flies, stomps, shoots, or otherwise involves mayhem and digital carnage, it probably hangs its gunbelt in Xtreme Games, the AOL Canada gateway to the best in action games. Whether your interests lean toward fantasy role-playing or high-tech vehicular battles, Xtreme Games includes something to make you smile. In addition to the games listed in this area, try keyword **Gamestorm** for still more multiplayer action titles. Like Xtreme Games, the goodies in GameStorm carry a per-hour fee, so choose wisely what you shall enjoy.

Game Guide

Keyword **Game Guide**

When you want gaming information of almost any kind, go straight to the Game Guide, the AOL Canada one-stop gaming warehouse. Game Guide links you to areas all over AOL Canada, including gathering places like Gamers Forum; news and help areas like Games Help; discussion areas for swapping tales of success and prowess; and GameViewz (keyword **GameViewz**), a forum that includes game news, reviews, downloads, and more. At the bottom of the Game Guide window, you'll also find links to other Computing & Games departments including shopping, message boards, and reviews.

Download Software

Keyword **Download Software**

When you want new software for your Windows, DOS, or Macintosh computer, start the search in the Computing channel's Download Software department. This area offers freeware, shareware, demonstration software, sound files, and graphics files in popular Windows and Macintosh formats; hundreds and hundreds of TrueType fonts; and ready-to-use template files for popular commercial programs like Microsoft Publisher, Aldus PageMaker, and many others. And, of course, you can plop down your credit card for some online software purchasing, too.

Help Desk

Keyword **Help Desk**

Did your computer ever go *ping*, *beep*, or (our personal favourite) *bzzzrp-sproing-wugga-wugga-wugga*? During the workday, those peculiar sounds usually mean a quick call to your friendly computer support technician (followed by a bit of a wait while the support folks draw straws over who answers your question). At home (and in many small businesses) those same sounds usually precede weeping, wailing, and gnashing of teeth as you try to figure out what on earth just happened to your faithful machine.

Rather than cry yourself a river (or at least a small in-office pond), sign on to AOL Canada (assuming that part of the computer still works) and check out the Help Desk. It's chock-full of hardware and software assistance, plus nightly *ask the expert* chat sessions.

Tutorials & Guide

Keyword **Computing Tutorials**

The name of this department pretty much tells it like it is. Here, you'll find *tutorials* on everything from downloading to playing digital music to building a digital darkroom. You'll find *guides* for new PC computer owners, new AOL Canada members, mobile computer users, and even health-conscious computer users — you know, the whole ergonomics thing. If you're ready to lay down a few bucks for your learning experience, be sure to browse the online classes available through the Online Learning forum (keyword **Online Learning**). Keep in mind that tuition prices are in U.S. dollars.

Your Web Page

Keyword **Your Web Page**

The Your Web Page department shows you how to create your AOL Web presence. Whether you need the let's-start-at-the-beginning basics or you want a piece of clip art to jazz up your Web site, Build Your Web Page contains stuff you can use to take advantage of the Web space that comes with your AOL Canada account. The Your Web Page area even offers daily help sessions and weekly classes to assist you in creating your own Web page.

Reviews

Keyword **Computer Reviews**

Owning a computer means many things, among them the freedom to spend every loose piece of money you have on new stuff to keep your machine happy (because, goodness knows, you don't want to upset the computer). Use the hardware and software reviews in this department to help you find the best digital goodies at the most wallet-friendly price. And talk about reviews! Here are a few of the options you'll find on the left side of the Reviews window (the right side is a features area — a good place to watch for review highlights):

- *Dijit's buying guides*: "Who's Dijit," you ask? Well, he's sort of like an electronic mascot to the online computing magazine *Viewz*. Dijit, you see, has a whole lot of information about everything from personal digital assistants (Palm Pilots and such), to digital cameras, computer monitors, scanners, printers, and more. If you're in the market for one of these items but you don't yet know the basics, use Dijit's guides as a starting point. Each offers clear explanations for the uninitiated (that's you!).

- *ZDNet Product Reviews:* ZDNet is, by its own account, a worldwide technology behemoth, offering consumers expertise in all manner of techno goodies. It's no surprise then that the site regularly ranks products in just about every computer-related category there is.

- *Parent Soup's Kid Software Reviews:* You've set your AOL Canada Parental Controls just so. You've spent time with your child exploring the Net. Good. Your job's nearly done. Now all you have to do is breeze through these reviews to be sure your child is getting the most out of his or her time with the computer.

- *The latest CD-ROM releases:* Another area brought to you by a partnership with *Viewz* magazine. CD-ROM fans that want to know what's up, what's out, and what's stocking the CD-ROM store shelves right now should be sure to browse this area.

- *Computer companies:* Do you have a name-brand computer? Would you like to learn more about what that company has to offer? Use this fairly exhaustive list for direct access to everyone from IBM to Intel. Keep in mind, sometimes these companies offer free downloadable demos of new software!

Newsstand

Keyword **Computing Newsstand**

Computer magazines have earned their stripes. After all, it's not 1980 anymore — these guys have been around a while. Use the Newsstand to find the magazine that's right for you. You shouldn't have much trouble. Start by subscribing to AOL Canada's free Computing & Games Newsletter. Take part in a Computing Poll (same as keyword **Computing Poll**). Then try a PC mag like Canada's own *Viewz*, a Mac users mag like *MacWeek* or *Macworld Online*, or even a magazine for young techies called *YouthTech*. It's all waiting at the Computing Newsstand.

The Computing & Games channel has still more features, and we're quite sure you'll dig most of them up over time, but before we switch to the next channel, we don't want you to miss the following.

Daily Byte

Keyword **Daily Byte**

You never know what's coming next at the Daily Byte, but it's always interesting. Pick up screen savers, music programs, games, graphics, and more in this never-ending parade of unique and useful software.

Computer Cartoon

Keyword **Computer Cartoon**

If you've recently considered throwing your computer out the window, it's time to lower your blood pressure with a laugh. Try the Computer Cartoon. It might just do the trick.

How to Play Games on AOL Canada

Keyword **How to Play**

New gamers may want to spend a little extra time in this area, where AOL Canada answers your questions and provides an A to Z list of the system's games.

Video Games News

Keyword **Video Games**

If your favourite games live on a Nintendo 64, Sega Dreamcast, or Sony Playstation, the Video Games News area has your name written all over it (and the maintenance crew wants to discuss that with you, by the way). Console games rule the day, with areas devoted to news, gossip, tips, and chat about your favourites.

Hot Tip: If you love classic arcade games (like Asteroids, Centipede, and Tempest) or home video-game systems (such as the Atari 2600 and the original Nintendo system), relive your glory days with a visit to Vintage Gaming (www.vintagegaming.com). This site offers *emulators* (programs to make your computer behave like the brains behind the video games of days gone by) and the actual programs for your favourite arcade and video game classics. It's all free (well, some of the emulators are shareware, so you should pay for one if you fall in love with it), so give it a try!

Entertainment Channel

If you asked Canadians to tell you what they found most entertaining in life and then digitally rolled all their answers

into one place, tossed in a chat or two, seasoned the concoction with a touch of glamour, and then threw Christmas tree lights on it, you would come close to the flavour of the AOL Canada Entertainment channel (keyword **Entertainment**). Close, mind you, but still not *quite* there.

This channel simply *is* entertaining. No matter what you're into, you can find it all here (within the bounds of good taste, of course — no accordion players need apply). Movies, theatre, music, trivia, entertainment news, online games, and even places to mix and mingle with new people — the Entertainment channel is all that and more.

The window layout puts you in the front row of an informational extravaganza. Sitting in the centre of the window like a bunch of studio executives are the channel's main areas. Each area focuses on a different facet of the entertainment industry, from movies (John's favourite) to books (Marguerite's top pick) and Celebrities (we'll admit to some star-watching — no one can be highbrow all the time). Arrayed along the right of the window are the featured areas, the online version of this week's hot entertainment properties. Like the real-life version (stars of the moment, as it were), the featured areas change daily. Finally, a group of four buttons at the bottom of the window whisk you away to AOL Canada's main entertainment content and e-commerce partners — including Chapters.ca, Tribute.ca, EntertainmentAsylum.com, and SamTheRecordMan.com. Here then, is a complete list of the channel's main areas.

Music

Keyword **Music**

Ah, music. What would we do without those soul-soothing melodies and beats? Okay, maybe some of us could live without the bagpipes, but that's beside the point. AOL Canada's Music department is a haven for music makers, listeners, and lovers. The areas in this department cover all kinds of music, plus the artists, labels, and technologies behind the beats. The right side of the music window is taken up with features that change regularly. Here's what you'll find in the rest of the window:

✔ *The Listening Booth* (keyword **Music**): Poised at the centre of the music window is, well, *music*! Aren't those programmers clever? The Listening Booth is your own private testing ground, where you can sample the latest offerings from your favourite artists in such diverse realms as classical, jazz, and Canadian music. Online audio is one of the great innovations of our time, so this option is a must-do for people who want to test-drive everything the online world has to offer.

✔ *Chat & Message Boards* (keyword **Music Community**): Music, as Madonna would say, brings the people together (or was that Bob Dylan?). So it is with the features in the Chat & Message boards. For example, if you're already a devoted fan of a particular artist, you can publicly proclaim your admiration by posting essays, Web pages, and more at the Fans & Followers area (keyword **Music Fan**). Not so keen on the new album by this or that *band-du-moment*? Write a review or compare notes with others in the Member Reviews area (keyword **MMR**). Finally, musicians can also meet, exchanges notes (no pun intended), and commiserate on the decline of pop music in the Music Professionals area (keyword **Musicians**).

✔ *Other Music Resources:* This pull-down menu probably holds enough music-related information and samples to make Michael Jackson blush. Just select one of the options and click Go to give it a try. Worth mentioning here are some very cool Canadian resources. One of our favourites is KickinTheHead.com, a superb Web site where you can read about and even sample music from over a thousand Canadian bands. Also check out *ChartAttack.com*, the Canadian online music magazine, and CBC Infoculture, our public broadcaster's insightful guide to the arts.

✔ *Much Music:* A direct link to your Nation's Music Station.

✔ *SamTheRecordMan.com:* If all the samples, features, and tidbits you come across at AOL Canada Music are driving you music-mad, by all means visit Sam's store, where you can buy CDs online.

Movies

Keyword **Movies**

Ah, the silver screen! The magic, the drama . . . the popcorn! If you love movies as much as we do, you can't afford to miss AOL Canada Movies. Whether you're a full-fledged film buff in search of obscure movie facts, or you just want to know which new movies are opening this weekend, you're bound to find something here that interests you. Tab between several main content areas, including Now Playing (where you'll find features on the hottest new flicks), Coming Soon (if you can't wait to see what

Hollywood has in store), Cinemaniacs (yeah, that's us!), and On Video (for the home theatre nut). With a host of other fun features to offer, including the Top Ten list of current box office winners, member movie ratings, downloadable trailers, links to major film studio Web sites, industry news, chat rooms, message boards, and more, AOL Canada Movies may just keep you too busy to *get* to the movies. So pace yourself and go back often!

Hot Tip: If you already know what film you want to see, but don't know where it's playing, look no farther than the Movie Showtimes service (choose AOL Services⇨Movie Showtimes from the toolbar, or use keyword **Movie Finder**). Brought to you by *Tribute.ca*, Canada's online movie magazine, the service provides listings for theatres across Canada.

Television
Keyword **TV**

Do you ever find yourself sitting down for a relaxing evening of television, only to end up, not much later, furiously clicking around, looking for something good to watch and wondering why you aren't online instead? Fear not, brave TV watchers! The new and improved AOL Canada Television will help take the anxiety out of your next TV night. How? Well, thanks to a partnership with TVGrid.com, you can now use AOL Canada to see what's playing right now, no matter where you live in Canada. Better yet, you can create your own personalized TV guide with just the channels and shows you want to watch.

To get started, AOL Canada will ask for your postal code and the name of your cable provider. After that, you determine what goes in the grid. *What's that?* The

latest Aaron Spelling production you loved so much has been cancelled? No problem. You can edit your grid anytime to remove programs or add new ones — Spelling is sure to cast something equally juicy and ludicrous next season. Want to know what's playing right now on Channel 25? Not a problem either. Enter the channel number in the Jump to Channel field, click Go, and you'll instantly find out what's on.

AOL Canada Television even has a search function to help you find the shows you want. You can dig through categories like Action, Soaps, and Sports, or try a Quick Search if you already have a show title in mind.

Hot Tip: Three more features will help you decide what's worth watching on the tube:

Use the *Top 10 Searches* to check out shows that other AOL Canada members have frequently searched for — a good sign you might want to tune in yourself.

Browse the *Canned Searches* for ready made lists of information on everything from the new fall TV lineup to past Oscar winners.

When in doubt about AOL Canada Television, your personalized grid, or the continuing popularity of professional wrestling, you can always turn to the *Help Centre*. It's prominently displayed no matter where you find yourself inside AOL Canada Television.

Books
Keyword **Books**

We love books. Period. Sure, we write them, but that's nothing compared to the joy of *reading* the product of someone else's creative labour. If you love books as much as we do, here's a spot for you. Turn to the Books department to indulge yourself in the latest tidbits about the newest titles and the hottest authors. You can even use the Book Finder at the bottom left of the window to search for specific titles. Much of the content here is brought to you through a partnership with the good people at Chapters.ca (keyword **Chapters**), who, of course, will also be happy to sell you one of the tomes you covet!

On the bottom right of the main Books window, you'll also find an extensive list of options in the pull-down menu called More Book Resources. Among the offerings: Book Club Canada, BookReviews.net, the Canadian Book Review, CBC Infoculture, and the world-renowned *New York Times* Books section (the latter giving you free access to a back catalogue of more than 50,000 reviews and author interviews).

Celebrities

Keyword **Celebrities**

Sure we love the movies, but we also know the personal lives of the stars are often stranger (and juicier) than fiction. Get the goods and gossip on all the celebrities you love (or just love to hate) at AOL Canada Celebrities. Thanks to partnerships with all the biggies in the entertainment world — including *People Magazine*, *E! Online*, *Entertainment Weekly*, and *Entertainment Asylum* — this area is your ticket to keeping up with what the stars are saying (check out the Celebrity Q & A's link), what they're wearing (via People.com's Style Watch and E! Online's Fashion Police), where they're going, and more importantly, who they left with! Still hankering for more info about the stars? Try the pull-down menu called Celebrities index, located in

the middle of the window. Here you'll find links to the AOL Entertainment Newsletter, transcripts from previous AOL Live Celebrity chats, celebrity interviews from *E! Online*, and more.

Hot Tip: Everyone knows Canada is "Hollywood North," including AOL Canada. That's why AOL Canada Celebrities has tidbits about your favourite Canadian stars, too. Whether they've gone South of the Border or they're busy being famous right here at home, be sure to check back often for coverage of events like the annual inductions into Canada's Walk of Fame at Roy Thomson Hall, in Toronto.

Videos

Keyword **Videos**

Remember when "watching a movie" involved leaving your living room? Thanks to videocassettes, laser discs, and DVD, your couch is the front row of the Bijou whenever you feel like watching a flick. If home is your video castle, pop over to the Home Video department. Pick up new release information, reports on the most popular videos, and general stories about the home video market.

Speak Out

Keyword **ECommunity**

Do you have a favourite movie star, follow a particular television series, enjoy a good book, or love great music? (Hey — how's *that* for an inclusive question?) Swap thoughts and trivia about your preferred media darlings in the entertainment message boards and chat rooms. The boards cover all facets of the frenetic entertainment industry. The chats include everything from spur-of-the-moment ranting opportunities to every-week scheduled fun.

Entertainment Search

Keyword **ESearch**

Thank goodness for the Search & Explore option! (Okay, so it's very late and our naturally nerdy side *is* showing a little — but can't a couple of authors get excited about something that takes your request, digs through a ton of material, and then delivers your answer in record time, all without asking anything in return?) The Entertainment channel's Search & Explore area uses the Web-based search system like its fellow channels, so you have a set of tweakable tools at your service, plus the ever popular A–Z Channel Guide. Whenever you simply can't find what you need (at least in entertainment information), turn to this area for help.

While we're at it, here are two more Entertainment areas you shouldn't miss:

Fun and Games

Keyword **Fun & Games**

Hollywood wants very little from us — just most of our money and all our attention (plus some well-timed applause). In exchange, the entertainment industry offers, well, entertainment. It's not a bad exchange, when you get right down to it. In keeping with the whole Good Times concept, the Entertainment channel presents the Fun & Games department. Enjoy all kinds of free fun, from trivia contests to little arcade games, and all with an entertainment industry twist. It's fun (and free)!

In the News

Keyword **Entertainment News**

It's like simple math: Stars garner attention; attention draws reporters; reporters write stories; stories become news. Thus, thanks to obscure and unmemorable theories learned to escape grade eight math class, you end up with the statement *stars equal news*. (Mark this page — you never know when some online math teacher may throw a pop quiz at you about this stuff.) Given the stars and news equation, it's no wonder that the Entertainment channel includes a direct link to all the entertainment industry news you could possibly want.

Each time you visit AOL Canada's Entertainment News area, you'll be greeted by the day's Top Stories, as well as several clickable headlines. Don't be shy! Check them all out. Thanks to AOL Canada's news providers, like Canadian Press and Reuters, you can rest assured that you're getting the latest and best coverage of Canada's entertainment industry, not to mention Hollywood and the rest of the entertainment world.

Health Channel

Everyone wants to be healthy. Millions of Canadians lower their fat intake, partially eliminate meat from their diets, and begin exercise programs in an effort to maintain or regain health. The AOL Canada Health channel (keyword **Health**) helps you along the way, with departments devoted to treating illness, improving nutrition, and keeping fit, as well as numerous resource links to Canadian health organizations and government health departments.

The channel window is divided into several main areas. First, under the heading Taking Care of Your Health, you'll find the channel's main departments (like Conditions and Treatments, Alternative Medicine, and Health & Beauty). Next come the four Health Issues areas — specific information for Men, Women,

Children, and Seniors. Near the bottom of the window, the two pull-down menus under the Resources heading are jam-packed with Canadian health agencies and government contacts. On the right side of the window, you can test everything from your Emotional Intelligence Quotient to your knowledge of nutrition in the Tests, Tools, and Support area, or use the links here to delve into health-related message boards, chats, or even expert advice. Finally, AOL Canada health has a Search function to save you time and energy when maneuvering around the channel.

Hot Tip: The upper right side of the AOL Canada Health channel window displays featured areas. These change frequently, so if something really appeals to you, save it in your Favourite Places (see Chapter 7 for more about that).

Warning! Health care is serious business. The resources you'll find in the Health channel should not take the place of the personal attention of your physician. Also, keep in mind that Canadian treatments, prescription drugs, insurance, and doctors are different animals from those in the U.S. When in doubt about something you read online, ask your own doctor!

Conditions and Treatments

Keyword **Conditions**

When you or a loved one suffer from an illness of some kind, you long to find more about it, discover ways to cope, and meet other people who can relate. In the Conditions & Treatments department, you can meet all three goals at one time. The department contains folders on many different illnesses and health issues, from allergies and cancer all the way down to skin conditions. Select one of the areas and find out about it. In most cases, the specific illness window contains

information about online support groups, where you can connect with members who understand.

Dieting and Nutrition

Keyword **Dieting**

Need to shed a few pounds before terming yourself completely healthy? Seek help and guidance in the Dieting and Nutrition area. Starting with the basics of good nutrition and losing weight, the area covers a lot of ground on the way to a newer, smaller you.

Fitness and Sports Medicine

Keyword **Fitness**

There's more to fitness than push-ups and jumping jacks. Perhaps you prefer burning calories with mountain biking, weight lifting, tennis, running, or walking. Whatever your activity, the Fitness and Sports Medicine area delivers the information you need. Swap ideas with fellow aficionados, explore a ton of fitness tips, and garner some insight on how your body works (and why it hurts when you put your arm waaaaay over your head, like this. *Ow!*).

Alternative Medicine

Keyword **Alternative Medicine**

As the health industry grew, so did health customer concerns over expensive chemical therapies, lengthy treatments, and complex drug regimens. As health technology advanced, many doctors rediscovered herbs and other natural remedies. Soon, alternative medicine itself grew into a full-fledged health industry. Learn about alternative treatments, herbal remedies, and much more in the Alternative Medicine area.

Health and Beauty

Keyword **Health & Beauty Tips**

Beauty means more than picking the right cosmetics and making sure that your clothing colours match. The Health and Beauty section guides you through the world of beauty from a healthy perspective. Covering everything from balding and body image to skin care and sun protection, this area provides the health information you need.

Health issues vary by age and sex. In a nod to this reality, AOL Canada has added four focus areas for health to the main channel windows. Here they are:

Men

Keyword **Men's Health**

Men have special health needs. That's why the Health channel created the Men's Health focus area — to discuss men's health issues apart from the general illness or healthy living departments. Look in this area for information specific to men and the bodies they inhabit: male baldness and hair loss, cancers that affect only the male body, and other illnesses and problems men may incur.

Women

Keyword **Women's Health**

Women's health demands specific information. Find what you need to know in the Women's Health focus area. From information about cancers that affect only women to eating disorders and pregnancy, Women successfully delivers information uniquely relevant to female health.

Children

Keyword **Children's Health**

Nothing is quite as joyful as a healthy child. Healthy children run, leap, jump,

and ask millions of questions. Use the Children's Health department for information to enhance the health of the children in your life. Look in this area for information about topics that range from the snuffly-nosed cold and otitis media (ear infection) all the way to extremely serious illnesses, such as leukemia. You also find info about school-related health issues, such as attention deficit disorder and other learning disorders. Pick a folder and dive in.

Seniors

Keyword **Senior's Health**

Just as children sometimes suffer with specific age-related illnesses, the senior set faces its own unique challenges at the other end of the age spectrum. Look in the Seniors department for information about arthritis, glaucoma, osteoporosis, and a range of other concerns. You can also find an option named Caregiving (keyword **Caregiving**), which takes you to AOL's Caregiving forum, designed to help the elder caregiver.

Resources: Organizations

Canada has one of the healthiest populations in the world, thanks in part to the work of our leading health organizations where people work tirelessly to promote education and research. The Organizations pull-down menu includes links to the online presence of prominent organizations like the Alzheimer's Society, the Canadian Liver Foundation, Epilepsy Canada, the Thyroid Foundation of Canada, and more. Each Web site offers background information, contacts, and ways you can help.

Resources: Government

It's no wonder that health care has become *the* hot button in Canadian politics. Everyone wants a quality health care system, and as taxpayers we want our dollars used efficiently. That's where the federal, provincial, and territorial health departments come in. They deliver the care we need, and each of them does it a little bit differently. For everything from forms to details on your health coverage to links with other health agencies, choose one of the departments from the Government resources pull-down menu.

Tests, Calculators, and Tools

For a little healthy fun in your day, visit the Test Yourself area. This area offers all kinds of healthy tests and quizzes (no surprise there), plus a variety of other interactive informational sources, like the calorie calculator, nutrition database, and recipe finder. Munch through the chocolate quiz, take an IQ test, measure your risk for Diabetes, check your nutritional knowledge, and much more.

Message Boards, Chats & Experts

Keyword **Health Talk**

You (or someone you love) struggles with a health problem, and you want to talk about it? Turn to the Message Boards, Chats & Experts department for support and help. Select the support group that interests you, and open its folder to find out more. Some support groups meet in scheduled chats several times a week to discuss various topics; others meet only once a week. Browse through the entries on your topic of choice for the details.

House and Home

Home. The mere mention of that word conjures up such warm and fuzzy feelings, doesn't it? Not to mention all the other

good stuff that goes along with it — like the care we take decorating our home in our own unique way, the meals we share there with family and friends, and the hobbies we pursue within its walls. Yep, home truly is where the heart is, and AOL Canada, always in tune with the times, has devoted an entire channel to it. So consider the House and Home channel your home away from home the next time you need fresh ideas for everything from pet care to recipes.

The channel window itself is kind of homey (all muted tones and subtle design). Under the heading Around the House, you'll find several of the main departments relating to the care of your house, including decorating and home improvement. Next comes the In The Kitchen heading, under which you can follow links to Food & Recipes and even a customizable cookbook where you can store all your favourite recipes. Now, tell us this doesn't feel a wee bit like home. Also, be sure to keep an eye on the timely features on the right side of the channel window. AOL Canada updates them all the time.

Hot Tip: The information you'll find under the Real Estate heading on the main House & Home window leads to mostly U.S. home-buying options. We recommend that you visit the Canadian Real Estate Centre instead. Get there through the AOL Canada Personal Finance Channel. (The Real Estate link is on the lower right side of the channel window.) For more information about the Real Estate Centre, see its entry later in this directory.

Decorating

Keyword **Decorating**

Bare walls do not a home make. All of us like to add a few personal touches, regardless of where we live. Whether you're painting your first apartment or you already have a seasoned flair for making things just so, the enormous content in the Decorating department is sure to provide you with ideas or, better yet, solutions. The main department window is divided into several areas. Follow the Room-by-Room links to find out everything you ever wanted to know about decorating all the rooms in your home, from bathrooms to home theatres. Each room on the list gets its own content page, where you'll find a welcome screen with timely features, an ideas area, and helpful links to areas inside and outside AOL Canada where you can dig up even more solutions.

Under the Essentials heading, you'll find the bulk of Decorating's departments. Here's a quick guide:

- ✔ *Decorating Basics:* Brought to you by Homestore.com, Decorating Basics is a learning area (everyone has to start somewhere). Read through the Facts on Fabric, get to know the power of natural light, or even tackle the world of flooring. It's all waiting in the Decorating Basics area.

- ✔ *Easy Projects:* You don't have to be Martha Stewart to brighten up your home. The Easy Projects window is packed with simple projects you can try right now.

- ✔ *Paint & Wallpaper:* Does the sight of a colour wheel at the local paint shop terrify you? All that choice! You need some guidance, and the Paint & Wallpaper area can provide it, with specific how-tos and advice on how to make your next paint job a successful one.

- ✔ *Handy Estimators:* You'd like to start redecorating your home, but how much will it cost? The people at

Homestore.com can help you with their cost calculators for everything from a paint job to drywall.

Hot Tip: Before you leave the Decorating area, be sure to check out Today's Decorating Talk, on the right side of the window, which leads to a topical decorating message board. You never know when another AOL member might have that one insight you've been waiting for.

Hot Tip: If you want to fill your home with antiques, check out the Antiques Primer in the main AOL Canada Antiques area (keyword **Antiques**), where you can learn where to buy and how much to spend on antiques.

Gardening

Keyword **Gardening**

Green thumbs take note! AOL Canada has a new and expanded gardening area. Front and centre on the Gardening window is the Plant Finder, one of our favourite tools. Just type in a plant or flower name, click Search, and AOL Canada comes back with vital information about its many varieties, often accompanied by a colour image (just in case you're having trouble identifying a mystery plant). On the left side of the window, under the Features heading, you can follow the links for information on everything from bulbs, to your lawn, to vegetable growing. Lower down on the left side, under the Essentials heading, you'll find useful services like a list of Gardening Basics and the Garden Designer. The Designer helps you draw up your dream garden using a virtual representation. Also worth checking out: AOL's resident gardener Rebecca Koll's Tip of the Day. And don't miss the gardening message board and chat possibilities. You'll find links to them on the right side of the main gardening window.

D-20 House and Home

Home Improvement

Keyword **Home Improvement**

We live in a do-it-yourself world. No longer willing to pay someone else top dollar for home improvements we can do ourselves for less, we Canadians have developed a hefty appetite for do-it-yourself magazines, Web sites, and TV shows. Now, you have an even better option: AOL Canada Home Improvement. This area has ideas and tips for remodelling just about everything in your home. Apart from the regularly updated features that you'll find in the centre of the main window, and the message boards located on the right, you can also dig up a plethora of tips by searching the How-To Library (it's at the bottom centre of the window). Just type in whatever needs improving in your home — a door, a window, a floor — click Search, and thanks to the Homestore.com Web site, you'll get back a list of search results, including how-tos and recent feature articles on that subject.

On the left side of the window, under the Projects heading, you'll find the bulk of AOL Canada Home Improvement's helpful information. In categories as wide-ranging as Baths, Kitchens, Masonry, and Walls, each link opens its own window, where, depending on the subject, you might browse through an introduction and planning guide for your next project, find expert advice, or even check out a photo gallery of the latest styles.

Hot Tip: The name Bob Vila has become synonymous with do-it-yourself expertise. Now, you can get tips from the man himself by checking out Bob Vila's Weekend Project (on the right side of the Home Improvement channel window). Sponsored by BobVila.com, the projects change all the time — but don't worry, you'll find links to previously discussed projects under the "More Weekend Projects" heading.

Household Hints

Keyword **Household Hints**

Have you ever noticed that every household does things just a little bit differently? Everyone comes up with their own solutions to make their home run smoothly. Well, consider AOL Household Hints your own personal kitchen party (except you don't have to bring brownies). This is the place for swapping hints and tips on everything from stain removal to defrosting freezers to catching mice (yikes!) to uncurling old photos (no kidding). There's even advice from Heloise, a woman who probably has more house-running advice than 10 grandmothers put together! Check out her Tip of the Day on the right side of the main window. If you think you've got the perfect solution to a household quandary, share your innovation by leaving a posting on one of the House & Home message boards.

Hobbies

Keyword **Hobbies**

Read reviews of new books on the market, find out who located that antique whatzit you've been looking for everywhere, meet fellow star gazers in Astronomy, or swap roots with researchers in Genealogy. No matter whether you enjoy creating items from scratch, rebuilding cars for fun, or collecting yesterday's toys, the Hobbies area leads to pastimes online. Check out this department to brush up on an old hobby, maintain your skill level in an interest you enjoy, or research a new hobby or two for the winter.

Pets

Keyword **Pets**

Sharing your home with a furry roommate brings its own set of challenges and joys. Whether your friend is a dog, cat, gerbil, mongoose, or tarantula, concerns abound. Is your pet getting the right food? What signs of sickness do you look for? How do you redirect those less-than-desirable behaviours? Find answers to these questions and more in the Pets department. You may even meet and fall in love with a whole new section of the animal kingdom. Among the services you'll find here are a test to determine which pet best suits you and a Search area where you can find information on an array of pet topics. If you just plain love your pet, go ahead and nominate him (or her) for Pet of the Day, or check out the pet-related chats and message boards.

Food & Recipes

Keyword **Food**

Humans don't survive long without food, but some of us have taken culinary interest to an art in itself. Make the Food area your destination when you don't know what to fix from the leftovers in the fridge, or when you have friends coming for dinner tomorrow night and you're at a complete loss for ideas. The Food area provides recipes, informational articles, and tips on a whole host of food-related topics. Personal pick? Find a Recipe, a really cool search system featured front-and-centre on the Food area window. We also like these Food & Recipe features:

- *Essentials:* Each category under the Essentials heading is packed with a delicious array of recipes, tips, and information. Entertaining this week? Looking for something exotic from another part of the world? Concerned about healthy eating? These and more topic areas are waiting for you at AOL Food & Recipes Essentials.

- *Food Index:* The last category under the Essentials heading is actually a guide to all the content in the Food & Recipes area. Use the alphabetical

list, or try the list of More Visited Topics to orient yourself to all the excellent content.

- *The Weekly Dish:* Even if you don't have time to come back to AOL's Food & Recipes area as often as you'd like, that doesn't mean you have to miss out on its up-to-date content. By subscribing to The Weekly Dish, a free newsletter, you can receive recipes, seasonal specials, and tips in your online mailbox. No fuss, no muss. Just follow the link on the right side of the main Food & Recipes window, click Subscribe, and you're on your way.

My Cookbook

If you're like us and your trusty cookbook is either lost or covered in molasses and flour, it's time to start thinking about customizing your own virtual cookbook. Powered by Personalogic.com, you can use My Cookbook to store only the recipes you love, and get rid of recipes you aren't using, with the click of a mouse. Are you just starting out in the kitchen? Don't worry, My Cookbook starts you off by adding some basic recipes to your personal list. You can even share your recipes with friends electronically.

Find a Recipe

Feel like you're constantly preparing the same dishes? Or are you just feeling especially creative today? In either case, use this handy Search function, powered by Personalogic.com, to dig up recipes for anything your heart desires. You can enter a cooking term, an ingredient, or a food you love (like brownies or chicken). Then click Search to receive a list of results. (Our search for "chicken" returned more than 2,000 recipes! How's that for new options?)

Kids Only Channel

"When I was a kid . . . ." Do any words strike as much fear and trepidation into a child as the threat of yet another parental tale of the good ol' days? (How about "We're disconnecting cable TV"? That may come close.) Kids, here's something for you to lob back when Mom and Dad get into reminiscence mode: "Yeah, but you didn't have your own online hangout. We're talkin' *digital treehouse* here."

AOL Canada set aside a channel just for kids and marked it plainly, too. Kids Only (keyword **Kids Only**) offers activities, forums, discussion areas, research sources, and interactive hangouts specially designed for kids ages 5 to 14. Heck, it even includes homework help (where was this channel when we were kids?).

While all AOL Canada members can access the Kids Only Channel (that's KO for short) from the floating channels toolbar, parents will want to consider setting up a KO account so their kids can explore AOL Canada independently. Setting up the account is easy. Just choose Settings⇨Screen Names from the toolbar and follow the steps to create a screen name. When it comes time to choose a Parental Controls Category, click the radio button beside the option called Kids Only.

Now, when your children sign on using their own screen names, they'll have access to all the services, games, and fun of the KO channel. What's more, they'll be greeted by their own modified toolbar and Welcome Screen.

Remember: When signed on to AOL Canada with a KO account, your child will have access only to approved Web sites (appropriate for kids 12 and under), text-only e-mail, and monitored chats. She or he will not be able to use Instant Messages, receive e-mail with attachments or imbedded pictures, access premium (fee-based) areas, or stumble into unsavoury Internet Web sites. For all the details on KO accounts, including how to tweak them to give your child slightly more access, visit keyword **Parental Controls**, or choose Settings⇨Parental Controls from the toolbar. Make sure you read through Chapter 6 of this book as well, where you'll find step-by-step instructions on how to protect your children online.

Warning! Most of the people who hang out in Kids Only are there to have a good time and learn stuff. Unfortunately, it seems like a few bad apples always try to spoil things for the rest of us. If you run into a person in a chat room who's being obnoxious, if someone sends you an instant message that makes you feel weird, or if *anyone* asks for your password, get help from a Kids Only guide. To do that, either click the Kids Help button near the bottom of the Kids Only Channel window or click in the address box on the navigation bar (the big white space just under the toolbar at the top of your screen), type keyword **KO Help**, and press Enter. Follow the instructions onscreen, and help will arrive shortly!

KO Welcome Screen

Hey, kids! If your parents have helped you set up your own screen name, you're in luck. Not only can you get online with your very own AOL Canada screen name (same as your e-mail address), but each time you log on you'll be greeted by a special KO Welcome Screen. It looks totally different from the regular (uh, adult) Welcome Screen. In the top left corner, you'll find a list of Cool Tips. These simple definitions and explanations are sure to make your time online more fun. On the top right corner of the Welcome Screen, you can dive right into a KO Chat, where other young people are waiting to share ideas, jokes, and stories. On the bottom left is your online mailbox. (You'll know right away if you have a new message because a yellow envelope will be sticking out of the mailbox and the red flag will stand up.) Finally, on the bottom right, there's a button that takes you straight to the Kids Help area. Whenever you have questions about what's happening online, this — and your parents — are the two places to get answers. So, are you ready to explore? Go for it!

KO Toolbar

The KO Welcome Screen isn't the only benefit you get from signing on to AOL Canada from a KO account. You'll also notice a unique toolbar across the top of your screen. Some features, like your online mailbox, are just like those on an adult account. But the rest is definitely just for kids. Here are some of the special icons you'll find:

✔ *Newsletter:* The green notepad icon is your ticket to the KO Channel's free newsletter. Just click the Subscribe button and you'll automatically get a free summary of what's new and hot on the KO Channel delivered to your online mailbox twice a month!

✔ *KO Chat:* The icon with the little people on it brings you into the world of KO chats, where kids — from Gander to Kelowna and the rest of the world, too — can meet, laugh, and make new friends.

✔ *Games:* What better icon than a video game control to represent one of the most popular areas on the KO channel? Yep, that icon is your ticket to games, games, and more games!

✔ *KO Search:* AOL has designed a special search engine just for kids. Click the globe icon and you'll see! By typing a word (or words) in the text box and clicking the Find button, you'll get back a list of Web pages and Web sites that contain related information.

✔ *KO Fun Spots:* If you've just set up your KO account and don't know where to start, KO Fun Spots (that's the one with the heart-on-the-envelope icon) is a good place to start. AOL Canada has already created links to some of the coolest and most fun areas inside the KO Channel. All you do is click one that sounds interesting and you're off!

News and Sports

Keyword **KO News & Sports**

Catch up on the news from a kid's point of view or play ball — or whatever other sport activity you enjoy — in the Kids Only channel's nod to the action-packed world of information: Kids Only News and Sports. In addition to all its regular sports coverage, the News and Sports department profiles well-known athletes and newsmakers, giving you some insight into what they like, how they started out, and what they do to stay on top in their area of sport. Uncover new tidbits about your favourite sports stars and swap notes about the sports you love on the News and Sports discussion boards (in the More News and More Sports windows) right here, in the KO News and Sports department.

Art Studio

Keyword **KO Art**

Expand your creativity in the Art Studio, the Kids Only channel's answer to arts, crafts, theatre, and writing all rolled into one. Try your hand at drawing, show off your poetic talents, and create some neat crafts. Wherever you go, the best and brightest minds in all of Kids Only are waiting to meet you.

Hot Tip: For a truly artsy time, take a side-trip to Blackberry Creek (www. blackberrycreek.com). It's a wild club for young writers, artists, and storytellers. Take a moment to check it out!

Clubs

Keyword **KO Clubs**

Come one, come all! Join a club and have a ball! (Sorry, no more poetry. Promise.) Taking its place as one of the best spots to have fun and meet new people on the whole Kids Only channel, the Clubs department gives you a place to follow your interests and find cool friends in the process. Just pick your favourite hobbies (or a hobby you've always wanted to try), find the club that matches them, and join the fun!

Homework Help

Keyword **KO HH**

Stuck on that geometry assignment? Need a little push to get through an English essay? When homework closes in around you, leaving you more than a bit frustrated and forlorn, turn to the Kids Only Homework Help department. You can find the energy and tips that help you over the hump (and, more important, open up time to spend in the Chat and Clubs departments with your friends).

Remember: The folks you find waiting in Ask a Teacher *don't* do your assignments for you, no matter how much you beg and whine. They *do* offer all the help they can and go to great lengths to make sure that you find the resources you need. Putting the pieces together, though, is still your job.

Games

Keyword **KO Games**

Games, John always says, are the only real reason computers exist. Well, games and AOL Canada access — but that's strictly it. Everything else is just icing on the digital cake. The Kids Only Games department takes this idea and runs with it, proving beyond any doubt that the best things in life explode, fly, drive fast, or make peculiar *boinging* sounds. The Games area offers so many diversions that we may find it hard to stay focused long enough to write this paragraph. (Whoops, sorry — it's now tomorrow. We got sidetracked, but we promise to finish this section without getting lost again. Really.) Take your brain for an entertaining and even *educational* (remind Mom and Dad about that one frequently) spin through some of the best games, puzzles, and contests anywhere in the online world.

TV Movies & Music

Keyword **KO TV**

Whether you love cartoons, comics, or celebrities, the TV, Movies, and Music department brings everything you want to know about your favourite shows and stars right to your computer screen. You never know exactly what (or who) you may find, so visit often. (After all, if you aren't *watching* television, you may as well *read* about it.)

Français

Keyword **AOL Junior**

If your child is enrolled in French immersion, by all means encourage him or her to sample the francophone version of the KO Channel.

Weather

Keyword **Weather**

The weather link transports your child to the Current Conditions screen of the AOL Canada Weather Channel.

Chat

Keyword **KO Chat**

Kids, like adults, *do* love to talk, discuss, and chat. Even though the topics may focus on some slightly different subjects from other online areas, the Kids Only chat rooms make great places to meet and be met by other online kids. The Chat department houses the channel's special chat and discussion rooms, plus a broad variety of kid-centric discussion boards.

The Kids Only channel sponsors six regular chat rooms, organized by topic. During the school year, these special chat rooms open up after school hours and close in the evening (so if you're home sick from school, no chatting for you — but you should be in bed anyway!). During the summertime, the rooms run most of the day, so when it rains, you may want to drop in for some online talking time. Specially trained Kids Only staff members hang out in the rooms to keep the chats moving and on-topic.

Hot Tip: It's easy to pick out Kids Only staff members because their screen names always begin with KO, for Kids Only. If you have a question or problem, always feel free to ask a Kids Only staffer — they want to hear from you!

Note to Parents

At the bottom left corner of the Kids Only Chat window, you'll find this important link. Kids will find it boring, but parents should read through the information here for more help in making the AOL Canada experience safe and fun for their brood.

Kids Only Search

Keyword **KO Web**

The Web (even apart from its fairly eerie name) sometimes sends stout adults into fright-filled spasms. Because kids aren't the least bit phased, of course, by little things like new technology, the Kids Only Web department focuses on getting around the Web and finding new places to visit, instead of spending a bunch of time explaining how the whole thing works.

Hot Tip: If, despite being a member of the techno literate younger set, you need some information about how the Web actually works, don't worry — we won't tell a soul. Find out everything you need to know about the Web in Chapter 17.

Cool Tips

Your kid will love this list of kid-specific keywords.

Kids Only Help

Keyword **KO Help**

When things aren't working quite right or something a little unexpected happens, it's time to get help. That's why the Kids Only Help department exists — to answer questions, help you through the technically tricky stuff, and generally make you feel comfortable in the big online world. Kids Only Help covers everything from basic online life to the perils of the Web. If you have a question, dive right in and find the answer. That's why Kids Only Help is there!

Life Channel

How do you show the world who you really are? What parts come together to make you unique? Your beliefs, ethnic background, and stage of life all play a part. Celebrate your uniqueness on the Life channel (keyword **Life**), and find other members who believe, live, and dream in much the same way as you.

Divided into eight departments, Life helps you connect with people who share your background, your dreams, and your views of the world. Don't be shy — select an interesting-looking department, hop right in, and explore a new facet of Life.

Ages & Stages

Keyword **Ages & Stages**

Drop in to Ages & Stages for age-appropriate fun, whether you're 23, 43, 63 or beyond. Toggle among the Chats, Boards, Home Pages, and Features tabs to find a forum and people like you, no matter which stage you occupy. Ages & Stages includes focus areas for retirees, baby boomers, Generation Xers, and more.

Faith & Spirituality

Keyword **Faith**

Your belief system helps shape your lifestyle. Dip into the Faith & Spirituality area when you need a little encouragement or you want to know more about others' belief systems. This area lists many of the major world religions, plus new religious movements and links to general spirituality-oriented topics. To access the main belief areas quickly, including some topical Web sites, click one of the yellow folders along the left side of the window. The Jewish

Community, Christianity Today, Catholic Community, Islam, and other folders take you to their featured areas in a flash. Given recent news reports showing that meditation can truly improve health and longevity, you may also want to use the blue globe link titled Meditation, which takes you to the Institute for the Scientific Study of Meditation Web site.

Parenting (Families)

Keyword **Parenting**

The kids are in bed (or safely packed off to university or college), the house is neat, and you're too tired to go anywhere. Maybe you spent all day matching wits with a four-year-old (and losing more often than you care to admit) or you need some advice on living day by day with a teenager. Rather than spend the last daylight hours sitting numbly in front of the tube, hop on to AOL Canada and nimbly check out the Parenting department.

The window's right side displays the current *featured areas*, which change frequently during the week (the digital equivalent of the seasonal-products aisle at your local department store). The left and centre sections offer the more permanent parenting-related options — your links to all the good stuff in the department. In the Parents Toolbox, you'll find calculators, tests, tips, advice, and more on subjects as wide-ranging as naming your baby, tracking male fertility, and even on how to interview new doctors and nannies. Under the Departments heading, there's so much to choose from, we can't resist giving you a brief synopsis here:

- *Parenting by Age:* These links explore parenting at different stages: babies, preschoolers, grade schoolers, and teens.

✔ *Pregnancy* (keyword **Pregnancy**): It's never too early to start playing your role as father and mother. For a guide to *in utero* parenting, try the Pregnancy area.

✔ *Family Issues* (keyword **Family Issues**): Divided into three main areas — Family Relations, Single Parents, and Grandparents, the family issues window has advice and support for all parents — at all ages. Check out the subjects in the How do I? pull-down menu, or find community with other AOL parents by reading through the subject-specific message boards.

✔ *Genealogy* (keyword **Genealogy**): Explore your history and your family tree in the Genealogy area, powered by Ancestry.com.

✔ *Family Entertainment* (keyword **Family Entertainment**): Choose from several areas, including TV & Movies, Toys & Books, or Travel & Activities, for new ways to entertain your brood. In the pull-down menu under the heading More TV and Movies, you'll even find expert advice on subjects like how much TV is appropriate for children, courtesy of iVillage.com.

✔ *Mom-to-Mom* (keyword **Mom to Mom**): What did moms do before AOL Canada? Here, you can commiserate, swap tips, and learn from fellow mothers using message boards, chats, and other resources.

✔ *Dads* (keyword **Dads**): Fathering is an art, too, and AOL Canada, in recognition of that fact, has designed a dads-only area where you can post tips on the message boards, learn from other dads in online chat sessions, and explore other fathering resources.

✔ *Search* (keyword **Parenting Search**): If you're having trouble locating a specific parenting topic in the AOL Canada Parenting department, turn to the Parenting Search function. You can either type in a subject name and click the Search button, or use the alphabetical content list — both excellent time-savers for busy moms and dads.

Health

Keyword **Cdn Health**

Good health is the starting point for a good life. In keeping with that adage, AOL Canada has included this link to the new and improved Health channel. Turn to it when you need information about conditions and treatments, when seeking community with others who share your health concerns, or if you need links to some of Canada's leading health organizations and government health departments.

Learning & Reference

The title of this department says it all: One click, and you can begin a research and learning journey through reference books, periodicals, history, the sciences, and more. Start by conducting a search using the Quick Reference text box. Depending on which radio button you choose, it will return results from the online encyclopedia, dictionary, or from AOL and the Net. Then take the time to explore the almanac (it's full of excellent tidbits like famous birthdays and anniversaries), the thesaurus (another word for aardvark, please!), as well as maps of the world and the A to Z index of everything in the Learning & Reference department. The Science area (keyword **Science**), which you can access by clicking the blue link on the right side of the main channel window, is particularly useful for parents with curious youngsters. In it, you'll find not just current news from the world of science, but information about space, our planet, and nature.

Hot Tip: There's one specifically Canadian research tool that we should mention while we're at it. They may cost a few dollars, but the services at Electric Library Canada (keyword **ELC**) will be worth their weight in gold next time you need in-depth reports on just about any subject. Instead of trucking off to library after library looking for just that document or just that microfiche, let these folks do all the scurrying around to dig up articles from newspapers, periodicals, archives, and even pictures for your next research project.

Love@AOL

Keyword **Love**

Neither man nor woman lives by bread (or even really good sushi) alone! Judging by the popularity of Love@AOL, a lot of members have already figured this one out. There are over 700,000 personal ads to browse or search here, and it's easy to add your own! Isn't technology grand? If you've already found a potential love interest online, try the electronic hugs or greetings options to show that special someone you care. Too shy to make direct contact? Why not start by getting your feet wet at the advice columns, by playing one of the games, or by reading your Daily Horoscope to see what the fates have in store. If you still need inspiration to motivate you, be sure to read through Love@AOL's Success Stories (the link is at the bottom of the Personals window). If you think you can handle the, um, "open-ended discussions" there, also try jumping into a chat room.

Teens

Keyword **Teens**

Nobody understands life as a teenager — except, perhaps, another teenager. That's why, in the name of preserving (or perhaps promoting) teenage sanity, AOL created the Teens department. With hot colours, cool topics, and a fast-paced flavour, AOL Teens fits the bill.

Looking hip and informative at the same time, the Teens department puts the online world at your fingertips. The right and left extremes of the window show off the featured areas for the day, the week, or the moment — these often include games, fun tests, and member polls.

In the middle, you'll find the main Teen department options, including Music, Movies & TV, Games, and more. There's a Search & Explore option where you can browse the entire department using the alphabetical topic list, the Search box, or even the list of Most Requested (that means hottest) areas.

One feature not to miss? Just under the main list of options, there's a link to something called Bolt (keyword **Bolt**). "What the heck is that?" you ask. Well, click once and you'll find yourself in an ever-growing, ever-sharing, and supremely cool teenage community. Once you create your Bolt member profile (yes, it's free), you can contribute opinions, read features by other teenaged Bolt members, join forces with new friends, and more. It's truly a place for teens to call their own.

Weddings

Keyword **Weddings**

Planning a wedding? Sure, you need flowers, invitations, dresses, and a great band for the reception, but the *first* thing you need is the Weddings area. Thumb through tons of message board postings, picture yourself in any of several thousand wedding gowns, set up a wedding (and beyond) budget, and research cool locations for the ultimate honeymoon. The Weddings area brings it all together for you — except the "find the mate" part, that is. (That's still up to you — and maybe a visit to Love@AOL, at keyword **Love**.)

Phew! Faith, Weddings, Health . . . life *is* strange and wonderful. But don't leave the channel yet. Still more options await you here! On the right side of the main channel window, you'll find two jam-packed pull-down menus. Here's where they lead:

Life Resources: Communities

The left pull-down menu is filled with links to people who can support, understand, and share your concerns. Among the communities you'll find here, a couple are worth special mention:

✔ *Ethnicity* (keyword **Ethnicity**): Where does your family originate? When did they arrive in North America? Connect with others who share your traditions and your background when you visit the Ethnicity department.

Warning! The department lists ethnic groups from all over the world, with the possible exception of Antarctica, but the focus is definitely on people who've settled in the U.S.

✔ *Gay & Lesbian* (keyword **Gay**; keyword **Lesbian**): Find lots of information and many kindred spirits in the Gay & Lesbian department. Visit all kinds of online services, including a great resource directory, or check out the cities most open to gay travellers. OnQ and PlanetOut in particular offer some well-developed online commu-

nities, plus solid information and discussion areas. Check out the PlanetOut News (keyword **PNO News**) for a well-focused look at important headlines from the gay, lesbian, and transgendered viewpoint.

Life Resources: Newsstand

What subject could be more inherently interesting to readers than life itself? Maybe that accounts for the myriad publications and Web sites devoted to discussing, informing, and dreaming about how life should be.

Whether you're looking for general lifestyles information (Canada's respected *Chatelaine* magazine), for romance (Harlequin online), for new views on the home and family (*Canadian Living* magazine), or even for age-specific articles (like the information and community you'll find on Fifty Plus online, a Canadian Web site by and for people over 50), the Newsstand has it all. There are also links to several more channel-specific AOL Canada Newsstands, including publications designed for Families, Teens, and Hobbyists (at the Interests Newsstand).

Local Channel

According to the wise old sage (who probably moonlights at the automobile club), "Getting there is half the fun." Thanks to the cool stuff on the AOL Canada Local channel (keyword **Local**), you may think that *not* getting there is almost *all* the fun (virtually speaking, of course).

The Local channel is AOL Canada's nod to our country's great regional diversity (after all, you'd be hard-pressed to mistake a Newfoundlander for a

Manitoban or a Quebecker). The channel chaperones you through a slew of Canadian cities from coast to coast, as well as cities big, small, and frankly obscure South of our border (boy, those Americans sure are numerous, eh?).

Occupying most of the Local channel window is the *HotMap,* a clickable map image of Canada and the U.S. On the bottom left of the window is a list of the Canadian cities currently accessible through the AOL Canada Local Channel (expect more in the future!). To get all the local goodies, you can either click the city name that interests you on the HotMap, or select a yellow folder from the list.

Now, the keenly attentive among you will notice right away that there's something fundamentally different between what happens when you click most of the Canadian city links on the HotMap (those for Calgary, Charlottetown, Edmonton, Halifax, Montreal, Ottawa, Quebec City, Regina, Saskatoon, St. John's, Victoria, and Winnipeg) and what happens when you pick a link for Vancouver or Toronto, or one of the U.S. cities.

Selecting the former replaces the list at the bottom of the Local channel window with a different set of options — actually links to local attractions. These generally include information from that city's tourist office, local theatre and entertainment facilities, newspapers, post-secondary institutions, and more. (You can get back to the main list of yellow folders by clicking the back-pointing arrow on the left side of the navigation bar.)

Selecting Toronto or Vancouver is a tad more exciting: You get a totally new window full of options. That's because these sprawling urban giants are part of

a virtual network called Digital City. (The U.S. cities are also part of this network.) Each Digital City entry offers the best in tourist information, city maps, travel tips, and hot sightseeing spots, all available without leaving the comfort of your home. Who could want more? You do? Okay, how about reading current news articles, finding out which movies fill local screens, reading personal ads, getting to know the local arts scene, and looking up current weather conditions? Told you it was exciting.

While the Toronto and Vancouver Digital City pages differ somewhat from their U.S. counterparts, you can usually find the following information somewhere in the window:

✔ *Entertainment:* Thinking about heading out to a movie tonight? What about a band or a play, museums or restaurants? The Entertainment area will lead you to local businesses, companies, and venues where you can plan to spend your next big night out.

✔ *News:* The Local News window offers your choice of the top local stories, as well as links to local news organizations. For example, Toronto's Entertainment link leads to all sorts of media outlets, including CityTV and TVOntario.

✔ *Other Cities:* If poking an online map with your mouse pointer doesn't sound like much fun, use the Other Cities option (sometimes called the City Index) to find the Digital City you desire. This link brings up a dialog box listing all the cities covered by the whole Digital City area. Scroll through the list, find the city you want, and double-click its entry to see everything there is to see.

✔ *People:* Personals, pen pals, message boards, local groups and associations, specialty publications, and more are waiting for you in the People area.

✔ *Personals:* Sometimes included under the People heading, the Personals deserve an extra mention, if only for their popularity. Looking for a friend? Seeking a companion? Trying just to find someone to do things with? Don't give up until you check the Personals area. Good luck!

✔ *Real Estate:* Before you pull up stakes and travel halfway across the country for a new job, use the Real Estate area to help you locate that perfect house or rental. Generally, this area offers links to reputable local brokers and listing agencies.

✔ *Shopping & Services* or *Marketplace:* Thinking of visiting a local shopping centre or boutique while on vacation? Save time and energy by checking the Shopping area first to pinpoint malls and stores that stock the kind of goods your heart desires!

✔ *Travel:* Speaking of visitors, check out the Travel area when planning your next vacation. Why? Well, one click and you'll find maps, travel guides, restaurant guides, events listings, and links to local tourist offices. Cool, eh?

News Channel

Keeping up with the news gets harder all the time — so much to think about, so many things vying for your attention, and so little time to pursue mundane trivialities like staying informed. What's a hoping-to-be-informed Canadian of the

new millennium to do? Check out the AOL Canada News channel (keyword **News**) — that's what.

The News channel delivers quick and timely stories, all at the click of your mouse. Whether it's a crisis in the Middle East or a federal election here in Canada, a political scandal in the U.S. or a fishing dispute in Nova Scotia, AOL Canada News is there to bring you breaking news and in-depth coverage of the stories that matter. You can even use a search function to pick and choose from the news of the day and keep up on the stories important to you.

For its size, the News channel window packs quite an informational wallop. Scrolling along the top portion of the window is the news ticker. Click a particular headline or anywhere in the Headline area and you'll get the full story.

Under the scrolling headlines, you'll find the hour's Top Story. Below that are the department buttons, leading to the various news detail areas. Each has a short headline to give you a taste of what's to come if you click the department heading. Along the bottom of the window are three utility buttons: Search News, News Poll, and In Toon. The latest (and oft-changing) breaking news and news features are located in the middle of the window, in the shaded area. To dive into any of them, click the blue link or the photo next to the story that interests you. Finally, rounding out the window are three more Canada-centric features located on the right side: the Local Forecast, Print Weasels, and Speak Out. Here are the details of all the News channel features:

National News

Keyword **National**

The National News department is the heart and soul of the AOL Canada News channel. After all, domestic news is something Canadians do very well. The attractively designed window has several timely features on the right side, including, notably, a Feedback button so you can send the AOL Canada News department your two cents' worth.

The left side of the window starts off at the top left with scrolling national headlines, followed by the Top Canadian Story, and several more featured news items (just click the blue links to see and read more).

If your appetite for news is voracious, click the More Stories button on the bottom left of the window. This brings up a whole slew of the latest stories from the Canadian news wire services. (The camera icons indicate that a story is accompanied by a photo.) Right next to More Stories are the National News Links, organized into a handy pull-down menu. Here you'll find all the big Canadian dailies, including the *Globe and Mail,* the *National Post,* and city papers across the country, as well as links to CBC National Radio News, Newsworld, and Canoe News.

Hot Tip: Two more National News links happen to rank as our personal favourites. *The Daily Planet* is a publication of the Humber College School of Media Studies (based in Toronto) that keeps track of events within the media industry. The *Bourque NewsWatch* (keyword **Bourque**) is an impressive news site maintained by one very devoted Canadian journalist named Pierre Bourque. A self-professed "neojournalist," Bourque painstakingly sifts through all the news he can get his hands on to bring you what he considers the best and the most insightful.

World News

Keyword **World**

While Canadians are renowned for our domestic news coverage, our multicultural makeup also makes us eager consumers of news from outside our national borders. The World News department is the place to go for global coverage on events that matter, regardless of citizenship. Begin with the now-familiar scrolling headlines along the top of the window, followed by the Top International Story and a few more clickable features, or jump straight to the More Stories button for a complete list of recent articles. In the World News Links, you'll find several of the world's top news agencies, including the British Broadcasting Corporation (BBC), CNN, the *New York Times,* and more. Just select an option from the pull-down menu and you're off!

Two features on the right side of the window are especially noteworthy: Camera's Eye and the AOL Canada Newsstand. Camera's Eye (keyword **Camera's Eye**) is a photojournalistic gallery of pictures that stand alone to tell their own story. The Newsstand (keyword **Newsstand**) is where you'll find the complete list of links to Canadian news-papers and magazines. (You worldly types should pay special attention to the International Papers folder under the newspapers heading, on the right side of the window. It's got an impressive range of publications from every continent.)

Entertainment News

Keyword **Entertainment News**

Stroll down the red carpet into the heart of Tinseltown with a stop in the Entertainment News area. One click and you're knee-deep in the top movie, music, and theatre stories. You also receive a selection of the best people-oriented tales rolling through the news wire. Topics in this area include the entertainment industry, online world, art, culture, film, theatre, music, television — the list goes on, as you can tell. Whenever you need to take a break from the stressful stories pouncing on you elsewhere on the News channel, chill out in this area. It really helps — we promise.

Hot Tip: We also like Jeff Craig's Hollywords's column (keyword **Hollywords**), located on the bottom right of the window. Craig is the proverbial insider-fish-out-of-water — yes, such a thing exists. You see, he knows his stuff about Tinseltown (that covers the insider part), but he's also a Canadian living in L.A. (thus, the fish out of water).

Business News

Keyword **Business News**

Ask any journalism student to tell you where they are likely to find their first job, and they'll probably say financial reporting. Business news is, well, big business. The appetite for stock market, industry, and consumer updates has grown by leaps and bounds in the past few years. AOL Canada is keeping pace with this trend in the Business News department.

Aside from the headlines and top stories, the Business News window also houses its own sub-set of departments, each focusing on a different area of the business news world, including:

- ✔ *Canadian Business:* All the general business news all the time, as well as a link to financial forum message boards, links to business publications,

and even editorials by financial experts through Investor Canada's Market Comment — they're all waiting for you in the Canadian business window.

- ✔ *International:* International business news stories are filed by country in this simply designed window. Just click the folder that interests you and read away!

- ✔ *Resources:* Canada lives and breathes natural resources. Find out the latest market prices for all the heavily traded metals, including silver, gold, and copper.

- ✔ *Markets:* Up-to-date news from the Canadian and foreign stock exchanges.

- ✔ *U.S. Business:* With 250 million citizens and a big portion of the world's wealth, the U.S. is an economic giant. Keep up with the latest headlines from the American business world in this window, which includes a handy search function.

- ✔ *Technology:* Dot.commers take note! Here's where you can stay on top of the latest information and technology news from around the world.

- ✔ *Consumer Briefs:* Even if business news tends to put you to sleep, you should be able to find something of interest here. (These are like general news stories with business leanings!)

- ✔ *Currency:* Dollar goes up. Dollar goes down. It's never quite a "new" story, but if you're a currency watcher, you can get the latest info here.

Fund News Network

Keyword **FNN**

Brought to you by TD Mutual Funds, FNN is sort of like an electronic version of the business summaries you see on TV. Every day, one of TD's financial experts delivers an audio summary of market and mutual fund news in Canada and around the world (complete with graphics and even a cute picture of your narrator). Play it, pause it, or even roll it back more than once to keep abreast of all the latest market action!

Today's Markets

On the right side of the Business News window, you'll find a daily summary of all the big business stories as reported by Canadian Press. Now you have no excuse not to know why your stocks have fallen. (Sorry 'bout that!)

Sports

Keyword **Sports**

Is news of the sporting scene important? Take a look at the Sports News department and then tell us what you think. With a myriad of main categories, plus the wonderful More Sports area, you can find more news in this area than any three fanatics could want. All the major sports (professional baseball, basketball, and hockey are just a few) have their own categories, although More Sports is probably the coolest area: Where else can you follow baton twirling, cricket, inline skating, and paintball from the same news window?

Hot Tip: Don Cherry has been called a lot of things (many unprintable), but never has he been deemed boring. Maybe that explains why AOL Canada has given him his very own forum. Spirited features, message boards, hockey trivia, and, yes, even shopping at the Don Cherry Emporium are all waiting at keyword **Don Cherry**.

Once you've loaded up on headlines and articles from all the departments we've just described (and if you've still got

enough energy left over), there are several more news features you absolutely *must* try on the News channel. Here they are:

Search News

Keyword **News Search**

If you're not a browser (and with the volume of stuff in the AOL Canada news area, we can hardly blame you), try the News Search feature. News Search thumbs through stories from the other AOL News Today sections, helping you to zero in on stories *you* find interesting, not the ones the helpful wire service editors chose for you (no offense to our journalistic leaders).

Use either keyword **News Search** or the News Search button to open the News Search dialog box. Type a few words that describe the kind of stories you're looking for, then click Search to see what's out there. After a few moments, the window fills with story headlines that contain the word or phrase you typed. See Chapter 14 for tips on searching the News channel.

News Poll

Keyword **Cdn Survey**

Do you think airline pilots should have the right to strike? Do you think school children in Canada should swear allegiance to the Queen? Do you think . . . well, you get the idea. News polls are fun, fast, and best of all, free. Just click Yes, No, or Undecided, followed by the Vote button, and you'll be added to a growing statistical sample of AOL Canada members on all sorts of news-related questions like these. If you've missed a recent poll, don't worry. You can read through earlier results using the News Poll Archives button on the bottom left of the window.

In Toon

Keyword **In Toon**

Sometimes, one picture can say more than an entire article, editorial, or opinion piece. That's the idea behind editorial cartoons, and the proud tradition of biting (as well as hilarious) visual commentary is alive and strong at In Toon. Sample the latest cartoons from across Canada on topical issues, read about the artists behind the witty scribbles, or even leave a posting on the In Toon Message Board. It's all at keyword **In Toon**.

Local Forecasts

Keyword **Weather**

Whether you're trying to figure out what to pack for your trip or wondering whether it will rain on your way to work, the Local Forecasts link at the top right of the News channel window has your info. It whisks you directly to the Current Conditions page of the AOL Canada Weather channel.

Print Weasels

Keyword **Weasels**

It's sort of a cruel moniker, but AOL Canada's seven print weasels can take it: they're a tough lot, not to mention well respected. The simplest way to get to know these national columnists and artists is to visit the Weasels window as often as you can. You can also fire back at the weasels by posting a note to their individual message board or e-mailing them directly. For the sake of clarity though, here are their vitals:

- John Daly: Senior Editor, the *Globe and Mail*'s *Report on Business*
- Andy Donato: Nationally syndicated editorial cartoonist

- Mike Duffy: Author, Ottawa Editor, CTV NewsNET
- Gary Dunford: Columnist, the *Toronto Sun*
- Brian Flemming: Columnist, the *Daily News* of Halifax
- Barbara Yaffe: Columnist, the *Vancouver Sun*
- Linda Barnard: Sunday Living Editor, the *Toronto Sun*

Speak Out

There's something about writing out your views on an on-going news story that helps clarify your thoughts, heighten your awareness, and, oh yeah, lower your blood pressure. If something in the news has you steamed (can anyone say "politics"?) or if you are simply moved by a story, Speak Out about it! Just click the Speak Out link at the bottom right of the AOL Canada News channel window, pick a topic that interests you, and post away! For all the details on message boards, flip to Chapter 11.

Newsstand

Keyword **Newsstand**

Welcome to the world of magazines and newspapers with windows rather than covers, with e-mail addresses rather than phone numbers, and with interactive chat areas rather than letters to the editor. This world is the Newsstand department, one of the News channel's most interesting areas.

Pick a hometown newspaper or try a daily from a different province. Try an international publication. Read one of Canada's prominent magazines. You'll soon find that time flies when you're absorbed by the news!

Personal Finance Channel

Money makes the world go around. (Some laws of physics are involved, too, but you get the idea.) It also keeps you up at night, makes you work 50 hours a week, and leaves you feeling vaguely defeated after paying the month's bills. (Where did it all go!?)

Suppose — just for a moment — that you controlled your money. Pretty neat thought, eh? That's what the Personal Finance channel (keyword **Finance**) is all about. It covers saving, investing, dealing with credit, owning a home, and lots of other stuff. You can find help for tuning your portfolio and for finding out what exactly a portfolio is and whether you can take it out in the rain.

The channel window is your doorway to the online world of personal finance. The prominently displayed quote box, exchange box, and market indexes welcome you at the top left of the channel. In addition to displaying the current value of these popular investment barometers, the index names link directly to the day's performance chart. This area also includes a button for the popular AOL Canada Portfolios system.

Below the stock area are several up-to-date business news headlines, followed by the department buttons that lead to the eight Finance focus areas. On the bottom right of the window are buttons for the four AOL Canada Financial Centres. Look there for online banking, real estate, brokerage, and mutual fund information. On the top right side of the channel window are today's featured financial areas.

Opinions aren't information

Before wading too deeply into the Personal Finance channel, we want to reinforce something you probably already know: *Opinions are not information, and vice versa.* Although you may not think that this statement is groundbreaking, it's important to keep in mind on the Personal Finance channel.

The forums and services on the Personal Finance channel contain a great deal of cold, hard data: financial calculations, sales reports, stock price fluctuations, and company histories. They also harbour many warm, soft opinions floating around in the discussion areas. To get the most from the Personal Finance areas (and not lose a bunch of money on wacky investments), you have to carefully discern the difference between the two. Suppose that someone posts a message saying, "You're an idiot if you don't buy SciPhone Video and Tanning because it's going through the roof!" That is an *opinion*. If you read a news story that says SciPhone Video and Tanning just won a huge contract to install hundreds of its patented combination satellite TV/video conferencing/pay phone/tanning booths across the country, that's *information*.

Our advice to you is simple: Don't let someone else decide on your investments for you. Everyone has a right to an opinion — just don't blindly adopt someone else's as your own.

Watch for sharks

A long time ago, a wise and learned person taught you an important lesson: Don't believe everything you read. Before you get too carried away on the Personal Finance channel, please write down that lesson in big letters and tape it across the top of your monitor.

Keep a particularly tight grip on your wallet while perusing the investment discussion boards throughout the Personal Finance channel. Most of the messages are from small investors like yourself — but some sharks can lurk in those waters, too. It's your money, so rely on *your* research and intuition.

If you're new to investing, do the smart thing: Remember the disclaimers in the Personal Finance areas. Nearly all the services have them. They say things like "Don't take this as professional advice" and "Watch who you give your private information to," and "Please, oh please, oh please, don't send money to anyone without reading the full prospectus."

Business News Department

Keyword **Business News**

Put your finger to the pulse of the world's business headlines with the Personal Finance channel's Business News department. It links you directly to the AOL Canada News channel's Business News area, offering up the latest in technology, the economy, the markets, and the international scene. To narrow down the number of articles you will read, try the Search button on the bottom left of the window. Type in a few words describing what you're looking for, and the Search engine returns articles relating to that subject. The Fund News Network (keyword **FNN**) also deserves special mention for its audio- and graphics-enhanced display of the day's market action.

Company Research

Keyword **Company Research**

Many people think that making money with investments is a matter of luck — a case of being in the right place at the right time with the right type of zebra on the right colour of leash during the right phase of the moon. Even though the Fates play a role in stock market success, the people who consistently win at the money game do it through careful research. The Company Research department puts a whole library of financial information at your fingertips (or at least at the tip of your mouse pointer). All the important corporate filings and financial statements live in this area, as do company profiles and detailed stock reports.

On the right of the window, you'll find several highlighted features, including a link to one of AOL Canada's content partners, Multex Investor (keyword **Multex**). It may have a techno-sounding name, but it's actually an impressive personal finance site, where you can get articles, opinion pieces, research reports, or just plain ol' stock quotes for a host of companies. Although Multex is a big company offering many fee-for-service options, the Multex Investor part is sponsored, meaning it's free for you, the little guy!

Along the bottom of the Company Research window are several service buttons. You can return to the Main Menu of the Personal Finance channel, dive in to a finance-related Chat, visit the Forums (message boards on things like stocks and mutual funds), find Help, or send Feedback to the AOL Canada gurus.

On the top left of the window are buttons leading to the popular Quotes and Portfolios services. Just under these, you'll find a list of Research Resources organized into a pull-down menu. And what a list it is! This is the meatiest portion of the Company Research window, and it's got some excellent Canadian options. You can do the following:

✔ *Search* financial news

✔ *Drop by* the AOL.CA Personal Finance Web Centre (powered by Quicken.ca) for a complete look at the financial world, including news, quotes, a portfolios service, and even company research

✔ *Read* through a mountain of news releases at CNN, one of Canada's biggest corporate news release services (formerly Canadian Corporate News)

✔ *Build* a clearer picture of your stock's long-term performance at BigCharts Canada (it's free!)

✔ *Trade* online or conduct in-depth company research with GroomeCapital.com

✔ *Listen* to a daily audio interview with one of Canada's leading financial experts, using Investor Canada's Investor Radio service (Marguerite likes this one because it's got that live feel to it)

✔ *Take* a trip to National Bank Financial

✔ *Stay* on top of your mutual fund's short- and long-term performance with Fundata Canada (this area includes a daily list of Top Ten performing funds, a glossary, a search function, and more)

✔ *Dig* up more corporate news releases from Canada Newswire

✔ *Unearth* a company prospectus or just about any other type of official corporate filing at SEDAR, the grand-mommy of respectable Canadian financial Web sites

✔ *Get* advice and more from one of the biggest Canadian producers of investment-related publications, MPL Communications (choose the

Carlson Online link, or type www.adviceforinvestors.com in the address box on the navigation bar.)

Hot Tip: If you've got a few loonies invested outside Canada, it pays to do some foreign research, too! There are lots of options for both U.S. investment sites and European information in the Research Resources list. Take some time to explore them all.

Warning! Some of the services we've just described are free. Others, including online trading and in-depth company research reports, will cost you.

Message Boards

Heard a hot tip about your favourite company? Want to argue the merits of one stock over another? Feel like venting about the performance of your mutual fund? For these and other communicative moments, turn to the Finance Forums, the community discussion areas on the Personal Finance channel. There are general investment message boards plus areas for mutual funds, stock index options, investor discussions, those dreaded taxes, and even RRSPs. The stock discussion boards are organized alphabetically by stock ticker symbol. Just browse through the board list, dive into the right letter, and find the folks talking about your favourite stock.

Warning! Remember that what you read in these areas are *opinions* that can be posted by *anyone*. Before pinning your life savings to some hot advice you discover in this area, be sure to read the sections "Opinions aren't information" and "Watch for sharks," a few pages back.

RRSPs

Keyword **RRSP**

All this finance stuff can get a little boring, right? We couldn't agree more. But before you get too sleepy-eyed, consider the power of the unglamorously named Registered Retirement Savings Plan, or RRSP: Place your savings dollars into one of these handy shelters, and not only will that money grow, but it does so *tax-free*! Hey! You're awake now! Okay, you're ready to start exploring the RRSPs department.

The window includes a lot of links to other areas of the Personal Finance channel. On the right, though, you'll find some unique features. One click of the RRSP Calculator link and you're knee-deep in a step-by-step RRSP Planner (part of Quicken.ca's Learning Centre).

Next, use the arrows beside the black RRSP, RRIF, and RESP titles to get an in-depth look at each of these savings tools. Each opens a brand-new window where you'll find Hot Links and Tools & Calculators on the left, as well as a 1-2-3 punch of features on the right.

Once you've spent time answering all your questions, such as, "Why should I invest?" and "Why are there so many confusing acronyms beginning with the letter R in this world?" you can even shop around online to buy your first RRSP. (Follow the links starting at "I'm ready to invest" in the RRSP information window.)

Investing Info

Keyword **Cdn Investing**

Attention new investors: Your informational ship just came in! For a good introduction to the basics of making money from investments, try some of the options available in the pull-down menu on the left side of the Investing Info window. Many of them are Canadian, many of them are free, and all of them are incredibly informative.

Try the glossary of investment terms — an essential weapon against the irritatingly confusing words that populate the financial world! Visit Fundata Canada for everything you ever wanted to know about your mutual fund investments and more. There's also a link to AOL.CA's very own personal finance Web Centre, which is designed specifically not to scare off non-expert types like you. You can visit the Toronto, Canadian Venture, or Montreal Stock Exchanges (no travel arrangements necessary), or even, heaven forbid, Canada Revenue, which actually has a ton of information available online for individual taxpayers and investors.

And we're not done yet! No, sir. You can also find links to a bunch more informational wonders, some Canadian, some international. So bone up, will ya?

Hot Tip: When you're learning, there's nothing like a good teacher to offer guidance and support. The same holds true in the investment world. Among the offerings in the Investing Info department (keyword **Cdn Investing**) are links to two very different kinds of teachers. First, there's Garth Turner (keyword **Garth Turner**), writer, advisor, and commentator. And then there's the Screaming Capitalist! Well, actually his name is Kevin Cork and he lives in Calgary, but he calls himself the Screaming Capitalist on his Web site, where Canadians can find a host of links and tips on making sound investments, not to mention a taste of Kevin's really good sense of humour.

Advice & Planning

Keyword **Advice & Planning**

Every stage in life comes with its own unique physical, emotional, and monetary challenges. Even though you just have to buck up and endure some of them (such as the teenage years), the right planning and advice promise to smooth the way during others. That's why the Advice & Planning department exists — to offer sage advice and an understanding shoulder, just when you need it most. Starting with the woolly world of singledom and carrying you on past retirement, the Advice & Planning areas offer sound suggestions for managing your money at every step along life's way. Take a look at the tips for where you are right now, as well as the ones covering where you're headed in the coming years. You won't find a substitute for good planning — but you can start here if you are trying to catch up on some missed years of investing. Don't let money slip through your fingers! Why not try a few of the Canadian offerings, such as the following:

- *Browsing* or buying a new or used car online at the AOL Canada Auto Centre (keyword **Auto**)

- *Comparing* two mortgage options to find out which is best suited to your needs (powered by Quicken.ca)

- *Getting* help for your home business at the online version of *Home Business Report,* a leading Canadian publication designed for at-home workers

- *Organizing* your financial documents, thanks to tools and tips from TD Bank

- *Looking* into your financial future with a free Portfolio Forecast

- *Visiting* the RRSP department (same as keyword **RRSP**)

- *Finding* advice and forms for this tax season (same as keyword **Tax**)

Insurance

Keyword **Insurance**

Insurance can be a confusing area for even the most dedicated among us (including your authors). If you feel the same pain and angst when faced with the myriad insurance questions of life, turn to the Insurance area for help. It explains the most common types of insurance, including home, auto, and travel, offers an online quote system (powered by Cowan Insurance Online), has multiple links to prominent Canadian insurers (they're listed in the Insurance Resources pull-down menu), and even provides an ever-changing roster of insurance-related Bright Tips provided by RBCInsurance.ca.

Taxes

Keyword **Tax**

Although some people would disagree, the word *tax* really contains three letters and not four. But that knowledge doesn't make its monetary bite any less painful. The only remedy for that is the advice awaiting you in the Personal Finance channel's Tax department. Rustle through the areas in the Tax Planning department for the latest tax news, forms, and planning tips, plus the best in tax-focused forums. Tax software is enshrined in its own special section, thanks to a partnership with *Viewz*.

Not ready to start inputting numbers just yet? Need some good news? Use the Tax Calculators to figure out what you can save on this year's tax bill from the GST credit, RRSP contributions, home business deductions, and more.

Mutual Funds

Keyword **Mutual Fund Centre**

If investing in individual stocks fills you with dread, don't let that stop you from putting money away for the future. Turn your investing sights on mutual funds, where the "pros" manage the details while you watch your money grow. The Mutual Fund Centre offers insight and information about funds from all over, plus a daily Top Ten performing funds list, brought to you by the people at Fundata Canada (keyword **Fundata**).

Banking

Keyword **Banking**

Banks are part of life, so banking information should be part of your world, too. The area offers some information about banking in general, plus several links to online banking companies. Personally, we'd like to see this area spend more time on education and less on marketing — but such is life sometimes.

Brokerages

Keyword **Brokerage**

Online trading has changed the face of Canada's brokerage industry, with companies scrambling to set up business on the Web and, lucky for us, also competing for investors by offering lower transaction fees! The AOL Canada Brokerage Centre is a good place to start if you're thinking of setting up an account online. You can use the pull-down menu of Brokerage Resources to locate many of the leading Canadian firms. Or, if you're still shopping around, try the link called "Which discount broker is cheapest for you?" — a useful tool powered by Quicken.ca.

Real Estate

Keyword **Real Estate**

Measured by total dollars spent at one time, the two largest purchases most people make in their lives are their home and their car. (For the nerds of the world, of course, it's usually home and *computer,* but that's another story.) Although the multi-thousand-dollar outlays demand special care and attention, their complexity often leaves us utterly bewildered and at the mercy of a sharp-tongued sales rep. To overcome the bewilderment and arm yourself for battle with real estate agents, turn to the Real Estate department. Search for a real estate agent in your province, get tips on preparing your home for resale, rate Canadian cities by cost of living, and even start your home search.

Before you leave the AOL Canada Personal Finance channel, you should also know about a few more crucial (yeah, we know that's a strong word, but we're talking about money here) features:

Portfolios

Keyword **Portfolios**

Good investors don't leave all their financial eggs in one basket (even if they do, you can bet that the basket lives in a bombproof refrigerator). Because most investments are a mix of stocks from several different companies, keeping up with your holdings on a symbol-by-symbol basis would take forever. You need a tool that monitors your whole stock portfolio at one time — and, as luck would have it, AOL Canada provides one in its Portfolios system. This system helps you manage your stocks by grouping them into one or more portfolios and displaying a single window that gives you an at-a-glance summary of how everything is performing. Because you are building the portfolios, everything about them is up to you. Create them according to industry, investment risk, or any way you want.

Quotes or Snapshot

Keyword **Quotes** or **Snapshot**

Many years ago, a brass-and-glass ticker-tape machine busily spewing forth a constant stream of letters and numbers in your office was a tangible sign of success. Today, society measures success differently (and it's a darn good thing, too, because those ticker-tape machines were noisy). Late-breaking stock market news isn't the sole domain of the rich and powerful anymore. Instead, this information is freely available to everyone on AOL Canada, through the Snapshot system. To check the current price (actually, the *mostly* current price because data in the system is delayed about 20 minutes) of a particular stock, just enter the stock's symbol in the Symbol box and click Get Quote. If you don't know the stock's ticker symbol, click the Symbol Lookup link for help.

Shopping Channel

Shopping is a drag. You leave your comfortable home, brave the wilds of modern transportation, and then walk around some glitzed-up store following carefully marked paths just the right size for a thin 11-year-old. After bumping into innumerable displays and more than a few other shoppers, you clutch the prizes of your quest and head for the recycled cattle queues — uh, sorry, that is, checkout lanes. After a certain amount of mooing time, you make your purchase and begin the trek homeward.

Online shopping is *nothing* like that. You don't mess around with crowded stores, pushy clerks, long lines, or wailing children (yours or anyone else's). Your goods arrive at the door of your comfortable home, which you never left. What a deal.

If this kind of stress-free shopping experience sounds interesting to you, the AOL Canada Shopping channel (keyword **Shopping**) is the place to go. This area has a variety of stores for your browsing and purchasing pleasure. Better still, many of the items for sale include online pictures to show you exactly what you're buying.

Like an unusually good mall, the Shopping channel is laid out in an easy-to-navigate format. The centre of the window features the various departments, where everything from apparel to zydeco CDs await you and your credit card. On the opposite side of the window are the Shopping channel's featured items. They change often, much like the seasonal goody aisles at your favourite department store. Almost hiding down at the bottom of the screen are the Customer Service and Gift Reminder buttons, to help you in times of gift-need.

Warning! Before you shop, keep in mind that some of the departments listed in the AOL Canada Shopping channel will lead you to U.S. sellers. There's an immense variety of goods to be had there, so before you turn away dejectedly from your computer screen, flip to Chapter 13 for more information on cross-border shopping online. It's painless, but can be a tad more expensive! AOL Canada also provides a currency converter whenever you enter a U.S. shopping area, so you can get a better idea up-front of what you'll spend in Canadian dollars.

Choose a Department

Keywords **Apparel & Footwear; Auctions & Classifieds; Health; Beauty & Wellness; Books; Music & Video; Computer Products; Consumer Electronics; Flowers & Jewelry; Gifts & Collectibles; Gourmet & Grocery; Home, Kitchen, & Garden; Office Products & Services; Sports & Outdoors; Toys, Kids & Babies**

There's nothing like starting big — and, on the Shopping channel, that means hitting the departments. With hundreds of stores spread across 16 departments, you're likely to find just about anything you want or need to purchase right there.

Each department contains a number of stores that either cater to the department's focus area or offer a selection of related products that's part of a bigger mix. Don't be surprised to find some of the larger stores, like Chapters.ca, listed in several departments.

Customer Service

Keyword **Shopping Services**

Shopping and customer service — you can't have one without the other. (Well, you *could*, but nobody would shop there.) To make the online shopping experience fun and hassle free, the Shopping channel offers all kinds of help in the Customer Service department. The area provides customer service links for Shopping channel vendors. If that doesn't work, e-mail AOL Canada Shopping directly with your concerns.

Free Gift Reminder

Keyword **Reminder**

Apart from the stores, our favourite item in the shopping channel is the Free Gift Reminder service (keyword **Reminder**), which reminds us of those important dates we simply *can't* forget (but which

we work so hard at putting out of our minds — why is that?). For a step-by-step guide to the service, go to Chapter 13.

Sports Channel

The smell of the engines, the roar of the crowds (or is it the other way around?), that little *schussing* sound the skis make right before the announcer says, "Oh, that had to hurt!" — the world of sports brings to life all kinds of sights, sounds, and fascinating medical opportunities. It also fills the news wires and magazines with scores, stories, gossip, and colourful photographs. In fact, the sports world generates so much information that, out of sheer self-defence, AOL Canada dedicated an entire channel to it: the aptly named Sports channel (keyword **Sports**).

Unlike many of its department-filled brethren, the Sports channel includes only three main areas: Scoreboard, Team Pages, and Talk About It. Each of these departments merits, of course, its own special coverage below it. In addition to the three departments, the channel window provides quick access to focus areas for hockey, Canadian football, basketball, baseball, and many other popular sports. Along the right side of the Sports channel window, you see the spotlight areas, highlighting the day's top sports stories.

Choose a Sports section

In the midst of the Sports channel sit a bevy of sports buttons — auto racing, baseball, golf, hockey, and more. Each button leads to a mountain of news, details, trivia, and such that sends even the most hardened fan into joyous overload. Each sport's window displays top stories for the sport in general, plus provides tabs for more information (things like schedules, organizations, and such). Drill down as far as you want, because you can find plenty of depth everywhere you look.

Hot Tip: Click the buttons on the channel window for easy access to the various sports, or use the name of the sport (**Baseball, Basketball, Auto Racing**, and too many others to list) as a keyword to zip straight to the window you want.

Scoreboard

Keyword **Scoreboard**

When you want the scores and nothing but the scores, turn to the Scoreboard area. As its name suggests, this is *the* place for fresh statistics on your favourite NHL, CFL, NBA, and NHL contests. In addition to quick scores, the Scoreboard department also serves a sampling of the day's best individual performances. As a bonus, the department also includes links to the top sports stories and a couple of often-changing feature areas.

The real gold in the area lives beneath the various league buttons. Each of these buttons leads you to a sports fan's dream scoreboard, filled with statistics for current games, previews of coming games, and enough raw box scores to put your calculator in a coma for weeks.

Team Pages

Fans, unite! If you love the Calgary Flames, the Toronto Raptors, the Montreal Expos, or some other brand of athletic animal, share your dedication with fellow fans in the Team Pages area. Every team in the CFL, NFL, NBA, NHL, MLB, and NCAA (and possibly a few stray university professors who were sucked into the initial-laden maelstrom) gets a whole page

of scores, stories, schedules, rosters, and every other piece of information a *true* fan needs. Add to that the message board links in the Grandstand area (the next section in the directory), and you have a fan paradise wrapped up in digital clothes.

Talk About It

Keyword **Grandstand**

Sports fans love their teams. They read about the teams, go to games, swap insight, and second-guess plays. Stringing together these disparate pastimes is the undying need to talk endlessly about *their* team. That's where the Grandstand enters the action. Talk about your favourite teams, engage in some fantasy league action, and generally indulge your sports fanaticism with others like you. The Grandstand (through the Talk About It link) makes a great home for online sports fans like you!

Travel Channel

Suppose that you're trying to plan this year's vacation. So, where and when will it be? Perhaps Carnivale on the French Riviera . . . Oktoberfest in Munich . . . or does your budget have something a little closer to home in mind, like the annual Ukrainian Garlic Festival in beautiful, metropolitan Sudbury, Ontario (hey, it's close to Marguerite's hometown and she happens to think it's awesome)?

Whatever your plans (or budgetary constraints), make the most of your vacation with the help and forums available in the AOL Canada Travel channel (keyword **Travel**). All kinds of news and information await you here. The area's hidden gem is the marvellous collection of member-populated discussion boards containing firsthand insights and tips of the travel trade (which help you find those wonderful out-of-the-way restaurants that make trips worth taking). You may even find out a thing or two about your own hometown, if you're not careful.

Like an old hand at globetrotting the days away, the AOL Travel window uses every bit of space to pack lots of goodies. Prominently featured on the left of the window is Today's Feature. It could be about wine tasting in France or Cuban beaches. Regardless, it's sure to make you long for a seat on the next plane out of town. Just below the feature are Today's Bargains. These travel deals change all the time, so be sure to come back often!

On the right side of the window are the Travel Tools, including an all-important weather link, maps, books, and more. Above the tools you'll find two pull-down menus. The first whisks you off to various types of Travel Guides for everything from Asian to golf vacations. It's also your route to the main Travel Features Page (but you can also use keyword **Travel Features**). The right-hand menu is actually a list of Vacation Destinations — including hot spots in this country, the U.S., Europe, Asia, and even sun, snow, and sea destinations.

Travel Features

Keyword **Travel Features**

Why do travel magazines seem to proliferate like weeds? Well, maybe it has something to do with dreaming, fantasy, a love of the good things in life . . . and a healthy dose of idealism! We all seem to love reading about places and things that exist outside our own sphere. The ever-growing number of AOL Canada Travel

channel features taps into this desire with its features page. Choose a feature from the list on the left side of the window and read about everything from Mystical Places like Machu Picchu, in Peru, to Festivals throughout the world.

Weather

Keyword **Weather**

Leaving tomorrow on your vacation? Want an idea of what to expect when you get off the plane, bus, or train? Use the Weather link to check out current conditions and forecasts for cities and towns across Canada and the U.S.

Hot Tip: Thanks to a partnership with lastminuteclub.com, you can use this link for vital info on travelling just about anywhere in the world, using the clickable map image.

Distances

Remember the awe that was once inspired by expressions like "Around the world in 80 days"? It just doesn't hold water anymore, in an age when the Internet makes travelling the globe, well, instantaneous! To get back in touch with the actual kilometres separating you from Portland, Paris, and Peru, try the Distances tool.

Maps

Keyword **Maps**

Sure, we live in a country dotted with CAA branches, but not even the automobile club knows where *all* the addresses are (and besides, they don't have all the maps). Thanks to the Maps area, maps aren't a problem anymore. Among the driving directions, the instant maps of addresses across the country, and the marvellous library of city, provincial, and regional maps, Maps is a cartographer's (or at least a traveller's) dream.

Books

If you've ever had the experience of landing in a foreign country without some kind of guide book, you'll know it can be a tad scary — especially if you don't know the language and there seem to be dozens of people yelling at you about cabs and hotels! Yikes! Use the Travel Books area, powered by Chapters.ca, to dig up the right guide, or, if you're more of an armchair traveller, pick up a travelogue by your favourite writer.

Currency

Keyword **FX**

Oh, we love the Universal Currency Converter! It's so easy to use. You'll wonder how the world ever got by without it. Just fill in an amount, choose what currency you have, what currency you want, and bam! You've got conversion! And it's all free!

Restaurants

Keyword **Restaurant Finder**

Eating out is one of life's great pleasures. If all goes well, you should end up with better service, food, and smiles than you could ever muster up on your own! Next time you decide to forgo the pots and pans in your kitchen for a restaurant experience, be sure to consult the Restaurant Finder. On the left side of the window is a list of cities where you can start your search. Each will bring you to a window where you can specify the area, price range, cuisine, and features you want. If you'd prefer to get specifics about a particular restaurant, use the Quick Search option on the right side of the window. Type in the name of your favourite haunt and find out how it's been rated for service, value, ambiance, and more.

There's still more available from the AOL Canada Travel channel (hey, that rhymes!). Get the best at our behest, we still have a few more features to get off our chest (sorry, couldn't resist):

Destination Canada

Among the options in the Select a Destination pull-down menu (on the top right of the Travel channel window), the first and most patriotic is also very useful. Use Destination Canada to link to provincial tourist offices and even a cool window called Virtual Atlantic Canada, where, of course, you can read more about the omnipresent Anne of Green Gables.

Member Opinions

Keyword **Member Opinions**

Particularly in the world of travel, nothing beats firsthand experience. Sure, the guidebooks paint swell pictures with broad brushstrokes. But that's nothing compared to the photographic detail provided by someone who has walked the streets, eaten in the cafés, and gotten lost in the subway system (and, for the record, we *weren't* lost — we just took the wrong train from the wrong platform). To help you soak up information from the experience of others, the Travel channel includes the Member Opinions department.

The message boards and chat rooms in this friendly haunt are great for swapping real-world answers to tricky travel questions. No matter what kind of information you need, the advice of a friendly, seasoned traveller is usually mere clicks away. This area is also the home of the Travel channel's newsletter, a must-have item for any traveller's kit.

Weather Channel

Maybe the question of whether it will rain or shine today is a bit too obvious to discuss. . . . Naaah! Let's face it: Canadians can't get enough of talking about or being shocked by the weather in this country. Vancouverites and the rain. Haligonians and the wind. Montrealers and the snow. These are serious on-going relationships we're talking about!

AOL Canada understands that what you need most is a quick reference for today's weather. That's what you'll get when you first enter the Weather channel at keyword **Weather**. The Current Conditions page literally takes over the screen. Along the left side of the window are service buttons that lead to more detailed weather information. Along the bottom are a bunch more service buttons that can help you search, learn, or even query a bona fide weatherperson about the sun, the rain, or the snow!

USA

Keyword **US Weather**

An impressive array of maps, information, and, of course, forecasts await at the AOL U.S. Weather department. We particularly like the information in the World area, where you can get local forecasts for an astonishing array of countries. (They're listed in alphabetical order.)

Current Conditions

Keyword **Weather**

Check out those puffy clouds and shining suns! Cute! Click any of the little red buttons on the Current Conditions page to get a more detailed weather picture for any province or territory. You can keep

clicking red buttons until you end up in the more detailed weather windows for specific towns and cities across Canada.

Hot Tip: If you find yourself in a weather area but would prefer to return to the main Current Conditions page, use the Back button on the top left of the window to retrace your steps.

Forecast

That romantic picnic you've been planning is finally happening tomorrow and you're already biting your nails and crossing your fingers at the same time, hoping for sunshine. Get the scoop on tomorrow's weather (and beyond) using the Forecast button. It changes the main map to indicate estimated temperatures, but you can also follow the red buttons to get to more detailed information.

Barometer

Another switch to the main Weather channel map awaits with a click of the Barometer button. If you understand something about changes to air pressure, good! This is for you! Marguerite's running the other way!

Winds

In Canada, winds are no joke, especially when winter starts to settle in. Brrr!! Get current wind conditions for the entire country using the Winds button.

Seasonal

Offered as a learning tool through a partnership with The Weather Network Online, this button leads to the Seasonal Information window, where you can read how the network prepares things like its UV and Pollen Reports.

News

Sometimes terrible, sometimes wondrous, the weather is the subject of news stories pretty much all year long and everywhere in the world. Read the latest in the Weather News window.

Search

Hey! This is handy! Type in a city name and get the five-day forecast, thanks to The Weather Network.

Travel

The Travel window provides a brief synopsis of the day's weather in all the big Canadian and U.S. cities where you might find yourself landing in the next day or so.

Messages

If talking about it with your friends and family still doesn't satisfy your appetite for weather repartee, visit the Weather message boards and post your thoughts for other AOL Canada members to ponder.

Learn

The Learn button is a good place to start if you've just recently landed in this part of the world and don't exactly understand the meaning of the word "drizzle" (believe us, you will!). More useful is the Weights and Measures feature, with its Imperial to Metric conversion table.

Weatherman

Got a suggestion for the Weatherman who maintains this channel? Send it using the Ask a Weatherman window. (Marguerite wants to know why it's not called Ask a Weatherperson, but she's picky that way!)

Women Channel

Sisters, you've come a long way since the days when the kitchen was the only place where you could run the show. Not that keeping a home isn't a big job — take a look at any single man's apartment for insight into the value of that kind of work! Ironically, with all their newfound rights and freedoms, some women, overwhelmed with jobs, kids, the home, relationships, and financial responsibilities, may find themselves looking back fondly on those old times.

AOL Canada's Women channel is designed to help women keep their eyes on the future by providing support and information for everything from becoming a better boss (no more glass ceilings for you), to more relaxing fare like women's sports info and beauty tips.

Timely features abound on the main Women channel window, but you'll also want to dig into the 10 departments that sit on the bottom left side. These include the following:

Beauty & Fashion

Keyword **Beauty & Fashion**

Just because you're a liberated woman doesn't mean you can't appreciate the value of good style and careful appearance. The Beauty & Fashion department is the home of advice and products to please just about every taste. The window contains several sub-departments, including Skin, Fashion, Make-up, Hair & Nails, and Spa. Click the link called "Talk about Beauty & Fashion" for message boards (not a bad idea for women needing advice on dressing for work, or more serious topics like body image), chat rooms, and even a free newsletter. On the right side of the window, you'll find a pull-down menu with a host of Beauty & Fashion resources. Among our favourites? The Daily Dilemma, brought to you by the U.S. television network called Oxygen. It's frivolous but fun!

Relationships

Keyword **Women's Relationships**

Women have historically been responsible for keeping family ties, friendships, and romantic liaisons alive. Whether or not that's changed is still a matter of raging debate! Regardless, women are keenly interested in relationships. In this department, advice abounds in each of the sub-departments of Dating, Sex, Couples, Romance, and Family & Friends. Take a relationship quiz or explore the scheduled chats and message boards. There's also a full menu of Relationship Resources on the right side of the window, including some areas inside AOL (Love@AOL, Weddings, AOL Health), and some out there on the World Wide Web (more offerings from sites like Oxygen and iVillage.com).

Wellness

Keyword **Women's Wellness**

A relatively new concept, wellness is all about taking care of your body and soul now so you can enjoy good health later. Two sub-departments complement the main Wellness window: Diet & Fitness, and Self-Discovery. Each comes complete with its very own window, quizzes, and tools, and a list of resources inside and outside AOL Canada — not to mention frequently updated articles and advice columns.

Living

Keyword **Women's Living**

It's something of a catch-all title, but the Living Department boasts some of the best content on the entire Women's channel. The three sub-departments give you a uniquely female take on some popular general interest areas. Women's Entertainment (keyword **Women's Entertainment**) zeroes in on fun stuff like star style, hunky leading men, and television programs with strong female characters. Activities (keyword **Women's Activities**) is a nod to the undisputed fact that women are often the ones who plan both romantic and family outings — not to mention all the independent women out there who are making plans to go out solo and loving it. Our favourite, though, is the Editorial & Opinion area (keyword **Women's Editorial**), where you'll find intelligent views on politics and current affairs, as well as links to women's organizations online. (The focus here is on the U.S. women's movement, but Canadian women should still find inspiration in most of the content.)

Money & Work

Keyword **Money & Work**

Women have special obstacles and challenges when it comes to managing a career and a portfolio: You want to be taken seriously, but you don't want to check your personality at the door! Find features, advice, and other women like yourself in the Money & Work area. The list of resources on the right side of the window includes Web sites and AOL content areas. One resource we particularly like is AOL's Marriage & Money forum (keyword **Marriage & Money**), where you can learn how to better strike the delicate balance between love and your chequebook.

Weddings

Keyword **Weddings**

Whether you're planning on a traditional wedding (big cake, big dress, and big hair) or something a little more innovative (skydiving nuptials, anyone?), you'll still need advice and information about the basics, like engagement to-dos and honeymoon suggestions. You can find it all at AOL Weddings. The bulk of information is stored in the Favourite Wedding Topics pull-down menu on the bottom left of the window. But be sure to check out the Tools & Resources menu on the right side, too. There, you'll find answers to all kinds of wedding questions, like how to write your own vows and how to pay off your wedding debts. (Then again, maybe you don't want to visit that area just yet!)

Women Talk

Keyword **Women Talk**

Since most of the departments at the Women's channel have some kind of community links, it made sense for the smart people in charge at AOL to create an extra department where you can find *all* the message boards and chats spread throughout the channel. Be sure to check out the A–Z list of boards and the Meet Our Guests link, where you can read about upcoming scheduled chats with prominent women. You can even talk back to the Women's channel with the Tell Us What You Think link on the top right of the window.

Horoscopes

Keyword **Horoscopes**

You're about to face a long day of meetings, followed by dinner preparations for your family, and a long-overdue volunteer meeting in the evening. Oh boy! Will it all work out? Relax and enjoy a peek into your immediate future at AOL's Horoscopes department. If you're really serious about astrology, there are even scheduled chats with famous soothsayers!

Newsstand

Keyword **Women's Newsstand**

Whether your tastes tend toward the racy (*Cosmopolitan*), the conservative (*Good Housekeeping*), or even the pastoral (*Country Living Gardener*), you should be able to find a publication to suit your lifestyle in the Women's Newsstand.

Search

Girls may indeed just wanna have fun, but the sheer amount of information and features on the Women channel is enough to overwhelm even the most astute lady. Cut a swath through all these departments and sub-departments with the Search & Explore service. There's a handy A–Z list of all the content in the channel, as well as a complete list of current features and the requisite Search box where you can type a few words explaining exactly what you're looking for.

WorkPlace Channel

Work makes the world go round. At least, it makes the economy go round. If you're like most people, you spend most of your waking hours at some sort of job. You wake up, putter off to work, make a difference in the world through what you do, and wander back home to collapse in front of the computer at night. Perhaps you own the business — in that case, you relax only when someone whisks you out of the country for a couple of weeks!

Filled with its ups and downs, its unique hassles, and the camaraderie that comes only from spending long hours together, the workplace is a fixture in Canadian culture. AOL Canada recognizes this and presents the WorkPlace channel (keyword **Workplace**). WorkPlace gives you business help, career guidance, and job-finding tips. You can network with others in your field, find out about a completely different career before you take the plunge, or discover how viable a home business may be.

The WorkPlace channel window is organized simply and efficiently. After all, this is serious professional stuff! Prominently displayed on a big orange button is the Find a Job function, followed by two related services: Post Your Resume and Jobs E-mailed To You. Farther down, you'll find the Career Resources, including tips on interviewing and a list of top-selling business book titles. At the bottom of the window is a pull-down menu of Career Essentials. Each category leads you to a different Professional Forum, where you can explore job opportunities, read articles about an industry, or even chat with others in your field. On the top right, you'll always find a timely feature to pique your interest, followed by the weekly WorkPlace channel poll. Finally, at the bottom right of the window is the Community area. This is where you get to relax with a bit of WorkPlace Humour, dig into the work-related message boards, or even dream a little about a job abroad.

Find a Job

Feeling a little out of place in your current job? Or perhaps your career grew in fits and starts, bringing you to a point where you aren't sure what happens next (and you *really* aren't sure if you even like the options)? Whatever the case, it might be time to start looking for a new job. Thanks to a partnership with Monster.ca, a massive job-finding Web site that you can also get to using keyword **Monster**, you can start your search online right now. With over 250,000 postings in all of Canada's regions, and in categories ranging from Administration to Telecommunications, you may find there's more choice than you can absorb.

Hot Tip: Not getting the results you'd hoped for? Be sure to click the link called Tips on Searching at the top of the Job Search window. The link brings up a window where Monster.ca neatly explains all the different ways of browsing or searching its job postings, depending on your needs and preferences.

Post Your Resume

Keyword **WorkPlace**

The online revolution touched everything. Communicating, buying goods, selling products, playing games — it's all online now. Since businesses took the online leap, it only makes sense that job hunters should take the plunge, too. The WorkPlace channel and Monster.ca put all the tools you need to send your resume into cyberspace behind a click of the Post Your Resume button. You'll be walked through the entire process, starting with a resume title and including all your vitals.

You'll have take a moment to register with Monster.ca before you can build and post your resume to the Web — but don't worry, it's painless and free. Be sure to store your Monster password and screen name somewhere safe, though, so you don't have trouble returning to make adjustments to your resume.

Job Alerts by E-mail

Keyword **WorkPlace**

Tired of being the early worm that gets up, reads the Help Wanted ads in the newspapers, and walks down to the Employment Office in search of a better job? Time to start taking control of your search the electronic way! AOL Canada and Monster.ca propose a simple solution: Receive information about the kinds of jobs you want in your online mailbox. It's easy. Just click the Job Alerts button, and you'll be walked through the setup process. You can create up to five different alerts, and you can have them delivered daily, weekly, or monthly.

Resumes and Cover Letters

Perfecting a resume and the all-important cover letter can mean the difference between snagging an interview for a job and being cast into the giant pile of never-again-seen candidates. Even veterans of the job market could use a bit of advice on spiffing up these tools of self-promotion. Monster.ca offers several resources, including a list of "don'ts" written by a leading expert in the field of resume writing.

Interviews and Job Hunting

Okay. You've made it to the interview stage. Take a deep breath. There's nothing to fear. You know you've got what it takes to do the job. Now all you need to do is convince *them* of that. Get help from Monster's Interview Tips. We particularly like the list of questions you might want to ask the interviewer. They're sure to impress!

Research Companies

A particular company catches your eye. Maybe you want to work for that company. Or perhaps you want to invest in the product or service it provides. No matter what your reason (even if you need a subject for your latest term paper), the Research Companies department offers several different online sources to speed your search, including the ability to research its reputation among employees and other employers.

Warning! This tool is of limited use for Canadian members, since searches focus on U.S. companies. If you want a more Canadian approach to researching, visit Monster.ca (keyword **Monster**) and click the Featured Employers link. This takes you to an alphabetical list of company profiles available for your perusal.

Quizzes & Tools

Are you a workaholic? Do you know how to manage your time efficiently? Are you a "team player"? Find out the answers to these and other fun and informative questions using the Monster.ca Quizzes and Tools area.

Top 10 Business Books

If you've taken a stroll through any book-store lately, you've probably noticed that the business section is sort of taking over the shelf space. Gurus of all kinds, from managers to spirituality-in-the-workplace types, have all put pen to paper to share their wisdom with the masses (not to mention collecting healthy profits from sales). Find out who's on top in the business-writing world with the Best-selling Career Books, as compiled by Chapters.ca.

Career Management

It's not easy to navigate the political pitfalls and delicate relationships of the workplace. So it pays to become your own career manager. Start learning at Monster.ca's Career Management area. With easy-to-understand advice in categories like Management and Teams, Networking, and Business Life, you're well on your way to solving whatever crisis happens to occur along your career path.

Career Essentials

Keyword **Professions**

How do you advance in your chosen career? Where do you find information about jobs related to yours? When you're looking for real-life information about a career different from yours, where do you turn? Begin your search in the AOL Professional Forums.

Professional Forums provide more than message boards. Look in the forums for scheduled chats that discuss your profession, recent news articles specifically related to what you do, and links to work-specific Web sites. Whether you're working in a particular profession or thinking about taking the plunge, check the Professional Forums department first.

You can zero in on a particular forum using the alphabetical list of career areas in the pull-down menu on the right side of the window, or start with keyword Professions for a complete list of industries and jobs.

Warning! While most of the articles, opportunities, and chat and message boards in the professional forums have universal appeal, they are primarily geared to U.S. users. Some stuff here, like lists of professional associations, for example, can feel more than a little un-Canadian.

Workplace Humour

Keyword **Lighter Side**

No matter how much you love your job (or how much like the rest of the world you are), sometimes you need a smile, a laugh, or some other quick recharge of your spirits. When the burdens of life weigh a little heavily on your shoulders, drop by the Workplace Humour department for a quick lift. With features like the Dilbert Zone (keyword **Dilbert**) and the member-submitted joke of the day from iVillage (keyword **iVillage**), you won't be morose for long.

Chats & Messages

Keyword **Business Talk**

On those days when you feel like connecting with someone, drop in to the Chats & Messages department for a rousing chat room conversation or to browse the business message boards. Two weekday standards, Your Business Lunch and Your Business Dinner, invite different special guests each day. Topics range from public relations to starting your home business and from Internet marketing to effective management.

International Work Opportunities

There's a lot of hype about "globalization," but when it comes to working abroad, modern travel, open borders, and technology really do seem to have shrunk the world. These days, depending on your skills, just about anyone can decide to spend six months tending bar in London, England, or crewing a yacht in the South Pacific.

Monster.ca has an array of information and listings for people looking to work abroad. There are feature articles on things like preparing yourself for culture shock; you can follow the links to other places on the World Wide Web where you can find international jobs; and, of course, you will also want to browse thousands of actual job postings from Germany to New Zealand.

Workers in this part of the world should also be sure to check out these AOL Canada job-related areas:

Business News

Keyword **Business News**

What happened today in your corner of the world? Is your company about to "restructure"? (That dreaded term!) Who knows? Maybe earnings are actually up this quarter! Keep current on business happenings, company news, the economy, investment markets, and technology through the AOL Canada Business News department. Rather than wade through the general news window for specific business news, go directly to Business News and read all the news you need to understand how your career fits into the changing world of business.

Home Business Report

If you haven't already packed up and moved your office into the home, you are bucking a trend that is truly sweeping the nation. With e-mail, fax machines, and the Internet, more and more people are choosing to do their work from home. Sadly, this has also led to a trend of people working in their pyjamas.

The Home Business Report, at www. homebusinessreport.com, has been helping Canadians adjust to working at home since the 1970s, so you know you can trust their advice and suggestions. Be sure to check it out, and for Pete's sake, get dressed!

International Channel

By virtue of our ethnic diversity, we Canadians tend to grow up aware that there's more to this planet than what lies atop the 49th Parallel. Africa, Asia, Australia, Europe, North America, and South America all await us in the Great Out There. Of course, all that travel takes either big bucks or lots of frequent-flier miles, so if you're a little low on both but still want to find out how the rest of the world lives, the International channel (keyword **International**) is for you.

Prominently displayed across the window is the *HotMap,* a highly technical and cool-sounding term that we made up just now. The HotMap's seven red buttons (one for each continent on the map) are your main links to the International area. They each reveal a pull-down menu of options, which in turn leads to windows filled with Web links, discussion boards, chat areas, and other information about the continent you clicked.

Some areas have local versions of AOL (who'd have know there's an AOL Brazil?). If the menu contains only an option called Access Numbers, there's no local version of AOL in that part of the world. For your real ticket to the content on the AOL Canada International channel, choose Explore All from one of the pull-down menus. This opens a window from which you can choose a specific country and find out more about its people and geography.

There's even more to the International channel than meets the eye. Here are some extra areas you won't find labelled on the main channel window, but that you should not miss:

Bistro

Keyword **Bistro**

If this world is really to become a global community, we all have to learn how to communicate. The International channel has stepped forward with one innovative way to begin: the Bistro. This area permits people from around the world to assemble in chat rooms to discuss serious and not-so-serious stuff pertaining to cultural diversity. (Like why is it that in Europe you sometimes have to pay to use public washrooms? Oh, mystery of mysteries!) The best part about the Bistro is its linguistic diversity. Some, like the main chat room, accept messages in any language, while others are designed for native speakers in French, Italian, Japanese, and more.

Warning! Before you start chatting, we strongly suggest you learn how to use the system by reading the About This Area article as well as the community guidelines. Also check out the Live Events at the International channel, where you'll find upcoming scheduled chats with celebs, thinkers, and leaders from different corners of the world.

Search & Explore

Keyword **Intl Explore**

Find out what gems await you on the International channel by taking a trip to the Search & Explore department. Another service of the U.S. version of this channel, Search & Explore is too cool to pass up just because you're a Canadian member. After all, we are talking about *international* features, right? Use the A–Z International Channel Guide for an alphabetical overview of the channel's contents. We also like the Best of International Channel link on the right side of the window, where you can learn a bit about the channel's features, then use the Go There button to try them out.

Fun & Games

Keyword **Intl Fun**

Quick! Think of your favourite online games. Name That Flag? Foreign Language Trivia? No? How about international trivia games, like Trivia Info in French or Tiger Trivia in German? If none of these comes to mind, you're missing some of the most unusual games on AOL. In these games, along with the other sections in the Fun & Games department, you find out about leisure-time events such as films and music and meet international friends-to-be, all while practising a foreign language. Not exactly your middle-school foreign language course, is it?

World News

Keyword **Intl News**

Nothing keeps you up-to-date on another country like reading its news. Stay on top of all the News channel's international headlines and features at the World News department. Even better, get local reports and opinion by following the Newsstand link on the right side of the window to browse International Papers from Latin America, Europe, the Middle East, Africa, Asia, and Australia.

U.S. Channels

Back when AOL first came on to the scene, it was known only as America Online, which gives you a pretty good idea where it was born! Yep, the Land of the Free, the U.S. of A., the United States. And the service is the country's most popular Internet Online Service Provider, bringing content and the Net into millions of American homes.

As we mentioned at the outset of this book, it's no surprise, then, that U.S. content is everywhere on AOL . . . and, uh, sometimes pokes its head into areas that would be strictly Canadian. No big deal, really. Our neighbours to the South are pretty cool, too, which is why you shouldn't be shy about visiting the U.S. channels.

Français

This country celebrates its bicultural beginnings daily with an official policy of bilingualism, French immersion schools, and, of course, the day-to-day workings of francophone communities across the country (not to mention the giant of francophone culture that is Quebec). AOL Canada also celebrates this heritage with its channel *en français*, at keyword **Francais**.

All the content here is either written in French or geared to francophone AOL Canada members. Occupying a prominent place in the window are news headlines from across Canada and the world, as well as business, sports, and lifestyles news. Just below the news area are links to both the Weather channel and even more headlines (that's *manchettes* to you Anglos).

On the right side of the window is a very full menu of options, including Le Bistro St-Denis, your portal to the francophone chat rooms. More must-sees include a site for francophone fans of technology and the Internet (at keyword **Branche**), a health department brought to you by GlobalMedic (keyword **Globalmedic**), a very cool kids play area called l'îlot de TFO (keyword **TFO**), where even anglophone children could benefit from the interactive games and quizzes, a play area (keyword **jeux**), a travel forum (keyword **Voyagez**), sports, and much, much more.

Whether you're French Canadian or just learning French as a second language, you're sure to find something informative, educational, and *excitant* at the AOL Canada channel *en français*.

Chapter 16

Loading Up, Loading Down, and Zipping All Around

● ●

In This Chapter

▶ Finding things to download

▶ Downloading a file

▶ Using the Download Manager

▶ Unzipping, unstuffing, and otherwise decompressing files

▶ Uploading your donations

▶ Logging everything you see

● ●

*I*magine a department store where everything is free — you just pick out what you want and carry your selections out to the car. Some items require a small payment directly to the manufacturer, but many don't. Sounds like heaven, right? (Well, heaven probably would be a computer superstore set up this way, but we digress.)

The scenario we just described already exists, except that it's not a department store — it's the hundreds of file libraries on AOL Canada. Just find something that interests you, download the file to your computer, and then, if it's a shareware program, pay a small fee to the author because you love the application so much.

Sounds too simple, right? There must be a catch. Well, it *is* simple, and there really *isn't* a catch. This chapter is your guide to getting a share of this digital bonanza. Read on and find out how to find stuff to download, how the download process works, how to share stuff you love by uploading it, and much more.

Welcome to Software Heaven. Come right on in.

Locating Likely Candidates

You're ready to storm the digital gates, eager to get your share of the software fortunes within. But where do you start? Jeez — hundreds, maybe thousands of places exist for you to look through. Nothing like having too many options to keep your mind spinning in circles, eh?

Start with one or two forums (another word for an AOL Canada content window) you particularly like. If you're looking for a certain kind of file (such as fonts or clip art), use the software library search feature to see what's available. This section explains both these options.

Forum and service libraries

Many of the AOL Canada forums have a file library. Libraries are sometimes listed among other clickable features in the main forum window (see Figure 16-1), or they're listed along with other resources (as shown in Figure 16-2), or you might have to dig around a little to find them. Ultimately, all these means lead to a file list window like the one in Figure 16-3.

Software Library Link

Figure 16-1: Look! Up there, in the sky! It's a library link in the Space Exploration window.

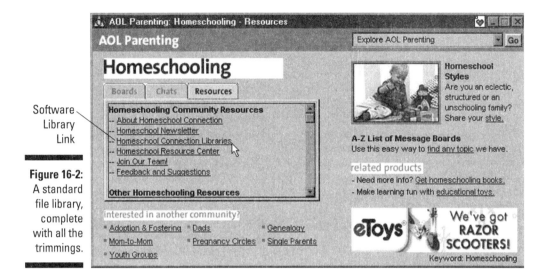

Software Library Link

Figure 16-2:
A standard file library, complete with all the trimmings.

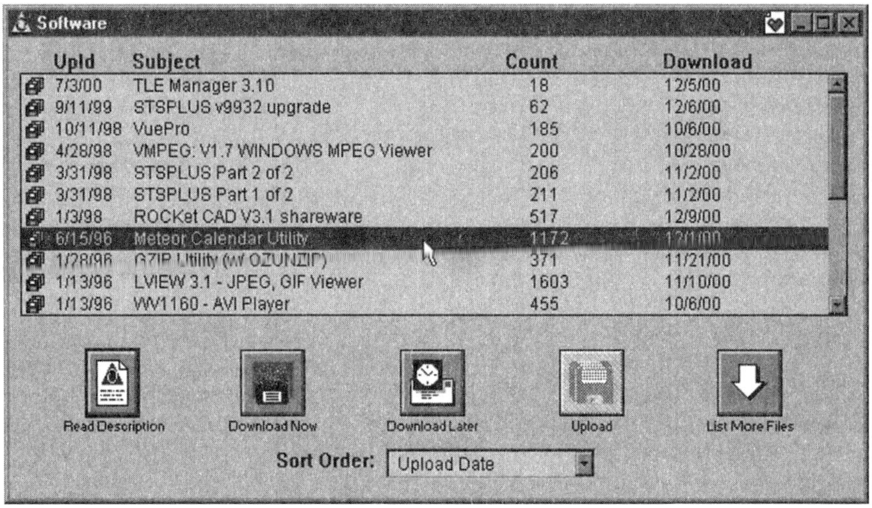

Figure 16-3:
All roads lead to a file list window.

> ✔ To find out more about a file, double-click its entry in the forum library window (or click the entry and then click the Read Description button). A page of information about the file appears, including its name, size, and author, plus a complete description (or as complete a description as the person contributing it provides).

Incidentally, if you're using a session log, all the file descriptions you view are saved there automatically. For more information about session logs, see Chapter 14.

✔ Downloading is a breeze with the Download Now and Download Later buttons (covered in the next section).

✔ Use the Sort Order pull-down menu to see the files by the date they were first uploaded or last downloaded, alphabetically by subject, or by download count (a relative measure of which files are the most popular). Just click the down arrow next to the Sort Order setting, choose your preferred order from the list, and wait a moment while AOL Canada organizes everything for you.

✔ Although most libraries have lots of files, the library's window only displays the first 20. That's why a List More Files button usually appears in the lower-right corner of the forum library window. Click this button to display more files in the window.

For leads on good downloads, read the forum's discussion areas to see what people are talking about, or post a message that describes your interests and asks for recommendations.

Look for files that are popular. The *count* column in the file list window is a good popularity gauge; this column tracks the number of times members downloaded that file.

File library search

If you're looking for something more general or if you just like knowing *all* your options before you start, try the software library Search feature. This feature browses through all the libraries in AOL Canada, looking intently for whatever you tell it to look for.

You must be signed on to AOL Canada to use the software library search system. Sorry, but that's just how life goes.

Here's how to do a search:

1. **Get into the file search system by using keyword** Download.

   The Download Centre window pops up, offering all kinds of software catalogues, plus two places to search for software.

2. **In the Download Centre window, click the Shareware button (or use keyword** File Search **to go directly to the search window).**

   The Software Search window *finally* appears.

   The other button in the Download Centre window takes you to the commercial software area, where the price of admission is your credit card number. That's great if you need a particular program for the office, but it's usually overkill for a home computer. Rather than plunk down the bucks for an over-packaged application, look for a shareware (or even a freeware) program that fits the bill.

For a Macintosh file search, click the Mac Search button along the bottom of the Software Search window.

3. **To limit your search to a particular time period (the past week, the past month, or since time began), select the appropriate radio button in the Select a Timeframe area.**

   Barring a specific, burning need to search only the most recent uploads, leave the time frame set to All Dates. The search system displays the file list presorted by category and date, with the newest files at the beginning of each category.

4. **Narrow your search if you want to.**

   Narrow your search to particular file libraries by clicking one or more of the check boxes in the Category area. To search everywhere, leave all the check boxes clear (the default setting).

   When you feel comfortable with the search function, try experimenting with these settings to see if they help you find more of what you want.

5. **Type a few words that describe what you're looking for.**

   See Figure 16-4 for an example.

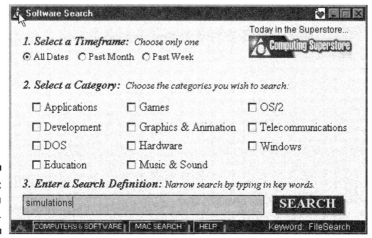

Figure 16-4:
The search
begins.

If you know the specific program you want (like WinZip, Paint Shop Pro, or PowerTools), type the program name in this area.

6. **Click the oversized and relaxingly coloured Search button at the bottom of the window (refer to Figure 16-4).**

   After a moment or two, the File Search Results dialog box appears, looking somewhat akin to Figure 16-5. The File Search Results dialog box is much like the forum's file list window, right down to the buttons along the bottom.

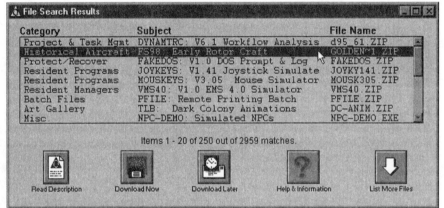

Figure 16-5: The results are in!

7. **Scroll through the list to see what your search uncovered. Double-click interesting-looking entries to see a full description of the file.**

   At this point, you're ready to do some downloading, which (surprisingly enough) is covered in the next section.

Incidentally, Paint Shop Pro, PowerTools, and WinZip are *great* shareware applications for everybody who uses Microsoft Windows and AOL Canada. If you don't have them yet, test your new downloading skills on them.

Downloads sources to check out

There are still more places on AOL Canada worth checking for interesting and, in some cases, even patriotic downloads. Here are some of the most fun, accompanied, of course, by a handy-dandy keyword to get you there faster than you can say "doowwnnlooad"):

✔ **Daily Download** (keyword **Daily Download**): Have you ever been in the kind of mood when you want something new but you won't know what it is until you see it? If so, give the Daily Download a try. It could be a game. It could be a picture. It could be just what you didn't know you were looking for but can't live without.

✔ **Cool Downloads** (keyword **Fun Stuff**): How can you go wrong with a name and keyword like that, eh? Just click the Cool Downloads folder for quick access to downloadable screen savers, games, and more.

✔ **Canadian Software Libraries** (keyword **Cdn Boards**): Get in touch with the maple leaf within by browsing the Canadian downloads. First, click the Software Libraries link at the main Canadian Message Boards window. Then, choose from several categories, including the Images of Canada Photo Libraries, the Canada Shareware and File Library, the Canada Artist Library, the Canada Wav and Sound Library, and last but certainly not least, the Partagiciels Francophones (that's franocophone shareware).

✔ **Viewz Software** (keyword **Viewz**): Viewz is a very cool online magazine for PC users everywhere, published right here in Canada. Just click Downloads on the left side of the window, and explore several categories of files (some free demos of commercial offerings by companies like IBM and Disney). While you're there, spend some time reading the magazine's news, reviews, and the weekly Dijit's Top Ten list.

Downloading a File Right Now

You finally found a promising file, checked its description, and decided that you simply *must* have a copy. Cool. You're ready to do the dirty deed, then — time to download a file.

Here's the procedure:

1. **Click the name of the file you want to download and then click the Download Now button (see Figure 16-6).**

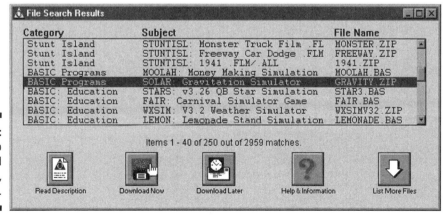

Figure 16-6:
Ready to
download
your file,
Captain.

If you're in the file list window, Download Now is a square button with a cool graphic of a disk "beaming down," as in *Star Trek*. In the file description window, the button is simply labelled (you guessed it) Download Now.

Clicking the Download Now button accesses the Download Manager's filename dialog box (but not the whole Download Manager itself — that's covered in the next section of this chapter).

The file's name is displayed in the File Name box (see Figure 16-7).

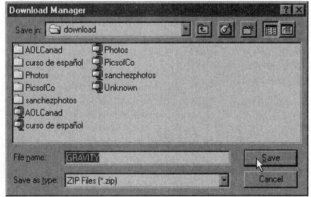

Figure 16-7:
Name the
file and it's
on the way.

2. **Change the file's name or its destination directory if you like. When you're satisfied, click OK.**

   Clicking OK starts the download. To keep you updated, AOL Canada displays a progress bar.

   The Download dialog box also has two control buttons: Finish Later and Cancel. If you suddenly need your computer for something more urgent than downloading this file, click Finish Later. AOL Canada remembers that you already received part of the file. When you start to download the file again, the download picks up wherever you stopped the first time. Cancel, on the other hand, is the abort button. Click it if you come to the conclusion that downloading this file is a terrible mistake.

   After the download is complete, a little dialog box pops up to gleefully announce the news.

3. **Click OK to make the dialog box go away.**

If something goes horribly wrong (for example, the download gets stuck for some reason), try downloading the file again. If it doesn't work that time either, try once more at a different time of day, particularly early in the day, just before you leave for work or school.

What if you're *not* on the unlimited time plan and you burn up a bunch of online time for a download that doesn't work? It's no problem — just go to keyword **Credit** and ask for a refund. Fill out the form, complete with the time, date, and minutes lost, and click Send Request. The AOL Canada credit elves should reply to you within a few days.

After you get the hang of the AOL Canada file libraries, check out the Internet Connection's FTP (File Transfer Protocol) feature. FTP is your link to millions of files available on the Internet. If instant access to file libraries all over the world already has you salivating, flip to Chapter 17 for details.

How Do You Manage This Many Downloads?

What if you find not one, not two, but 47 fascinating files? Well, you can spend much of your copious free time watching the computer draw progress bars (how exciting). Or you can use the Download Manager to automate the whole sordid process. The Download Manager's main goal in life is to help you download tons of stuff from AOL Canada. Really — that's it.

Using the Download Manager is a two-stage process: You mark the files you want to download and then you tell the Download Manager to get them. The best thing is that you don't need to be present for the second step of the process; your computer happily sits and catches all the files you want while you're off doing something really fun.

Here's how the process works:

1. **Click the name of a file you want to download and then click the Download Later button.**

   The file hops into the Download Manager's queue (see Figure 16-8). By default, the AOL Canada software throws up an annoying little window that *helpfully* explains that you just decided to download this file later (assuming that you mistakenly thought that the Download Later button actually washed your car or something).

   If you plan to use the Download Later feature frequently, turn off the this-is-what-you-just-did dialog box. To do that, open the Download Manager (as described in Step 3) and click the Download Preferences button. When the Download Preferences window appears, de-select the Confirm When I Add Files to My Download List check box and click Save. Finally, close the Preferences window and take a moment to smile smugly in the knowledge that you've silenced yet another silly dialog box.

2. **Repeat Step 1 for all the files you want to download.**

3. **Open the Download Manager by choosing File⇨Download Manager from the menu at the very top of your screen.**

   The Download Manager window appears, looking like the one shown in Figure 16-9 (except that your list of files in the middle looks different from these).

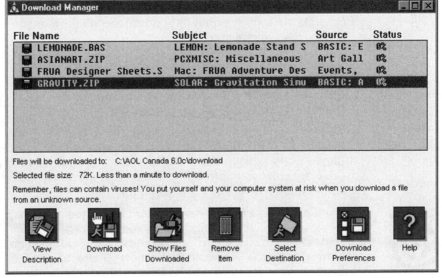

Figure 16-9:
The
Download
Manager is
your digital
shopping
cart, filled
with the
goodies
you've
selected.

To see the file description one more time, double-click the filename in the Download Manager window. The description appears, just as it did in the file list window.

If you have sudden second thoughts about a file and decide that you don't want to download it, click its name on the Download Manager list and then click Remove Item. Repeat the process as many times as you want.

4. Click the Download button to put the Download Manager to work.

Two windows appear onscreen, as shown in Figure 16-10. One window shows the overall status of your massive download. The other window displays a progress bar for the file that's downloading right now.

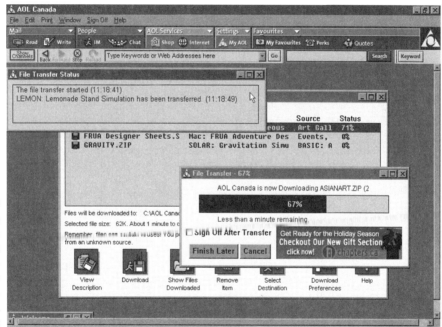

Figure 16-10: Two windows show you the downloading status.

If you have *lots* of files to get, select the Sign Off After Transfer check box. That option tells the Download Manager to go ahead and sign you off from AOL Canada after the last file arrives. This feature is handy (and makes sure that you don't waste online time if the download finishes before you expect it to).

Remember that Automatic AOL sessions work with the Download Manager. You can mark a bunch of files and download them in the middle of the night, when AOL Canada is the least busy. Chapter 8 explains the basics of Automatic AOL from an e-mail perspective, but you need to check the Help menu for details about scheduling the sessions.

The Joys of Stuffing and Zipping

Many files in the various and sundry AOL Canada file libraries end in ZIP, SIT, or ARC. These letters don't mean that they're fast or resting or that they date from the time of Noah; rather, the letters indicate that the files were compressed so that they take less time to download (and less space inside the AOL Canada computers). ZIP files come from the PKZip or WinZip programs, and SIT files are created on the Macintosh by StuffIt. ARC files are in an old and rarely used format, but some are still around.

Before using a compressed file, you have to decompress it. To do that, you either need a copy of the right program (as mentioned), or you can let the AOL Canada software handle it by itself.

To simplify your life, the AOL Canada access software will automatically unpack compressed files if you want, either when the download is complete or when you sign off the system. (Those programmers are amazing, aren't they?) To make sure that this setting is set the way you want, choose Settings⇨ Preferences. Click the Download link under the list of Organization preferences to open the Download Preferences dialog box. Make your selection, then leave the decompressing to AOL Canada. If you're comfy with a program like WinZip (which, by the way, is one of the most useful programs ever invented for Windows users), select Do Not Decompress Files and do the unpacking yourself.

Installing programs on your computer involves many little niggling details — too many, unfortunately, for us to go into here. We won't leave you high and dry, though (we'd never do that to you!). Take a look at these resources for more about both downloading and installing programs:

✔ For a great view of the whole download-and-install thing, try keyword **Download 101**. This interactive area offers tips and instructions covering the entire download process as well as lots of links to great file libraries all over AOL Canada. And every now and then, the area offers free, live training chats.

✔ Still more downloading help awaits you at keyword **Download Info** in the form of a very complete list of FAQs. From "How do I deal with a slow or bad download?" to the perennial "What about viruses?" — it's a resource you'll use over and over again.

✔ If the mere thought of folders, directories, and software installation makes you pass out on the floor, put some soft blankets down there to cushion your impending arrival. When they're safely in place, pick up a copy of *Windows 98 For Dummies*, by Andy Rathbone, or *Macs For Dummies*, 7th Edition, by David Pogue (both from IDG Books Worldwide, Inc.), hit the blankets, and catch up on your reading.

Well, now it's yours — sort of

Three kinds of programs exist in the world: freeware, shareware, and commercial software. If this sounds like horribly dry, technical drivel, you obviously aren't a lawyer (you did seem rather likeable). Please bear with us (and stay awake) while we explain.

Freeware, shareware, and commercial software are the three most common ways in which a program is licensed for use. *Freeware* costs nothing; the author has graciously donated it to the public. *Shareware* is software you can download, try, and pay for if you like it. *Commercial software* is what you buy at the local computer superstore, from companies such as Borland, Lotus, Microsoft, Novell, and Corel.

Here are a few basic rules regarding the three kinds of software:

✔ **Freeware:** Download it, use it, give a copy to your friends. Isn't freeware great?

✔ **Shareware:** Download it and give it a try. If you don't like the program, don't pay for it. If you think it's great, get out your chequebook and send in the registration fee. Whatever you do, don't keep using an unregistered shareware program because you don't think that you should have to pay for something you downloaded from AOL Canada. That would be like stealing a book from the library and then saying that it's okay because the library doesn't charge for books anyway. Shareware is often high-quality work and well worth the minimal registration fee.

✔ **Commercial software:** Never, under any circumstances, upload or download something that claims to be a commercial program. If you like Corel's WordPerfect, that's fine — just don't show your admiration by giving copies of it to your friends. We won't get on our "pirated software" soapbox, we promise. But we will say this: If you like a program, buy your own copy. Okay?

 Whether or not you plan to download lots of files and programs, we *highly* recommend downloading and registering a copy of WinZip, a Windows-based archiving program. This one program knows how to handle almost any type of compressed file thrown at it. That alone makes WinZip worth the minimal registration fee. But all the other tricks it knows (like making a ZIP file on the fly by dragging and dropping files into it from Windows Explorer) make WinZip truly indispensable.

Donating Your Own Efforts

Most file libraries not only offer files for your downloading pleasure but also accept *uploads* — files donated by other AOL Canada members. After all, the library files had to come from *somewhere,* so why not let members chip in things they like?

To upload a file, you need to know the file's name and location on your computer. You also have to find a potential home for it somewhere on AOL Canada. Look for a place that accepts uploaded files (this step is a must) and has other files like the one you're sending. If you're sending a game, utility, or other program, use your antivirus software to be extra sure that you're not donating a computer virus, too.

✔ Not every file library accepts uploads. If you're looking at a file list and the Upload button is dimmed, it's a good sign that you're browsing a read-only library.

✔ Only public domain, freeware, shareware, or items of your own creation can be uploaded to AOL Canada. If you aren't sure about the appropriateness of something you want to upload, post a message to one of the forum hosts (you can usually find their screen names in a welcome-to-this-forum type document on the forum's main screen). Describe your file and get the host's opinion about your uploading it. Check out the sidebar "Well, now it's yours — sort of," earlier in this chapter, for a little more information about the whole freeware, shareware, and commercial software issue.

✔ Don't upload something on your first day on AOL Canada. Wait a little while. Get involved in a forum or two, meet some people, post some messages, and generally get a feel for what goes on before you upload anything to a library.

At this point, you're ready to upload the file. Here's what to do:

1. **Display the file list window of the file library to which you want to upload.**

   Get there through whatever combination of keywords, menus, and mouse-clicks works best for you.

2. **Click the Upload button at the bottom of the file list window.**

   The Upload File dialog box appears.

   If the Upload button is dimmed, this file library doesn't accept uploaded files. Sorry, but that's how things go sometimes. Also, AOL Canada may tell you that the library is full. In that case, post a message on the forum's discussion boards asking whether there's a place for you to upload the file you want to share.

3. **Carefully fill out all the information boxes in the Upload File dialog box.**

   Be as specific as you can. The more that people know about this file, the more likely they are to download it.

4. **Click Select File to display the Attach File dialog box, double-click the name of the file you want to upload, then choose OK to close the dialog box.**

5. **Double-check all the text you typed; after you're happy with it, click Send.**

Don't be surprised if your uploaded file doesn't immediately appear in the file library. Most, if not all, AOL Canada forums check uploaded files for viruses before setting those files free in the library.

Logging Isn't Really Downloading, Although It's Close

Sometimes, you want a record of where you were and what you saw. If you didn't, most of the photo film and developing market (as well as a large chunk of camcorder sales) wouldn't exist.

In AOL Canada terminology, what you're looking for is a *session log*: a file that stores the contents of every document you touched during a particular online period. The session log grabs every e-mail, news story, and bulletin board posting and stuffs them into one long text file.

For all the details on the AOL Canada logging features, flip to Chapter 14.

Chapter 17

Cruising the Internet

• •

In This Chapter

▶ Checking out the Internet

▶ Getting started: A brief Internet primer

▶ Skimming the resources

▶ Using Internet e-mail

▶ Trying a mailing list (or two)

▶ Leaping through the World Wide Web

▶ Newsgroups: The Internet's answer to discussion boards

▶ Downloading the world with FTP

• •

*T*urn on the TV news and what do you hear being discussed? The Internet. Go to lunch with some friends and what's bound to come up either in conversation at your table or in a loud debate at the one next to you? The Internet. Attend a cocktail party and what's on everyone's minds? Well, if it's boring, they may be thinking about how much better the *last* party was; but to pass the time until they can make a polite departure, they're talking about the Internet. (What's wrong with these people? Don't they have real lives?)

Rising from technoid obscurity to media-star status in just a few short years, the Internet is still a mystery to most people. Frankly, it was a mystery to your co-authors until a few years ago. In the hope of sparing you additional moments of fear and anxiety, this chapter explains a little about the Internet (just enough to get you going) and a lot about the powerful AOL Canada Internet Connection. It also unmasks the odd language of the Internet, introducing and explaining terms such as *World Wide Web*, *FTP*, and *newsgroup*.

A big electronic world is out there, just waiting for you to visit. Grab your modem and get ready to go Internet surfing!

You can get online today using the AOL Canada Version 6.0 access software. It's easy! Just follow the instructions in the appendix to install the software from the free CD-ROM in this book, which comes with a trial period of 540 free hours in your first month (communication charges may apply). After your trial period, you will be charged a monthly membership fee of $22.95 plus applicable taxes for unlimited Internet and unlimited e-mail. Online registration will give you the complete details.

Internet Basics

Like everything else on AOL Canada, the Internet is just a hop, skip, and a click away from wherever you are. In fact, it's even a little closer than that because AOL Canada has a toolbar icon for it too: the cleverly named Internet icon.

Click this button to quickly get you where you want to go: the AOL.CA home page. You can also try using keyword **AOL.CA**. Either way, it's your launchpad for a journey *out there* on the Net. At the centre of the AOL.CA home page, you'll see a big horizontal red banner, where the intelligent programmers have placed a search system. Along the bottom of the page, you'll also find several columns of links to some very cool stuff, including extra search functions, the AOL Canada Web Centres (which we'll discuss at length later in this chapter), and online shopping links.

So Just What Is This Internet Thing?

Hang on to your seat — we're about to explain the Internet in four (yes, just *four*) paragraphs. This may get a little hairy at times, but you have nothing to worry about because we're trained professionals. Kids, don't let your parents try this stuff at home.

The Internet started as a big U.S. Department of Defense project somewhere back in the 1960s, slowly expanding through the '70s and '80s, and coming into its own in the '90s. It was originally supposed to help university researchers exchange information about super secret defense projects, thus decreasing the amount of time necessary to find new and ever more fascinating ways to end life on the planet. The U.S. government linked computers at colleges, universities, research labs, and large defense contractors. The Internet was born.

At the same time, the seeds of today's digital anarchy were sown. This research network connected lots of bright, intelligent people, and those people started coming up with bright, intelligent ideas about fun, new things to do on the research network. "How about a discussion area where we can swap notes — kinda like a bulletin board?" *Poof!* The network newsgroups were born.

Then anarchy took over. Discussion areas originally intended for deep conversations about megaton yields and armour deflection/implosion ratios carried witty repartee about Buddha, the Rolling Stones, and kite flying. Everyone with an opinion to share was welcome, as long as they could get there in the first place.

Although the Internet continued to slowly bubble and ferment throughout the 1980s, things suddenly changed when the 1990s arrived. In the span of a couple of years, the Internet simply exploded. Thousands of computers and networks around the world joined the fun. Newspaper articles and TV news stories appeared, introducing this electronic colossus to the normal world. Non-computer companies linked up to the network as business e-mail use blossomed. Millions of average people began poking around on the Internet through online services such as AOL Canada.

With that brief bit of background under your belt, ponder these important tidbits before venturing out into the online world:

- ✔ No single computer or place is called the Internet. The Internet is a collection of millions of computers all over the world.

- ✔ Nobody's really in charge of it all. Nope, nobody. Some committees and groups attempt to keep everything headed in the same direction, but nobody actually leads the parade.

- ✔ No one knows how big the Internet is. Suffice it to say that it's really, *really* big — and still growing.

- ✔ The Internet is not free (even though you don't pay extra for it through AOL Canada). It kinda looks like it's free because you just pay for your AOL Canada account — you're not charged for the telecommunications time between AOL's main computers in the State of Virginia, USA, and the rest of the Internet world (including all us Canucks). We only bring this up so that you remember that *someone* out there is paying the bill; it's good netiquette to use Internet resources wisely, particularly FTP (covered later in this chapter).

- ✔ Believe it or not, all this anarchy works if everyone's nice about it.

Free speech is the *rule* on the Internet, not the exception. If you see a Web page, read something in a newsgroup, or find a document through gopher that's offensive to you, you have our personal apologies. But that's all the sympathy anyone's going to give you. The communications code of the Internet is simple: If something offends you, either ignore it or disagree with it, but *don't* post a message suggesting that "somebody ought to shut those people up." An action such as that is sure to fill your mailbox with angry e-mail questioning your parentage and suggesting that you do some biologically impossible things in the corner.

E-Mail the Internet Way

Perhaps you joined AOL Canada solely to use Internet e-mail. (It wouldn't surprise us at all.) An Internet e-mail account is an absolute must these days, particularly in the business world.

The AOL Canada e-mail system makes Internet e-mail a snap. You don't have to remember any special commands or visit any obscure corner of the service to send an e-mail message through the Internet. Just create the message as you would normally, type in the person's Internet mail address, and click Send. If you need a quick review of the how-tos of AOL Canada e-mail, flip to Chapter 8 or choose Mail⇨Mail Centre from the toolbar and poke through the information there.

Here are a few notes about e-mail that we just couldn't fit anywhere else:

- ✔ An e-mail message takes anywhere from a few seconds, to a few minutes, to a few hours to make its way through the Internet and find its destination. If you send a message and it doesn't arrive by the next business day or two, consider the message lost.

- ✔ Yes, Internet mail messages sometimes get lost. No, it's not the fault of Canada Post or any other postal service.

- ✔ Your AOL Canada account can receive mail through the Internet as well as send it. Your Internet e-mail address is your screen name — minus any spaces in it — with @aol.com appended to the end. For example, John's Internet mail address on AOL is jkaufeld@aol.com (his screen name first, then the extra Internet stuff tacked on to the end). If his screen name included a space (making it J Kaufeld), the Internet e-mail version would still be jkaufeld@aol.com, because the Internet doesn't like spaces in e-mail addresses.

- ✔ Look through Chapter 8 for all the particulars about using e-mail both through the Internet and within AOL Canada.

Join a Mailing List for Fun and Full Mailboxes

Swapping letters through a mailing list is about the simplest form of information exchange on the Internet. You don't need any special software, you don't have to buy anything, and no salesperson calls. Everything comes straight to your mailbox; you don't even have to go find it. You can find lists for everything and everybody covering hobbies, music groups, religion, mine-proofing military vehicles, motorcycle repair, world history, and Canadian culture too — the list goes on and on.

Consider getting an Internet book

If one of the main reasons you joined AOL Canada was for its Internet services, we highly recommend getting a good book about the Internet. We personally suggest *The Internet For Canadians For Dummies Starter Kit* (by Andrew Dagys, John R. Levine, Carol Baroudi,

and Margaret Levine Young), and MORE *Internet For Dummies*, 4th Edition (by John R. Levine and Margaret Levine Young), both from IDG Books Worldwide, Inc. (No, it's not because we *have* to suggest them — we really like them.)

Finding and joining a mailing list

Before enjoying the wonders of discussions that take place in your mailbox, you have to sign up. AOL Canada makes that simple with easy access to *Liszt*, a searchable database of Internet mailing lists. To get there, click in the address box on the navigation bar, and then type www.liszt.com and press Enter (or click the Go button to the right of the text box). On cue, your Web browser opens and displays the Liszt mailing list directory (as shown in Figure 17-1).

Figure 17-1: The Liszt mailing list search system makes finding an e-mail discussion easy.

Liszt includes a searchable database (containing nearly 100,000 mailing lists) and a browsable subject-oriented directory named Liszt Select.

- ✔ **To search the database:** Type either the list name or subject in the search box and then click Go. Liszt thinks for a moment and then returns a report of what it found. Browse through your results and click anything that looks interesting.

- ✔ **For a relaxed browse through the subjects:** Scroll down a little in the Liszt main window until the topic lists appear. When you find a topic that looks interesting, click it to see what Liszt offers there. Remember that the subject listing includes only a small portion of the total Liszt database, so if you don't find something of interest, try the search option mentioned in the first bullet.

When you find an interesting list, follow the subscription instructions to join. Usually, you need to send an e-mail message to either the list moderator or a program that maintains the subscriber list. If the instructions say something about putting the phrase SUBSCRIBE listname your-name in the body of a message, you're dealing with an automated list-keeping program. If you're supposed to send "a politely worded request," a human's doing the work. (Don't sign up for a human-maintained list and then ask to be removed a couple of days later. The poor person on the other end is usually overworked as it is.)

Save the *welcome to our list* message that usually arrives after the list accepts your subscription. It contains all kinds of useful information — most importantly, it tells you how to un-subscribe from the list, should you ever want to quit.

If you can't find the list of your dreams through the Liszt database, try the CataList catalogue, at www.lsoft.com/lists/listref.html, or the massive Publicly Accessible Mailing List site (also known as PAML because computer people can't resist a cute acronym), at www.paml.net.

Sharing your wisdom with everybody else

Belonging to a list means both reading what others have to say and tossing in your own two cents every now and then. To send a message to the entire list, write your thoughts in an e-mail and send it to the submissions or articles address — *not* to the address you used to subscribe to the list. Your important thoughts find their way out to everybody within a day or so — or at least they may.

Keep your thoughts clear and concise, with emphasis on the word *concise*. People on the Internet appreciate brevity. Remember that some of your readers have to pay for each message they receive; others are charged by the size of the message. Keep your messages short, clear, and to the point, and you will be adored by millions.

Just because your thoughts are lucid and fascinating doesn't guarantee that they'll actually be shared with the rest of the mailing list. Here's a brief guide to help you understand the three basic types of lists and how each affects your chances of sharing your thoughts:

- **Unmoderated:** Accepts whatever you send; posting is automatic, as long as your contribution makes its way successfully back to the listkeeper (be it machine or otherwise).

- **Moderated:** Edited and controlled by someone. Everything that goes out to the list's subscribers is okayed by the moderator. If your posting doesn't meet the standards or requirements of the list, it's not distributed. You can ask the moderator why your posting didn't pass muster, but simply whining doesn't do any good.

- **Announcement-only:** Doesn't accept submissions from you, the listening audience. They send out information only from a particular source. Writing an article for one of these lists is like trying to convince the recorded weather information to say something else for a while.

Un-subscribing from a list

Yes, the time does come when you must bid adieu to the things of youth and flights of information fancy. And so it is that you may, one day, want to get the heck off that mailing list that fills your mailbox with messages every day.

To un-subscribe from a list, turn back to the information page you so carefully printed or saved when you joined the list. Buried among everything else on the page is a notation about "un-subscribing from this list" or something like that. Just follow the instructions, and soon the digital torrents wash through your mailbox no more.

If you lost, erased, or otherwise can't find the information sheet, just search the mailing list database and find it. Send your "I wanna quit" message to the list administration address, not the submission address. You don't want everyone to know that you're quitting, do you?

Topic Hopping in the World Wide Web

It's huge. It's interconnected. It has a funny name. It's the most exciting, promising part of the Internet. It's also the newest addition to the AOL Canada suite of Internet services. It's (electronic drumroll, please!) the *World Wide Web*.

The Web is a most amazing place. Where else can you find newspapers, technical information, company product catalogues, a library of folk song lyrics, far too many personal biographies, and a clock that displays the current time with fish sponges? (Not at the local mall, that's for sure.)

So just what *is* the World Wide Web? Like the Internet, it's not a single, unique "place" out there somewhere. Instead, the *Web* is a collection of interlinked *sites* containing millions of interlinked *pages*). The links between the various sites and pages are what make the Web a truly cool place.

Ever hear of something called hypertext? (You probably know what it is but don't know that it has a name — trust us for now and read on.) Although the term sounds like a book on a sugar high, *hypertext* is a neat way to organize information by *linking* related topics.

Suppose that you're reading an encyclopedia article about wombats and find out that the wombat is an Australian marsupial. Like most rational humans, your next thought is "I wonder what's for lunch." While foraging for food in the wilds of your refrigerator, you casually wonder precisely what a marsupial is. Abandoning your meal in search of knowledge, you pull out the *M* volume of the encyclopedia and look up marsupials. You discover that kangaroos are also marsupials, a fact that sends you racing for the *A* volume to determine whether the Australian government is aware that the country is brimming with marsupials.

If this keeps up much longer, you may as well move in with your encyclopedia.

What if you were using a hypertext encyclopedia on the computer? In the wombat article, the words *marsupial* and *Australian* would be highlighted to let you know that they're links to related articles. You click *marsupial* and immediately see the marsupial article. Another click takes you back to the first article so that you can explore the *Australian* link. Talk about fast information — you didn't even have time to eat!

The World Wide Web works just like the hypertext encyclopedia we described. The onscreen page offers information, plus it contains links to other Web pages. Those pages have links to still *other* Web pages. That cloud of links is where the name *Web* comes from — it's a Web of links. It's an information browser's dream come true.

A quick stop at the terminology shop

The Web just wouldn't be a computer thing if it didn't have a whole slew of new terms and acronyms to baffle and amaze you. Here are the terms you need in order to make sense of the Web:

✔ A *Web page* is the smallest building block of the Web. It's an electronic page with information and links to other places on the Web.

✔ A *Web site* is a collection of Web pages. A site may have just a few pages or more than a hundred. It depends on the site's purpose and how much time, energy, and effort the site's builder puts into it.

✔ Every Web site has a *home page*. It's usually the first page you see when you visit that site. The term also refers to your own personal Web page (if you created one) or the page that appears when you start your *Web browser* (the software you use to browse the Web — see the next section for more info about the AOL Canada browser).

✔ To find something on the Web, you need to know its *Uniform Resource Locator (URL)*. This special code tells the browser software what kind of site you're visiting. All World Wide Web URLs start with `http://`, although `gopher://` and `ftp://` sites are out there, too.

✔ *HTTP* is half the magic that makes the Web work. The abbreviation stands for *HyperText Transfer Protocol*. All you need to know about it is that every Web site address starts with `http://`.

✔ The other half of the Web's magical underpinnings is *HTML*, the HyperText Markup Language. HTML is the programming language of the World Wide Web. If something has `.html` (or sometimes `.htm`) appended to its name, the odds are that it's a Web page. In everyday conversation, HTML is a spelled abbreviation (such as "I'm working with H-T-M-L").

✔ *Links* (or *hyperlinks*) connect Web pages. When you *follow a link,* you click a button or a highlighted word and go careening off to another destination in the online world.

✔ Because having only one term for things often fosters understanding and comprehension, the World Wide Web goes by several monikers. It's also referred to as *the Web, WWW,* or *W3.*

For more information about how the Web works, see *The Internet For Canadians For Dummies Starter Kit.*

Taking the Web browser for a spin

AOL Canada did a great deal of work to integrate to the World Wide Web as seamlessly as possible. It was quite a trick, too, because you need special software (called a *browser*) to look at Web pages.

The Web browser shown in Figure 17-2 is built right into the AOL Canada access software. The navigation bar, just underneath the toolbar at the top of the screen, contains all the goodies you need to traverse the Web. Flip to Chapter 3 for details about the navigation bar.

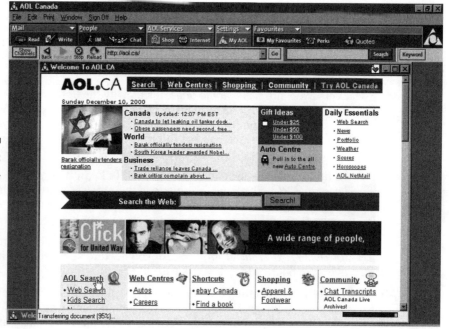

Figure 17-2:
The AOL
Canada Web
browser,
doing its
Web
browsing
thing. It all
starts at the
AOL.CA
home page.

✔ Don't be surprised if your AOL.CA home page looks different from the ones in the figures. World Wide Web pages change all the time — it's a natural part of online life.

✔ Your World Wide Web browser understands gopher and FTP sites, too. Some pages have links to Internet newsgroups (more about those later in this chapter), which, unfortunately, your browser *can't* understand. If you click a link and the browser displays a window that says something like `Cannot interpret link`, it's a clue that you just clicked something beyond the browser's comprehension. We hope that this difficulty gets fixed, but so far, wishing isn't working!

✔ The most common Web-oriented error you see is something to the effect of `Sorry, I can't contact that site` (although the computers don't say it that nicely — they intone more ominous things, such as `Error 404 Requested URL not found`). Double-check the address and try it again. If it *still* doesn't work, either AOL Canada is too busy to be bothered with the Web right now or the Web page you're looking for isn't available at the moment. Either way, try again later.

✔ In case you're interested, the foam bath fish clock is at `www.savetz.com/fishtime/fishtime.cgi`.

✔ For some cool (and free) fun, try sending your friends some virtual flowers, an electronic postcard, or even a marvelously smelly goodie you find in a digital Dumpster. For a quick start, send virtual flowers to friends and loved ones from www.virtualflorist.com or visit www.regards.com to create a free online greeting card. When you're ready for more, flip over to Chapter 27 to pick up several other sites.

✔ When you find sites you absolutely love, add them to your Favourite Places window by clicking in the little heart-on-a-page icon in the upper-right corner of the Web browser. For more about Favourite Places, see Chapter 7.

Opening a specific page

Even though the AOL.CA home page offers lots of interesting links to explore, sometimes you want to hop directly to a particular page. Maybe you saw the address in a newspaper ad or TV commercial, or perhaps you're champing at the bit to see the fish clock. No matter where a Web address comes from, explaining it to AOL Canada is a piece of cake.

Direct your attention to the navigation bar (parked just under the toolbar on your screen). To go directly to a particular page, click in the address area (the big, white box that probably says Type keyword or Web address here) of the navigation bar and then type the address of the page you want to see, just as in Figure 17-3. You don't need to include the http:// part in front of the address, but it doesn't hurt if you feel like doing it anyway. When the address is in there, press Enter or click Go. Shortly, the built-in Web browser comes to life, displaying your page in glorious colour.

Figure 17-3: For faster service, sidle up to the navigation bar and order your Web page there.

Newsgroups Talk about the Craziest Things

The Internet newsgroups are a collection of, oh, about 30,000 discussion topics, from artificial intelligence applications (the comp.ai newsgroup) to the latest Kennedy assassination theories (try alt.conspiracy.jfk or alt.assassination.jfk). Newsgroup discussions get pretty wild sometimes, with ideas flying thick through the network. The language is often fairly (ahem) to the point, so if you're easily offended, you may not want to venture too far into the newsgroups. We tell you how to get to the newsgroups a little later in the chapter, under the heading "Finding and subscribing to a newsgroup."

We want to be *very* clear on this point because if you can't trust us, who *can* you trust? When you venture into the Internet newsgroups, you're leaving the friendly, trusting, caring community of AOL Canada and venturing out into the wild, uncontrolled reality of the Internet. It's the difference between the lawns of suburban Victoria and the pavement of Yonge Street in Toronto. The Internet has no Terms of Service agreement — anything goes (and usually does).

That's not to say that the Internet has *no* rules, because there definitely are some. They're simple and unwritten, and they apply to almost every newsgroup:

- ✔ You're welcome to join the discussion, as long as you take the time to understand the newsgroup before contributing anything. Read a newsgroup for *at least* a week or two before posting something of your own. Also read the newsgroup's Frequently Asked Questions document (known as the *FAQ*). If you can't find the FAQ anywhere in the current newsgroup postings, post a message asking someone to point you toward it.

- ✔ Stick to the topic of the newsgroup. Posting get-rich-quick schemes and business advertisements to the newsgroups is in very poor taste. People do it, but they're the exception, not the rule.

- ✔ You may agree or disagree with anything that's said. You may agree or disagree as loudly as you want. If you disagree, focus on the point — don't degenerate into personal attacks.

- ✔ You may *not* question a person's right to say whatever comes to mind. Yes, some points of view are, shall we say, distasteful, but some people feel that way about what you think too.

- ✔ If someone disagrees with you rather abusively (known on the Internet as *flaming*), the best thing you can do is ignore the message. If you can reply in a level-headed tone, that's fine, but it probably won't change what the other person thinks. It's best to let the flames die down and just go on with other conversations.

By now, we hope that we've scared you a little about the Internet newsgroups. Well, *scared* really isn't the right term. How about *educated* instead? The newsgroups really aren't as wild and vicious a place as we're making them out to be, but you need to understand that they also aren't part of AOL Canada — they're completely outside the mores of the AOL Canada world. If you visualize yourself stepping from your neighbourhood into a completely foreign environment every time you use the newsgroups, you have the right frame of mind. The newsgroups work much like the AOL Canada discussion areas. They're different from mailing lists, though, because mailing lists come *to* your mailbox; you have to *go* to the newsgroups. Check out *The Internet For Canadians For Dummies Starter Kit*, for a more complete explanation of newsgroups.

Finding and subscribing to a newsgroup

As we've said, you have literally thousands of newsgroups to choose from — and AOL Canada carries them all. To keep things from getting too out of hand, the newsgroups are organized into categories by topic. Table 17-1 briefly explains the main categories. Other categories certainly exist, but we'll let you explore those on your own. Each category contains a bunch of related newsgroups (or, in the case of the alt and misc categories, a bunch of newsgroups related only because someone said so).

Table 17-1	Newsgroup Category Names
Name	*Description*
alt	Alternative — home of freewheeling discussions on just about any topic
aol	AOL — articles of interest to AOL members
biz	Business — topics generally relating to business on the Internet
comp	Computers and computer science — where the nerds hang out
misc	Miscellaneous — all the stuff that doesn't fit under one of the other hierarchies
news	Network news and information — discussion and information-only groups about the Internet itself
rec	Hobbies and recreation — think sports and hobbies, and you have this one figured out
sci	Science and research — if you thought that nerds were in the comp group, just wait until you look in here
soc	Society and social commentary — focused mainly toward both sociologists in the audience
talk	Talk — talk, talk, talk, talk (get the idea?)

Your search for an interesting newsgroup starts by guessing which hierarchy the topic belongs in and then browsing through that hierarchy's available newsgroups. Simple enough, right? Here's how to do it step by step:

1. **Use keyword** Newsgroups **to begin your adventure.**

   The Newsgroups window pops up.

2. **Click Add Newsgroups.**

   The Add Newsgroups Categories window appears.

3. **Choose a category.**

   Scroll through the list of available categories until you find one that looks interesting. Double-click a hierarchy to see which newsgroups it contains.

   A window listing all the category's newsgroups elbows its way to the screen.

4. **Scroll through all the listed newsgroups, find one that looks interesting, and double-click its entry in the list.**

   Yet another window, which may or may not tell you anything helpful about the newsgroup, appears, looking something like Figure 17-4.

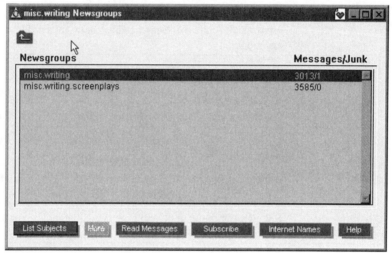

Figure 17-4:
Hmm — a
writing
newsgroup.
Sounds
interesting.

5. **Sample some messages and subscribe to the group if you like what you see.**

   For a look at the messages in this newsgroup, click Read Messages. When you're sold, click Subscribe to include the newsgroup on your subscription list. To pretend that you never saw the newsgroup in the first place, just close the window and go about your business.

   Subscribing to a newsgroup may take a minute or two to allow the AOL Canada computer to think, ponder, and snicker at its ability to make a human wait for something.

   For more about reading messages in a newsgroup, see the next section.

6. **When the Confirmation dialog box pops up, click OK to reassure it that you know what you're talking about and that you really want to read that newsgroup. When the Group Preferences dialog box appears, click Save to make it go away, too.**

After a great deal of digital consternation, AOL Canada displays a brief dialog box saying that the newsgroup is now on your list. Click OK to make the confirmation dialog box go away and leave you alone.

Likewise, the Group Preferences dialog box offers some advanced tools for simplifying your newsgroup experience. (In one of those odd paradoxes of technology, the tool for making newsgroups easier is itself almost too complex to use.)

For now, don't worry about the group preferences settings. You can always get back to the window by clicking on the newsgroup name in the Read My Newsgroups window and then clicking the Preferences button.

7. **Subscribe to more newsgroups if you want.**

   To subscribe to more newsgroups, just close the last few windows (click the upper-right corner of the window) until you work your way back to the Add Newsgroups window.

   Congratulations — you did it!

If someone describes a marvellous newsgroup and gives you the Internet name of it (which looks like `alt.folklore.urban`), you can use the Expert Add button and skip this whole menu-driven process. However, you must know the exact name, complete with all the required (and occasionally odd) punctuation marks. The Expert Add button is also handy for checking out newsgroups recommended by one of those clever Internet books that we suggest you buy.

Reading messages

Subscribing is, of course, only the first step. Your next task is finding time to read all the stuff you subscribe to. Unlike mailing lists, newsgroup messages don't stack up in your e-mail box — they collect in some mysterious place deep within AOL Canada. To read what's new, you have to pay another visit to the Newsgroups window. Here's what to do:

1. **Start with keyword** Newsgroups.

   The Newsgroups window pops up.

2. **Click Read My Newsgroups.**

   After a few pensive moments of waiting, thc Read My Newsgroups window pops into being. It shows the name of the newsgroup, the number of messages you haven't read, and the total number of messages in that newsgroup.

   Even if you subscribe to only one or two newsgroups, your newsgroups list comes preset with some suggested reading, courtesy of AOL Canada.

3. **Double-click a newsgroup to see what's new.**

   A window that's more a scrolling list than anything else (see Figure 17-5) pops into being. The window shows the article title and the number of responses in the *thread* (that's the newsgroup term for *discussion*).

   To see all the articles in the newsgroup (whether you've read them or not), click the newsgroup name and then click List All.

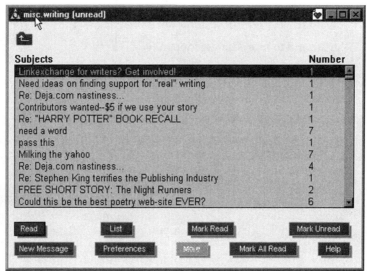

Subjects	Number
Linkexchange for writers? Get involved!	1
Need ideas on finding support for "real" writing	1
Re: Deja.com nastiness...	1
Contributors wanted--$5 if we use your story	1
Re: "HARRY POTTER" BOOK RECALL	1
need a word	7
pass this	1
Milking the yahoo	7
Re: Deja.com nastiness...	4
Re: Stephen King terrifies the Publishing Industry	1
FREE SHORT STORY: The Night Runners	2
Could this be the best poetry web-site EVER?	6

Figure 17-5:
So many articles, so little time.

4. **To read an article, double-click its title.**

   A window containing the message text opens. Read to your heart's content and then close the window after you're done.

   To reply to a message, click Reply to Group. To see the next message in the thread, click the button labelled Message→. For the preceding message, click the button labelled ←Message. If you're thirsty, get something to drink.

   If you have a specific question for the person who wrote the article, click the author's blue highlighted e-mail address rather than post a reply to the newsgroup. (You should see the address at the very top of the posting.)

5. **When nothing else looks interesting enough to read, click Mark All Read.**

   Click OK in the dialog box that wonders whether you really want to do that.

   This last step tells AOL Canada to pretend that you read all the messages in the newsgroup. Therefore, you can quickly tell which messages are new the next time you wander through.

Contributing something

Reading a newsgroup is fun, but soon enough you decide that it's time to post a few messages of your own. Adding a message to a newsgroup isn't hard, but it does take a couple more steps than your average e-mail message. Here's what to do:

1. **Pretend that you're going to read the messages in a newsgroup, and go through Steps 1, 2, and 3 in the preceding section.**

   At this point, the window for whatever newsgroup you want to post an article to should be onscreen.

2. **Click the New Message button.**

   A Post New Message dialog box appears onscreen.

3. **Type a descriptive subject in the Subject area, press Tab to move down into the Message block, and type your message.**

   A check box marked `Use Signature (set in Preferences)` sits underneath the Message block. If you want to sign all your newsgroups postings in a standard way, such as *John Doe — Ace Contractor, Incorporated,* or *Sven, Lover of Adventure,* you can write your signature once and then check the box to sign your name the same way with each posting you send.

   Oh — by the way — although it says that the signature is set in global preferences, you actually find it under the Set Preferences button in the main Newsgroups window.

4. **When the message looks groovy, click Send.**

   Click OK when the system asks whether you're serious about posting the article. Click Cancel if you suddenly decide that the world would be a better place without your message in the newsgroup.

   When you're writing for a newsgroup, be brief and to the point. Say what you want to say and then stop. Don't go on and on and on. Whatever you do, don't ramble. Try to imagine how you would enjoy reading someone else's ramblings . . . yeah! "Not" is right!

Un-subscribing from a newsgroup

Getting out of a newsgroup takes a whole lot less time and effort than getting into one. In fact, it's so quick that you'll hardly believe it:

1. **Open the Newsgroups window with keyword** Newsgroups.

   The Newsgroups window reports for duty.

2. **Click the Read My Newsgroups button.**

   The now-familiar Read My Newsgroups window appears.

3. **Click the name of the newsgroup that you want to kick off your subscription list and then click Remove.**

   With only a moment of digital concentration, AOL Canada un-subscribes you from the selected newsgroup and announces the fact in a little dialog box. Click OK to make the box go away.

Automating your newsgroups

Here's a little piece of advice about getting involved in newsgroups: The words *addictive* and *newsgroups* naturally belong in the same sentence. Although they're not as bad as the People Connection chat rooms, following a newsgroup does rack up your online charges if you use one of the AOL Canada measured billing methods.

Does that mean that you shouldn't do the newsgroup thing? Not at all! You should just do it *smarter* and *quicker* by using an Automatic AOL session — the same familiar technique that prevents your voluminous e-mail traffic from overwhelming your credit card each month. With some careful tweaking, the messages from your favourite newsgroups stream right into your mailbox just the way your e-mail does. How could it possibly get better? Actually, we're glad you asked.

Frankly, it could get better if doing newsgroups through Automatic AOL were slightly easier than disarming a thermonuclear device with a bobby pin and a bag of nacho chips. Unfortunately for you, it seems that the bomb folks moonlighted on the newsgroup Automatic AOL design team.

Before giving this task a try, you must thoroughly understand both the newsgroups you want to keep up with and your AOL Canada Filing Cabinet (having a degree in nuclear engineering doesn't hurt either). Newsgroups are covered in the preceding pages; notes about the Filing Cabinet reside in Chapter 8. The details of making it all work are too complex to attempt here — trust us. If you're still convinced that flashing the newsgroups into your computer sounds like fun, follow these steps for all the details:

1. **Use keyword** Newsgroups **to open the Newsgroups window.**

   As expected, the Newsgroups window appears.

2. **Click the Read Offline button.**

   The Choose Newsgroups window hops into action.

3. **In the Choose Newsgroups window, click the Help button in the lower-right corner.**

   Yet another window piles on the stack. But don't fret — you're done. A text window steps forth, revealing the secrets of this mystic feature.

If merely getting to the instructions sounds like a journey across the Himalayas (with or without a nuclear device), don't attempt to do newsgroups through Automatic AOL. The steps you just scaled were only the foothills — the peak is still waaaaay up there somewhere. Good luck, brave newsgrouper (we're heading back down the mountain for a nap).

A brief word about parental controls

The newsgroups offer a wild array of useful and interesting information, but some of the stuff could send a shipload of sailors into a collective blush. Thanks to the Parental Controls section, you can prevent such a thing from happening at your house (assuming you have a shipload of sailors huddled around your AOL Canada account).

The parental controls for newsgroups are available under the cleverly labelled Parental Controls button in the Newsgroups window. These controls let you do the following:

- ✔ Block the Expert Add feature, which limits a screen name to only the newsgroups that AOL Canada chooses to list under the Add Newsgroups button.
- ✔ Block access to the newsgroups entirely.
- ✔ Prevent program and file downloads from the newsgroups.
- ✔ Block specific newsgroups you choose.
- ✔ Block newsgroups with "adult" content.
- ✔ Block any newsgroup that contains certain words in its name.
- ✔ Grant a screen name access to the complete list of available newsgroups.

If you have a child using AOL Canada, we *highly* recommend blocking the Expert Add feature for that child's screen name. You may want to go farther, but you can worry about that later.

Because little eyes and fingers often get into the darnedest places, AOL Canada offers a strong, flexible group of parental controls. For all the details about your online child-management options, flip to the section "Parental Controls: Taking Away the Online Car Keys" in Chapter 6.

FTP Downloading for the Nerd at Heart

If you think that the file libraries in AOL Canada are a hoot, you haven't seen *anything* yet. Welcome to *File Transfer Protocol,* more commonly known as *FTP.* FTP is the Internet's answer to the Copy command. And you'd better believe it's one serious answer.

You're about to enter [bring up geeky music in the background] the Technoid Zone, so keep a pocket protector handy. Working with FTP definitely isn't like using gopher or the Internet newsgroups. You're interacting directly with computers all over the world without the benefit of software like gopher to protect you. It's you against the computer. If using the Macintosh Finder or Windows File Manager to track down an errant file on your disk drive makes you queasy, you don't want to try FTP.

You can use the AOL Canada FTP service in two ways: by going to the built-in FTP sites or by typing an address on your own. We suggest using the built-in options at first because you can be relatively sure that they work. After you have some experience under your electronic belt, get brave and flip to Chapter 27 for some other FTP sites to try.

- We're deliberately a little vague in our how-to-use-FTP instructions later in this chapter. The reason is simple: FTP really *is* more advanced than the other Internet services. You need to understand a lot of nerdy stuff, such as subdirectories and file compression (including ZIP files and many, many other kinds), before FTP is of much use to you.

- If you're absolutely dying to discover FTP, check out the Using FTP option in the main FTP window (keyword **FTP**), the FTP help section of Member Services (keyword **Nethelp**), or the Internet help section of the AOL Canada Web site (www.aol.ca/nethelp).

- Trust *nothing* you download from the Internet via FTP. Assume from the start that it's completely virus-infested, like a little digital epidemic just waiting to break loose on your computer. Virus-check absolutely *everything* that comes to roost in your computer from the Internet.

- Yes, we're serious about the virus checks. We perform them for our own downloads.

- Watch out for files with odd extensions like .Z, .gz, or .tar.z. They are compressed files, but they're *not* normal .sit or .zip files. To decompress them requires special software, the patience of Job, and often the rest of your day. If you're intent on trying anyway, get a copy of either GZip or MacGZip from the /pub/compress subdirectory of ftp.aol.com (which just happens to be on the FTP menu). If that last sentence didn't make *any* sense to you, don't try to mess with these files.

✔ FTP is also called *anonymous FTP* by Those Who Know. That's a fancy way to say that you don't need a special access code or anything to download files. Because the computer sending the files doesn't know who you are, it's an anonymous service. Aren't those computer nerds clever?

All it takes to use FTP is a strong stomach for the technical side of life and these instructions:

1. **Dive into the FTP system by selecting A̲OL Services⇨Internet⇨FTP from the toolbar, or with keyword** FTP.

   The FTP (File Transfer Protocol) window opens.

2. **Click the Go To FTP button. The Anonymous FTP window opens.**

   Finally, the File Transfer Protocol window shows its face (see Figure 17-6).

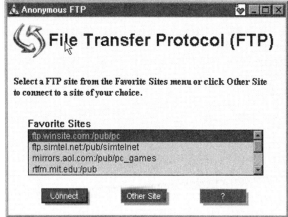

Figure 17-6:
The Anonymous FTP window offers to whisk you away to File Transfer Land.

3. **Scroll through the Favourite Sites list and double-click one that sounds interesting.**

   After a moment or two (or perhaps three, if the Internet is having a busy night), another window pops up, explaining where you're about to go. Click OK and proceed directly to the directory listing of whatever computer you just attached yourself to (see Figure 17-7).

4. **If something looks interesting, double-click it.**

   Different things happen depending on the icon that's next to the item. If the icon is a file folder icon, that entry is a directory; double-clicking it brings up a new window showing you what's in there. If the icon is a document, a dialog box pops up and offers you a View File Now button.

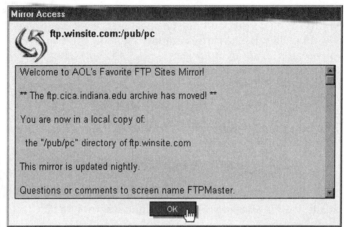

Figure 17-7:
Welcome to
winsite.

To view the document without downloading it, click the button. If the icon is a bunch of disks, you're looking at a program or a compressed file that's available for downloading. Sometimes you also see the funny-looking handshake icon; it stands for a pointer to a particular subdirectory.

5. **Keep poking around, and have a good time.**

Part IV
Going Your Own Way

The 5th Wave   By Rich Tennant

"IT'S ANOTHER DEEP SPACE PROBE FROM EARTH, SEEKING CONTACT FROM EXTRATERRESTRIALS. I WISH THEY'D JUST INCLUDE AN E-MAIL ADDRESS."

In this part . . .

With 26 million members around the world (and more joining every day), 19 Canadian content channels of information, education, and entertainment, and hundreds of bulletin boards and chat rooms populated by interesting people from around the world, you never lack options on AOL Canada. Where do you start? What should you see first?

If you have questions like these, you're in the right place. Each chapter in Part IV looks at AOL Canada from a particular point of view, with suggested destinations galore. Everywhere you look, it offers ways to solve problems and actually get things done in your life.

Pretty radical, huh?

Browse through the chapters and see what you can find. They're designed to draw you in, fill your head with ideas, sweep up a little as long as it's in there, and send you on your way with a neat, tidy mind. Use your creativity to take the suggestions that suit you, and find still better ways to do stuff all by yourself.

Chapter 18

The Student's Guide to Online Life

*E*ducation is where you find it these days, and you can find a great deal of instructional goodies around AOL Canada. When you're stumped with a problem, digging for facts, or trying to make a perfect (or at least airworthy) kite, plenty of online resources await your call for help, no matter what time of the day or night you yelp.

This chapter, like the others in this part, provides direction rather than answers. It offers some suggestions to get you started but encourages you to think creatively and come up with your own resources as well. We know you can do it — now *do it!*

Places to Start

Even in a digital wonderland such as AOL Canada, you still have to start somewhere. A couple of places stand out as excellent jumping-off points:

> ✔ The hub of any campus is its student centre (after all, that's where the food is). It works the same way in online student life, thanks to the AOL Teens area (keyword **Teens**, as shown in Figure 18-1). As the name implies, this one window offers links and resources for everyone traipsing through the tumultuous teens.

✔ What can't you find on the Internet these days? This international network of networks is definitely worth a look. AOL Canada offers lots of Internet services, beginning with the Internet icon on the main AOL Canada toolbar. See Chapter 17 for all the details.

Figure 18-1:
Celebrate
teen life, in
full colour
and at full
volume, in
the Teens
window
(keyword
Teens).

Getting Help When You Need It

When you're stuck on a homework problem and need some help to get over the hump, fire up the computer and sign on to AOL Canada. Look for your much-needed help in these areas:

✔ When tough homework is on your mind (eww — get it off, get it off!), drop by Ask-A-Teacher (keyword **Ask-A-Teacher**) for help and advice. To reach assistance from the main Ask-A-Teacher window, first choose your grade range (elementary, junior high, and high school, or beyond). Each level's section provides discussion boards and tutoring rooms, plus a database of previously answered questions on nearly any subject. If you need help with a complicated or unusual topic, e-mail a teacher with your question, and in the best of all worlds, a real teacher responds to your query within about 48 hours.

✔ More homework help is available at keyword **HHK** — short for Homework Help for Kids, of course. Choose from the four main options, including *Look It Up* (where you'll find links to useful online resources like a dictionary and encyclopedias), *Ask a Teacher* (send your questions about English, math, science, or social studies to a professional!), *Discuss It!* (which has a lot of American content, so we'd give that one a skip), and *Explore*.

✔ Need a topic for that research paper? Flip to Chapter 13 for direction to the numerous AOL Canada search tools. These doorways lead to an almost endless supply of online information (and almost all of it is free).

✔ The annual science fair looms before you, and you can't think of a great project to save your life. AOL Canada comes to your rescue again, with science fairs (keyword **Science Fair**). Get project ideas, tips for making your project (and its presentation) super, and Web sites where you can begin your research.

✔ Looking at life through another's eyes takes an open mind and an open heart. Of course, it also requires another open-minded person for discussion (after all, unless two of you are in there, it's tough to get a second opinion from yourself on much of anything). Whether you need insight for a creative writing project, a term paper, or a drama course, or simply have a desire to expand your personal horizons, gain a taste of life through new eyes in the Ethnicity area (keyword **Ethnicity**), the Faith area (keyword **Faith**), or try a specific cultural community area like the AOL Canada Jewish Community Online (keyword **Jewish**).

✔ Speaking of culture, why not mix some cultural and geographic learning by taking a trip to AOL Canada International. Find out how others live. Exchange messages and postings with people from around the world. Think of it as training for your eventual appointment as an ambassador for Canada. And yes, we did say this to make your parents smile. (To get there, just click the International option on the channels window on the left side of your screen.)

✔ Stuck trying to understand the *Aeneid*? (Goodness knows, you would *not* be the first.) Turn to Barron's Booknotes (keyword **Barron's**) for downloadable study guides and plot synopses. Also try the granddaddy of study guides, the indomitable CliffsNotes series, at www.cliffsnotes.com. For a pretty much boundless book search, head to AOL Canada's bookshop (keyword **Bookshop**) and see what Chapters.ca has to offer in terms of study guides.

A Trip to the Virtual Library

Research was never easier. Between the online encyclopedia (keyword **Encyclopedias**), the magazines (keyword **Newsstand**), and the whole Research & Learn area (keyword **Research**), you may not have to look anywhere else.

✔ Some things in life are free, some cost money, and some tempt you with free stuff in the hope of ultimately costing you money. The Electric Library Canada (keyword **ELP**) lives in this last category. The helpful service includes free searching in an incredibly broad magazine and newspaper database. The search results provide the article title and publication details. (We particularly love the Search Canadian Content feature, that lets you narrow your search to bring back specifically Canadian information.) As you may guess, the pay part of the equation begins when you want to read the articles online. AOL Canada offers 45 days of free access when you subscribe. At the time we wrote this book, a one-year subscription cost just under $90, which isn't a bad deal at all when you factor in all the research trips to the library that you don't need to make now.

✔ This next option isn't Canadian, but it sure is cool. The University of California Extension Online (keyword **UCAOL**) offers an incredible link to the collection in its Public Library area (click the Public Library button in the main University of California window). Invest some time (well, a *lot* of time, because this area is big) to check out what's available — it's a gold mine!

✔ An even broader area of the Internet is the World Wide Web (keyword **WWW**). Start out with AOL Canada Search (keyword **Search**) and then try the Other Searches option (including the book search, maps search, newsgroups search, and more). At the AOL.CA home page (keyword **AOL.CA**), your launchpad to the Web, check out the Web Centres and Shortcuts. Both contain an incredible array of information and links on a whole lot of subjects.

✔ The Internet newsgroups are another great source of information and discussion. Use keyword **Newsgroups** and then try either Add Newsgroups or Search All Newsgroups to see what strikes your fancy. Chapter 17 covers the Newsgroup beat, so check there for more tips.

✔ If your search is of a cartographic nature (yeah, we know that you know this is just a fancy term for maps, but this is supposed to be serious, so go with it), try the AOL Canada Travel channel's maps service. Although it's intended to help plan road trips, you can use it to pull some excellent regional and territorial maps from all over the country. You can also access this service by choosing AOL Services➪Maps & Directions.

Thinking about That Job

If you're over the age of eight, you're probably starting to think about that career at the end of your school years. AOL Canada has some great places that can help you get the education you need, and maybe even figure out what you want to be when you grow up. (And if you find something good, can you e-mail us? Neither of us is sure either!)

✔ Here's one that's definitely a sign of the times. The RESP area (stands for Registered Education Savings Plan, one of the options you'll find in the RRSP forum at keyword **RRSP**), will give you plenty of info and guidance for saving money for your post-secondary education within a registered (and tax-sheltered) plan. While you're there, and if you're serious about saving, read up on RRSPs in general — your parents will thank you.

✔ If you're considering career options, knowing what the job entails is helpful. Read up on different careers and browse through job postings at AOL Canada WorkPlace (keyword **Workplace**). The jobs database is powered by the aptly named Monster.ca Web site (at www.monster.ca), and contains thousands of job postings in just about every field imaginable.

✔ Find out what real people do in a particular industry in the Professional Forums (keyword **Professional Forums**). Some of the stuff you'll read in here is directed at the U.S. job-hunter, but most of it is universal enough for us Canadians as well.

✔ Researching a particular industry or company? Investment Research (keyword **Company Research**) contains stock reports and other financial information for recent years. For up-to-the-moment (or at least *through the past two weeks*) news from Reuters and the Associated Press, use the Search Company News by Ticker system (keyword **Company News**). If your class is studying mutual funds, get with that program using the Fundata service (keyword **Fundata**).

As If One School Weren't Enough

If you're one of those people who just wants to *learn, learn, learn,* good for you. The ever-changing technological workplace of today makes constant education (and re-education) a vital part of every career. Whether your aspirations are for a new degree, some enhanced understanding, or just for the heck of it, AOL Canada has some educational opportunities for you:

✔ For computer know-how (particularly in the programming arena), check out the noncredit (and no-fee) computer classes in the Computing Online Classroom (keyword **Online Classroom**). You can find classes listed for everything from DOS for beginners to programming in Visual Basic 5.0 (keyword **Computing Tutorials**).

✔ Occasionally, there are even more computer learning opportunities on AOL Canada. Computer Camp 2000, for example, was a virtual summer camp for people of all ages. Keep your eyes and ears open for similar featured lessons coming your way!

✔ The Online Campus (keyword **Online Campus**) offers "personal enrich-ment" classes in almost any topic for a small fee — usually $30 to $50. (Keep in mind, that charge is in U.S. dollars, so expect the real cost to be higher.)

Time to Relax and Recharge

Remember to have some fun. All work and no play makes you a financially secure, crotchety old nerd (and the world's got enough of them already). Take some time to meet people, play games, and enjoy your online life:

- ✔ Three easy options right off the bat are Life (keyword **Life**), Hobbies (keyword **Hobbies**), and the People Connection (keyword **People Connection**). Browse around and see what's out there — and who.

- ✔ The Gamers area (keyword **Games**) is home to all kinds of interesting pursuits, including computer games, board games, role-playing, online simulation games, and collectible card games.

- ✔ If you love music, theatre, or dance, mark Extreme Culture (keyword **Extreme Culture**) on your Favourite Places list. This area offers student discussion boards, scheduled chats with both arts professionals and university-level arts faculty, and lots more. Take a poll, win a prize, sign up for the newsletter, or just relax with people who share your passion for performance.

- ✔ If you're at all interested in music, books, movies, theatre, politics, life, and Toronto (hey, how did that last one get there?), *Now Magazine* (keyword **Now**) is for you. It's cool, edgy (see Figure 18-2 for confirmation of a very funky layout as well), and yes, a tad Toronto-centric. But don't hold that against them — it's their home.

Figure 18-2: The arts are where you find them — often that means Toronto! Check it out with *Now! Magazine Online.*

✔ Teens who love to program computers find a home at Youth Tech (keyword **YT**). Learn the answer to that sticky coding problem in the chat shack, read computer game reviews, or find some top Web sites — whether you're looking for school help or techy news sites.

✔ You might like to pretend that they're old-fashioned, but we've seen people your age do crosswords. If you visit keyword **Crossword**, you'll get a new AOL Canada puzzle every day — and we promise not to tell any of your cooler-than-thou friends.

✔ If fashion is your thing, curl up with the online edition of *Elle* magazine (keyword **Elle**). Get the scoop on the latest in looking great, feeling good, and emptying your chequebook (sorry — no one ever said there's no price to pay for being fashionable).

The Sweet Sound of Song

Techno. Hip-hop. R&B. Reggae. World music. Rock. Rap. Christian thrash metal. The music of our time is as beautiful as it is diverse (depending on your tastes, of course). And we know through a study or two that you teens are still the number one listeners out there. We also know that finally technology has caught up with your tastes, putting the freshest tunes online for you to download.

So we thought we'd better mention a couple of very cool music-related areas that we know you're going to groove on:

✔ AOL Canada Music (keyword **Music**): If you wanna rock on AOL Canada, start here (the main window is on display in Figure 18-3). In The Listening Booth, you can sample new music by your favourite artists (you'll need an audio player such as RealAudio to hear it). If you like what you hear, you can indulge your musical tastes at SamTheRecordMan.com (there's a link at the bottom of the Music window). Check out the record reviews and band interviews at magazines like Canada's own ChartAttack, or Billboard (you'll find links to both these mags in the pull-down menu at the bottom of the window).

✔ MuchMusic on AOL Canada: It's already your favourite station on TV, so why not make it one of your favourite places to visit on AOL Canada? Just click the MuchMusic link (at the bottom of the main Music window) to start a wild ride through Much. Check concert listings, watch videos, get to know more about popular musicians in the MuchMusic Spotlight, chat with other fans about what makes music so great, or post a message at the virtual Speaker's Corner. And don't forget to rock on! (Yes, we know this is a dated expression. We were just testing you.)

Figure 18-3:
AOL Canada
Music can
be music to
your ears.

Chapter 19

Parenting Your Offspring (in Diapers, Online, or in Between)

In This Chapter

▶ Staying about even with the kids

▶ Being wise about parental controls

▶ Keeping the kids safe

▶ Remembering what fun's all about

▶ Surviving the work-at-home life

Some days, it seems like the sole goal of parenting is to make sure that everybody arrives at the dinner table at roughly the same time. On other days, the incredible size of the job looms like a monster in a bad 1950s horror film, doesn't it? Well, you're not alone in your concerns.

Judging by the resources available to parents through AOL Canada, it looks like parents are finally going to get some help. This chapter points out the best of the resources and gives you a gentle push along the way.

All the resources in the world aren't any good unless you take the time to use them.

Keeping Up with the Kids

Parents have to learn about all this parenting stuff the hard way — by trying something, either getting it right or messing it up, and then trying again. AOL Canada gives parents some unique opportunities to simplify this shoddy arrangement and share information and experiences with one another (and to voice opinions about topics of concern):

- ✔ At keyword **Familles**, you're ushered into the AOL Canada parental information refuge. Start here for links to just about every family-related goodie on AOL (and a bunch of Net-based places, too).

- ✔ Take some time to find out about the Internet and what it offers. As a parent, you need to understand the wonderful resources on the Net and comprehend the potential dangers as well. The AOL Canada Internet connection at AOL.CA (keyword **Internet**) is the place to start. If you're completely new to the Internet, take a stroll through Chapter 17 for a bout with the basics.

- ✔ Next on the hit list is Child & Family Canada (`www.cfc-efc.ca`), a Web site that brings together more than 50 nonprofit agencies, all with the goal of providing resources for parents and families. Use this site to access Web sites for those agencies, or read through the extensive documents related to parenting.

- ✔ If you're a home-schooling family, link up and swap tips with others in the Home Schooling forum (keyword **Homeschooling**). For still more informational wellsprings, search for the term *homeschool* through AOL.CA (keyword **Internet**), Yahoo! Canada (`www.yahoo.ca`), AltaVistaCanada (`www.altavistacanada.com`), or any of the other Internet search engines mentioned in the Search Engines table (Table 13-1), back in Chapter 13.

Protecting Your Online Kids

This section of the book isn't particularly funny, but it *is* very important. Please take time to read it and then act on what you find.

You already know the bad news: Some sick people are in the online realm, and some of them are trolling for kids. The good news is that you *can* protect your kids — you're not powerless in this frightening mess.

Although it's important that you, as a concerned parent, do *something* to protect your children, knee-jerk reactions are not the answer. Remember that AOL Canada and the Internet are much like sprawling digital cities. Just as you don't want the kids visiting certain parts of your own town, you also find areas of the online world that are definitely for adults only. Cancelling your account or erasing the access software doesn't protect your kids — doing so just teaches them fear. Instead, you need to interact with your children, help them understand this crazy online world, teach them how to respond appropriately, and take the responsibility that's yours as a parent.

With all this in mind, here are some ideas, tips, and suggestions for keeping your online kids safe; please take them to heart:

✔ **Educate your kids.** Remind them that just because the person they met online sounds like a kid (or even claims to be one) doesn't mean that it's necessarily the truth.

✔ **Teach your kids what not to say online.** Make sure that they never give out their address or phone number. Never.

✔ **Observe what your kids do.** Ask to join them for an evening online. If they know more about how this stuff works than you do, ask them to teach you. If you ask, be ready to take notes and really learn — don't merely nod and comment about how amazingly far technology has come. Think of the online system as a hobby your children enjoy. Your goal is to share that hobby with them.

✔ **Report questionable occurrences.** If your child tells you about being approached in a questionable way, get the user ID of the person your child was interacting with and report it to the online service. Those folks will help you deal with the problem.

✔ **Take the time to find out about the online world.** Reading this book is a great start — congratulations! Beyond that, invest the time to understand AOL Canada's Parental Controls (keyword **Parental Controls**). These controls let parents determine the level of access that their kids have to various AOL Canada features (like instant messages and chat) as well as limit World Wide Web access. You select the limits; they can explore everything else. Look at Chapter 6 for the details of setting and tweaking the Parental Controls.

✔ **Encourage your kids' offline activities and friendships.** Offer to throw a pizza party, game night, or movie extravaganza for your children and their friends. The cost is minimal, but the rewards are many.

✔ **Don't presume that bad things *won't* happen to your kids.** Denial is a marvellous breeding ground for the worst of problems.

✔ **On the flip side, don't automatically assume that everyone your child meets online is a wacko.** Lots of real kids just like yours populate the online world.

✔ **Don't interrogate your children about their online use. Be interested, but don't accuse.** Show interest, but don't presume guilt. You didn't like it as a child, and neither will they.

Have Some Fun? What's That?

If your kids can have fun on AOL Canada, why shouldn't you? Hmm. . . . You were a kid once, right? AOL Canada makes family outings a snap, and offers lots of tips for some parental fun, too. Here's a quick look at great places to start:

✔ We love movies (particularly when they're at the dollar cinema). So much happens behind the scenes, so much money is spent to create the masterpiece, so many people with odd job titles — it almost makes you want to take part in the movie biz yourself. Wander over to Movies (keyword **Movies**) and catch some of the excitement. As Figure 19-1 shows, this area is packed with movie and video information. Read about new flicks, join a movie chat, and catch up on the industry buzz from this window. When you find a movie you *must* see with the kids, search AOL Canada's Movie Showtimes (choose <u>A</u>OL Services⇨Mo<u>v</u>ie Showtimes, or use keyword **Showtimes**) for a local theatre.

Figure 19-1:
Come here
when you
want to
know what's
new at the
movies.

✔ For a more parental twist on movies, check out some family movie guides. Start with the Entertainment Asylum Family area (keyword **EA Family**), which reviews movies, home videos, and even TV programs.

✔ Movies are great, but nothing quite matches the thrill of live theatre. To keep up on the latest in Broadway, off-Broadway, regional, and even international professional theatre, check out *Playbill* Online (keyword **Playbill**).

✔ Looking for a night out *sans* children? Then visit the Ticketmaster Canada Web site at www.ticketmaster.ca. It has a searchable list of all the events that Ticketmaster covers around the country, and you can place your order online.

✔ Few things are more relaxing than a casual shopping excursion. Why not wander the online gifts selection, or choose from among the computing products available for purchase online? For both these options, or any of the myriad other buying opportunities available through AOL Canada, visit the Shopping channel (keyword **Shopping**) and click the category that suits your whim.

✔ To unwind after a hard day's work, pick up a new hobby or follow an old one in the Interests areas (keyword **Interests**).

✔ We're willing to bet that more than one hockey parent is out there reading this book. Hey, we respect every 6 a.m. January morning you've ever invested in your child's love of the game. But if you still want more of Canada's favourite pastime, visit AOL Canada hockey (keyword **Hockey**). And while you're at it, check out Don Cherry's Coach's Corner (keyword **Don Cherry**).

✔ If you're a crossword fan, put down that pencil, throw out the newspaper, and give electronic crosswords a try. For a new puzzle every day, try out the crossword (keyword **Crossword**).

✔ Want something a little more interactive? Try the People Connection (keyword **People Connection**), the AOL Canada interactive chat area. Also check out AOL Canada's Computing & Games (keyword **Games)** for all kinds of online games and game clubs.

Bringing School Home to Meet the Kids

Who says that you have to leave the house to get a good education? You don't need to leave for entertainment — and there's no reason to take off in the name of learning stuff. Home schooling is growing fast all over the country, as parents look for quality alternatives to the public school system.

AOL Canada offers lots of resources to support and connect home schoolers. Here are some to get you started:

✔ A good general place to start is the Homeschooling forum (keyword **Homeschooling**), although you probably found this one on your own. The area features regularly scheduled chats, a wide variety of lively discussions, and links to education-related areas within AOL Canada. As well, Homework Helper is a growing area that has resources for students from elementary to high school.

✔ Home schoolers come from all backgrounds and beliefs, especially in a country as ethnically and culturally diverse as ours. If you'd like to share ideas on education from a different perspective — be it Christian, Islamic, or Jewish — AOL Canada's Faith area (keyword **Faith**) is the place to start. Just click the folder that interests you, and explore the message boards for postings related to education.

It's worth noting here that when you click the folder titled Jewish Community in AOL Canada's Faith area, you will be guided to an extensive and entirely Canadian forum called the Jewish Community Online Canada. You can also access all of this community's message boards, chat areas, news, and information by using keyword **Jewish**.

Doing the Work-at-Home Thing

More and more families have at least one parent working at home. This exciting lifestyle change has lots of positive aspects, but it also brings some, uh, *challenges*.

One of the hard parts of working at home is feeling disconnected from people — missing the impromptu hallway meetings (also known as chats) and unscheduled personal refreshment intervals (or coffee breaks) that often precede them. AOL Canada has some great places to build a group of friends and acquaintances who understand this crazy lifestyle. Here are some top picks (although one is, admittedly, biased):

- ✔ If online business interests you, visit the Online Business area (keyword **Online Business**). For everything else related to the wonderful world of work, visit AOL Canada WorkPlace (keyword **Workplace**). For more specifics on the Workplace forum, flip to Chapter 21 of this book.

- ✔ If you're having a sudden attack of the lonelies, jump into the People Connection (keyword **People Connection**) and see who you can see. The rooms are always hopping, even in the middle of the day and night. Honestly, we don't know what all these people do for work, but whatever it is, it pays their AOL Canada bills.

- ✔ Fellow writers, check out a few of the scheduled chats in the Writers Club (keyword **Writers**) and focus on romance, historical, poetry, technical, or the business of writing. Use the keyword to bring up the Writers Club window and then click the Chat button to open the Writers Chat window. Double-click Writers Club Chat Schedule for all the chat and conference information.

Chapter 20

The Well-Connected Teacher

Creating an interesting, involving, and intellectually stimulating classroom environment isn't easy these days. Arguably, it *never* was easy, but when you're dealing with attention spans measured in seconds, that sure cranks up the old challenge metre a few notches.

Whether you teach at a public or private school or you're leading a home school, AOL Canada has plenty of resources just waiting for you. This chapter points out the highlights, offers you some ideas to start the creativity gears grinding, and sends you off toward other relevant chapters of this book. Keep your mind open as you read through this chapter — you can find a way to use almost *everything* educationally.

The Ultimate Learning Resource Centre

As resource centres go, you can't beat AOL Canada. It's open 24 hours a day, it's stocked with everything from lesson plans to clip art, and it has a friendly face that doesn't yell at you when things go wrong (unlike many resource centre keepers that you meet in the offline world).

Here are some ideas to help you begin your quest for resource material:

> ✔ Take a look at the Research & Learn area (keyword **Research**) for online forums, reference material, and Web sites that concentrate on content areas, such as history, science, business, health, geography, reading, and writing. Take a look at Figure 20-1 to see your many options.

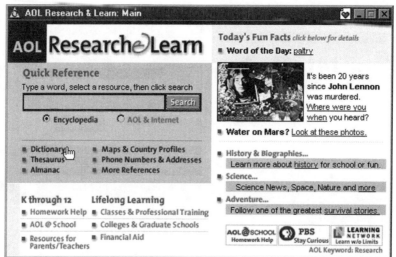

Figure 20-1:
Choose a
subject and
find gems
to take back
to your
classroom.

✔ When looking for children's books, general education titles, or literature, browse through the AOL Canada bookshop (keyword **Bookshop**). Or get there by dropping by the Shopping Channel, and clicking Books & Music. AOL Canada's partner, Chapters.ca, is always open — that means easy access for busy teachers.

✔ And then you have the Internet. For a massive infusion of lesson plans and ideas, check out D-CIPHER News Education (`www.newseducation.com`), where Canadian teachers can find lessons relating to this small planet's latest goings-on. Having trouble getting your head around media literacy? Visit the Media Awareness Network (`www.media-awareness.ca`), where you'll find support for all manner of media education. Play with gopher (keyword **Gopher**) and poke around on the Internet mailing lists (visit `www.liszt.com`) to find more educational goodies than you can imagine. (See Chapter 17 for more about the Internet in general if you need some help with that.)

✔ Speaking of awesome resource materials, how about picking up electronic copies of classic literature? They're available for downloading from a site called the Etext Archives at `www.etext.org`, as well as through the Online Book Initiative (type `gopher://ftp.std.com/11/obi` into the Navigation bar text box at the top of the screen and click Go!). For theatre buffs, try Scripts For Schools at `http://scriptsforschools.com`, a very cool Canadian site where you can purchase plays and skits for young thespians of all ages.

✔ Covering weather in science class this year? Keyword **Weather** gets you to the Weather channel (see Figure 20-2). There, you'll find a great current national weather map that prints beautifully on a colour ink-jet printer.

Figure 20-2:
Whoa!
Check out
that
weather
forecast at
AOL
Canada's
Weather
channel.

For weather-related resources, visit Canada's Weather Network Online at www.theweathernetwork.com, or try Environment Canada's national Weather Office at www.weatheroffice.com.

✔ Speaking of the Web, don't forget about the mind-boggling sites waiting for you there. For starters, use AOL Canada Search (keyword **Search**) and try a search for *education* — or any other field of specialty, such as *science* or *special education*. When AOL Canada Search returns a list of sites, find one that sounds appealing and click it to go there.

It's an Online Louvre

When you're looking for the perfect addition to a bulletin board, worksheet, or professional presentation, check out these resources and prepare to say "Whoa!"

✔ AOL has a veritable treasure trove of images in its photography libraries. You just have to know how to get there. First, go to the House & Home channel (keyword **Home**). Next, click the Crafts & Hobbies link. Scroll down the list of hobbies and choose the Photography folder. Once you're there, scroll through the menu (yes, there are layers within layers in this system), until you can see Photography Libraries. For all the ups and downs of downloading, see Chapter 16.

Taking Your Class to See the World

If you have a computer in the classroom and access to a phone line, your students' world doesn't end at the walls of the room. Consider the following ideas for field trips without even leaving the school:

✔ Check out today's news (keyword **News**) before class and at lunch. Discuss a current story and follow its development by making "today in the news" a part of your students' day. This idea works well for a unit study (the study of several school subjects around a single item, such as news) because you can concentrate on whatever kind of news you want — sports, business, world, and Canadian politics, for example.

✔ Highlight social studies with information from the Travel channel (keyword **Travel**). Students can plan an entire trip with information about airline and train fares, where to eat, weather predictions, and more.

✔ If you're from small-town Canada, like Marguerite, your school might consider planning a student trip to this country's biggest (and yes, most self-absorbed) city: Toronto. If so, don't miss Toronto.com at keyword **TourismToronto**. Read up on the ol' standards (the CN Tower, the Metro Toronto Zoo), and find out what's new and exciting (browse the photo gallery, read through news releases).

✔ The new AOL Canada International expansions put a wealth of foreign-language material at your disposal. Whether you're looking for texts or live interaction with native speakers, it's all waiting for you behind keyword **International**. For all the details, flip to the International information in *AOL Canada For Dummies Channels Directory* (the yellow pages in this book), or, to try it right now, sign on and visit the Bistro (keyword **Bistro**).

✔ Combine listening and research skills by visiting CBC's Infoculture. (Get there by using keyword **Music**, then choose CBC Infoculture from the drop-down menu at the bottom of the window, and click Go.) Infoculture has a tremendous range of news, reviews, downloadable audio samples, and downloadable reports about all kinds of musical styles and happenings. Go ahead, get your tax dollars' worth!

✔ Pay honour to this country's bicultural roots by browsing with students through AOL Canada's Français channel (keyword **Français**), and while you're there, be sure to visit "l'îlot AOL de TFO" — as seen in Figure 20-3 — where kids can play high-quality francophone word and strategy games. (You can also get there by using handy-dandy keyword **TFO**.)

✔ Follow local coverage of news events in every part of Canada by using the AOL Canada Newsstand (keyword **Newsstand**) to access newspapers from all over Canada.

Figure 20-3:
Mais oui!
It's the AOL
Canada
francophone
kids' area at
keyword
TFO!

✔ For the best in cool Internet stuff for kids, have a look at the Kids Only Top Internet Sites (keyword **Kids Only** and then click the Web button).

✔ Take advantage of live conferences on AOL Canada. Business leaders, writers (yes, even people like us), media favourites, and all kinds of other people appear in the large conference areas to discuss their areas of expertise and answer questions. What an opportunity for your class! Check out AOL Live (keyword **AOL Live**) for upcoming events.

The Involved Teacher

There's never enough time for you, the teacher. To make the most of the time you do have, the Internet newsgroups are an excellent resource. Using newsgroups, you can instantly call upon the knowledge of people just as dedicated (and probably harried) as you. Check out Chapter 17 for all the details about using newsgroups, then try these out for size:

✔ Canada's got its very own cluster of newsgroups devoted to all things educational and teacher-student–related. It's called Canada's Schoolnet, and you can find these groups by using keyword **Newsgroups**, then clicking Search All Newsgroups, and look for can.schoolnet. The search results will contain an impressive list of groups devoted to everything from math to the social sciences.

- ✔ You can find out more about Canada's Schoolnet by visiting their site on the World Wide Web. Just click into the white space in the main rectangular AOL Canada navigation bar, type www.schoolnet.ca, click Go, and read away!

- ✔ Still looking for fresh ideas for your class? There's a newsgroup called alt.teachers.lesson-planning where, as the name implies, you can find other souls just like yourself, willing to share, commiserate, and, hopefully, inspire!

Chapter 21

Help for the Worker, the Saver, and the Entrepreneur

. . . .

In This Chapter

▶ Looking for a new career

▶ Collecting news of the business world

▶ Promoting and building your own business online

▶ Finding a little something for the female upstarts

▶ Hopping on the highway

. . . .

*T*hanks to the wonders of computer technology, the title of this chapter can easily apply to you. The process of changing careers, investing for your future, or even starting up your own small business can be as easy as sitting down at your keyboard. Looking for job postings? Want inexpensive global e-mail? Tips on where to put your hard-earned loonies so they'll grow? No problem. Special help for female or young entrepreneurs? It's a cinch. Sniffing around for product and service ideas? Get ready to find them. This chapter introduces you to the AOL Canada and Internet resources available to start up, start over, put away some cash, and expand and promote yourself and your small business.

A Place That Works for You

The AOL Canada WorkPlace channel (keyword **Workplace**) is the best place to start if you're itching to make a career move. Powered by the aptly named Monster.ca (a Web site that maintains a list of more than 250,000 jobs online), it makes sure your job search is simple. Click the Find a Job button, then pick a location and job category, or enter a keyword into the text box provided, then click Search For Jobs. *Voilà!* You've got listings! At Work Place, you can also post your customized resume, or sign up to have new job postings delivered to your e-mail inbox. (Your mom did say the early bird gets the worm, didn't she?)

Feel like you need to bone up before you tell your boss you've got better things to do? Bone up on the do's and don'ts of resume writing, check out the top business books in Canada (as compiled by Chapters.ca), or even take a quiz to determine your "promotability." You'll find it all under the heading Career Resources, at the bottom left corner of the main AOL Canada Work Place channel window.

While you're at the Work Place channel (we did say it's working for you, remember?), also take the time to delve into the voluminous information available in the Career Essentials area. Each folder in the pull-down menu opens to reveal newsgroups, chat groups, bulletin boards, and more related to each main category — like media, entertainment, and financial services.

Had enough of the serious stuff? After all, this job stuff is pretty draining. Try clicking the Workplace Humour link in the main AOL Canada Work Place window to dig up a laugh or two. Daily funnies, links to some very cool Internet sites, and more are waiting for you.

Figure 21-1: AOL Canada Work Place — a good place to start when looking for a new job.

Taking the Pulse of Business News

Being in business means staying on top of what's happening in the business world. Information is power in business. With AOL Canada, you have access to far more information than your offline competitors do:

✔ For general business news, look to the Canadian Business News window (keyword **Biznews**). Here you'll find up-to-date reports from Canadian Press (CP) and Reuters Canada (including the very cool daily CP Business News Summary), as well as a search function (click the red Search The News button). Choose from categories including Canadian Business, U.S. Business, Resources, Markets, Currency news, and more (see Figure 21-2). In the category called Canadian Business, you'll also find a link to the online version of the world-famous *Financial Times* newspaper.

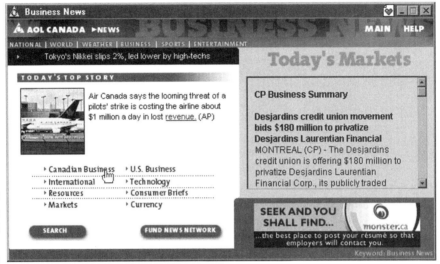

Figure 21-2:
Business
news to go!

✔ Newspapers aren't the only source of business information on AOL Canada. Look for some of the top business magazines as well, like the U.S. publication *Business Week* (keyword **BW**), *Economist Intelligence Unit* (keyword **EIU**), *Canadian Business* (`www.canadianbusiness.com`), and *IE:Money* (`www.iemoney.com`). For the most complete list, visit the AOL Canada Newsstand (keyword **Newsstand**) and click Business under the Magazines heading at the bottom left side of the window.

✔ If you're looking for information about a particular company, you'll want to check out the Research Companies link in AOL Canada Work Place channel (keyword **Workplace**). Be forewarned, some of the search functions in this research area are premium services, meaning they cost money.

✔ Dig up regional business highlights in newspapers from across Canada by visiting the AOL Canada Newsstand (keyword **Newsstand**) and scrolling through the regional newspapers.

Resources to Relish

When do you sit back, rest on your laurels, and say, "Whew! I've done enough! No more working this month (or year)"? If you're a small-business owner, the answer is — never! Just as you never stop thinking, planning, or advancing your business, you also never have enough business resources at your disposal. Who knows what you'll need next? In addition to the areas listed earlier in this chapter, you may use some of the following resource areas online:

- Find millions of listings for Canadian businesses and organizations at the AOL Canada Business Finder (keyword **Business Finder**).

- Get all the banking information your little business-starting heart desires at the AOL Canada Banking Centre (keyword **Banking**). Check out the drop-down list under the heading Banking Resources, at the bottom-left side of the main Banking window. That's where you'll find links to the big players in Canadian Banking, all of whom have pages dedicated to both individual and business-owning investors.

- Stimulate debate and discussion by using keyword **Investor Canada**, then clicking Market Comment. This takes you to the latest Op-Ed by one of Investor Canada's contributors. You can read previous Market Comments by clicking the See Prior Commentaries link.

- Stimulate even more discussion by pouring over the latest column by resident financial guru Garth Turner (keyword **Garth Turner**) and decide if you want to aim your financial strategy in the same direction!

- Use the home business tax calculator (powered by Quicken.ca) and generally keep on top of your whole responsibility-as-a-democratic-citizen tax burden at the AOL Canada Tax Centre (keyword **Canada Tax**).

- Relax a few minutes with daily *Dilbert* cartoons (keyword **Dilbert**). Everybody needs a good laugh to keep the doctor away.

If you have equity in a home, or you're thinking of taking that kind of plunge with your investment dollars, try keyword **Cdnrealestate**. Get the latest mortgage rates or link to Century 21 or to MLS (Multiple Listing Service), which offers Canada's most extensive database of homes for sale.

Blowing Your Online Bassoon

Now that you and your business are online, advertise your arrival! Be careful, because promoting your business online isn't as easy as it sounds. Sure, lots of prospective customers are out there, but you have to approach them appropriately. *Slow* and *subtle* are the keys to your success.

Build Your Nest Egg Now!

Want to start saving for the future but don't know how? Get a head start by heading to Personal Finance and clicking on Investing Info, or use keyword **RRSP**. Here, you'll find information and online services relating to RRSPs, mutual funds, and stocks in plain language that everyone can understand. Click the Chat button to access AOL Canada scheduled chats on investment topics — one recent chat we saw focused on investing in developing markets.

As well, try a column by AOL Canada's own John Daly (a.k.a. "the business weasel," not to mention Senior Editor at the *Globe and Mail*'s Report on Business) — and don't forget you can keep up with all of AOL's columnists at keyword **Print Weasels**.

If it's RRSP season but you don't know a registered plan from a registered nurse, get with the program at keyword **RRSP**. Start with the basics, by clicking the "Why you should invest in an RSP" link, and then fan out to information about mutual funds, RRIFs, and even figure out exactly what you should be putting away using the RRSP calculator. It's (almost) never too late to start saving in a tax-sheltered RRSP, so go ahead and read up.

For those who already know the basics (and beauty) of compound interest and RRSPs, take advantage of the services you can access through keyword **RRSP**. Set up an online trading account with one of Canada's top brokerage firms (also at keyword **Brokerage**), buy shares in a mutual fund (also at keyword **Mutual Fund**), or download this year's tax forms (also at keyword **Taxes**).

For starters, let your customers know that you're online by printing your company's AOL Canada screen name on business cards and brochures. Depending on how familiar your clientele is with online services and the Internet, you may want to list your address twice. First, identify it as an AOL Canada screen name for your customers who subscribe to AOL Canada. Next, format it as an Internet mailing address by taking out any spaces in your screen name and then adding @aol.com to the end of it. For example, John's AOL Canada screen name is JKaufeld, so his Internet address is jkaufeld@aol.com. Notice that the Internet version is all lowercase — it's a subtle thing, but it shows that you know about the Net.

Here are some other tips to keep you ahead of the game:

✔ Obey the rules of the digital road. Inside AOL Canada, sending unsolicited (read that as "junk") e-mail messages is a violation of the Terms of Service agreement. Likewise, some discussion areas on the Internet don't appreciate blatant advertising.

✔ When you're posting a message in a newsgroup or online discussion, pick an area that's relevant to your business *and* accepts business-related postings. If you're promoting financial planning services, don't post an ad in a cancer support discussion because you reason that terminally ill people need lots of financial planning help. If you have to make excuses about why you're posting in a particular area, it's probably not the right place for your message.

Discussion Builds Business

How can your small business even hope to compete with companies that can afford such "luxuries" as extensive market research, product development staff, and customer focus groups? By leveraging your business acumen with the power of AOL Canada, that's how. Here are some ideas to get you started:

✔ Thinking about taking your company into the wilds of digital space? The Financial Forums (go to the Personal Finance channel and then click on Message Boards) are where you'll find discussion boards dedicated to cyberbusiness.

✔ Also use the Message Boards to access the Garth Turner Message boards (yes, *the* Garth Turner, financial advisor to sooo many Canadians) and the U.S. Investing Message Boards (choose US Channels on the channels toolbar and click Personal Finance). These two areas are sure to keep you on top of the latest money-growing strategies, tips, and pointers.

✔ Want to know what's on your customers' minds? Find the forums they frequent and monitor the discussions.

✔ If children are part of your market segment, don't forget about the discussion boards in the Kids Only area. Let the kids themselves keep you abreast of new trends and interests.

✔ Discover new product lines by listening to the complaints and discussions of your customers. No better product idea exists than a customer's hopeful prayer of "Wouldn't it be great if . . . ."

✔ Conduct live, online meetings in the People Connection area (keyword **People Connection**). Use them for brainstorming sessions with other businesspeople, online meetings among your outside sales staff, customer focus groups, or anything else you can imagine.

If your new business is going to mean a lot of driving, visit AOL Canada's Auto Centre (choose AOL Services⇨Car Buying), powered by Chariots.com, one of Canada's biggest online car-buying Web sites. Here, you can read up on all this year's latest models, find out what kind of car is right for your needs, price shop, read automotive reviews, or even request a quote on a new or used car via e-mail. Whoa! It's all waiting for you at the AOL Canada Auto Centre. Just pull on in. If it's insurance you're looking for, try keyword **Insurance** to request a quote from several resources.

And Now, Something for the Ladies

If you're like Marguerite, you get a tiny bit tired of business journalism, business manuals, and business advice being directed mostly at the male mind. Don't despair, sisters! AOL Canada has a feature that you should check out to feel a little less left out!

The AOL Women's channel has an area called Money and Work (keyword **Money&Work**) where you can get expert advice on everything from work-stress to work-dress, subscribe to one of the woman-focused online newsletters, or, if you prefer a more informal approach, quiz your fellow female AOL members by posting your query to one of the many women-and-work message boards. You'll find it all by choosing Women from the channels window on the left side of your screen.

Self-Help for the Computer

Small businesses, particularly small home-based businesses, often rely heavily on a computer but lack the support resources to haul themselves out of trouble when problems strike.

Take a peek into the Computing & Games channel (keyword **Computing**) for some great places to find the computer help you need. Also, check out the Computing Newsstand (keyword **Computing Newsstand**) for news, features, equipment reviews, Web links, and a buyer's guide. For some good discussion areas, filled with ideas for getting the most from your sometimes-reluctant hardware and software, dive deeply into the Computing channel (keyword **Computing**).

Joining the Information Superhighway

If the new millennium can already be said to have a theme emerging, it's got to be "cyberworld." For a small-business person, the Internet and cyberspace represent an information source you can't afford to pass up. The AOL Canada links to the Internet are very impressive in this respect. Chapter 17 explores the Internet and explains all those crazy terms, like *FTP*, *WWW*, and *USENET*. Here are some other small-business helps to try on the Internet:

  ✔ Join some Internet mailing lists. Visit the Liszt mailing list server, at `www.liszt.com`, to find the lists you seek. Either enter a word or phrase about your business, your customers, or whatever else interests you, or browse through the topical list on their Web page. Either way, you're only moments away from a great mailing list!

✔ Internet newsgroups are a great place to hear your customers. With well over 30,000 newsgroups out there (and more being added every day), monitoring a few well-chosen newsgroups is almost like target marketing. Look through Chapter 17 for more details.

✔ Put your business in front of millions of potential customers by building a site on the World Wide Web. Many businesses offer their services on the Internet with this graphical, point-and-click system. You're halfway there already because your AOL Canada account includes storage space for a Web site! To find out more about the Web and how to use it in your business, check out Online Business (keyword **Doing Business Online**). Although some of the information here is specific to American AOL members, it's more than worth your while to check it out for general information on everything from what kind of computer hardware you'll need, to hosting an online business, to advice on writing that all-important appeal to potential customers.

✔ That new Web site comes together pretty easily with AOL Canada's free Web site development tools. My FTP Space, the quick and easy AOL Canada Web publishing tool, lives over at keyword **My FTP Space**.

Trading on an International Scale

If you've never envisioned your business moving in the realm of international trade, it may be time to think again. World trade is the order of the day, and the Internet can help you join the club. Start with a quick search of the Internet Mailing List database for the International Trade List (see the first bullet in the preceding section to find out how). Subscribe to this list, read it awhile, and get ready to go international.

Part V
Secret Tricks of the AOL Gurus

The 5th Wave   By Rich Tennant

In this part . . .

In addition to its great content areas, strong Internet links, and dandy little triangular logo, AOL Canada harbours secret powers known only to a select few. In the past, only the Acolytes of the Great Circle–Triangle–Thingie knew the twists and turns of the system's hidden paths — only they were admitted to the powerful inner sanctum of AOL Canada, where customized profiles, Internet software tricks, and personalized menus are part of everyday life.

The chapters in this part tear away this veil of secrecy, exposing the steps that bring these extraordinarily cool extras into your online life, too. With these powerful techniques in your hand, you too are ready to join the ranks of the initiated — the ranks of the AOL Gurus.

Chapter 22

Making a Truly Cool Profile

In This Chapter

▶ Unlocking the secrets of the custom profile

▶ Making your profile a thing of personalized beauty

After joining the digital world of AOL Canada, one of your first meet-the-neighbours tasks is filling out your member profile with the My Profile button at keyword **Profile**. Depending on how you fill it out, your online profile may describe who you are and what you do when you're not online (you know — in that *other* world), offer a little peek into your cyberpsyche, or paint a picture of your character in a role-playing game. The space is yours, so use it well!

Unfortunately, the basic member profile offers little flexibility. It's so, well, *basic* — state your name, birthday, occupation, marital status, blah, blah, blah — uh, is this a tax office or a neighbourhood?

To avoid that federal office building feeling, spice up your profile with some custom categories and simple formatting. Thanks to careful research and lengthy undercover investigation (okay, accidentally bumping into someone in a chat room who willingly shared the secret counts, doesn't it?), this chapter reveals the details of the once-clandestine steps to making a perfectly cool profile.

It's All in the Wrists (and the Tabs and Colons)

Customizing your profile involves fooling AOL Canada into doing what you want. (Yes, you're playing tricks on the software — isn't that a wonderful feeling?) When you build a normal profile, it's a fill-in-the-blanks experience. You type some clever thoughts, click Update, and AOL Canada does the rest.

Behind the scenes, AOL Canada adds some extra control characters to your words. When the system displays your profile, it automatically looks for these special characters and uses them to figure out how to display your information.

These special characters are the key to the whole customization process. By typing them in the profile, you can add new categories and generally make your member profile look awesome.

The characters in question are Ctrl+Backspace and Tab. For reasons beyond comprehension (and, frankly, beyond our interest), the AOL Canada programmers chose Ctrl+Backspace to mark the start of a new category and Tab to mark the break between a category heading and its associated text.

Profile Remodelling for the Do-It-Yourselfer

Enough of this dreadful theory — the time has come to haul out the implements of destruction and make a cool, custom profile. Best of all, unlike the folks on those let's-remodel-the-house-in-30-minutes TV shows, you don't need any special equipment, extra software, or even a witty sidekick to accomplish the job. What a deal!

Before signing on to the system and starting profile surgery, take a few minutes to jot down your profile ideas on a handy piece of paper. (You can get some ideas by looking at Marguerite's profile under construction in Chapter 6.) Just as good blueprints keep a building project on track, knowing precisely what headings and information you want to put in the new profile makes creating the profile much easier.

With your paper-based sample in hand, get ready to join the ranks of Those with Cool Profiles. Here's what to do:

1. **Sign on to AOL Canada.**

   Since the profiles live on the big AOL computers out at AOL's massive hub in Dulles, Virginia, you can't do a thing with the profile before signing on.

2. **Open a blank document window by either selecting File⇨New from the menu or pressing Ctrl+N.**

   This prepares you for capturing a Tab character, a hard-to-find little creature that plays a vital role in your custom profile. (Yes, these steps really *do* lead to customizing your profile — have a little faith.)

3. **Press Tab to insert a tab character into the blank document.**

   The blinking toothpick cursor moves over a bit on the screen. That space is really a *tab* character, just like the ones you get in a word processor by pressing the Tab key. Because pressing Tab in the Edit Your Profile window moves the cursor from one field to another, you have to cheat and find another way to insert a tab character — and *that* is what you're about to do.

4. **Press Shift+Home to highlight the tab character, then press Ctrl+C to copy the character for safekeeping (and even safer inserting).**

   This step copies the tab character into the Windows Clipboard. With the tab character in hand (or, more specifically, in Clipboard), you're ready to create a masterpiece.

   Follow this step *very* carefully. More than anything else in the instructions, your success with custom profiles depends heavily on catching the Tab character.

5. **Take a deep breath in heady expectation and then click on MY AOL and choose My Member Profile from the Menu.**

   A screen containing your existing profile pops into view.

6. **Pick one of the current entries (Your Name, Hobbies, or one of the others) and click in its text area. When the flashing toothpick cursor appears, press End.**

   The little toothpick cursor moves to the end of the entry.

7. **Press Ctrl+Backspace and then type the name of a new category for your profile. Put a colon (:) after the category name just to make everything look official.**

   If the process worked right, your entry now contains a box (from the Ctrl+Backspace key combo), the category name, and a colon.

   To make a new line without a category heading (it makes long entries look good), insert the Ctrl+Backspace character, but leave out the category and colon. Instead, skip straight to the next step.

8. **With the new category in place, press Ctrl+V or choose Edit⇨Paste from the main menu.**

   The cursor jumps over a bit, thanks to tab character you borrowed from the blank document window. Despite the screen's increasingly odd look (the screen should look like Figure 22-1 by now), you're doing just fine.

9. **Type the text that goes with your new category.**

   This step works just the way it always did — no surprises here.

10. **Repeat Steps 6 through 9 to add more new categories and entries.**

    Feel free to keep adding new categories and information to your profile.

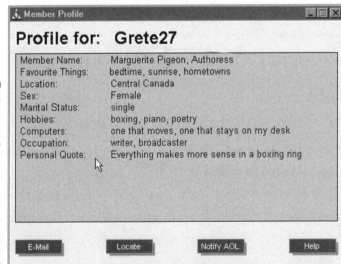

Figure 22-1:
The Your
Name field
looks weird
as a new
category
(Favourite
Things)
takes shape.

Although each profile entry holds a limited number of characters (see Table 22-1 for the details), that's not a big problem. When you run out of room in one entry, just go to the next one on the list!

11. **After you're done, cross your fingers (this is very important) and click Update.**

After a moment, AOL Canada acknowledges your request and updates your profile. If all worked well, your new headings and entries tell your story with panache (just like in Figure 22-2).

Figure 22-2:
The finished
product,
with new
headings
and extra
white space
to make the
profile
informative
and pretty.

A personal Web page is the ultimate profile

Even though you can add new categories to your member profile, the process still suffers from some frustrating limitations. To escape those restrictions and discover a whole new world of possibilities, check out AOL Canada's My FTP Space (keyword **My FTP Place**) and build your own World Wide Web page.

Want to change fonts? No problem. How about adding a picture? It's a snap. You don't need to know a bunch of technical mumbo jumbo to

make it work, either. My Place puts you in the creativity driver's seat while it handles the digital details.

For even more profile options, why not try creating your very own Web page using Groups@AOL? Every member of the group can create a profile that you can choose to display on your main page. For details about Groups@AOL, visit Chapter 12.

Table 22-1	Category Sizes
This Category	*Holds This Many Characters*
Your Name	128
City, Province, Country	255
Birthday	32
Gender	Radio button
Marital Status	32
Hobbies	255
Computers Used	128
Occupation	128
Personal Quote	255

Check the finished profile to make sure that it comes out just as you envisioned. Do that by pressing Ctrl+G and typing your screen name in the dialog box.

When the time comes to update your cool profile, use the same techniques described above, but with a twist in the process. When you open up the profile for changes (just like in Step 5 in this chapter), each category area displays only the *last* set of information you entered — in fact, it looks like the computer ate most of your profile! Don't panic like we did (we positively came unglued the first time we changed our profiles because we thought they were gone), because your whole profile is safe and sound.

To see all of the text in each category area, use your cursor keys. Table 22-2 explains how the keystrokes work in the profile window. (And remember to click Update when you finish reworking the masterpiece!)

Table 22-2	Cursor Key Actions in the Profile Window
This Keystroke	*Moves the Cursor as Follows*
Home	Puts the cursor at the start of the current custom heading
End	Sends the cursor to the end of the current custom heading
Ctrl+Home	Moves the cursor to the beginning of the category
Ctrl+End	Dispatches the cursor to the end of the category
Right and Left arrows	Move the cursor one character in each direction
Ctrl+Right, Ctrl+Left arrow	Jumps word by word in each direction

Chapter 23

Dressing Up Your Software with Fresh Buttons and a New Menu

In This Chapter

▶ Building a better toolbar

▶ Creating a menu, one item at a time

*C*ustomizing means extraordinarily different things to different people. To one person, it means adding a pinstriped dash of colour to the exterior of a car; to another, it involves some light-hearted reorganization of the vehicle's body parts with the help of a handy acetylene torch. (Okay, maybe that's *art* rather than customization, but you get the point.)

In the world of software, customer-customizable features started out small ("You want to change the colour of your screen? You got it!") and gradually grew to the point where we are today. With many applications on the market, you can adjust almost anything — including the menus and the toolbars.

The new AOL Canada 6.0 software rides this trend by including customization features. You, the non-programming AOL Canada member, can add new buttons to the toolbar and create your own navigational menu system (complete with hot keys). This chapter explores the ins and outs of these two great customizing features. First tackling the toolbar and then illuminating the My Hot Keys menu, this chapter makes both these great tools easy to understand and use.

Although building your own toolbar buttons and menus isn't hard, the task will be easier if you know about the Favourite Places heart-on-the-paper icon and also understand how keywords work inside AOL Canada. To find out about them both in one easy step, flip to Chapter 7.

Not that you need reminding, but it's our job to make sure you know that the new 6.0 access software is loaded onto the CD-ROM that came with this book. Install it and you can benefit from 540 free hours within your first month on AOL Canada (communication charges may apply). Go back to Chapter 1 for details.

Dancing the Toolbar Tango (or Is That the New Button Bop?)

Until now, the toolbar just sorta hung out at the top of the screen and stared at you. Granted, it was very useful (and colourful), but it wasn't terribly interactive. The AOL Canada programmers put a great deal of thought into precisely which buttons should appear on the toolbar, and they put them there carefully. So, if you didn't like one or another, you couldn't do anything about it.

With the AOL Canada 5.0 and now the 6.0 software, however, the programmers discovered customization, and now the toolbar (or at least a little corner of it) is your personal navigation playground. Although most of the toolbar is still locked in place, the plum-coloured area on the far-right end of the toolbar (shown in Figure 23-1) belongs to you. Fill it with buttons pointing to your favourite AOL Canada areas, chat rooms, or Web sites.

Figure 23-1:
The six customiz-able toolbar buttons live on the far-right end.

Customizable
Area

If the online area for your prospective toolbar button has a Favourite Places icon in its window, you're only a few moments away from adding that area to your toolbar buttons. Just look at the following steps for all the details. However, if the window *doesn't* have a Favourite Places icon on it, you can't create a toolbar button for the area. Sorry, but that's how it goes. (Even flexibility has limits.)

To put a button of your own on the toolbar (or to replace an existing button with a new one), follow these steps:

1. **If the customizable area of the toolbar is full, decide which of the customizable buttons you don't need anymore.**

   Granted, it doesn't seem fair that you need to lose a button to gain one, but that's how things go.

2. **Right-click the button that's going bye-bye.**

   A short pop-up menu (if a menu with only one item can be called a menu) appears next to your cursor.

3. **Click the Remove from Toolbar option on the pop-up menu (it's the only one, as you can see in Figure 23-2) and then click Yes in the Are You Sure dialog box.**

   Quick as a wink, the toolbar button vanishes, leaving an open space on the right side of the screen for your button.

Figure 23-2:
Just one
click and
the button is
history.

4. **By whatever method you usually use (keyword, Favourite Place entry, or menu browsing, for example), view the online area destined for its own toolbar button.**

   Just as it always does, the online area of your heart hops on the screen.

5. **Drag-and-drop the little heart-on-a-page icon into the customizable toolbar area (see Figure 23-3).**

   When you let go of the cursor, the Icon Selector dialog box hops on the screen.

   It doesn't matter where in the customizable section you drop the Favourite Places icon. The AOL Canada software always adds the new button in the last position on the far right side of the toolbar.

Figure 23-3:
Drop the
icon on this
end to make
a new
button.

6. **Scroll through the collection of pictures until you find one that looks vaguely like what you want, click it, and type a short name (up to eight characters long) that will appear along with the image in the Label text box.**

   By the way, you can't add your own pictures to the icon list. For now, you simply enjoy the opportunity to use the artwork graciously provided by the AOL Canada developers.

7. After you're done, click OK.

The button proudly takes its place on the toolbar, looking something like Figure 23-4.

Each screen name gets its own custom toolbar buttons, so don't be surprised when your new button vanishes the moment you switch to a different screen name. When you change back to the original screen name, the custom button comes back.

To use the button with other screen names on your account, sign on with each of the other names and go through this whole make-a-button process for each one. If you have multiple copies of the AOL Canada software (one on your home computer and one at work, for example), you need to add the buttons in both places. Custom toolbar buttons aren't stored in the AOL Canada computers; they're stored on your computer.

Also, you can't create custom toolbar buttons when you're signed on with the Guest option — it works only on your very own copy of AOL Canada.

A Menu to Call Your Own

My Hot Keys is your very own customizable menu space. Load it with as many as 10 of your favourite online destinations. This menu comes preloaded with entries for nine popular parts of AOL Canada, but you can easily change those entries to things *you're* interested in:

✔ Why go to the trouble of putting something in My Hot Keys when it's so easy to add things to your Favourite Places list? Good question — glad you asked. In addition to appearing in My Hot Keys, every item on this special menu gets a *hot key* assigned to it — something that Favourite Places can't do. Rather than work your way through the menu or manually type the area's keyword, you can press a Ctrl-key combination (Ctrl+1 through Ctrl+9, depending on which position the item holds in My Hot Keys) and go there immediately.

✔ You need to keep just one rule in mind: Only services and areas with a keyword can be on the special My Hot Keys menu. If you can't get there with a keyword, you can't get there with the My Hot Keys menu, either.

✔ We probably shouldn't tell you this, but you can bend the only-keyword-areas-go-here rule just a bit. In addition to keywords, you can include Internet locations, such as Web sites or gophers. Type the address exactly as you do when you're using your Web browser to get there. That means using what the techies call URL *format*, including the `http://` part in front of the site's address.

✔ Some of our picks for a starter My Hot Keys menu include Canadian business news (keyword **Business News**), Stock Quotes (keyword **Quotes**), and the nationally renowned columnists in Print Weasels (keyword **Print Weasels**).

Here's how to customize the My Hot Keys menu.

1. **Find something you want to add to the menu, and get its keyword or Internet URL and name.**

   Make sure that the keyword is correct; otherwise, the menu option doesn't work (and the programmers of the world don't need *any* help in developing software that doesn't work).

2. **Choose Favourites⇨My Hot Keys⇨Edit My Hot Keys.**

   This step displays the Edit Hot Keys dialog box.

3. **Decide which key you want to use for the new item and click the Shortcut Title box for that key.**

   The first time you open your Edit Hot Keys dialog box, there should be a space at the bottom of the window to add another shortcut. If the box already has an entry, press Backspace or Delete to remove it (see Figure 23-5).

Figure 23-5:
Typing in a new entry in the extra space at the bottom of the Edit My Hot Keys window.

Hot Key Title	Keyword/Internet Address	Key
Buddy List	buddyview	Ctrl + 1
Chat	chat	Ctrl + 2
Calendar	fav36	Ctrl + 3
Help	help	Ctrl + 4
Internet	internet	Ctrl + 5
Member Benefits (Perks)	perks	Ctrl + 6
News	news	Ctrl + 7
Shopping	shopping	Ctrl + 8
Stock Quotes	quotes	Ctrl + 9
Those Wacky Col		Ctrl + 0

Edit Hot Keys

Save Changes   Cancel   Help

4. **Type the name of the item in the Menu Entry box.**

   Whatever you type appears on the My Hot Keys menu, so keep it kinda short — one to four words, at most.

5. **Press Tab to move to the Keyword/Internet Address box.**

   If you're replacing an existing entry, press Backspace or Delete to remove it.

6. **Type the keyword or Internet address for your new menu item in the Keyword/Internet Address box (see Figure 23-6).**

Figure 23-6: Watch your spelling (after all, nobody else will).

Hot Key Title	Keyword/Internet Address	Key
Buddy List	buddyview	Ctrl + 1
Chat	chat	Ctrl + 2
Calendar	fav36	Ctrl + 3
Help	help	Ctrl + 4
Internet	internet	Ctrl + 5
Member Benefits (Perks)	perks	Ctrl + 6
News	news	Ctrl + 7
Shopping	shopping	Ctrl + 8
Stock Quotes	quotes	Ctrl + 9
Those Wacky Columnists	print weasels	Ctrl + 0

(Edit Hot Keys window; buttons: Save Changes, Cancel, Help)

   Double-check your typing to make sure that the keyword is correct. If you entered a Web site address, make sure that you include the `http://` part at the beginning!

7. **Click the Save Changes button to make the new entry part of your My Hot Keys menu.**

   Your new menu item is ready to test!

   If you have a sudden desire to forget that you ever considered changing the menu, click Cancel in Windows or close the window on a Macintosh.

8. **Choose Favourites➪My Hot Keys and choose your new item from the list of Hot Keys (see Figure 23-7).**

If you've misspelled a keyword while creating a new entry for My Hot Keys, the AOL Canada software will try to help you by launching a search through AOL.CA, which would be very nice, except you wanted to go to a very specific, keyword-named place inside AOL.

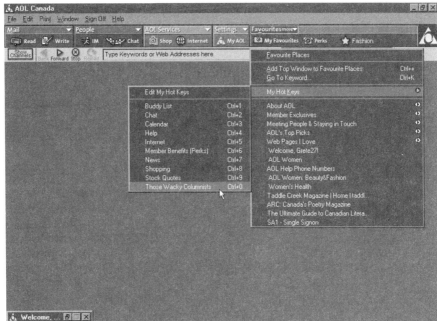

Figure 23-7:
Your new entry looks great strutting on the My Hot Keys menu.

If this happens, just go back to Favourites⇨My Hot Keys⇨Edit My Hot Keys, click into the Keyword/Internet Address box and check the spelling. If you've got something that looks like Gaymes, or Print Weesils, there's your problem right there!

Chapter 24

So You Wanna Go Faster?

In This Chapter
▶ Bantering about bandwidth
▶ Touring the technologies at a high rate of speed

*W*hen it comes to technology, we humans have a serious attachment to speed. Fast is good, faster is better, and *really* fast takes our breath away. We expect speed from our cars, our computers, even our cameras (how else do you justify instant-print film and Hello Kitty photo sticker kiosks?).

Online connections live under the same speed demands as every other technical piece of our world (we want information *now*, darn it), and the computer industry has risen to the occasion. Over the past few years, connection speeds have risen steadily while prices have dropped like an old modem thrown from the 53rd floor.

Of course, new technologies bring new terms, concerns, and costs — all of which add up to frustration for people trying to sit on the safe side of the technological cutting edge. This chapter attacks the problem head-on by exploring and explaining the most popular high-speed connection options available on the market today (and a couple coming out tomorrow). Flip through here before plunking down the money for a high-speed Internet connection — you'll be glad that you did!

High Bandwidth Doesn't Mean Oversized Musicians

There's a funky give-and-take relationship between the speed of your online connection and the things that you do online. Every boost to your connection speed opens up new vistas of online content. For example, the Reuters and Canadian Press news photos adorning the AOL Canada Today channel load faster. Samples from AOL Canada's Online Listening Booth (keyword **Music**) load almost instantly. Files that took an hour or more to download hop onto your hard drive in a matter of minutes. This increased speed is pretty close to digital Nirvana.

As you start looking at high-speed connections, the term *bandwidth* pops up over and over. (Once the nerds find a word they like, they use it as much as possible). Bandwidth describes how much data moves through an online connection over a period of time. Modems, for instance, are a low-bandwidth connection that measure their speed in "bits per second" (the bps thing again, which we tell you about initially in Chapter 1). High-speed (or high bandwidth) connections measure speed in KBps, or *thousand bits per second* (recycling the popular nerd convention of substituting "K" for "thousand" whenever possible).

Browsing the Net through Rose-Coloured Wires

High-bandwidth connections come in all shapes, sizes, costs, and acronyms. The specific connections available where you live depend quite heavily on exactly *where* you live within your city, province, and region of the country. (Remember that there are somewhere between 600 and 2,000 Internet Service Providers in Canada — no one knows exactly how many, and the landscape is changing as fast as you can say Internet!) Even though one of the high-speed services might be available in your city, you could discover that it *isn't* in your neighbourhood yet.

Don't automatically assume that high-bandwidth connections don't exist in your neck of the woods just because you live far away from a booming metropolitan area. Some of the coolest high-speed projects take place in smaller, more rural areas, because those areas understand the economic importance of the online world better than their big-city brethren.

The following sections look at the most common high-speed technologies for the home and small office/home office market. Big businesses, with their equally big budgets, need more speed than these connections provide, so those folks are on their own (but they can afford a consultant).

TIP

Doesn't bandwidth cost money?

In the world of automobiles, speed costs money. There's no way around it — if you want to go *vroom*, then your budget goes *zoom*. Generally speaking, it works the same way with the wild world of high-speed Internet connections, but the *zoom* factor causes a lot less budgetary stress than in, say, rocket car drag racing.

Although high-speed connections cost more than plain modem connections, the difference isn't exorbitant. In fact, it's probably more inexpensive than you think.

For instance, if you have an extra phone line for your computer (those computers tie up the phone like a caffeinated teenager), you pay about $25 per month (plus applicable sales taxes, which goes for all the prices we discuss). A cable modem connection, which runs up to 100 times faster than a regular dial-up modem, costs around $40 per month. Add another $15 per month to rent the cable modem (although this fee is sometimes waived), and you get a total monthly cost of $55 for cable modem service. The *net* cost (because you don't need the extra phone line now) drops to $30.

But the calculation doesn't stop there. High-speed connections usually include their own

Internet connection, which drops your AOL Canada fee dramatically. Instead of paying $22.95 per month for AOL Canada, the cost drops to $13.95 per month (using the Bring Your Own Access plan, at keyword **BYOA**). Now the high-bandwidth connection only costs $11 extra. Hmm. . . . Sounds enticing, doesn't it?

Also, AOL Canada will be introducing its own AOL PLUS High Speed Service! AOL Canada 6.0 software is broadband enabled, meaning it comes with the appropriate tools necessary to experience broadband content like RealPlayer and Flash. AOL Canada will introduce its AOL PLUS High Speed Service in a few select markets sometime in 2001. You can obtain more information by contacting AOL Canada Member Services toll free at 1-888-265-4357.

Don't arbitrarily dismiss a high-bandwidth connection without running the numbers yourself and checking the actual costs in your area. Fees vary by region, and depend on your Internet Service Provider (ISP). When you look at the costs, remember to factor in the money that you *already* spend before making your final decision. The outcome may surprise you!

Data over cable: Good speed when it works (but don't tell your friends)

The first time we heard about "Internet access via cable TV systems" a few years ago, we thought that the person telling us about it was joking. What do the online world and a cable TV company have in common? Sure, they both involve screens, but there had to be something a little more meaningful than that.

After thinking about it more (and doing some research), the idea made a lot more sense. Moving television signals around a community is a lot like moving data around a network — heck, even some of the wire is the same. It took a few years to get the act together, but the cable TV industry made great strides along the way.

Today, cable companies all over the country provide high-speed Internet access over the same cable lines that deliver *The Beachcombers* reruns to your living room. (There's some kind of poetic justice there, but not an easy one to nail down.) What's more, since the end of 1999, the Canadian Radio-Television and Telecommunications Commission (CRTC) has made it possible for other companies, like your local Internet Service Provider, to act as resellers of cable access to the Net.

In addition to the cable line itself, cable access requires two special pieces of equipment. First, your computer needs a network card that supports *10baseT Ethernet* connections (which is a fancy way of saying "twisted-pair network wire that looks like overgrown phone cord"). Lots of new machines include a network card as part of the standard configuration, but if yours doesn't, it's not a big deal. Every computer store, and many home electronics places, like Future Shop (www.futureshop.ca) and Business Depot (www.staples.ca) carry the cards, and cable ISPs will also provide you with one when you sign on (it's included as part of their installation charge). You can either have the card installed by an expert, or get real friendly with your computer and do it yourself.

The other technical goodie that makes cable communication possible is the *cable modem* itself. This box translates between the cable wire and your computer, moving data back and forth at astonishing speeds. Depending on the policy of your cable provider, they may include the modem as part of your monthly fee, waive the cost (at least in the short term, in order to get people interested in the new technology), or sell it to you for a one-time cost.

Most, if not all, cable companies bundle their own Internet service (e-mail accounts, newsgroup access, and such member networks) into the price of the high-speed access. Even so, the fee is pretty darned fair considering what you get for the money. When the line works like it should, cable access really screams. It's quite an experience to watch a 12MB file pour into your computer in minutes instead of an hour or more.

A potential downside of cable access is its "shared resource" concept. Due to the cable system's design, the subscribers in a given area share their Internet access (just like you share the neighbourhood roads, particularly during rush hour). If everyone uses the system at once, response time plummets because each person takes his or her own increasingly small slice of the total bandwidth. If you work at home, your access flies all day, because you aren't sharing bandwidth with anyone (everybody else is at work, so the roads are clear).

Cable's other main issue is reliability. Unfortunately, the key phrase for cable access is "when the line works like it should." The cable companies try hard, but they wrestle with the computer side of their business. Although reports of slow (or no) cable connections abound on the Internet newsgroups (check out `comp.dcom.modems.cable` for the latest tidbits), the performance is just too good to dismiss because of glitches.

Since cable connectivity depends entirely on your local cable company, call them first to find out if they do data over cable lines yet. To learn more about the cable industry's approach to the Internet, you can also visit the Canadian Cable and Television Association's Web site and read a document called The Internet and Beyond, at `www.ccta/ca/TRASH/beyond/firstpg.html`.

Coming soon to AOL Canada: Hold your breath! Cable access to your AOL Canada account in a select number of communities through a service called AOL PLUS High Speed Service.

DSL: Fastest of the bunch, but not available everywhere

Considering their huge investment in copper wire, it's no wonder that the phone companies looked far and wide for a high-speed solution that leverages all of that old copper wire into a competitive advantage. At first, they thought that the grail carried the name ISDN (covered in the next section), but in the late 1990s they started to change the tune to DSL. DSL stands for *Digital Subscriber Line*, a very cool technology that could herald some exciting new dimensions for the online world.

DSL, like ISDN, runs through your existing phone lines. Unlike its slower brother, DSL is only a data link — telephones and fax machines need not darken DSL's doorway. Connecting your computer to the DSL line requires a DSL modem. (It has a more technical name, but most everybody simply calls it a "DSL modem," since that describes what it does.)

Blazing, consistent speed gives DSL a slight advantage in the market. Cable systems claim to run at 10 times the speed of a standard 56K modem. DSL delivers up to five times the cable connection's speed, but without the "shared resource" problems that the cable folks calmly describe as a "feature" of their system.

Like cable connections, vendors usually package an Internet Service Provider plan with the DSL line, which brings the cost to between $30 and $50 per month. DSL subscribers here in Canada not only provide you with the modem, but the network card as well. The software is a little different; users log on with something called an Access Manager. This Access Manager gives the user control to log on and off the service. Cable, on the other hand, is "always on." As soon as you open a browser, you are online.

Also coming soon to AOL Canada: Yes, the programmers are busy setting up AOL PLUS High Speed Service using DSL connections that will be made available to AOL Canada members in select markets.

ISDN: Great flexibility, but expensive

ISDN, short for *Integrated Services Digital Network*, arrived on the scene well before either cable access or DSL. It won a dedicated following among small business and advanced home users thanks to its guaranteed connection speed (either 64KBps or 128KBps), and the fact that, for a long time, it was the only high-speed game in town.

Unlike its competitors, ISDN service replaces your existing single phone line with a pair of new, *super* phone lines that operate on the same old piece of wire already installed in your house. Using a special ISDN adapter (an extra piece of gear that you usually purchase from your ISDN provider), connect your computer directly to the ISDN line for either 64KBps (using one of the two lines) or 128KBps (with both lines) of connectivity to the Internet.

The ISDN line basically takes the place of your old phone line, and its price reflects that idea. ISDN service usually pays for *only* the communication line itself, not your ISP account. For most home users, the cost will probably be out of range.

Since it only provides a 64KBps or 128KBps data connection, it sits at the very bottom of the speed contest. Considering what DSL and cable can do (and at a much lower price point), it looks like ISDN only makes sense for people who *need* a fast online connection, but don't mind paying an arm, a leg, and half a sideburn for it.

Part VI
The Part of Tens

The 5th Wave   By Rich Tennant

THAT'S RIGHT, THE UPPER-CASE BUTTON WORKS ON SCREEN, BUT THEY'RE NOT COMING OUT ON THE DANG PRINTER! HOLD? SURE, I'LL HOLD.

Poet e.e. cummings makes his last service call.

In this part . . .

As expected, the book closes with The Part of Tens, the ...For Dummies answer to all the silly things you had to memorize as a child in school. Don't memorize them — don't even try. Instead, read them, laugh with them, and put them to work for you.

Chapter 25

Ten Fun Things to Do Online

In This Chapter

▶ Deciphering obscure computer terms

▶ Venturing onto the Internet

▶ Tracking long-lost friends, online buddies, and even packages

▶ Exploring obscure online areas with the Search system

▶ Downloading great software

Depending on whom you ask, the online world and the Internet are either chock-full of the latest information about every topic under the sun or they're factual mirages that look promising from a distance but disappear as you arrive. Why do people hold such radically different views on the subject? Because the first person *found* what she looked for, and the second didn't.

The key to finding stuff, of course, is knowing where to look. In the online world, that's quite a challenge because you have so many places to look. This chapter provides some starting locations as you search for fun people, nifty places, and various online features.

Always watch for new resources — you never know when you may find one. Feel free to jot down the area's keyword or address here in this book, too, so that the address doesn't accidentally get lost in the shuffle. (After all, it is your book, so you can write whatever you want.)

Start enjoying the Internet goodies we discuss in this chapter today. All you have to do is install the AOL Canada Version 6.0 software from the CD-ROM that came with this book. The instructions are easy to follow — see the appendix, "On the CD," for details. If this is your first experience with AOL Canada, you can use the software for 540 hours (whoa!) in 30 days (communication charges may apply) before deciding whether you want to stick around and join the AOL Canada community as a member.

Decoding Digital Terminology

The computer industry turns out new technology quicker than you can say, "I just bought a new computer." (The lesson here seems to involve announcing PC purchases with shorter sentences, but let's move on.) But computers are the industry's second most prolific product. More than anything else, the computer nerds make amazing new names for things.

To keep a handle (or at least get a grip) on the wild world of computerese, visit the Webopedia site at http://webopedia.internet.com. Decipher specific terms by typing them into the Webopedia search box or browse a list of related terms by picking a category. The site also features a Term of the Day, for those days when you need a cool new techo-term to impress the computer folks.

Seeking Out a Chat Room

The People Connection ranks as one of the top AOL Canada destinations. Finding the room that's right for you may take some time, particularly because the area contains hundreds, if not thousands, of active chats all the time.

To simplify your chatting life (and find interesting chats quickly), use Find a Chat, the People Connection search feature:

1. **Click the Chat icon on the toolbar to bring up the People Connection window.**

2. **Click the Find a Chat link to bring up the Find a Chat window, then click Search All People Connection Chats on the bottom left of the window.**

   (If that doesn't work, choose People⇨Find a Chat from the toolbar, and then click Search All People Connection Chats on the bottom left of the window.)

3. **Type a few words to describe the room you're looking for and click Search. Type it carefully — spelling counts!**

   AOL Canada lists rooms matching your description. For rooms that are always open, the list shows only the room name. If the search system finds a special scheduled chat, it shows the name and time of the chat.

4. **Scroll through the list until you find a likely candidate and then double-click the chat room's name.**

   AOL Canada displays a brief description of the chat.

5. **To hop into the chat room, click the big Go Chat button in the description window.**

   If there's space for you (remember that each chat room holds between 1 and 23 people), you immediately pop into the room. If the room is full, the software lets you know.

This set of steps searches all of AOL Canada, looking for interesting chats sponsored by various online areas. It *doesn't* search the general People Connection chats, though. The only way to find a chat in there is by old-fashioned browsing in the main Find a Chat window (choose People⇨Find a Chat from the toolbar).

 After you get into the room, add it to your Favourite Places list by clicking the little heart-on-a-page icon in the chat room's upper-right corner. For more about Favourite Places, see Chapter 7. To delve into the depths of chatting, see Chapter 9 — and don't miss the section called "Can(ada) We Talk, Eh?" all about the regularly scheduled Canadian chats.

Staying on Top of Important Dates

AOL Canada gets it. And by that we mean that the people who work for this amazing organization have foreseen one of life's worst, uh, "discomforts": that of missing a significant other's birthday or anniversary. And in their wisdom, these same people have built into the AOL software a mechanism that can save you the tears or flying plates that can accompany this particular oversight. It's called the AOL Canada Gift Reminder, and it works like a charm.

To use it, just use keyword **Reminder**, and click Create Your Reminder. AOL walks you through the process, asking for the name of your loved one, the type of occasion, and, most importantly, that elusive date. Once you've saved the information (which is, of course, kept confidential by the AOL Reminder Team), you will receive an e-mail a full 14 days before the big event. Hey, if you can't get to the mall in 14 days — including Sunday shopping — then you may be beyond help. And speaking of shopping, you can find out more about the AOL Canada Shopping channel by flipping back to Chapter 13, or consult the *AOL Canada For Dummies* Channels Directory that is oh-so-neatly tucked into the yellow pages in the middle of this book.

Ferreting Out Long-Lost Friends and Businesses, Wherever They May Be

Want to find your old flame from high school? Interested in seeing your college roommate again? (Maybe he finally has the rent money he owes you!) You've already searched the Member Directory but found nothing. Is there anywhere else to turn? Yes!

Finding a person's e-mail address, street address, and phone number can't get much easier than it is with the AOL Canada People Finder. Get there by using keyword **People Finder**, or by choosing AOL Services⇨People Finder. (To find a business, choose AOL Services⇨Business Finder.)

Tripping through the Coolest Online Areas

After spending some time on AOL Canada, it's easy to fall into a rut. You find a few areas that match your interests, visit them regularly, and get to know the members there. However, after a while you may long for something new — a change of pace and scenery, perhaps.

When the urge strikes, answer it with a quick trip to the Search system. Interested in education? Type that word into the search box on the navigation box and click Search. A page of results will almost immediately come into view.

To use the Search categories, begin with keyword **Search** to bring up the AOL Canada Search page. Under the Canadian Search categories, click the Education category. This takes you to another page of subcategories, including Associations (9+ sites), as well as Colleges and Universities (a whopping 280 sites and counting).

Using this system, Marguerite recently found a Web site devoted to the Year 2000 Canada Women's History Month. (She found it via these categories and subcategories: Society/History/Canada/Women. And by the way, that Web address is http://victoria.tc.ca/community/whist.)

Speaking Your Mind in a Cancon Kinda Way

Okay, so you know from Chapter 14 that AOL Canada brings you the latest news from across this fair land every day. So what's so special about that, you ask? Well, this *is* a community, right? So go ahead and talk back about what you read in the news (keyword **Cdn News**) by clicking the arrow beside the Speak Out section at the bottom-left corner of the main News Channel window. This takes you to the channel's ever-changing message board, and if you ever doubted that Canadians, despite our politeness, can get a tad testy about everything from gun registry (343 postings at last count) to the so-called brain drain (102 postings at last count), think again!

Sending Online Cards, Flowers, and Other Things That Smell

The online world brings people closer in amazing ways. Distance makes no difference on the Internet, so your circle of online friends quickly includes people from everywhere on the globe. Unfortunately, distance does make a difference when you want to send greeting cards and other gifts to your buddies. Popping an e-mail over to Guam is one thing, but shipping a batch of Montreal-style bagels is quite another.

The good news is that programmers love these types of problems and they quickly developed a solution. If your friends exist in the digital world, why shouldn't your cards and gifts live there too? Thanks to these clever programmers, the Internet is chock-full of digital postcard, greeting card, and flower delivery services. With a few quick clicks, e-mail your sentiments to friends and family. Best of all, most of these services are free!

The following list includes a variety of greeting cards, postcards, and flower bouquets (well, at least *pictures* of flower bouquets — but they don't need any water). We couldn't resist including one off-the-wall delivery service, but we figure you can pick it from the list without further explanation.

To use one of these sites, just type its address in the address box on the navigation bar and then press Enter (Return) or click the Go button. AOL Canada automatically starts your Web browser and sends you off to the site. Enjoy!

What It's Called	Web Address
Blue Mountain	www.bluemountain.com
Corbis E-Cards	http://ecard.corbis.com/
Electronic Postcards.com	www.electronicpostcards.com
Greet Someone.com	www.greetsomeone.com
Postcards From Ontario	http://204.101.2.101/pcard/
Prince Edward Island Greeting Card Centre	http://www2.gov.pe.ca/card/index.asp
Send My Postcard	www.sendapostcard.com
Virtual Florist	www.virtualflorist.com

For a fancier card, check the American Greetings card centre (keyword **American Greetings**). It offers a wide variety of high-quality animated cards for all occasions. They're a hoot! Or for something both multicultural and Canadian, try a site called Our Image Greeting Cards at www.our-image.com, where you can purchase cards designed by and for the Afro-Canadian card-giver.

Hanging Out with Your Favourite Celebrities

Sure, the stars come out at night — but at AOL Live, they shine the rest of the day, too. Some people appear regularly on their own shows (like John's *America Online For Dummies* chat at 9:00 p.m. Eastern time on the third Monday of every month), and others drop in for a one-shot event.

To check the schedule for upcoming AOL Live appearances by your favourite entertainment, sports, political, and business personalities, use keyword **Live**. AOL Live features new chats each night that are always promoted on this page. Click Search, and enter your luminary's name. If that person has an event coming up, a dialog box containing all the details appears onscreen. Try Coming Attractions if you're still just browsing.

To search for transcripts of previous events, click Event Transcripts in the AOL Live window (keyword **AOL Live**). For info about John's monthly AOL Live event, check his online profile (press Ctrl+G, type **JKaufeld**, and press Enter). For more about AOL Live, check out Chapter 9.

Downloading the Best Software

You can't beat a huge, free collection of programs for bringing out the computer person in anyone (it always works for us, but then again, we may not be the best sample population). Let your inner nerd run free in the DOS, Macintosh, and Windows software libraries on AOL Canada. Download some business programs, home-management tools, or even a few games — everything is yours for the taking.

To search the libraries' Windows, Macintosh, or DOS software, use keyword **FileSearch**, click a category that interests you, then type a few descriptive words into the text box under the heading Enter a Search Definition (or, better yet, enter the name of the program if you already know what you're after). By default, the system searches for Windows and DOS software. To search for Macintosh software, click the tiny Mac Search button at the bottom of the Software Search window.

For more about the perils and pleasures of downloading, see Chapter 16.

Tracking Packages All Over the World

Depending on what you do for a living, following the progress of little boxes as they wing around the world may (or may not) be of particular importance to you. If you ship a number of things, though, or if you work from home, knowing the current location of a much-needed carton or document envelope often makes or breaks your whole day.

Thanks to the Internet, package-tracking information is only moments away. Sign on to AOL Canada and then type the appropriate shipping company address from this list into the address box on the navigation bar and click the Go button:

Carrier	*Web Site Address*
Canada Post	www.canadapost.ca
Federal Express Canada	www.fedex.com/ca
Purolator	www.purolator.ca
UPS Canada	www.ups.com/canada/

AOL Canada automatically launches your World Wide Web browser and opens the page. Carefully follow the onscreen instructions to find your package.

Collecting Free Stuff from the Government

Okay. We know this is Number 11 Cool Thing to Do and we only promised 10, but we just couldn't resist including this one. The federal government has an entire department devoted to serving the needs of you, the consumer. Not known for their flare for naming these things, it's called the Office of Consumer Affairs, and guess what — they understand the average consumer's obsession with all things free of charge. Here you can read dozens of federal publications for free.

"But how can it be?" you ask.

"Well, Johnny, tell the folks at home how it's done." "That's right. For the low, low price of your annual tax bill, you get pamphlets and links for information on just about everything a Canadian might care about. You got your composting info from the Government of New Brunswick, your sunglasses safety info courtesy of Health Canada, your papers on Canada's policy regarding e-commerce, not to mention up-to-date lists of recalls and telemarketing scams."

To find all these goodies, just visit the Canadian Consumer Information Gateway at `http://consumerinformation.ca/`.

Chapter 26

Ten Common Things That Go Wrong (and How to Fix Them)

*I*t's easy to start imagining that computers and software were invented by a cabal of psychiatrists and psychologists as a long-term project to ensure that Western civilization would have trouble coping in the 21st century — therefore needing their services for many years to come. With that paranoid fantasy out of the way, it's time to consider the problem at hand — namely, the one you're having right now. Look for your problem in the following sections. If you find it (or one much like it), read the information in that section and try the suggested solution.

If you can't find your problem here, try the Doctor Tapedbridge Miracle Elixir: When things start failing for no apparent reason, quit the program, restart your computer, and try again. If that doesn't solve things, check keyword **Help** for more suggestions. If you can't get online at all, either use the Offline Help system (choose <u>H</u>elp⇨O<u>f</u>fline Help from the menu at the top of your screen), or call the friendly AOL Canada technical support folks at 1-888-265-4357.

There's a .MIM File Motioning from My Mailbox

You never know where a mime may show up next. At the amusement park, in the local shopping mall, or perhaps as a wandering entertainer during dinner, you can't beat a mime for hilarious hijinks (particularly when the mime focuses his attention on someone else). But a mime in your online mailbox? Now that's another matter.

We're not talking about a real mime, of course (although this book may prompt some adventuresome soul to create a routine called *You've Got Mime*). Instead, we mean a MIME file — a file that ends with a .MIM extension — attached to an e-mail message in your box.

The MIME tools (short for *Multi-purpose Internet Mail Extensions*) work behind the scenes to send programs, documents, spreadsheets, and other files through the Internet e-mail system. When someone outside AOL Canada sends software, documents, or other files to you, their e-mail program translates the files with the special MIME tools, giving the file that funky .MIM extension in the process. The program then attaches the translated file to an e-mail message and ships the whole thing off to you.

When the message (and its attached MIME file) arrives at AOL Canada, the e-mail system automatically converts the MIME file back into whatever it was originally (an .EXE, .DOC, .JPG, or such). At least that's how it *should* work.

Unfortunately, AOL Canada's e-mail system gets confused sometimes and can't translate the MIME file back into its original form. Instead, the e-mail system shrugs and simply drops the .MIM file into your mailbox without a single word of condolence, apology, or (worst of all) instruction about what to do next.

When that happens to you, just download the file as you normally do, then use WinZip to translate the file back to normalcy. Yes, in addition to all the tricks that it does with ZIP files, WinZip also knows the secrets of unlocking MIME files.

For help with both downloading and the wonders of WinZip, flip back to Chapter 16.

The Computer Almost Signs On

Your password is in, the modem is singing, and all is well with the world. At least it was until you couldn't complete the connection to AOL Canada.

Usually, this happens at Step 6 of the connection process — the one that says `Connecting to AOL Canada`. This problem isn't your fault; the fault belongs to AOL Canada. For some reason, the AOL Canada computers didn't acknowledge your existence. Perhaps the computers have so much going on that they can't spare a moment from their busy schedule for you. Perhaps the computers aren't running. Whatever the reason, wait a while (15 to 20 minutes) and then try again. If this behaviour keeps up for more than an hour or two, call the AOL Canada technical support number 1-888-265-4357 and find out what's happening.

The Host Isn't Responding to You

This message is nerd lingo for "the computer didn't answer your request," usually expressed in human terms as "Huh? What? Were you talking to me?" You wanted to do something simple (like display the Channels menu), but the big computers at AOL Canada weren't paying attention. Isn't that just like computers? Give them a little power and they walk all over you.

Stuff like this happens when a large number of people are using AOL Canada at the same time. Don't be surprised if you get these errors in the evening, because that's when *everybody* is usually signed on. When this happens to you (and if it hasn't yet, don't feel left out; it will eventually), the first thing to do is try again. This time, it should work. If you're still having problems, sign off, sign on, and try again. Beyond that, throw up your hands in defeat and go have some ice cream. (Sometimes, that's the only thing that helps.)

 If you find you're frequently having trouble signing on, not only in the evening, there might be a problem with your modem setup or the access number. If this is happening to you, give the AOL Canada technical support folks a call at 1-888-265-4357.

The System Rudely Kicks You Off (Punted, Part I)

You're minding your own business, wandering online through this and that, when WHAM! — Dorothy, you're not in Kansas anymore. The technical term for this is being *punted*, as in "Rats, I was punted."

It happens for no particular reason. It could be noise in the phone line; it may be your call-waiting feature kicking in; perhaps the digital gremlins are at work. Whatever the cause, sign on again and continue your pleasurable labours. If this happens frequently (more than about five times a week), call the folks at the phone company, tell them in a confident voice that you "recently lost numerous connections with your online provider" (which is a fancy way of saying that you get punted a lot), and ask them to check your line for interference.

There's usually no charge for checking your phone line, but the phone company only tests your line to the point where it comes into your home or apartment. If they find a problem in the Great Out There, then they fix it for free. If the problem is inside your walls, then someone else (probably you) pays for the repairs.

AOL Canada Doesn't Say a Word

Your friends said that AOL Canada would talk to you. They even demonstrated it to really sell you on the point. So you went to the local computer store and spent big bucks on a sound card and speaker system. For that much money, AOL Canada should say, "Welcome" or "You've got mail" once in a while, if not perform entire Wagner operas. Instead, the service is mute — nothing changed. This situation quietly bothers you (as well it should).

First, make sure that your speakers are turned on and that the computer's sound system works with other programs. If your favourite game or multimedia program brings forth glorious melodies, the sound card is working just fine. If those programs can't make a peep either, double-check your new sound card to make sure that it's working. (Look for troubleshooting information in the sound card's documentation.)

When you know that the sound card is okay, make sure that the AOL Canada access software knows that it's supposed to use sounds. Sign on and choose Settings⇨Preferences from the toolbar, then click the Toolbar option from the Preferences Guide. Make sure the last box is checkmarked to Enable AOL sounds and click Save. Sign off and then sign back on. You should be greeted by a friendly "Welcome" just before the Welcome window appears. If the sound still isn't working, look for assistance in the Member Services area (keyword **Help**).

Your Computer Locks Up While Downloading Files (Punted, Part II)

You started with a simple goal to save some time. You invested in a 56,000-bit-per-second modem. You carefully searched the download area until you found precisely the program you wanted. It's a great plan — except for one tiny little detail: Your computer loses its connection to AOL Canada almost every time you try to download a big file. Whoops.

Don't worry — you're not the target of an electronic conspiracy. Believe it or not, the odds are good that this problem belongs to your AOL Canada software (or maybe your phone line).

When you run the AOL Canada software for the first time, it automatically searches the computer, looking for your modem. After it finds the modem, the software carries on a brief discussion with it. The AOL Canada software wants to know what kind of modem it is, how fast it can communicate, what its favourite colour is, and other things like that. Based on what it finds out, the software automatically configures itself.

The problem with this seemingly wonderful process is that modems aren't particularly communicative. In fact, they're pretty stupid. As a result, the AOL Canada software may confuse your modem with another one from the same manufacturer. In the worst cases, it may think that you have a completely different kind of modem than you do!

To fix this problem, you must manually tell the AOL Canada program what kind of modem you have. Luckily, AOL Canada anticipated this problem, so it completely outlined the steps in the program's Offline Help system. Without signing on, choose Help⇨Offline Help from the Menu to bring up the Offline Help window and then click the Index tab. In the box near the top of the Help window, type **modem**. As you type, the help system locates the modem help files. Near the top of the window, you should see an entry that says Modem. Just below that should be another entry called Expert Add/Edit Modem. Double-click that entry. The help system displays all the steps you need to fix your modem configuration.

If you're still stumped, there's a bounty of information about modems at keyword **Modem**, or try choosing the Connecting to AOL option from the list of help topics at keyword **Help**. One sub-topic in particular, called "Setting AOL to work with your modem," walks you through the whole ugly modem thing step by step.

File Downloads Take Too Long

When you look at a file description, it displays a statistic labelled DL time, which is the approximate time the file will take to download in a perfect world with whatever speed of modem you're using right now. The most important phrases in that sentence are "approximate time" and "in a perfect world." You see, approximations are rarely correct, and the world is most certainly not perfect. Don't computers make stupid assumptions about real life?

Here's the reality of this download-time thing: The actual time it takes to download something depends on how busy AOL Canada is, how noisy the phone line is, and the current phase of the moon. If your download is really big (like multiple megabytes in size), the AOL software may not even try to make an estimate, but instead present you with an approximate download time it picked out of thin air. (Seriously!)

If a download seems to take forever, first be patient. If it looks as though the download really will take forever, cancel it; then try again or use the Download Manager and an Automatic AOL session to resume the download at a less busy time. See Chapter 16 for more information about that.

Automatic AOL Mail Goes Undercover

Automatic AOL sessions are great things that save you time, money, and effort. (See Chapter 8 for more on Automatic AOL.) Of course, they also kind of hide your incoming mail from you.

Your mail really isn't hidden; you just have to access it through your Filing Cabinet. To get there, choose Mail⇨Filing Cabinet from the toolbar.

Your Internet Mail Is Undeliverable

The AOL Canada Internet mail gateway is great if you have friends or business associates on the Internet. Unfortunately, the Internet is a technologically wild place. Mail messages that are misaddressed in even the smallest way come screaming back into your mailbox, sent by angry computers with names like MAILER-DAEMON@mail02.mail.aol.com (which sounds like a character from *I Know Who You E-Mailed Last Summer*). The nice thing — if you can really say that about returned mail — is that these computers usually tell you what's wrong with the message.

If your friend's Internet mail address is minstrel@linguaplay.com, minstrel is the user part of the address (the person's screen name on that system), and linguaplay.com is the name of the host, server, domain, or system, just as aol.com is the system name for AOL.

Such technical drivel is necessary for understanding the two most common mail errors: User Unknown and Host Unknown. Both messages mean that the address you entered has a slight problem. A User Unknown message means that the problem is with something to the left of the @ symbol in the address; Host Unknown means that the problem is to the right of the @ symbol. The error code appears in the subject area of the returned e-mail message.

Whatever is wrong, check and double-check the address to which you're sending mail. Be particularly alert for hostnames ending in something other than `.com` (such as `.org` or `.net`), because more and more of those sites appear on the Internet each year. Also, watch the difference between the number one (1) and the lowercase letter *L* (l), as well as the number zero (0) and the uppercase letter *O*. Computers get all hung up about this stuff.

If the address seems okay but the message still doesn't go through, try having the other person send a message to you. After you get that message, click the Reply button to insert the sender's address automatically. Click the Add Address button to create a new entry in your Address Book. Now you know that the address is correct.

The New Item on Your Go To Menu Goes to the Wrong Place

In Chapter 23, you skirt the frightening realm of nerddom by creating your own items on the Favourites⇨My Hot Keys menu. Now, however, the item is there in the menu, but it doesn't quite work. Don't let this little setback worry you. It usually takes a professional to make a menu item that doesn't work; you managed to do it with little or no training!

This glitch is relatively easy to fix. The problem is the keyword you entered in the Edit Hot Keys box — the odds are high that it suffers from a slight spelling problem. Choose Favourites⇨My Hot Keys⇨Edit My Hot Keys from the toolbar and look at the keyword you entered for the non-working menu item. You'll probably discover that the keyword is just the tiniest bit misspelled.

Use the menus to get back to this favourite of your online places and note the keyword when you arrive. Then go back to the Edit My Hot Keys dialog box and type that keyword *very carefully*. Save your changes by clicking Save Changes. Then try your new item. Isn't programming fun?

Chapter 27

Ten Internet Resources Worth Checking Out

* *

In This Chapter

▶ Checking out the coolest newsgroups and mailing lists

▶ Finding fun-filled gopher, Web, and FTP sites

* *

*T*he Internet is a most amazing place. With connections to most of the countries in the world and a truly daunting array of services and information, the Internet is like a giant library, discussion group, and digital department store all rolled into one. (And best of all, nobody hangs over your shoulder reminding you to keep quiet when you visit.)

This chapter gives you the expected 10 interesting things to try on the Internet, plus a couple of bonus items. The goal is to pique your interest in the Internet and give you a sample of the incredible range of stuff you can find out there.

To use these Internet services, choose <u>A</u>OL Services⇨<u>I</u>nternet on the AOL Canada toolbar and choose the appropriate option from the menu (like Go To The Web, Search The Web, Newsgroups, and so on). If you need some general help with the Internet, see Chapter 17.

alt.folklore.urban (Newsgroup)

Heard the one about the beached whale the Oregon Department of Transportation blew up with dynamite? Or about the Proctor & Gamble logo being linked to "forces of evil"? These are *urban legends* — stories that get told and retold until they take on lives of their own. And they have a home on the Internet.

If you like this kind of thing (or if you've heard a legend and want to know whether it's true), check out the alt.folklore.urban newsgroup. You find discussion and commentary on all things odd, improbable, and larger than life. Sign up at keyword **Newsgroups**. In the Newsgroups window, click Expert Add, type **alt.folklore.urban**, and then click Add.

can.politics (Newsgroup)

You know the expression "Build it and they will come"? Well, that's the essence of newsgroups. Create a subject area and, lo and behold, people will toss in their two cents, which is exactly what makes newsgroups ideal soapboxes for political debate.

Using the same method described above, we encourage you to subscribe to can.politics. Got something to say about the state of health care? Immigration? Or would you like to exercise your right to comment on our beloved and not-so-beloved federal leaders? You never know who might be reading and become inspired by your words.

The OCF Online Library (Gopher)

A delicate balance keeps the world in order. No, not the balance of military power — we're talking about the Balance of Normality. Some places on Earth (like Britain and Cape Breton Island) are particularly level-headed. Others, like Berkeley, California, aren't.

So what happens when you give those zanies at Berkeley a bunch of networked computers? They come up with the OCF (Open Computing Facility) Online Library. Who else could (or even would) compile a collection that includes NAFTA (the North American Free Trade Agreement — remember that one?), Shakespeare plays (choose from the comedies, tragedies, or histories), a parody of Edgar Allan Poe's *The Raven* ("Once before a console dreary, while I programmed, weak and weary. . . ."), and a wonderful set of transcripts from *Monty Python* movies and TV shows?

To check out this place for yourself, click in the navigation bar's Address box, and then type gopher://gopher.ocf.berkeley.edu/11/Library and press Enter. By the way, capitalization counts in gopher addresses, so be sure to type **Library** with a capital *L*.

The Mother of All Gophers (Gopher)

It's the "Big Gophuna" — your link to the gopher world. With one connection to this service, you can reach almost every gopher in the whole world. (No joke.) And it's available right from AOL Canada.

To get there, type `gopher://gopher.tc.umn.edu` in the Address box on the navigation bar and press Enter (or Return).

InterText Magazine (Mailing List)

If you like to read, the Internet has plenty to offer — and it comes right to you. If fiction is your interest, subscribe to the *InterText* online magazine, and, every two months, it appears in your AOL Canada mailbox. *InterText* is a moderated collection of subscriber-submitted fiction, which means that it won't necessarily include your story just because you send it in. You can check out the magazine at `www.intertext.com`.

Subscribe by e-mailing a request to `subscriptions@intertext.com`. On the Subject line, type either **ASCII** (to show that you want the magazine e-mailed to you) or **NOTIFY** (you receive an e-mail when a new issue comes out, but you must go to the Web site and pick up a copy on your own). Your subscription starts when the next issue comes out.

NETHUMOUR (Mailing List)

The NETHUMOUR mailing list offers a daily dose of humorous Web sites, mailing lists, and other Net resources. It includes the site address, general information, and a brief sample of the site's humour. The listing also notes whether the site offers any (ahem) mature jokes that aren't fit for kids (and some accountants).

To add some fun to your life, send an e-mail to `majordomo@bapp.com`. The subject can be anything, but in the body of the message, type **SUBSCRIBE NETHUMOUR** and then your Internet e-mail address (that's your AOL Canada screen name with `@aol.com` after it). Because John's screen name is JKaufeld, his subscription request was SUBSCRIBE NETHUMOUR `jkaufeld@aol.com`.

Trojan Room Coffee Machine (World Wide Web)

This entry falls under the heading Technology Run Amok. A bunch of computer people at Cambridge University decided that walking down several flights of stairs for a cup of coffee, only to find out that the pot was empty, was too much trouble, so they devised a clever solution worthy of their time and talents: They put their coffeepot on the Internet.

Yes, from anywhere in the world, you can see a digitized video image of the coffeepot and find out whether those folks are low on java. The address to use is www.cl.cam.ac.uk/coffee/coffee.html.

WimpyPoint Slide Presentations (World Wide Web)

Looking for a quick, easy, and free way to create professional presentations for your next business meeting or Internet chat? Do you need to collaborate with someone across the city or around the world on a presentation? Would you like a simple way to give a presentation using any Internet-connected Web browser on the planet?

If anything in the previous paragraph sounds appealing, take a trip to wimpy. arsdigita.com and try WimpyPoint, the Web-based answer to a laptop presentation system. The service costs nothing to use, requires no special software (other than a Web browser), and takes only a couple of moments to learn. WimpyPoint stores your presentations on its server, which makes working on a presentation with your friends and cohorts easy. In short, WimpyPoint makes a great example of how the Internet puts a new (and highly useful) spin on an old idea.

Even though the WimpyPoint site doesn't start with the standard www moniker, it's still a Web site. Just feed it to the address box on the AOL Canada navigation bar, press Enter, and watch it appear on your screen.

Net Search Services

After using the World Wide Web and the rest of the Internet a few times, you start wanting more. It's addictive — like eating a handful of popcorn out of your friend's bucket at the movies . . . before you know it, you're standing in line for your own. Luckily, some highly technical people got themselves addicted to the Internet and created a variety of indexes all over the Internet.

To get more of the Net than most television production companies want you to have, check out these indexes:

All search engines (Web)	www.allsearchengines.com
AltaVista Canada (Web)	www.altavistacanada.com
AOL.CA (Web)	www.aol.ca (or keyword **aol.ca**)
Copernic (Web)	www.copernic.com
DejaNews (Newsgroups)	www.dejanews.com
Dogpile (Web)	www.dogpile.com
Excite Canada (Web)	www.excite.ca
Google (Web)	www.google.com
Gopher Home	gopher://gopher.tc.umn.edu
Go.com (Web)	www.go.com
Lycos (Web)	www.lycos.com
Mining Company (Web)	www.miningco.com
Publicly Accessible Mailing Lists	www.paml.net
Yahoo! Canada (Web)	www.yahoo.ca

MS-DOS, Macintosh, and Windows Software Archives (FTP)

These last three entries are software libraries (or FTP sites) on the Internet. Each library has a bunch of software: business programs, utilities, virus detectors, and (of course) games. Each site specializes in programs for a different platform, so be sure to hook up to the right one for your computer.

MS-DOS	oak.oakland.edu
Macintosh	mirrors.aol.com/pub/info-mac
Windows	ftp.winsite.com
A little of everything	mirrors.aol.com

For more about FTP in general, flip to Chapter 17.

Chapter 28

Ten Terms for the Chat-Room–Challenged

In This Chapter

▶ Telling people when you leave, come back, or feel tickled pink

▶ Expressing your heart in four letters or less

*N*o matter where you go in the People Connection area (or any of the other AOL Canada chatting areas), odd abbreviations and wacky terms wait to prey upon you. This chapter unmasks 10 (or so) of the most common abbreviations and terms skulking around out there. Read about them, memorize them, and use them — it's for your own safety (and to keep you from ::blushing:: too much in the chats).

Away from the Keyboard (AFK)

You're chatting the night away in the People Connection and suddenly hear the call of nature — or you're assailed by the Call of the Small-Bladdered Dog Who Needs to Go Outside Right Away. (It happens, you know!) Well, it takes too long to type "I have to go let the dog out before she detonates all over the kitchen floor like she did last week when I was in a chat room and ignored her because I was having too good a time." (Besides, nobody really wants to know that much about it.) It's rude to just pop out of the room without saying goodbye to everyone. (Besides, you're having too much fun to leave now.) But the dog's timer is ticking, and the linoleum's looking scared. What to do, oh, what to do?

Here's your solution: Type **AFK**, press Enter (or Return), and then put the pupster on a trajectory for the backyard. *AFK* is the universal chat room notation for Away From the Keyboard — online shorthand for "I'll be right back." Just remember to let everyone know that you're BAK (covered in the next section) when you return!

If someone you're chatting with types a quick **AFK**, you should reply **K** (short for "okay") so that the person knows that you understand and that you are waiting for him or her to return. Kinda scary that something as wild and frolicsome as a chat room is so darn organized, isn't it?

Back at the Keyboard (BAK)

Telling folks that you're AFK is common courtesy, but it's equally important to let them know when you return from your task, suffused with the glow of a Job Well Done (or a Dog Well Launched, as the case may be). A quick **BAK** is all it takes to announce your re-entry into the conversation.

Drinks and Glassware

Nothing soothes the soul (or makes friends faster) than a couple of digital drinks in your favourite chat room. If bartending duties fall to you, be sure that your bar stocks all the best in online glassware. After all, serving coffee in a martini glass certainly won't win you any friends!

c(_)	Coffee cup
c|_|	Root beer mug (of course!)
_/	Double old-fashioned or generic bar glass
|_|	Water or generic kitchen glass
Y	Martini or stemmed wineglass (yes, it takes some imagination)

As you see other cool glasses wander by online, jot them down here or on the Cheat Sheet in the front of this book. You don't want to drop a good glass!

Emoticons

Sometimes you need to say more than mere words can convey (which explains why we have comic books). But how do you include a picture in a typewritten message? Easy — with *emoticons*, or emotion icons.

Feel free to use these symbols in your e-mail messages, bulletin board postings, and everyday conversation. Emoticons make up for the facial expressions and other kinds of body language that are missing from electronic communication. And they're kinda fun to type, too:

:-)	Smile
;-)	Wink
:-/	Befuddled
:-(	Frown
:-p	Bronx cheer
8-)	I drew a figure eight on my face (actually, it's a smiley wearing glasses)

For a more complete list of the best emoticons that typing can make, check out the Smileys button behind keyword **Mail Extras**.

Emotion and Action — ::Smiles and Waves::

If you hang out in the People Connection too long or accidentally wander into one of the online simulations (keyword **Games**; then click the Simming button), someone may enter the chat room and ::wave to all:: or ::looks bewildered, walks into a wall::. These folks don't love colons that much (only a doctor can muster that much affection for a simple organ). No, they're doing something in the chat room. Items encased in double colons usually indicate action (::swinging on the chandelier::), show a facial expression (::looking completely puzzled;;), or disclose thoughts (::wondering if I should even answer that question::).

Hugs { } and Kisses*

Have a friend who's feeling glum? There's nothing like a hug or two to keep someone going. You can give someone a little hug, { }, lots of little hugs, { }{ }{ }{ }, or a great big hug, {{{{{{ }}}}}} — the choice is entirely yours.

These days, the online kiss (*) is one of the best ways to show affection. The kiss can be quick or long — *really* long if need be. And it's safe because it doesn't lead to anything, except perhaps an online hug ({ }).

Laughing Out Loud (LOL)

Although LOL isn't a computer acronym, you certainly see it all over the place these days. *LOL* is Internet shorthand for "I'm laughing out loud!" A variation on this theme is LOLOLOL, which means "That's really, really funny" or "I particularly like consonant-vowel combinations tonight and wanted to share one with you."

Lofting

Conversations flow wild and free in a busy chat room, but sometimes you want to share a private thought with that special someone. Or course, one thought quickly turns to many, and before you know it, the chat room banter leaves you far behind. Focusing on a private, instant-message–based conversation while in a chat room is called *lofting*. Often someone types a message like `Greetings from the loft!` to show that he or she is still around, but not really listening to the chat room right then.

Rolling on the Floor Laughing (ROFL)

Use this abbreviation when someone *seriously* tickles your funny bone. Like its little brother `LOL`, `ROFL` is a communication shortcut that most everybody on AOL Canada understands. Expect to find it in the People Connection and on various message boards.

Swatting IMsects

Instant messages are wonderful things — at least until you get inundated with them, that is. If a swarm of IMs distracts you from the chat room, let everybody know by dropping in a quick comment like `Sorry I'm not paying attention — I'm busy swatting IMsects!` Although it's a small thing, it assures your chat room buddies that you aren't ignoring them (at least not completely).

Appendix

About the CD

*I*n this appendix, we tell you how to install the CD-ROM that comes with this book. The people at AOL Canada have made it as simple as possible for you to go online right now! Just pull out the CD-ROM that came inside the cover of this book and follow the steps below.

If you received this book from a friend (or found it at the library), and the CD-ROM has gone AWOL, don't panic. You can order a FREE AOL Canada Start-Up Kit by calling 1-888-382-6645.

Installing the CD

1. **Turn on your computer.**

2. **Pop the CD into your computer's CD-ROM tray.**

3. **Follow the Installation instructions that appear on your screen.**

    The computer takes over at this point, going through a bunch of strange steps (most of which don't involve you, and even if they do, it won't require much more than clicking a button called Next).

    If the installation doesn't start by itself (rats!), click the Start button on your desktop and select Run. Type D:\Setup and click OK once with your left mouse button. If your CD-ROM drive isn't drive D, type the letter appropriate for your drive rather than dD. If you're not sure which letter to type, see the paragraphs that begin "If you don't know the letter of your PC's CD-ROM drive," later in this appendix.

    During the actual installation process, a *status* bar (like a little horizontal meter with a percentage number on it) lets you track your computer's progress. (To imitate computer experts everywhere, just nod a lot and look serious. If someone comes into the room, tell them you're focused on an installation procedure and you're watching its status. Good. Bill Gates would be proud.)

    When the process is complete, the computer may send you a message telling you it's necessary to restart your computer to complete installation. Click OK and it will restart for you.

4. **Double-click the pretty little AOL Canada triangular icon on your desktop (in Windows 95 and 98), and follow the instructions to set up your AOL Canada temporary account.**

   Remember, the CD-ROM in this book comes with a trial period of 540 free hours in your first month. After your free trial you will be charged a monthly membership fee of $22.95 plus applicable taxes for unlimited Internet and unlimited e-mail. Communications surcharges, premium services, and local telephone carrier charges will apply, if you use these services, even during trial period. Online registration will give you the complete details.

When setting up your AOL Canada account, you'll need a registration number and password. Don't worry. These came with the CD-ROM in this book, or you'll find them with the Start-Up Kit you ordered from 1-888-382-6645.

If you don't know the letter of your PC's CD-ROM drive: Most PCs assign the letter D to a CD-ROM drive. Here's how to find out which letter your CD-ROM drive uses:

- If you use Windows 95 or Windows 98, double-click the My Computer icon on your desktop. A window appears that lists all your drives, including your CD-ROM drive (which is usually represented by a shiny disk icon), and shows you the letter of each drive. When you're done examining the My Computer display, exit by clicking the window's Close button in its upper-right corner or choosing File➪Close from its menu.

System Requirements

Make sure that your computer meets the minimum system requirements listed below. If your computer doesn't match up to most of these requirements, you may have problems using the contents of the CD.

- A Pentium-class processorPC.
- Microsoft Windows 95 or later, and Windows 2000.
- At least 16MB for Windows 95 or 98 (64MB recommended).
- At least 130MB of hard drive space available (Windows 95); 113MB available hard disk space (Windows 98/Windows ME) to install all the software from this CD. (You need less space if you don't install every program.)
- A CD-ROM drive.
- A monitor capable of displaying 640 × 480, 256 colours or better (optimized for 800 × 600) at least 256 colors or grayscale.
- A modem with a speed of at least 14,400 bps, preferably 33,000 or 56,000.

If you need more information on the basics, check out *PCs For Dummies,* 7th Edition, by Dan Gookin; The iMac for Dummies, by David Pogue; *Macs For Dummies,* 6th Edition, by David Pogue; *Windows 95 For Dummies,* 2nd Edition, by Andy Rathbone; *Windows 98 For Dummies,* by Andy Rathbone; (all published by IDG Books Worldwide, Inc.).

If You've Got Problems (Of the CD Kind)

We tried our best to compile a system that works on most computers with the minimum system requirements. Alas, your computer may differ, and some programs may not work properly for some reason.

The two likeliest problems are that you don't have enough memory (RAM), or you have other programs running that are affecting installation or running of a program. If you get error messages such as Not Enough Memory or Setup Cannot Continue, try one or more of these methods and then try using the software again:

- ✔ **Turn off any antivirus software that you have on your computer.** Installers sometimes mimic virus activity and may make your computer incorrectly believe that it is being infected by a virus.

- ✔ **Close all running programs.** The more programs you're running, the less memory is available to other programs. Installers also typically update files and programs; if you keep other programs running, installation may not work properly.

- ✔ **In Windows, close the CD interface and run demos or installations directly from Windows Explorer.** The interface itself can tie up system memory, or even conflict with certain kinds of interactive demos. Use Windows Explorer to browse the files on the CD and launch installers or demos.

- ✔ **Add more RAM to your computer.** This is, admittedly, a somewhat expensive step. However, if you have a Windows 95/98 PC, adding more memory can really help the speed of your computer and enable more programs to run at the same time.

If you still have trouble installing AOL Canada 6.0 from the CD, please call AOL Canada's technical support line at 1-888-265-4357.

Index